Thoughtful Teachers, Thoughtful Schools

Issues And Insights In Education Today

Editorial Projects In Education

Allyn and Bacon

Boston • London • Toronto • Sydney • Tokyo • Singapore

Series Editor: Virginia Lanigan
Design and Layout: David Kidd/EPE
Editorial Coordination: Laura Miller/EPE
Series Editorial Assistant: Nicole DePalma
Manufacturing Buyer: Louise Richardson
Cover Administrator: Linda Knowles
Cover Designer: Suzanne Harbison

Copyright © 1994 by Allyn and Bacon
A Division of Simon and Schuster
160 Gould Street
Needham Heights, Massachusetts 02194

ISBN:0-205-15520-0

Printed in the United States of America.

10 9 8 7 6 5 4 3 2 1 98 97 96 95 94 93

Contents

W H A T W E W I L L T E A C H

About Editorial Projects in Education

Since its inception in 1958, Editorial Projects in Education's primary mission has been to help raise the level of awareness and understanding among professionals and the public of important issues in American education. A nonprofit, tax-exempt organization, EPE's first publishing ventures were in higher education. Beginning in 1958 and continuing for more than two decades, the organization published annual reports on major issues in higher education. These reports were bound into more than 300 college and university alumni magazines and, at their peak, reached more than 3 million readers. In 1966, EPE founded *The Chronicle of Higher Education*, which it sold to the editors in 1978. In September 1981, *Education Week* was launched as American education's newspaper of record. And in 1989, EPE created *Teacher Magazine*. In the winter of 1993, *Education Week* and *Teacher Magazine* became available online through GTE Educational Network Services. In the fall of 1993, EPE began syndicating articles via computer for daily newspapers across the country. More than 30 foundations have made grants to EPE in support of these ventures.

COMMENTARY AND FREELANCE AUTHORS

Eleanor Armour-Thomas *is an educational psychologist in the school of education at Queens College, City University of New York.*
Bruce S. Cooper *is a professor at the Fordham University Graduate School of Education.*
Larry Cuban *is a professor at the Stanford University Graduate School of Education.*
Colette Daiute *is an associate professor at the Harvard University Graduate School of Education.*
Chester E. Finn Jr. *is a director of the Edison Project and a former Assistant U.S. Secretary of Education.*
Marilyn Gootman *teaches early childhood education at the University of Georgia.*
Daniel Gursky *is a writer with the American Federation of Teachers and was formerly a staff writer at* Teacher Magazine.

Susan Harman *is director of evaluation for Community School District One, Lower East Side, in New York City.*

Willard L. Hogeboom *is a freelance writer and a retired social-studies chairman from Babylon High School on Long Island, N.Y.*

David W. Hornbeck *is co-director of the National Alliance for Restructuring Education and a former Maryland state superintendent of schools.*

Paul DeHart Hurd *is professor emeritus of science education at Stanford University.*

Mary Koepke *is a freelance writer and was formerly an editor at* Teacher Magazine.

Robert Lake *(Medicine Grizzlybear) is a member of the Seneca and Cherokee Indian Tribes and was an associate professor at Gonzaga University's School of Education.*

Joseph P. McDonald *is senior researcher at the Coalition of Essential Schools at Brown University.*

Jeff Meade *is a book editor for Rodale Press and was formerly an editor at* Teacher Magazine.

Ruth Mitchell *is associate director of the Council for Basic Education.*

John Morris *teaches 1st, 2nd, and 3rd graders at Marlboro (Va.) Elementary School.*

William A. Proefriedt *teaches philosophy of education at Queens College, City University of New York.*

David Ruenzel *is a freelance writer and a former teacher.*

Morris J. Vogel *is professor of history at Temple University's Graduate School of Education. He is working with the Philadelphia Schools Collaborative on the restructuring of that city's 22 comprehensive high schools.*

Judy Westerberg *is a mathematics teacher at Heritage High School in Littleton, Colo.*

Tim Westerberg *is principal of Littleton (Colo.) High School.*

William B. Wood *is the geographer for the U.S. State Department.*

E D U C A T I O N   W E E K   A N D   T E A C H E R   M A G A Z I N E   S T A F F

Michael J. Aubin *is Production Coordinator at* Education Week *and* Teacher Magazine.

Ann Bradley *specializes in writing about teachers and urban education.*

Jennifer Chauhan *is Assistant Managing Editor of* Teacher Magazine.

Gregory Chronister *is Managing Editor of* Education Week.

Deborah L. Cohen *writes mainly about early childhood and parent issues.*

Karen Diegmueller *concentrates on state policy.*

Harrison Donnelly *is a Senior Editor of* Education Week.

Virginia B. Edwards *is Executive Editor of* Education Week.

Lonnie Harp *specializes in school finance.*

David Hill *is Senior Editor at* Teacher Magazine.

Millicent Lawton *writes about women's issues.*

Tom Mirga *is News Editor of* Education Week.

Lynn Olson *covers national policy issues in education.*

Mark Pitsch *writes about federal affairs and programs.*

M. Sandra Reeves *is a Senior Editor at* Education Week.

Joanna Richardson *writes about teachers and administrators.*

Blake Hume Rodman *is Executive Editor at* Teacher Magazine.

Robert Rothman *specializes in assessment, accountability, and educational research.*

Peter Schmidt *focuses on minority affairs.*

Elizabeth Schulz *is Managing Editor of* Teacher Magazine.

Meg Sommerfeld *covers partnerships and philanthropy in education.*

Debra Viadero *writes about special education and curriculum.*

Peter West *specializes in technology and mathematics and science curricula.*

Ronald A. Wolk *is Editor and Publisher of* Education Week *and* Teacher Magazine

A Season Of Change

The primary mission of public education is to prepare people for productive work and effective citizenship. It hasn't changed in 150 years, since Horace Mann transformed local free elementary schools in Massachusetts into a public school system and instituted compulsory attendance. But though the mission remains the same, the requirements for productive work and effective citizenship have radically changed—and keep changing. And that is the essence of the crisis in public education and the present efforts to reform schooling.

All of the accumulated knowledge about science in the 19th century could have fit on a few bookshelves in Thomas Jefferson's library, and he quite likely could have discoursed on it at length. As the 20th century draws to a close, vast libraries are needed to store what we know about the sciences, and information pouring forth is sometimes obsolete before it is published.

This extraordinary explosion of knowledge, the incredible advance of technology that has accompanied it, and profound demographic and economic developments are like hurricane-force winds hurling mankind into the future. We have moved further faster in the past 75 years than in all the previous years combined.

No wonder all of our social institutions are creaking and trembling under the strain. Designed in part to provide stability and continuity to society, our political, economic, legal and judicial, health care, and educational systems struggle to respond rapidly. They were designed to solve yesterday's problems.

In 1918, the Commission on the Reorganization of Secondary Education said that, to adequately prepare a high school graduate, the objectives of the school should be: "1. Health. 2. Command of fundamental processes. 3. Worthy home-membership. 4. Vocational education. 5. Citizenship. 6. Worthy use of leisure. 7. Ethical character."

Workers in the 21st century will need more than elementary basic skills to maintain the standard of living of their parents. They will have to think for a living, analyze problems and solutions, and work cooperatively in teams. And responsible citizenship will entail understanding and reacting to a host of problems so complex that 19th-century Americans couldn't even have imagined them.

Moreover, to be productive workers and effective citizens, today's students will need to learn continuously throughout their lives. Most will likely have two, three, or even four different careers during their life-

time. That is the challenge confronting public schools in the 1990s: to equip young people to cope with changes that they cannot yet envision.

Americans expect schools to meet that challenge. We have always believed deeply in the value of education; it has been called our secular religion. We credit it, with good reason, for our astonishing progress and prosperity. Not surprisingly, then, when our progress and prosperity seem to be in peril, as is now the case, we look for the fault in our schools.

This *Education Week/Teacher Magazine* reader offers a snapshot of American education in the midst of the most dynamic period in its history. The articles in the pages that follow were written day by day, week by week, on the scene as events unfolded. Inevitably some of the material will be dated, but the stories are ongoing; themes echo across chapters, issues wind like sinews through the text, and voices intermingle.

Education is by no means the dry, static, systematic accumulation of facts it is often thought to be. It is a dynamic process involving values, politics, and aesthetics. And it is, first and last, a human endeavor—a matter of relationships among people, of hope and aspirations, of personal success and failure.

Those who become teachers in the next decade will have the opportunity to be in the vanguard of a movement to redirect the course of American education and, through it, the course of the nation. No previous generation of teachers has faced problems and issues as complex as those facing us today.

The domain of tomorrow's teachers must go well beyond the classroom; to have some control of your own destiny and that of your students, you must be able to see and understand the entire terrain of education—the structure of the system, how power and money flow, the politics, the dynamic relationships between the players. The most important and enduring impacts of the school reform movement may well turn out to be the empowerment of teachers as true professionals.

The philosopher Alfred North Whitehead wrote that, on occasion, powerful forces combine in "driving mankind from its old anchorage." "Sometimes," he said, "the period of change is an age of hope, sometimes it is an age of despair. When mankind has slipped its cables, sometimes it is bent on the discovery of a New World, and sometimes it is haunted by the dim sound of breakers crashing on the rocks ahead." Whether this season of change will be one of hope for America or one of despair may depend on how well our educational system can adapt to new demands.

—The Editors

Who We Will Teach

"This nation cannot continue to compete and prosper in the global arena when more than one-fifth of our children live in poverty and a third grow up in ignorance. And if the nation cannot compete, it cannot lead. If we continue to squander the talents of millions of our children, America will become a nation of limited human potential."

—Report of the Committee for Economic Development, 1987

1.

America's Changing Students

Today's students are different from their predecessors, and they pose formidable challenges to schools and teachers.

Demography is destiny. And nothing has had more impact on America's schools than the profound demographic and behavioral changes in the nation's population. The challenge of nurturing, educating, and socializing the young was once shared by the family, the church, and the community. Increasingly, that responsibility has passed disproportionately to the schools.

University of Chicago sociologist James Coleman has written that public schools came into their own when America began to industrialize and men had to leave the farm in search of work and could no longer take responsibility for teaching their sons. Today, he notes, we are living through an equally significant sea change as women leave the home to work and our public schools struggle to adapt.

The majority of women between the ages of 17 and 44 are working full time; more than 80 percent of children under the age of 18 now have working mothers. An increasing number of women are living alone, and more and more of them are raising children. Some 6.6 million households are headed by single women raising some 13.7 million children.

Clearly, the family—the backbone of American society—has been undergoing major upheaval. Only about 6 percent of families today fit the description of the "traditional" household: a working father, a mother at home, and two or more school-age children. In 1965, about 60 percent of the nation's households matched that image.

Studies indicate that in the 1980s the nation lost ground on almost all measures of child well-being. There were more children living in poverty, more births to unmarried teenagers, more latchkey children, and more young people involved with the criminal justice

system. Said one report: Shifts in the economy, changes in "the routines and realities" of family life, and the failure of institutions to respond to those realities have severely hampered "the capacity of typical families to raise their children well."

Not surprisingly, the children who enter school in this decade will bring with them a heavy burden:
• 1 out of 4 will be from families who live in poverty;
• 14 percent will be the children of teenage mothers;
• 15 percent will be physically or mentally handicapped—often the result of low birth weight or drug use during the prenatal period;
• 15 percent will be immigrants who speak a language other than English;
• 15 percent will be children of unmarried parents;
• 40 percent will live in a broken home before they reach 18;
• 10 percent will have poorly educated, even illiterate, parents;
• Between one-quarter and one-third will be latchkey children with no one to greet them when they come home from school;
• 14 percent will be without health insurance;
• And a quarter or more will not finish school.

Obviously, the majority of American students will not live in poverty, will not be special education students, will speak English and come from two-parent, middle- and working-class families. But even these more fortunate young people will not be as easy to teach as their counterparts in previous generations. They have been reared on television and movies, during an age when standards of public morality and ethical behavior often seem to have slipped badly.

More than half of all high school students report on surveys that they have had sex. Moreover, a substantial proportion engage in behaviors that place them at risk for HIV infection—such as having intercourse with multiple partners and not using condoms.

A 1992 survey of some 9,000 teenagers and adults by the Edna Josephson Institute of Ethics found that an "unacceptably high" number are willing to lie, cheat, and steal. Some 61 percent of high school students admitted to having cheated on an exam during the past year, and 83 percent said they had lied to their parents during that time. A third said they had shoplifted, and a third said they would lie on a résumé or job application if necessary to get the job.

Materialism and selfishness are too often the motives for students to work part time. According to the 1992 report by the National Safe Work Institute, 5.5 million high school students have part-time jobs. The average 15-year-old worker works 17 hours a week in addition to a 32.5-hour school week. Sixteen- and 17-year-olds work 21 hours a week on average.

That kind of work schedule offers students little time for studying. And students working late at night may be coming to school too tired to learn, the report says. That may account, in part, for the consistently poor showings of American students on academic achievement tests.

Under pressure to conform, to achieve, and to make money, an increasing proportion of American students are suffering from problems of stress. The suicide rate for adolescents ages 15-19 has quadrupled over the past four decades, from 2.7 per 100,000 in 1950 to 11.3 in 1988. Two percent of high school students, or 276,000 young people, sustained medical injuries while attempting to commit suicide during the past year. According to the federal Centers for Disease Control, approximately one in four students acknowledged thinking seriously about attempting suicide during the past year.

Not surprisingly, a disproportionate percentage of the most troubled young people are from racial minority groups. Surveys of youth deviance consistently reveal minority students in the most endangered brackets. Minority students are also particularly at risk of dropping out of school.

About one-third of the nation's students are from racial minority groups, and the proportion is growing. They tend to be concentrated in, but by no means limited to, the larger inner-city schools (and scattered throughout rural areas, particularly in the South). Within 15 years, the student bodies in a number of our most populous states will have a majority of minority students.

Behind all of these numbers are real children, and you will find them in your classrooms. Indeed, teachers will bear the brunt of trying to find ways to reach these young people and help them forge the tools they will need to survive and succeed in a changing world.

It will not be easy. The majority of teachers responding to a 1992 survey by the Metropolitan Life Insurance Company expressed dismay and frustration over their students' lack of readiness for school; and

National Indicators of Child Well-Being

Indicators	From		To		Difference
Percent low birth weight babies	1980	6.8 %	1989	7.0 %	+0.2 %
Infant mortality rate (per 1,000 live births)	1980	12.6	1989	9.8	-2.8
Death rate Ages 1-14 (per 100,000 children)	1980	39.5	1989	32.4	-7.1
Violent Death rate Ages 15-19 (per 100,000 teens)	1984	62.4	1989	69.3	+6.9
Percent all births that are to single teens	1980	7.5 %	1989	8.6 %	+1.1 %
Custody rate, ages 10-15 (per 100,000 youths)	1985	142	1989	156	+14
Percent graduating high school	1982	69.7 %	1989	69.6 %	-0.1 %
Percent children in poverty	1979	16.0 %	1986-90	19.5 %	+3.5 %
Percent children in single-parent families	1980-84	21.3 %	1987-91	24.1 %	+2.8 %

SOURCE: Center for the Study of Social Policy; Annie E. Casie Foundation

they worried that they are ill-equipped to deal with the range of problems their students present.

Among teachers citing student preparedness problems, 65 percent pointed to a lack of parental support as a serious hindrance to students. More than 40 percent cited poverty as a major problem, while 32 percent identified parents' drug or alcohol use as a cause of trouble. Teachers mentioned physical and psychological abuse, poor nutrition, student drinking, violence, language difficulties, and poor health as serious obstacles to teaching and learning.

In the face of such problems, teachers acknowledged that they often feel stymied and do not know how to help their students. More than two-thirds thought that their own education and training had not prepared them well to deal with these social problems.

But if such social and demographic forces have made teaching much more difficult, they have also made it more crucial to the welfare of the nation. As one teacher said during an open discussion at a national meeting of educators: "We as teachers may lament and resent that we are being asked to cope with problems that schools are not organized to deal with and we are not prepared to solve. But these are America's children, our students. We cannot turn them away or walk away from them. We cannot exchange them for students with less baggage. We must accept them as they come to us and do our best to help them learn and succeed. We owe that to them; we owe it to ourselves as teachers; and we owe it to this country." □

Discipline Problems

Percentage of teachers indicating the extent of certain problems in their school: United States, 1990-91

Problem	Extent of problem			
	Serious	Moderate	Minor	Not a problem
Student tardiness	10	29	39	22
Student absenteeism/class cutting	9	28	38	24
Physical conflicts among students	6	22	46	26
Robbery or theft of items over $10	3	9	38	50
Vandalism of school property	5	17	44	34
Student alcohol use	7	16	22	55
Student drug use	3	14	29	54
Sale of drugs on school grounds	1	5	25	69
Student tobacco use	5	19	26	50
Student possession of weapons	1	4	25	70
Trespassing	2	7	32	59
Verbal abuse of teachers	8	22	39	32
Physical abuse of teachers	•	3	18	78
Racial tensions	2	12	30	56

• Less than 0.5
Note: Percentages are computed across each row, but may not add to 100 because of rounding
Source: National Center for Education Statistics

2.

Getting Ready For School

The first national goal may be the hardest one to reach—and the most important.

By Deborah L. Cohen

The success of the six national education goals hinges to a great degree on the first: ensuring that, by the year 2000, all children enter school ready to learn. If children are already at risk when they enter school, it will be that much harder to meet the other five goals—raising high-school graduation rates, boosting students' competency in key subjects, making U.S. students first in the world in science and mathematics, ensuring that all adults are literate, and ridding schools of drugs and violence.

But the readiness goal itself may be the most difficult one to meet. It will require overcoming a complex set of obstacles and implementing a set of interventions far more comprehensive than anything now in place. Consider some of the obstacles:

There is still no broadly agreed to definition of the age group, range of services, or outcomes that determine readiness—though most agree that readiness must include health, support and education for parents, and good early-childhood care.

The readiness goal involves three objectives:
• Ensuring that all disadvantaged and disabled children have access to high quality, "developmentally appropriate" preschool programs;
• Seeing that all parents get the support they need to act as their children's first teachers and spend time each day helping their preschool children learn; and
• Improving access to prenatal and other health care to reduce the number of low-birthweight babies and ensure children get adequate nutrition and health care.

One fundamental problem with the goal, many maintain, is how it is worded. While the goal is most frequently associated with the preschool period, some experts have begun to advance a definition that extends beyond the earliest years. Advocating that the health, social, and emotional needs of families and children don't go away when a child enters school, top scientists in the field recently proposed abandoning the concept of school readiness and substituting continued readiness to learn. Experts have also proposed expanding Goal 1 to ensure that "every child comes to school every day ready to learn" and that "every school is ready for every child."

The goal's wording troubled early-childhood experts from the outset, some said, because it implied that a child didn't do any learning prior to school, and that any difficulties they encountered were their own fault. Teachers' differing expectations of what constitutes readiness could also unfairly pressure or penalize children or foster inappropriate classroom practices. Some school programs, for example, have been making kindergarten more stringently academic, a trend that has predisposed a number of children to unhappy experiences.

The National Association for the Education of Young Children argues for teaching approaches and policies that respond to the wide variations in young children's development, help compensate for inequities in their early-life experiences, and shift the onus to schools to be "ready" to meet young children's needs.

There is uncertainty about how to assess progress toward universal readiness. And that's important

---

because the measures used to assess readiness will in part determine the strategy used to achieve it. In addition to perpetuating a narrow definition of readiness, some experts fear that Goal 1 could encourage testing practices that they consider unreliable for young children.

"Just using the word has the potential of inviting more readiness tests," said Lorrie A. Shepard, a professor of education at the University of Colorado. Ms. Shepard has collected data suggesting that children held back or tracked into special classes based on readiness tests do not fare better than those of similar capacity who enter 1st grade on time—and may actually suffer harm. Readiness, she said, "is so evocative of the misuse that we've been seeing of school districts giving tests to decide if kids are ready and either not letting them in or relegating them to two-year kindergartens if they are not."

One of the biggest problems in testing readiness is that schools tend to reflect middle-class values and knowledge systems, which automatically set poor children at a great disadvantage. Measuring readiness, in fact, has been one of the thorniest issues faced by the National Education Goals Panel.

One of the biggest problems in testing readiness is that schools tend to reflect middle-class values and knowledge systems, which set poor children at a disadvantage.

When the group last year was unable to identify an acceptable readiness test, panel members divided along party lines over whether the first progress report on the goals should instead include data on prenatal and child health, preschool enrollment, family life, and other factors affecting a child's ability to learn.

An advisory group to the goals panel issued a report in the fall of 1991 proposing an in-school assessment process to gather data on children during their kindergarten year. Using parent and teacher observations, individually administered profiles of skills and knowledge, and a portfolio of children's performance, the assessment would gauge children's physical well-being and motor development, social and emotional development, approaches to learning, language usage, and cognition and general knowledge.

To avert "potential misuse," the report "assiduously avoids" the term readiness. It also stresses that results should not be used to "label, stigmatize, or classify" individual children or groups. Frustrated, some early childhood activists charge that the whole education-goals-panel activity has concentrated on how to measure progress rather than on how to achieve the goal.

Others believe the key to achieving Goal 1 is more resources. "There's just one obstacle," says Keith Geiger, the president of the National Education Association: "money."

Increasing numbers of states are investing in initiatives—from preschool programs to parenting education—that target high-risk groups or address pieces of the problem. But the cost of making full-day, high-quality preschool programs universally available makes the goal elusive.

Some, like Mr. Geiger, say federal, state, and local resources should be tapped to fund preschools through the public schools. In the past, there has not been the willingness to invest that kind of money. Even with the additional funding Head Start has received in recent years, it still falls far short of serving all the disadvantaged preschoolers who are eligible.

The funding gap is also impeding expanding children's access to health care, improving youngsters' nutrition, and ensuring that all children are immunized. "It's an outrage that we don't use the knowledge we have to assure the physical and emotional health of children when they enter school," says Jack Shonkoff, the chief of developmental and behavior pediatrics at the University of Massachusetts Medical School. "For preventable, treatable, or curable problems to appear at the schoolhouse door is unacceptable."

But as fiscally strapped states cut programs ranging from welfare benefits to school aid, advocates of early services will be doing well just to hold their own.

There is a complex group of players whose support and collaboration will be needed. "It just isn't a mystery in terms of what we ought to be doing," says one expert. "The problem is, how do you wrap it up so it's a coherent program?"

The problem is compounded by a lack of an "infrastructure" for reaching children from birth to age 5. "There is no one institution or set of institutions that has access to all of those families, so it's a hit-or-miss proposition," says Douglas R. Powell, the head of the department of child development and family studies at Purdue University. "It takes time to work through all those layers of bureaucracy."

Meeting the goal's objectives—especially in the current fiscal climate—will require unprecedented coordination among health, education, and social services agencies and also among groups that are themselves fragmented.

The link between health and school success, for example, could be made by placing a medical professional on the search committee for a school superintendent, or education people on a public-health advisory committee. Easing the funding restrictions that keep agencies from pooling and coordinating resources could also help cut across old lines that block progress toward Goal 1.

Educators can also play a key role in helping make progress toward Goal 1. Schools could begin by:

• becoming more adaptable to the range of children entering school and what they bring with them;

• minimizing retention and early categorization of children by responding to developmental and cultural differences among children;

• establishing non-traditional mixed-age grouping and team-teaching practices;

• recruiting, hiring and training early-education staff members;

• promoting programs that ease the transition between

Teachers could benefit from a human-development framework that would highlight the need to involve parents and meet kids' needs beyond mastering skills.

Head Start and school, to sustain the gains made by children in preschool.

Researchers are also calling for interdisciplinary training to ensure that professionals across sectors have a broad perspective and can pool their expertise.

Teachers, for example, could benefit from a human-development framework that would highlight the need to involve parents and meet children's needs beyond mastering skills. In addition to curricular reforms, though, schools' role must be redefined and facilities revamped to make them the primary contact point for the referral or delivery of a wide range of services to families. And for such efforts to succeed, many agree that parents must play a pivotal role.

Rather than focusing on counting to 10 or knowing the alphabet, advocates say, interventions should help parents bolster children's social and organizational skills and zeal for learning. "Readiness is really civilizing people," says Dorothy Rich, the president of the Home and School Institute Inc.

For disadvantaged families in particular, intervention with a child is much more effective if it causes a positive change in the parents' behavior as well. Ideally, family intervention would help some parents improve their literacy skills, education, or training, which would bolster their self-esteem and greatly enhance the readiness capability of their children. But many agree that creating the ideal conditions for a generation of young children to succeed will require large-scale societal change.

Besides ensuring families access to the support and services they need, says one skeptic, "You wouldn't have any homeless children, any unimmunized children, or children not covered through health insurance. No child would be living in poverty. . . . Even in affluent homes, you wouldn't have exposure to horrible, violent television or bad care. You would have high-quality child care for all who needed it. And then you would still have to make sure that what schools expected was appropriate."

But perhaps the most daunting challenge in the effort to achieve universal readiness is marshaling the "political will." Early-intervention activists complain that Goal 1 has not been made part of the political agenda; often, businessmen understand the need for early services better than politicians. Moreover, the United States is way behind other industrialized nations in offering broad support for young children in the form of child care, preschool, and paid family leave.

The broader public needs to start seeing young children as a priority, needs to understand that readiness is everyone's business. Such political, economic, and social obstacles make some experts skeptical about achieving the readiness goal. But they say they see it as a rare chance to spotlight the early years. Having readiness as a national priority gives the opportunity to launch initiatives that are good for states, regions, and localities. In the words of one expert: "We want to seize the moment!" □

From Education Week, *Feb. 12, 1992*

3.

Teaching A Moving Target

Children with attention deficit disorder are human dynamos who need lots of time and care.

By Jeff Meade

Adam Berard is not an easy child to teach. Even his mother acknowledges that. "His body moves before his mind can think," she says. "He's got as much energy as the sun. He never runs out." But Adam, now 9 years old and in the 4th grade at W.A. Bess Elementary School in Gastonia, N.C., isn't just a little boy with a lot of energy.

Adam suffers from attention deficit disorder, or ADD, a disturbance in the elaborate chemistry of the brain. Roughly 2 million children between the ages of 6 and 18 are believed to have ADD, making it one of the most common psychiatric disorders in school-age children. Children with ADD are obviously different. They're unpredictable, unfocused, and often wildly active. Children like Adam exhaust most teachers, taxing their patience and understanding to the limit. Such was surely the case as Adam began 2nd grade. "If he had something to say, no matter what else was going on in the class at the time, he'd just get right up and say it," recalls Cecilia Berard, Adam's mother. "He had a hard time getting along with other kids. Adam's teacher sent home ugly notes. He'd cry every Sunday night. He just didn't want to go to school."

Ultimately, Adam's classroom behavior led to conflict between his parents and his school. At issue: whether the schools of Gaston County were obligated to provide and pay for special education for Adam, a child whose disability wasn't spelled out in federal special education regulations.

Adam's parents believed the district was obliged; local school officials did not agree with them. The Berards pressed the issue and, with the help of the U.S. Department of Education's Office for Civil Rights, eventually prevailed.

But the complex issues raised by the case are central to a growing national debate over the education of children with ADD. The focus of that debate is the Individuals with Disabilities Education Act, formerly known as the Education of the Handicapped Act, which requires schools to provide appropriate programs for children with a wide variety of handicapping disabilities. Passed by Congress in late 1990, IDEA mentions a number of handicaps by name, but not specifically ADD. As a result, teachers, parents, and administrators have been struggling to more clearly define ADD and to decide how schools should handle students who suffer from it.

Causes of ADD Unknown

The specific causes of attention deficit disorder are unknown. Researchers understand that a specific class of brain chemicals, known as neurotransmitters, are involved in ADD, but, according to James Swanson, director of the Child Development Center at the University of California at Irvine, they don't know how the disturbance in those chemicals triggers attention deficits. A recent article in *The New England Journal of Medicine* reported that people with ADD exhibit reduced glucose metabolism in certain parts of the brain, but the reason for this cerebral slowdown remains unclear.

Whatever the underlying mechanism, children with

ADD have trouble focusing on relevant information—for example, following simple instructions such as "open the book, turn to page 10, and read down from the top of the page." When trying to complete such a task, children with ADD are distracted by all the competing sights and sounds of the day, from the hiss of the radiator to the squeak of the audiovisual equipment cart as it's wheeled down the hall. Children with ADD understand the instructions, Swanson says, but they have difficulty following through with an appropriate or disciplined behavior. An ADD child may sit down with every intention of completing a reading assignment, but he or she is soon overcome by an impulse to jump up and splash a hand in the goldfish bowl.

To make matters worse, children with ADD are often—but not always—hyperactive. These children are wildly impulsive, with boundless energy and no sense of danger; they leap before they look.

Other children with ADD are placid as a pond, though they also have great difficulty focusing on the work at hand. ADD children may be quite intelligent, giving rise to teachers' complaints that they just don't work hard enough. As far as learning goes, it is the distractibility—not the hyperactivity—that sets ADD children apart from other children.

A Challenge for Teachers

For teachers, understanding and dealing with ADD children is often easier said than done. Many students with ADD can be quite disruptive in class: They fidget; they blurt out answers to questions; they interrupt other students; they lose homework assignments; they flit from one task to another.

"It is very frustrating for a teacher," explains Betty Matre, a behavioral specialist at the Lloyd Estates Elementary School in Broward County, Fla., who is also the mother of a 7-year-old ADD child. "Many times you want the students to control their behavior and to be attentive, but they're not physically able to do those things. You really have to tailor teaching to them."

ADD children respond to one-on-one attention, but one-on-one is a physical impossibility for most teachers. "They're able to respond to you," says teacher Alice Meyer of Pederson Elementary School in Eau Claire, Wis. "But there's only one of you."

Because children with attention deficit disorder can be hard to control in class, teachers and administrators often press parents to treat the syndrome with prescription drugs. In many cases, the wilder impulses of ADD children can be curbed through the use of either central

RHODA BAER

nervous system stimulants (such as Ritalin, Dexadrine, and Cylert) or antidepressants. It may seem odd to prescribe stimulants for these children, but ADD is actually a disorder that involves slow brain function—hence the distractibility. The stimulants, in effect, wake up the brain, enabling the children to focus their attention longer.

Drug-Use Controversial

Roughly 700,000 children under treatment for ADD now take Ritalin, the drug most commonly prescribed for the disorder. For many children, this drug is essential to their treatment. But its use is controversial. Critics warn, for example, that some children are on the drug because of misdiagnosis. Others say they are concerned because the drug can produce disturbing side effects—such as insomnia, loss of appetite, irritability, weight loss, and stomach aches—in a small number of children. The mild appearance of such side effects, however, may represent the lesser of two evils for genuine ADD sufferers. Clinical studies demonstrate improved behavior in about 75 percent of all children taking stimulant medications. Parents, too, report dramatic improvement in their children's behavior. And experienced teachers say they can always tell when an ADD child has missed a daily dose of the drug.

"I have six children with ADD in my homeroom," Meyer says. "All, on occasion, go without their Ritalin, and that, for me, is a real long day."

But the problem with Ritalin and other drugs is that they don't necessarily improve the ADD student's ability to learn. "There's no clear evidence that Ritalin alone has any effect on educational performance," Swanson explains. According to a recent article, co-authored by Swanson, in *The Journal of Learning Disabilities*, less than 20 percent of the children who are treated with Ritalin show improvement in math, spelling, or reading.

Children with ADD often do experience success, however, when a program of behavior management and positive reinforcement accompanies the use of drugs. Since children spend a great deal of time at school, teachers must be part of the behavior management program; in many cases, a little extra help is all that's needed. "For 50 percent of the kids," Swanson says, "either common sense intervention in a regular classroom or supplementary services with extra aides or pullout programs will work just fine."

Broward County teacher Betty Matre helps other teachers in her school learn how to establish a productive learning environment for ADD children. As part of her job, Matre patrols the halls in the morning, visiting classrooms and chatting with children who have been identified as having attention deficits. "I hug my kids," she says. "I encourage them and give them pep talks. I visit them throughout the day. I also have a walkie-talkie, so if there's a problem during the day, teachers can call me immediately."

Without this kind of appropriate and consistent help, children with ADD often grow up with negative self-images and eventually turn to destructive behaviors. A high percentage—more than 40 percent—have trouble with the law as adults. "Eventually, they get older, more frustrated, and more aggressive," Swanson says. "Then, they get into the juvenile justice system instead of the education system; they're getting taken care of but in the wrong way."

Given such dire consequences, a parent of an ADD child might assume that a diagnosis of attention deficit disorder automatically entitles that child to special services—either within the regular classroom or in the form of pullout classes. But special treatment is more likely to be the exception than the rule, mainly because ADD is not formally recognized as a disability in federal aid programs.

The Individuals with Disabilities Education Act defines—and requires appropriate school programs for—a wide variety of handicapping disabilities, ranging from mental retardation to epilepsy to tuberculosis; districts receive federal money under IDEA for each qualifying child. But nowhere in the act is attention deficit disorder listed as a specific disability that entitles a child to special services from a school.

Therefore, to qualify for special education, children with ADD must also have another emotional problem or learning disability that is specified by law. Children who qualify fall into one of three general categories: severe emotional disturbance, specific learning disabled, or a catch-all category called "other health impaired." Under the third category, a child with ADD might receive extra help from the school system, if the school system decides to respond to the child's needs by defining ADD as a qualifying medical disorder.

All this could change, members of the ADD lobby say, if Congress makes attention deficit disorder a separate, distinct disability under IDEA. Late last year, the U.S. Department of Education began efforts to clarify the legal status of children with ADD. If Congress acts, the decision to amend IDEA could have a profound effect on schools as early as this school year.

Confusion Over the Exact Causes

Efforts to amend IDEA to include children with ADD have been stymied by confusion over the exact causes

and definition of the disorder. Over the years, ADD has gone by many other names—from minimal brain damage to hyperkinesis—each with a different shade of meaning. Many suspected causes also have been considered, from too much sugar in the child's diet to food allergies. These theories have been largely discredited, but they have an extraordinarily long shelf life.

Take, for example, the runaround Mary Cahill Fowler of Fair Haven, N.J., was put through before her son, David, was diagnosed as having attention deficit disorder.

"At the time he was diagnosed, he was in a private kindergarten," explains Fowler, a former teacher and author of *Maybe You Know My Kid*. "We had a county child-study team evaluate him.

"During the evaluation, David was sent to a pediatric neurologist, who told us he had attention deficit disorder with hyperactivity. Prior to that, David had had a series of misdiagnoses. We ran the gamut, from 'There's nothing wrong with him' to 'He's just hyperactive.' We took him to an allergist, who gave him shots for dust. And, when that didn't work, they had us put him on an elimination diet to see if foods were causing the problem. At one point, a child psychiatrist suggested he was suffering from an 'individuation separation complex' brought on by the introduction of a sibling. That was my favorite."

All told, it took about a year and a half of chasing down doctors and consulting psychiatrists before the Fowlers obtained the right diagnosis. During this time, David put his parents through hell.

"From the moment this child was born, I could do very little to quiet or amuse him," Fowler says. "If he was hurting and I tried to hold him, he would just become more active and try to wiggle away. I assumed there had to be something intrinsically wrong with me. After all, what mother can't nurture her own baby?"

The Fowlers consider themselves lucky to have found the right diagnosis. "If parents find out the problem is ADD, they're fortunate," she says. "If they aren't fortunate, they think they are bad parents or the child is a bad child, and the seeds of failure get planted."

Because there is so much confusion over identifying children with ADD, many educators are reluctant to support a law that would require them to label children with the syndrome. As a result, groups as diverse as the National Education Association, the National Association of State Directors of Special Education, the National School Boards Association, the Council of Chief State School Officers, and the NAACP Legal Defense and Education Fund have come together to resist any effort to establish a special category for attention deficit disorder within IDEA.

Their concern, spokesmen say, is that including ADD in the federal law could result in teachers inaccurately designating unruly children as ADD children, as many now designate slow children as educable mentally retarded. This kind of labeling, they agree, can be harmful to students. "Everybody disagrees on what ADD is and what it means," says William Schipper, executive director of the NASDSE. "The medical procedures for pinning the label on a kid are not universally well-accepted."

ADD Probably Overdiagnosed

Few within the ADD research community would dispute that there is often confusion about ADD. Even researcher Swanson concedes that "ADD is probably overdiagnosed. Estimates that as many as 15 to 20 percent of school-age children have it are wrong."

Nevertheless, he says, there is a commonly accepted definition of the disorder. To arrive at a diagnosis of ADD, Swanson says, it isn't enough to document signs and symptoms of rambunctious behavior and maddening distractibility; one also must rule out all the non-organic factors that might account for the symptoms, such as anxiety or depression. A child who is being abused or adjusting to his or her parents' messy divorce may show many symptoms similar to ADD.

Another reason some groups object to including the disorder under IDEA is the increased cost of providing special education services to so many children. As a rule, special education programs cost local districts about two and a half times more than the cost of regular education.

But Swanson believes there would be no drastic growth in the number of children requiring special services if the federal law were revised to recognize ADD as a categorical disability. "Half the kids with ADD probably don't need anything from the schools," Swanson says. "Of the half that do need something, perhaps 70 or 80 percent just need supplementary services in a regular education classroom. A small percentage might need special education."

The difference, he says, will be in treatment: "A good many students with ADD are in special education programs, but not getting appropriate treatment. Often, these kids are just in the wrong setting."

Schipper and others argue, however, that existing laws provide adequate care for children with ADD. "The great majority of the kids with ADD, as we are informed by the experts, are not necessarily in need of special education," Schipper says. "They may need some accommodation in the regular class."

At the moment, Schipper adds, most educators are satisfied that a seriously impaired child with ADD would receive an appropriate evaluation and an individual education plan, if necessary, under IDEA. He says a child might receive placement in a special program "if he or she's obviously well behind his [or her] peers, or totally disruptive or uncontrollable in the classroom, and none of the techniques the teacher uses to help are successful."

But ADD lobbyists point out that many school

systems take the view that they are precluded from spending federal funds on any disability that is not clearly enumerated in IDEA. Such was the position taken by officials in Gaston County, N.C., where Adam Berard lives.

What the officials in Gaston County didn't realize was that another federal statute—Section 504 of the Education Rehabilitation Act—also regulates special education policies. Unlike IDEA, which clearly defines qualifying disabilities, Section 504 broadly defines a handicapped person as one whose disability substantially limits one or more major life activities. Schools that don't appropriately respond to a parent or teacher's request for an evaluation could lose federal funds.

Cecilia Berard says she heard about Section 504 from the head of a support group for children with learning disabilities. In July 1990, she says, she wrote a letter to the Office for Civil Rights "just to see what would happen." On Sept. 17, OCR ruled in favor of the Berards, requiring the district to provide educational services for Adam, and for other children with ADD in the district, or face a full investigation of district policies regarding the education of the handicapped; for the duration of the investigation, all federal funds would be suspended. The district complied.

"We have always tried to put the child first, both in terms of what is best for the child, and in terms of fulfilling our responsibilities under the law," explains Superintendent Edwin West. "Once we were made aware of what Section 504 required, we complied."

However, West notes, following the law may become a financial hardship for the district. Because ADD isn't recognized under IDEA, the school system receives no supplementary federal funds to provide treatment for children suffering from the disorder. "The programs all come out of local funds," he says.

Despite the cost, Berard has her own idea of what's fair. To her, district compliance with her request was the right thing to do. Last year, Adam began attending a special class two hours a day. "He seems to enjoy school a lot better," she says, "and he's getting along better with kids."

Many experts in the field of attention deficit disorder view the Berards' triumph as one in a series of important victories for children with ADD. But most won't be satisfied until Congress amends IDEA to recognize attention deficit disorder as a categorical disability.

In the meantime, the ADD child's struggle goes on, far from the halls of Congress, in the halls and the classrooms of America's schools. From teacher Matre's perspective, teachers still have much to learn. "ADD affects a great many children in our classrooms," she says. "More and more teachers are learning about ADD every day, but there are many teachers who think they don't need to know. They do." □

From Teacher Magazine, *October 1991*

4.

Programs For Gifted Kids?

In the competition for resources, programs for the gifted are losing out to programs for special-needs students.

By Debra Viadero

Once educators in his community decided he was gifted, Marcus Simpson began to do wonderful things in school. He created inventions, spent hours working on complex problems, and visited with a local television station to find out how weather reports are produced. He gave a presentation on meteorology to his classmates and spoke for more than half an hour, without notes, because the subject excited him so much.

Marcus lost some of his enthusiasm for school, however, after the local school board voted to eliminate his gifted-and-talented program. Back in his regular classes, his mother noticed, Marcus began to grow restless. Last fall, six weeks into the 8th grade, he transferred to a private school.

"You're watching your child just sort of becoming bored and unmotivated," Marcus's mother, Janney Simpson, says. "It's hard to decide to make a transfer six weeks into the year."

Experts in the field of gifted education say Marcus's situation may become increasingly commonplace in the future—not only because funding for such programs is scarce, but also because school reformers consider gifted education a form of tracking.

Some education reforms have called for schools to move away from the traditional practice of grouping students according to their ability in favor of more heterogeneous classroom settings. And that trend, along with such other reform-minded innovations as site-based management and cooperative learning, has put traditional gifted-education programs in jeopardy.

"We believe that the field of education for the gifted and talented is currently facing a quiet crisis," two researchers in the field, Joseph S. Renzulli and Sally M. Reis, wrote in a recent paper, "and that this crisis is directly related to the educational-reform movement in America."

'Rich Get Richer'

To a large degree, school programs for gifted students have always been engaged in a struggle for survival. Despite a boom in support for gifted education in the 1980's, the programs have long been criticized as elitist or unnecessary.

"Every time the legislature deals with this issue, the first question is: Why should the rich get richer?" says Lee Sheldon, a consultant in gifted-and-talented education to the California Department of Education.

Gifted-education advocates worry that that attitude will erode their programs even further. They point to recent developments in several states. For example:

• The number of towns with programs for gifted students in Connecticut, Marcus Simpson's home state, has declined by 20 percent over two years as state reimbursements for the programs have dried up. And Gov. Lowell P. Weicker Jr. has proposed eliminating state support altogether.

• State funds for gifted programs in Massachusetts have been reduced from a high of $1 million two years ago to zero last year. Michigan, Vermont, and New York have also reported cuts in their gifted programs.

• New Hampshire lost its only state coordinator for

gifted programs last year in a budget-cutting move. Gifted-education advocates in the state say that loss, along with the elimination of a state-grant program for gifted education, has also prompted a college in the state to drop its teacher-training program for instructors of gifted students.

"It's been disastrous," says Ms. Reis, a principal investigator for the National Research Center on the Gifted and Talented at the University of Connecticut. The center, the first of its kind, was established in 1990 with a $7.5-million federal grant.

There were so many programs being cut and so many people losing their jobs that the center decided to change the direction of its research to focus on how gifted children are faring in their regular classrooms. Those studies, three of which were released in early 1992, "paint a pretty sad picture," Ms. Reis says.

They found that gifted pupils in regular elementary-school classrooms typically receive the same curriculum as academically average students and that they are usually asked to revisit material they have already learned. The researchers concluded that gifted students would be better served if they were freed from covering up to 70 percent of the standard curriculum or were grouped by ability.

"They spend years and years learning what they already know and, sometimes by 3rd or 4th grade, their affective feelings about school have already changed," Ms. Reis says.

Pamela Thompson, the mother of another gifted student in Marcus Simpson's town, agrees. Her daughter had spent her time in gifted classes honing her writing skills. After the program was cut, however, her daughter, who was then in 6th grade, spent some of her spare time in study hall learning to knit.

"If she's bored now, I really fear what's going to happen in the future," Ms. Thompson says.

Eighty-five percent of the parents of gifted pupils in that community said the loss of the program had had a negative effect on their children, according to another University of Connecticut study. The researchers declined to reveal the name of the community. Nearly half of the parents had, like Ms. Simpson, considered putting their children in private schools after the program was cut.

Researchers and advocates say that gifted programs

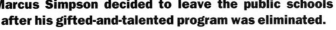

Marcus Simpson decided to leave the public schools after his gifted-and-talented program was eliminated.

are particularly vulnerable to budget cuts because 24 states do not mandate them. In Connecticut, for example, schools are required to identify gifted students but not to serve them. The programs are more vulnerable because they benefit only a small number of students—usually 3 percent to 5 percent of schoolchildren in most states.

Faced with a decision of whether to increase class sizes for all students or reduce gifted programs for a few, many local school boards may be right in choosing the latter, some gifted-program supporters concede. But, in some states and communities, the motivation to do away with gifted programs also has something to do with changing educational philosophies.

In the early 1980's, when the education-reform movement was stressing economic competitiveness, gifted programs experienced a small boom. Both state and federal support for programs meant to nurture the "best and brightest" increased for virtually the first time since the Sputnik era. Now, however, a number of education reforms have called for an end to traditional classroom practices of grouping students by ability.

Both the National Governors' Association and the Carnegie Council on Adolescent Development have, for example, issued reports in recent years that have been critical of such practices. The problem with ability groups, some reformers say, is that students get locked into a particular academic track at an early age.

While higher-ability students may continue to thrive in homogeneous classroom settings, pupils consigned to lower-level tracks are less fortunate. Studies show that such students get fewer classroom resources, inferior teachers, a less challenging curriculum, and fewer opportunities than do the better students. Moreover, in many communities, these pupils are disproportionately poor or members of minority groups.

"There is a strong recognition that, when we separate off the top 5 percent or 10 percent of kids in an attempt to give them special programs, we lose sight of what happens to the education of the other 90 percent of kids," says Jeannie Oakes, a professor of education at the University of California at Los Angeles.

"Most of us see any kind of whole-class grouping and most pullout programs as simply another form of tracking," she adds.

Advocates of gifted education say, however, that

schools should draw a distinction between tracking, in which students are homogeneously grouped in every subject and for every grade level, and ability grouping, in which students may be with students of similar ability in some subjects but not in others.

"We are anti-tracking," says Peter D. Rosenstein, the executive director of the National Association for Gifted Children. "However, though children are born deserving equal opportunity, they're not born with equal potential."

Some parents of gifted students also complain that their children tend to fare poorly in the kinds of cooperative-learning groups that characterize instruction in many of these new mixed-ability classrooms. These groupings usually involve children of varying academic abilities who work together on a project or a complex problem. Teachers evaluate pupils both individually and as a team for their work in these groups. Parents of gifted pupils say, however, that, in practice, their children often end up doing all the work in the groups or teaching their less able peers.

"Kids are suffering the social consequences—they get called 'geek,' 'nerd,' or 'dork'—to a level they've not experienced before because they're being held accountable for the learning of a group of kids," said Ms. Reis of the National Center for Research on the Gifted and Talented.

However, Robert Slavin, who has led much of the research on cooperative learning, disputes such contentions. Preliminary statistics from his own ongoing studies indicate that gifted and higher-ability pupils in properly run cooperative-learning groups gain as much from the group interactions as do lower-achievers. He notes, however, that in the classrooms he studied, the more academically advanced students were permitted to do some accelerated work in reading and math.

"I don't see any reason at all to provide separate gifted programs at any level," says Mr. Slavin, who is the co-director of the elementary-school program at the Johns Hopkins University's Center for Research on Effective Schooling for Disadvantaged Students.

"The main thing to do is accommodate the rate of learning for these kids," he argues. "If that means grouping within a class, where they go at different rates, O.K." He adds: "If it's letting a 6th grader take math with the 7th graders, I think that's reasonable. But if you're given a stark choice, if someone's going to provide $1,000 for an additional enrichment program for gifted kids, I would say $1,000 worth of one-to-one tutoring for a kid struggling to learn to read can make a big difference."

Partly as a result of such criticisms of gifted education and partly because of new theories of "multiple intelligences," advocates in recent years have taken steps to "open up" their programs. In an effort to bring more minority, non-English-speaking, and special-education students into gifted programs, for example, researchers have begun looking for ways other than traditional I.Q. tests to determine if a student has gifted abilities.

"We believe that our field should shift its emphasis from a traditional concept of 'being gifted' [or not being gifted] to a concern about the development of gifted behaviors in those youngsters who have the highest potential for benefiting from special-educational services," Mr. Renzulli and Ms. Reis wrote in their paper last year in Gifted Child Quarterly.

Some newer models of gifted education also strive to provide schoolwide "enrichment," with gifted-education teachers acting as resources for regular classroom teachers. Such models include projects or activities in which a wide range of students can participate.

"To a good degree, gifted education is good education," says James Delisle, the president of the Association for the Gifted of the Council for Exceptional Children. "If we're guilty of anything, it's probably being too isolated in a resource room on the corner."

Many educators of the gifted maintain, however, that their pupils still need a certain degree of separation from regular classrooms. "One mind sharpens off another," Mr. White of Connecticut says. Moreover, he adds, gifted children often feel pressured to "hide their light under a bushel" in the regular classroom because of the social stigma associated with giftedness.

Site-Based Management

Coordinators of gifted programs in several states also see a threat to their programs in the movement toward site-based management, in which more of the control for how schools are run is placed in the hands of teachers and principals.

In California, for example, schools using such management arrangements can often obtain waivers from state education-department rules, including those governing gifted programs.

"Usually, when a district goes to site-based management, one of the first casualties is the district-level person who coordinated the GATE [gifted and talented education] program," Mr. Sheldon says.

It is too soon to tell how much of the retrenchment in gifted-education programs is the result of changing educational philosophies and how much is the result of limited resources. In many locations, education reforms are coexisting peacefully with gifted-education programs. Concepts currently at the heart of education reform—such as hands-on learning and the use of authentic databases and information in classroom instruction—have been a part of gifted-education programs for years. To abandon the field now, in order to embrace some other reforms, some say, would be like "throwing the baby out with the bath water."

After all, says Mr. White: "These kids will be our future leaders, discoverers, and great performers." □

From Education Week, *March 18, 1992*

5.

Kids Just Ain't The Same

Teachers say students are becoming apathetic, impatient, self-centered, overwhelmed, and harder to motivate.

By Mary Koepke

If anyone is in a good position to determine how students have changed over the years, it's Allen Weinheimer. The 65-year-old has been teaching calculus at the same suburban Indianapolis high school for the past 36 years. And if anyone has a good chance of giving today's kids a thumbs up, it's Weinheimer. His students—the type who take the challenging, elective math course—are considered to be among the most highly motivated in the school, and his school—North Central High—is considered one of the best in the country.

Yet here is what the popular math teacher has to say: "Kids don't have time to do assignments. They seem to be satisfied to make a 'C.' It's a waste of talent. They know that to do any better will require more effort, and they are at the limit. They don't have any more time or effort to give." Weinheimer isn't alone. He expresses a concern that many experienced teachers are voicing about student motivation. As 25-year Ohio veteran Chris Hayward puts it, "It's harder for teachers to be teachers."

These aren't the teachers of inner-city teens plagued by urban violence and poverty; everyone knows that their jobs have gotten tougher. Weinheimer and Hayward are the teachers of kids who attend model schools, who live in suburban communities that are relatively safe and still fairly homogeneous. The students about whom they're talking are not the small percentage who drop out, or fail. They are the ones who succeed.

Increasingly, these teachers say, their students are becoming apathetic, impatient, self-centered, over-whelmed, and harder to motivate; they demand more, yet aren't willing to work for it. According to a recent poll of more than 21,000 teachers by the Carnegie Foundation for the Advancement of Teaching, 71 percent of teachers agree that students in their school "want to do just enough to get by."

Charlotte Huggins, who has been teaching English at New Trier High School in Winnetka, Ill., for the past 27 years, watched in horror recently as a cheating scandal unfolded at her nationally respected school. A group of students, who clearly did not need to cheat, had been stealing material from a teacher's file over a period of time. "Fifteen years ago, you wouldn't have seen this. You were still getting neck-craning, shouted whispers—the sorts of things kids were ashamed of when caught," says Huggins. "Now they're not even ashamed. They're only sorry that they got caught."

Although the unfortunate drama did not occur in Huggins' classroom, she has her share of frustrations. "What I see in this school is that kids aren't willing to accept lower grades," she notes, "but they aren't willing to work harder to raise them." After midterm grades have been sent to colleges with applications, she watches sadly as the vast majority of her seniors lose interest in their studies. "Of course, to some extent you saw that before," she admits. "But it's getting worse."

Private schools aren't immune, either. High school art teacher Chris Hayward at the Cincinnati (Ohio) Country Day School has similar problems. Recently, a gifted student in Hayward's video class decided it wasn't worth the effort to finish a meaningful long-term project. "She is not alone," says Hayward.

"Students are losing sight of their priorities."

Compared with the challenges faced by some inner-city teachers, these problems may seem minimal. But as the nation reels with more and more bad news regarding its schools, as the reports about poor test scores flood in, to think that even the kids with all the advantages are sliding into mediocrity is depressing. It symbolizes the overall concern that America is losing its edge.

But, wait a minute—is there really something wrong with the typical suburban teen or are teachers just idealizing the past? Something *is* wrong, according to David Elkind, child psychiatrist and author of *The Hurried Child* and *All Grown Up and No Place to Go.*

"Of course, in one respect kids and teenagers really haven't changed," says Elkind. "I mean they still go through puberty and all those things." And there is some truth to the notion that every decade of adults feels compelled to ask, what's the matter with kids today? Rewind a couple of thousand years, and you'll even hear Aristotle whining about the laziness of the youth in his day. "Even though children have been here forever," Elkind explains, "they are always new for each generation."

But Elkind and researchers who have been studying adolescent behavior and development understand why teachers are frustrated by students' behavior and performance. Today's teenagers are different from previous generations in many ways—in their attitudes, their values, and their behavior. Considering the changes that have reshaped society in the past 50 years, it would be miraculous if kids hadn't changed.

So how are young people different? And what does it mean for teachers? Are kids collapsing under the weight of societal pressures? Or are schools remiss in placing too much emphasis on rote learning and superficial test scores? Who's the culprit? Bad kids? Bad parents? Bad schools? Too much television? A combination of one or more of the above?

Although opinions and theories vary, one common word pops up in all the explanations for why kids are acting the way they do: stress. It is harder these days for teachers to be teachers; but that's because it's harder these days for kids to be kids. The world is changing more rapidly and more dramatically than ever before; and it's becoming a more stressful place for young people—even those children of reasonably affluent families who seem to have it so easy.

Young people today seem to have lost some of the natural optimism that has always been characteristic of youth. Only 17 percent of high schoolers feel that life in America will get better 10 years from now, according to the 1992 Scholastic Poll of American Youth. "Kids used to be basically optimistic," says Elkind. "But there isn't this sense of progress that was once present. We don't see the world progressing, necessarily." News of global warming, the deterioration of the environment, the increasing problems of homelessness, racial intoler-

ance, violence, AIDS, and teenage pregnancy abound. With recent innovations in video and television technology, bad news reaches us faster and in more graphic detail.

Hayward can practically monitor the increases in societal stress by looking at the topics of her school's recent assemblies. "One of our Alumnae was date-raped; she came in and talked to students," says Hayward. "Last week, we did a thing on AIDS. Three weeks ago, we did one on drugs. And tomorrow night, 75 students have signed up to learn how to defend themselves against aggressors."

The bad economic situation and the growing national debt aren't exactly relieving any of the pressure. This generation senses that it will be harder to "make it" in the new world. And as the media constantly point out, a bachelor's degree or even a graduate degree is no longer a guarantee to good jobs and prosperity. "Kids are not stupid," says Elkind. "They see that no matter how hard they work, they still might not find jobs."

But the heart of the problem lies much closer to home than the ozone hole and the economy. Psychologists believe that the messages that kids are getting from society—particularly parents—are adding pressure to the pot. On the one hand, we expect too much from adolescents; and on the other hand, we don't expect enough. It may seem paradoxical, but the two notions are not so far apart.

We send them the message: Don't just be all that you can be; be perfect—and be grown up about it.

One of the most fundamental changes in society is that we now believe that life ought to be perfect, argues Glen Elliott, head of Child and Adolescent Psychology at the University of California, San Francisco, and co-editor of a definitive new text, *At the Threshold: The Developing Adolescent.*

Teens are bombarded with the message that perfection is not only attainable but also a must. Television tells them that they should have the perfect body and wear the perfect clothes. It's not enough to own a pair of sneakers for the basketball court. You have to own a pair of sneakers perfectly designed for basketball.

And society is setting standards that are intrinsically impossible for most people to meet. "Take sports, for example," explains Elliott. "We have this extraordinary value for certain kinds of sports figures. Starting in about the 5th grade, we have created a structure that promises kids that if you're at the very, very top you're worth millions. But if anything happens to you—if you're not that good or if you get injured—then you're not worth anything."

This message is especially devastating to teens. "Kids don't know how to process that," explains Elliot. "All of those things speak to the very fears that adolescents have to begin with: i.e., 'I'm not perfect.'"

Today's teenage girls face particularly difficult standards, notes Cornell historian Joan Jacobs Brumberg, who has been studying girls' diaries from the past and present. "Girls face a particular anxiety about appearance and have serious body-image concerns," she notes, and writes about in her book, *Fasting Girls: the History of Anorexia Nervosa*.

And teens are not just getting these messages from the 3 hours of sitcoms and MTV that they supposedly watch each day. Parents have a lot to do with it, too. Harold Stevenson, psychology researcher and co-author of *The Learning Gap: Why our schools are failing and what we can learn from Japanese and Chinese Education*, believes that American parents are sending their kids the wrong message.

Today's parents don't just want their kids to be good students, they want them to be everything. Parents value education, but the problem is that they also place as high a value on lots of other things. "The demands on youth have increased greatly," says the University of Michigan researcher. "Kids are supposed to do well in school and be popular, help around the home, look better, do better in sports." And on top of all that, get

---

In the 1960s, educators became excited about the idea that IQs could actually be raised with early intervention—a notion that has led to all kinds of miseducation.

---

jobs. Kids in the United States are working at paying jobs more now than they used to and are working more than kids in other countries, according to Stevenson.

Teacher Allen Weinheimer hates to ask how many of his algebra students work 20 or even 40 hours a week in addition to carrying a heavy academic load. He can spot them anyway by seeing whose heads are down on the desk first thing in the morning. "Sometimes you think that students have gotten lazier," explains Weinheimer. "But priorities are changing. School used to be 'Number One,' but now it isn't."

Kids get caught up in so many other things that they're stretched to the limit. Weinheimer recalls the smart senior boy who was failing his calculus class—not because of a lack of ability, but because, with a 40-hour-a-week job, he simply didn't have time for his schoolwork. Did he have to work to support his family? "No, he said it was important that he work because he wanted to buy a car," says Weinheimer, frustration still audible in his voice.

In extensive cross-cultural studies of students in the United States and other countries, Stevenson found

that over 70 percent of U.S. students felt stress once a week or every day. The surprise here is that U.S. kids scored higher on the stress tests than Asian kids; meanwhile U.S. educators have been criticizing Asian education for being too stressful. We've assumed that such high academic standards must drive kids crazy.

The reason that Asian countries produce good students who are not totally stressed out, Stevenson says, is because everyone there still believes that school is the student's number one priority; school is the student's job. In interviews with parents, Stevenson hears the message repeated in many different variations. "An Asian mother said, 'I don't expect my child to do chores. It would break my heart because it would take my child away from his studies,'" he recalls.

Not expecting 14-year-old Jack and Jill to mow a blade of grass or wash a dish might seem a bit extreme to suburban moms and dads. They find nothing wrong with the good old tradition of wanting kids to help around the house. It is also normal for them to want their kids to be well-rounded individuals who can play a tune on the piano as well as tell you the difference between an atom and a molecule.

But a change in attitude toward children has caused us to go overboard, says Elkind. In the 1960s, educators became excited about the idea that IQs weren't fixed but could actually be raised with early intervention—a good notion that has since led to all kinds of miseducation, in Elkind's mind. Now, too many parents believe and expect that if they teach a subject or task early enough, their children can become Einsteins at anything. "It used to be that you wanted your kids to be normal. Precocity was looked upon as irregular: Early ripe, early rot," Elkind explains. "Now, everybody wants their children to be gifted."

As a result, parents push their kids into more and more activities at an earlier age. According to Elkind, it's much more prevalent today than 15 or 20 years ago.

Consequently, by the time kids get to high school, some of them burn out. "For example, we see a million fewer kids going out for sports in high school, and I think that has to do with the fact that so many kids have been in competitive sports since the age of 5," he notes. "At a time when their bodies are physically able, and they could really do well, they get turned off." And some very good students, if their parents would let them, would prefer to postpone college for a year or two in order to try something else; they feel like they've spent their whole life in school.

The root of the problem, as Elkind sees it, is that adults are putting their own needs above the needs of children and young people. Ever since those tumultuous 60s, a shift has slowly worked its way into the fabric of our everyday lives. The shift is to value autonomy, the individual needs of self-realization and achievement, over those of the family and community.

It's not all bad, Elkind notes. There are healthy and

beneficial aspects of self-realization. Before, the individual was too submerged in the family, but now we've swung the balance too far in the other direction; sufficient attention isn't given to the needs of children. "Parents and society as a whole have abrogated their responsibility to young people," says Elkind. "And the kinds of things that we're seeing from young people is a response to that."

Before, children were seen as being in need of adult guidance and protection. Society, overall, took much more responsibility. Adults watched what they said and did around young people; Hollywood made sure that messages on film and television were appropriate for all ears; advertisers didn't attempt to sell 11-year-old girls cosmetics and other accoutrements of adult life. But things have changed. Busy, self-realizing adults perceive children to be much more mature and independent than they really are. "Children have come to be seen as competent, ready and able to deal with all of life's vicissitudes," says Elkind. "And teenagers are seen as sophisticated and knowledgeable about everything from computers to sex and so on."

Children are expected to make more decisions. At the same time, the number of choices has increased dramatically. Everyone—adults and children—has more options before them now than ever. In some ways, that's good; social prohibitions were constricting. But something that is beneficial for adults is not necessarily good for kids. Too many options are not healthy for young people, insists Elkind. "They get overwhelmed by all these choices."

Parents and society need to take more control, giving children stronger guidance. At the same time, parents need to avoid taking too much control over the activities that their kids get involved in. If kids don't have time just to play without pressure to perform, they can explode when they hit their teenage years. If pushed and pushed, kids can become resentful. "Kids feel that they've been doing all these things to meet adult needs, and their own needs haven't been recognized," says Elkind. "One of the things that happens is to say 'To heck with it, I'm going to do what is right for me, I'm not going to play this game anymore.'"

Another message is broadcast to children and teens. It goes like this: You don't have to work hard to be successful. All it really takes is a good set of genes; and, either you have it, or you don't.

In his cross-cultural studies, Stevenson found that Japanese parents rate "hard work" as being the most critical determinant for success in school. In contrast, American parents cite "innate ability" as being the most important factor. "Society is saying that innate ability is a very important modifier," states Stevenson. "If you are highly able, you don't have to work hard—you'll get it."

As Stevenson conducted interviews, this new American motto kept rearing its ugly head. When he asked mothers of young children to say when they thought

students were ready to be given college entrance exams, Asian mothers gave their kids time to get smart through hard work and years of study: They said the 11th or 12th grade seemed an appropriate time for testing. American moms, on the other hand, didn't believe little Jill needed time to study or years of academic preparation to determine whether or not she should be Harvard-bound: They thought she was ready to test by the end of elementary school.

And Jill seems to be getting the message. When Stevenson asked students to identify the most important thing that helps them do well in school, Japanese and Chinese students said, "to study hard." The answer chosen most often by American kids was, "the teacher."

In other words, Asian kids believe that diligence makes all the difference. American kids believe that the intelligence that they need to succeed is ready and waiting right inside of them, and they just need a good teacher to bring it out.

Society is in denial. And it's not just kids. Parents are as outraged as their children when their children

---

'Children have come to be seen as competent, ready and able to deal with all of life's vicissitudes,' says Elkind. 'And teenagers are seen as sophisticated and knowledgeable.'

---

don't get the grades or treatment they believe they inherently deserve. More often than not, many teachers say, parents complain to the teacher rather than the child about their child's grades. And that goes for discipline as well. Recently, in suburban Virginia, parents at one school opposed a new attendance policy for being too tough while at another school parents of students caught with water balloons protested the punishment—school suspension—saying it was too severe.

"It used to be that the teacher was right," says Weinheimer. "I'm not sure they always were. But parents supported the teacher. If I called home to talk about a problem, the parents used to say: "Gee, what can we do?"

The structures teachers once relied on are simply no longer there. And that undermines the teacher's job. "If teachers set down rules, and it turns out that the parents don't support them, then the system no longer works," says Elliott. "You've got a serious problem."

Part of the problem, according to Elliott, goes back to

the fact that society has set higher stakes for success. Parents know that grades and test scores are important for their children to succeed. So, they place more emphasis on what scores their children get than on how their children get the scores. Add to that the fact that high school has become a minimal expectation. A high school education is no longer seen as a valuable thing in and of itself, for this population. College attendance and success is all that really matters.

When the cheating scandal erupted at Charlotte Huggins' school, parents were not exactly pushing for serious penalties. "At one time, we could depend on families to be just as horrified as the school system," says Huggins. "Now, all they do is worry about whether the colleges will find out."

The other thing that happens is that today's parents are simply too overextended themselves to take an active, participatory interest unless a crisis occurs. Fifteen years ago, on "Parents' Night," Weinheimer's room would have been overflowing. Last year, there were plenty of empty seats. "Parenting is much more complicated," agrees Elliott, father of two. "Because of the consuming nature of our jobs, school is seen as a way to get kids out of our hair."

The bottom line is that kids are growing up with the belief that they don't need to work too hard or follow all the rules in order to make it. Put this message along with the "perfection is attainable" message and you've got a particularly confusing brew. Kids learn that life ought to be easy and painless; that they should be able to succeed at everything without putting in too much effort.

But, what about the fact that more students have jobs? Isn't that helping to teach a meaningful work ethic? Unfortunately not, says Elliott. The kinds of jobs at which kids are employed today, such as fast-food service, offer few valuable interactions with adult role models and little responsibility or challenge.

The dilemma many teachers face is perplexing: How can you expect very much of students at school if they are so overextended and stressed? But, at the same time, how will they ever learn the value of hard work if you don't expect a lot of them?

Elkind emphasizes the value of talking with kids about the pressures they face. "It's important not to lay the blame on kids but to show how a lot of the things they are feeling are part of a social system."

But if we blame everything on society and parents, then aren't we teaching students not to accept responsibility for their own behavior? The healthy response is not only to talk with students about the societal baggage that they carry, but also to give the firm message that they have to work hard in order to succeed.

"It's critical to acknowledge the problem," says Elliott. "But also to say that the solution is for them to take responsibility."

Educators who lower their standards only contribute to the problem, says Stevenson emphatically. Overly concerned with building and maintaining a positive sense of self-esteem in their students, teachers often reward kids for easy work. "Too many teachers have such a hollow response to children," says Stevenson sadly. "When children read three words, teachers say, 'That's wonderful!' And then the children go on to the next grade, and everyone laughs at them."

The best dose of self-esteem comes when students work hard to reach a tough goal, the psychologist says. Teacher Charlotte Huggins agrees. "I haven't given up. The integrity of classroom standards is the heart and soul of the school," she says.

But just because the English teacher hasn't changed her standards doesn't mean she hasn't changed as a teacher. She continually works to make her curriculum relevant to the experiences of today's students.

Teachers who expect kids to sit still for a dry lecture pulled directly from a 20-year-old lesson plan will be frustrated by the results. No doubt, some of the apathy and unwillingness to work that some teachers see in their students is a direct result of an archaic teaching style or curriculum. "Teachers who are unwilling to adapt," says veteran Weinheimer simply, "lose their effectiveness."

When art teacher Chris Hayward realized her students were changing, she realized that she had to change, as well. In Hayward's own experience, learning was an intellectual venture; but today's kids expect learning to be a visual adventure. "Kids want you to do more of a song and dance than you did 15 years ago," she insists. "The impact of the media and new technologies has given them immediate access to everything. And they want you to bring all the technologies into the classroom."

Hayward worked hard to create an unconventional art curriculum that met her own standards and the needs of her students. Far from seeing the change as selling out, she sees the transformation of her classroom as positive. "It's been a trip to Candy Land, for me," she exclaims. "Getting into video and media has advanced my ability to teach. It's been another way to show my students the world."

In spite of some of the negative changes, teachers do see some positive changes in their students. Kids today are more communicative about their problems, more willing to talk about a variety of topics in class. They are more globally aware, more in tune with nature and environmental concerns. Some teachers say that lately kids have become more interested in community service, in reaching out to help others.

"It's important to remember that our times are bad, it's not the kids," says Hayward, who is also a mother. "There are times when you want to grab them around the throat. But the goodness is still there." □

Written for this book by Mary Koepke, former Associate Editor of Teacher Magazine

6.

The Baggage Of Abuse

Teachers can help their students overcome the trauma of mistreatment.

Commentary By Marilyn Gootman

Millions of children in our country carry more than their book bags to school each day. They also haul into the classroom the baggage of abuse. What do they unpack? Pain masquerading in the wraps of misbehavior and underachievement. And who gets blamed? Teachers. When troubled children misbehave and underachieve, their teachers are often accused of incompetence. Feeling like failures, teachers also blame themselves when they are unable to reach these children.

Teachers are not to blame. Standard classroom management techniques do not work for these children the way they do for children who misbehave and underachieve for reasons such as immaturity, lack of motivation, and attention deficit disorder. Baggage abused children bring to school is too heavy.

Even after teachers report suspected abuse, they still have to contend with the leaden contents of this baggage on a daily basis. In the classroom, many abused children act out their searing pain because they cannot express it in words. They act out this pain in disruptive, annoying, and frustrating ways—through aggressiveness, hypervigilance, and spaciness and by hurting others without seeming to care. Of course, not all children who behave this way have been abused, so these behaviors should not be used as the sole criteria for reporting suspected abuse. But if any of these behaviors appear in children who are known to have been abused, teachers must stop blaming themselves and the children for the problems. Instead, they should view the behaviors as a signal for help. By understanding their causes, teachers can help teach these students socially acceptable coping strategies.

Can teachers who see these students for just a few hours a day for less than a year really make a difference without devoting their full attention to one child or becoming therapists? Absolutely. Alice Miller, author of several books on abused children, argues that teachers, among others, can be "enlightened witnesses" for abused children. By believing that there is a core of goodness within each child and that children are not to blame for their abuse, teachers can help these students overcome the trauma of mistreatment.

Trust, empathy, and patience plant a healthy seed within these children that will flower in the future. The key lies in acknowledging that these children are not at fault, understanding the nature and origin of their behaviors, and then using direct teaching strategies to counterbalance the situation.

Following are several of the more common dysfunctional behaviors manifested by abused children in the classroom.

• *Aggressiveness*: Abused children often spill their rage over their mistreatment on "safe" targets, such as classmates and teachers, rather than on those who deserve it. Many are aggressive and rarely hesitate to hit when angry. They seem to be bullies who pick fights for seemingly trivial reasons. These children carry the aggressiveness they have learned at home into the classroom. They can and must be taught how to deal constructively with their anger. A teacher who remains calm yet firm when angry can replace the aggressive parent model and become a constructive source of identification for children. Staying calm does not mean ignoring inappropriate behavior; it just means "keeping your cool" when dealing with it. Children who act aggressively can be taught how to recognize that they're getting angry, how to cool down, and how to put their feelings into words.

Some abused children are terrified of re-experiencing the feeling of utter helplessness and powerlessness they suffered when being abused. When they fear that their safety or self-esteem may be threatened again, they try to replace helplessness with power and become aggressive and lash out in the process. The key to helping these children lies in giving them a positive sense of power and control over their own destiny. They need to be allowed to make choices about their work. With the other children in the class, they need to be involved in determining classroom rules. When a rule is broken, they can help decide an appropriate consequence.

• *Hypervigilance*: Abusers are impulsive and often lash out unexpectedly with no rhyme or reason. Their victims, therefore, never know when they are going to "get it" next and, as a result, have to remain constantly on guard. Many abused children remain on guard in the outside world lest an event occur that might trigger the same feelings of helplessness and panic. In school, these children may seem fearful and suspicious, on the lookout for potential dangers. They are acutely sensitive to mood, tone of voice, facial expression, and bodily movement. Often they are afraid to express their own ideas. A predictable school environment is essential for these children. Clearly stated routines, rules, and consequences that are consistently followed can gradually help reduce their hypervigilance. These children also benefit from teachers who remain calm and do not explode in unpredictable outbursts.

• *Hurting others without seeming to care*: Many abused children are hurt so often that the only way they can tolerate it is by suppressing their feelings so they are no longer aware of them. Children who cannot feel their own pain do not know that others feel pain. Therefore, they may hurt others without seeming to care that they have done so. They seem cold, hard, and unfeeling. Such children must be directly confronted and told that they are hurting others: "Stop that. When you poke Billy with the ruler, it hurts." Because they

BOB DAHM

have numbed themselves to pain, these children often don't even know when they have been hurt. They may, for example, act totally unaware of an injury, such as a cut or a bruise. Saying, "that must have hurt when you fell off the swing," helps them acknowledge their own hurts. Once they feel their own pain, they will learn to acknowledge the pain others feel, as well.

• *Spaciness*: Many abused children dissociate or hypnotize themselves to escape overwhelming thoughts, emotions, and sensations they experience during abuse. In school, they may become spacey, forgetful, and frequently daydream if they experience an echo of their painful experience. Even a seemingly innocuous story in a reading book can trigger such a reaction. Teachers can bring such children back by gently touching them or softly calling their name. They should not reprimand these youngsters for dissociating. Instead, they should privately help these children become aware of what is happening: "Billy, I notice that when . . ."

Teachers can also help students identify and sort out feelings, such as sadness, anger, and happiness, and become aware that thoughts and feelings are not the same as actions. Reassurance that nobody will punish or reject them for their thoughts and feelings is important.

Often teachers solicit parents' help when their children are being disruptive in the classroom. It certainly makes sense for parents and teachers to work together to solve problems. If you suspect, however, that parents may be abusing their children, don't make demands on them or ask them to help you with the disruptive behavior. This could generate further abuse. Instead, try to be as positive as you can when talking with them about their children.

The baggage that abused children bring to the classroom poses a challenge to the best of teachers. Their behavior is often exasperating, but it is important to remember that it is a direct result of the weight they must carry. An enlightened witness can do a great deal to ease the burden. □

Marilyn Gootman teaches early childhood education at the University of Georgia and has written two brochures for the National Committee for the Prevention of Child Abuse.

From Teacher Magazine, *September 1992*

7.

Back Home In Indiana

Curious about the fate of her students, a former special education teacher returns to the rural community where she first taught.

By Mary Koepke

Last autumn, I received an unexpected letter from one of the students in my first class as a teacher. Now a 21-year-old woman, she wrote that she was married, pregnant, working at a fast-food restaurant, and living in a rental trailer. The news shouldn't have startled me, but it did.

For two years beginning in 1983, I taught 7th and 8th graders in semi-rural Brown County, Ind. Most of my students came from poor or working-class families that had been living in the region for generations. They were the kind of students whose lives could have been changed by a good education: Most were eager and bright but, for some reason, struggling academically. Of the 32 students on my caseload, all had some kind of special "label." Most were considered learning disabled; a few had been diagnosed as emotionally or mildly mentally handicapped. Mainstreamed for most of their classes, they came to my room only for math, English, or extra help in a study hall.

As I read my former student's letter, I wondered about all the others, now at the threshold of adulthood. Were they working in minimum-wage jobs? Had they already begun families? What had their years of schooling done for them? Did their special education classes do any good? Were they caught in dead-end situations, or were they happy?

I decided to find out, to do what many teachers would love the chance to do: I set out to visit my former students to see what has happened to them. I arranged interviews with the first 10 students I could track down and set aside 10 days to do them. As the leaves were just starting to blush with color, I traveled to Brown County, where I began my teaching career a decade ago. What follows are a few snapshots from the journey.

Penny

The young woman who steps out of the house to greet me is and isn't the Penny I taught. I have chosen to visit her first because I think she will be the easiest. In junior high school, Penny was tiny and natural, eager to please the teachers she liked. That young girl has become a beautiful woman—still on the short side at about 5 feet 2 inches tall—with silky blond hair and large brown eyes.

In the 8th grade, Penny got caught in the cross-fire of her parents' impending divorce. Despite her family troubles, I didn't worry about her as much as I worried about some of the other girls. I assumed that she would find projects and activities in high school to help her get through hard times. I thought that she could have been anything she wanted: student council representative, cheerleader, homecoming queen, drama club star. And with the academic assistance available for learning-disabled students at many universities, I figured that Penny could succeed in college. I always thought that she would make a great teacher.

Now, as I walk toward her, my stomach is dancing. I haven't seen Penny since I left the county in 1985. I don't know what to expect. I only know from my telephone call that she, like so many of the young women here, is already a mother.

"It's so good to see you," she says and hugs me. Her words trigger a wave of unexpected relief. Until that moment, I hadn't realized how unsure I was of my standing. I thought I had been liked and would be remembered, but I wasn't sure; one sentence from Penny confirms it. In one of her many books, kindergarten teacher Vivian Gussin Paley admits that she needs to be liked as a teacher. I now realize that I share that need. I can tell that Penny liked me; and, even though that is not what I came here to find out, the discovery is gratifying.

Inside, I meet her tall, mustachioed husband, Tony, and gush over their 8-month-old daughter, Taylor, who is curled in sleep on the living room floor. This is Penny's family now, her home. The rental house is modest. The worn, unmatched sofa and chairs are typical of relative newlyweds. But it is much nicer than the college apartment I lived in when I was her age. Everything is clean; the baby looks well-fed. I breathe a little sigh of relief. Penny and Tony are OK.

We chat for a while about Taylor and the three toddlers Penny babysits at her home during weekdays for extra money. Then we look over pictures in her wedding album. "Penny, you looked like a princess!" I exclaim as I see a photo of her in white lace.

"She did," Tony says, looking at his young wife fondly. "She still does."

This expression of love releases another wave of relief. Penny is making it, I think to myself, she is well loved. I am surprised by the depth of emotion stirred from just this short encounter so far. Penny and I are not relatives, not comrades, but something lasting has linked us together. Although I haven't kept in touch with her, I realize how deeply I care about what happens to her.

After a while, Penny and I move to the kitchen table and begin talking about school. She enjoyed elementary and junior high school, but as each year passed, she liked school less and less. I had always

Penny

imagined that being pulled from the mainstream was most difficult in the elementary years when kids so openly tease each other. But Penny says that social pressures to conform to a "norm" were much fiercer in high school. And then there was the boredom. After years in special education classes, she felt that she was just going over and over the same material. In her junior year of high school, Penny asked, and was given permission, to try a regular English class.

She remembers her first day vividly. "The teacher made it clear that he didn't think I should be in there. He was doing verbs and all this, and I told him that they didn't do that in special education," she recalls. Her voice is quiet, gently plied with a slight country twang. Her vowels stretch out like warm taffy. "I told him that I would try but that I'd like to sit back and listen for a little while to catch up. He said OK. But then he called on me constantly. In front of the whole class, he said, 'If you don't know this, you shouldn't be in here.' "

This humiliation wasn't an isolated incident. Softly and slowly, Penny narrates other subtle and not-so-subtle occurrences. When she told a guidance counselor during her sophomore year that she was interested in studying child psychology after high school, the counselor told her to forget it.

I am stunned. I never imagined that Penny would be so actively discouraged in high school. As a teacher, I spent all day in my classroom teaching a diverse and lively bunch of kids. It was easy for me to see them as students, not as special education students. I forgot that Penny had to weave in and out of the mainstream and that people with labels are often stereotyped.

"Did anyone ever explain to you why you were in special education classes?" I ask, realizing that I don't know what she knows about her own label.

She says that she remembers taking special tests in elementary school and recalls hearing the word dyslexia. She wasn't told much other than that—except that special education classes would be easier. As she talks, I see how kids like Penny could mistakenly assume that they had failed the tests, that they were too dumb to make it in regular classes and were being relegated to a life of baby work.

I now explain the whole process: how a child is referred for testing, what kinds of tests are given, and how a conference is called to discuss the results. I let her know that having a learning disability doesn't mean that her IQ is low. I watch her face as she absorbs the information. It is all new to her, and that strikes me as tragic. Undoubtedly, the single thing that most affected Penny in school was her label, yet she knows little about it.

The system is careful to consult parents or guardians when it applies a label to a child in need of special services. Legally, everything has to be explained, put in writing, and signed. But I've been at the meetings. School psychologists and special educators often use sugarcoated or vague words to explain what will happen to the child if he or she is placed in special education. The benefits are emphasized: Class sizes will be smaller, and the special educator will use a variety of modalities to teach lessons and modify standard work sheets, texts, and tests to help the child succeed. But the stigma of the label, the hazard it poses to a child's self-esteem, is rarely even mentioned. The assumption is that the benefits of specialized instruction far outweigh any negative consequences. Now, the lack of in-depth, open dialogue between parents, teachers, and students seems like a travesty.

"Do you think that being in special education hurt you?" I ask bluntly.

Penny struggles with this. We talk for a long time about the pros and cons, but she keeps coming back to one point. What you are labeled, the kind of classroom you are put in, doesn't really matter. What does matter is your teacher. She remembers some good teachers. But she also recalls the teachers who just picked up their paychecks, the teachers who didn't bother to look her in the eyes, and the teachers who kept promising to give her extra help but kept giving her work sheets instead.

As I listen to Penny, I find myself wincing. So much is expected of teachers. But I also share her frustration. I remember my own junior high history teacher who sat behind his massive desk droning every day. Although my friends and I were usually honest, we developed an elaborate system of cheating on his weekly multiple-choice quizzes simply because we were desperate with boredom. He never caught us—or bothered to try.

Whenever we mentioned the history teacher's name to our parents and favorite teachers, they rolled their eyes and shook their heads, silently informing us that they, too, knew about him. But they didn't stop him—or even try to change him. These were the same caring adults who told us that we wouldn't get anywhere in life unless we strove for excellence. But our history teacher was proof to the contrary. His poor performance was rewarded not only with a paycheck but also with the power to influence children. How many children? Perhaps 100 a day for 30 years—3,000 in a career. I might not have learned any history that year.

But I did learn about the hypocrisy and cowardice of a school system that purports to care about quality while shrugging its shoulders at its own demerits. Penny learned the same lesson.

"You have to have something different in you to want to be a teacher," Penny is saying. My ears prick up. "You have to want to be a teacher," she declares.

I tell her that I had wanted to be a teacher but that when I was, I often felt the system didn't take me or my students seriously. I relate how shocked I was by my first evaluation. I'd been hungry for professional feedback. But the principal didn't even bother to come into my room; he just checked off the words "satisfactory" and "outstanding" on the required form. "That's one of the reasons I left," I say.

"*That's* why you left?" She asks as though she has been wondering about it for a long time.

"Well, it's more complicated," I say, thinking about the various teaching positions I later held. "But I didn't think the system really worked."

"You shouldn't have quit," she reprimands. "I had two teachers who thought about kids as individuals—Donna Reed and you—but you both left."

Her revelation catches me off guard. I had no idea that, for all this time, she has thought of me as one of her best teachers. I should be delighted, but I feel sad. I know I wasn't that good. I was a first-year teacher; the students' learning problems often stumped me. Still, I must have conveyed a sense of caring—and that is obviously what Penny believes is the most important quality in a good teacher.

I don't know what to say. I try to imagine myself in Penny's shoes. Was Penny's greatest need to have someone in her life who believed in her? If she had had that consistently, would things be different for her now? My next question is awkward and vague. "Do you feel as though how people treat you has the greatest effect on what you do?"

"I like what I'm doing now," she begins after a long pause. "I don't have the same discouragement that I had in high school. My husband tells me I can do anything. I don't know. I still feel like I'm not as capable as all the other people who have diplomas." Penny continues, barely moving a muscle. "In high school, I had an uncle who said, 'Enjoy it now.' Sure I had some good times with friends, but the pain that you go through doesn't pay for it."

When I ask her to tell me her worst and best memories about school, she doesn't miss a beat in relating a negative memory. "I was standing up at this teacher's desk with some friends. And he was talking about a dream he had. I said, 'I had this dream last night about snakes.' And he said, 'When you dream about snakes it's supposed to be sexual. Are you going to have your first time or have you had your first time?'" Penny looks at me, blushing at even the recollection.

Then there is a long pause. "The best moment was

probably my Enjoli commercial." Penny looks at me to see if I remember. It takes me a minute, but I do. In math class, I had invented a game show to motivate students to practice solving word problems. The students were contestants, and I filmed the shows with the school's video camera. "You were filming and said, 'Now, let's pause for a commercial,' " Penny says. "And then you turned the camera on me. I sang that song, remember?"

An image of Penny bursts onto my memory screen. There is this bright fireball of a girl framed by the blackboard, singing a gutsy perfume jingle that was popular at the time: "I can bring home the bacon! Fry it up in a pan! And never let him forget he's a man! 'Cause I'm a woman . . . Enjoli!"

We both laugh. But I am on the verge of tears. Suddenly, Penny speaks again. She puts her slender hands on the table. "I had this dream in high school," she says gently. "I had it twice." The dream was plotless and peaceful, she says. "You and I were just walking, side by side, down a long hill."

Greg

On top of a hill of knee-high grass stands a red and white house. The old wooden frame looks as if it were blown in from Kansas by a tornado over 100 years ago and has since taken root. Except for the zigzag of laundry hanging in the front yard, the place looks completely abandoned.

I pause, uncertain. No path cuts through the thick grass to the front door; the back entry looks boarded up. I knock anyway and hear a gruff male voice inside, but I can't make out what he's saying. No one answers my call.

The voice inside is silent. All I can hear is the wind rustling through the trees. I look around and, for a moment, lose myself in the beauty of the countryside. No other house is in sight, only hills of prairie grass and the fierce tangle of oak and pine. I take it all in with heady awe. The wind shifts, and I am instantly aware of my isolation. According to the directions Greg gave me over the telephone, this should be his parents' house. Did he forget I was coming? Maybe I am knocking at the wrong red and white farmhouse. I may have gotten turned around.

My heart races. What am I doing here, standing at the back door of a farmhouse in the middle of nowhere? What if the man inside is crazy? What if he doesn't like strangers on his property? I get into my only resource—a rented car—and pull back onto the road. At the nearest farmhouse, a neighbor informs me that Wayne—Greg's dad—does live in the old two-toned house.

I return. This time, an old man, wearing a T-shirt, torn, faded jeans, and a denim jacket, appears at the front door. For a moment, I can't tell if I am welcome. Then he grins and waves me forward. I scuff through the grass and duck under a scallop of plaid flannel

shirts hanging from the clothesline. The man steps out from the entrance and stares at me.

"Why, you're not old enough to be Greg's teacher!" he says, an absence of teeth slurring his speech. He looks about 70 years old. He has wide eyes, a pointed nose, and scruffy gray whiskers.

I remember him. Faithfully, he and his wife attended every parent-teacher conference. They always wanted to know if Greg was behaving. I had assumed they were Greg's grandparents.

As the old man repeats his surprise at my youthful appearance, my eyes take in the living room. Clothes are strewn everywhere. They must not have a dryer; I wonder if they have a washing machine. With its wooden frame and hand-planed doors, the house itself qualifies as an antique (Greg later tells me that it was built before the Civil War), but there are no quaint adornments—no gingham curtains, dried wildflower wreaths, or wrought-iron candlesticks. The wood burning stove that dominates the living room and the patch of dirt and wood chips beneath it speak only of cold winters. This is shelter for an aging couple and their only son: a nest in the wild.

Greg's mom, Pauline, steps into the room, apologizing for the mess. She must be about 60, slightly crippled by bad knees. She is clad in a dress as black as crow feathers. "Greg's just gettin' out of bed. He was out coon huntin' last night," she explains.

I perch on the edge of an old easy chair by the door. Greg appears, rubbing his eyes. He is a tall, handsome young man zipped into a pair of jeans and pulled into a T-shirt. He nestles a green cap over golden blond hair that has grown past his collar bone.

"Good morning," I say. We smile silently at each other, both aware how strange it is for me to be here. He picks up a couple of sweat socks from a pile of clothes nearby and sits on the floor to pull them on while his father rattles away.

The old man's questions about my age and marital status make me blush awkwardly. Greg jumps in—perhaps sensing my nervousness—and changes the subject, telling his dad the story of last night's hunting adventure. Colloquial language rolls off his tongue as wild and fast as a careening pickup truck. I am left in the dust, my mind wrapped around the only word I can understand: coon. He laughs as he tells his tale, oblivious of my incomprehension.

I am dumbstruck. This is the Midwest, not a foreign country. I grew up in neighboring Illinois and spent seven years here in Indiana, and yet I can't understand a word Greg is saying. The 13-year-old Greg who walked into my classroom every day must have adapted his language for me.

"Greg was always a good boy, wasn't he?" the old man suddenly asks, and I snap out of my daze.

"Yes, he was," I say, smiling again at Greg. I get up to look at the many photographs tacked on the paneled wall. "There you are," I say to Greg, pointing at his 7th grade school photo. I stare at the blond-haired boy in the picture—the one I knew—and find it hard to believe that he grew up in this setting. I knew Greg as a boy with a cute sense of humor who preferred being outdoors to reading a book. Yet this environment is a shock. How could I have taught him for two years without knowing what his life was like?

Pauline fixes me a cup of instant coffee while Greg and I sit down at the kitchen table to get reacquainted. The kitchen is crowded and dirty, so cluttered that it's hard for my eyes to focus on anything. Pauline stirs powdered milk into my coffee, and I wonder how far it is to the nearest grocery store.

Greg yawns. I can't tell if it's a genuine or a nervous reaction. I search my brain, trying to figure out where to begin. In this setting, we seem so far away from school. I try to imagine Greg as a kindergartner, hopping on a school bus. "When you first started school," I venture, "did you like it?"

"Uh-uh," he grunts negatively. His mom laughs.

"Why not?"

"I guess I'd just ruther be out here runnin' around all over these woods than bein' in school," he says. His mom nods her head in perfect agreement and swats at a fly that has landed on the table.

Greg tried to make the best of it, though. Although he admits now that he didn't always try as hard as he could have, he did his schoolwork throughout the years and enjoyed being with friends. In the 6th grade, he was referred for testing because he was lagging behind grade levels in both English and math. He was told that special education classes would be better—slower. He and his parents agreed. He had always thought of himself as a slow learner—not dumb, just slow. If anyone made fun of him, Greg says he didn't notice. "I didn't think nobody was better than me or that I was better than anyone else."

Greg relates no particularly negative memories, no complaints about his regular or special education classes. One positive experience stands out: high school shop classes—woodworking, drafting, and especially a class called "Building Trades." "In that class, we built two houses from the ground up," he explains. "It was three hours a day, and I did it for two years."

I am impressed. I didn't know the high school had

Greg

such comprehensive vocational classes. "Would **you** have learned those skills anywhere else?" I ask.

"No. We did electrical wiring, hung lights, everything. It was moved into after we got done with it," he says proudly. Just then, Greg's mom whops him on the arm with her fly swatter.

"I've been wantin' to kill that fly!" she exclaims triumphantly. I burst into laughter, and they join in.

We talk for a while about what happened immediately after high school. He tried married life and even had a baby boy; but he and his wife couldn't get along. When they divorced, he moved back in with his parents. He tried working at a veneer mill but missed the freedom and joy of being outside, working the land. Now, he picks tobacco for a local farmer. During the winter, his boss will probably keep him on to cut firewood. Greg says he is content to live one day at a time, just making enough money to get by. He imagines that he'll always live in this house.

His mom nods pleasantly. "I need him. It's hard to keep up," she whispers, gesturing toward her husband who is sitting in the next room. "Wayne has had four heart attacks and a stroke, and now his mind isn't so good."

Wayne—a farmer who made his living growing sorghum—was born in this house and was given the deed to it so long ago he can't remember when. With no rent or mortgage payments, all the family has to worry about is food, electricity, and phone bills. They get by on $500 a month—the combined total of their social security and disability benefits. Greg kicks in whenever his mom needs extra money.

The family does what it can to cut down on expenses. Out in the barn, for example, Greg and his parents raise and butcher all kinds of animals. Pauline can hang a hog on a hook and have it ready for the freezer in a couple of hours. "Ain't no sense sending carcasses over to the locker plant so that they can spend your money when you can do it yourself," says the practical Greg. Although he hunts mainly for sport, rabbits and squirrel occasionally end up in the frying pan. And if he gets a deer, then there's a feast.

When I ask him to tell me more about hunting, Greg warms. Hunting is what keeps him out late on Friday nights, and talking about it is what wakes him up on Saturday mornings. He proudly shows me his rifle, which has an elaborately engraved wooden butt, and the secondhand bow he bought last week for 117 hard-earned dollars. When we step outside to meet Belle, his hunting dog, I notice an immediate and utter change in Greg. He opens. Suddenly, he is able to breathe.

Greg stoops down and points out the nicks and scars on Belle's ears and face, all from fighting with raccoons. "Me and her get along just fine. She don't gripe, she don't grouch, and she does what I tell her to," he says with total admiration. "The other day, my girlfriend asked me if I thought more of my coon hound than of her," he adds with a smile.

"What did you say?" I ask curiously.

"I pleaded the Fifth," he says. We laugh.

Then, he shows me the wild red fox he has captured and is trying to tame, the barn (which has at least 200 squirrel tails hanging from the rafters), and the cleaning shed. I stare up at a menacing-looking hook used to suspend carcasses ready for skinning. I try to imagine myself functioning in this environment. I wouldn't know what to do, how to behave, or how to occupy my time. On his territory, I am learning disabled.

The bewilderment must show on my face because Greg is grinning, obviously getting a kick out of hosting a city mouse like me.

"I didn't know it was this different here," I confess. "Indiana University, where I went to college, is just in the next county. When I got the job at Brown County Junior High, I thought, 'This is only 16 miles away. It's going to be just the same.' " Greg nods.

We walk through the grass in silence. I think about Greg and wonder what it was like for him in my territory—the school. It must have seemed foreign. The consolidated junior high was housed in a brand new building, spanking clean with bright walls, matching furniture, wall-to-wall carpeting (even in the cafeteria), and manicured lawns. It looked a lot like the junior high I attended in a modest suburb of Chicago. Back in 1983, the sanitized familiarity of the school environment deceived me. I saw Greg only in that environment, so I assumed that his life was more like mine than it really was. Seeing him there was like watching a Disney version of Huck Finn.

I tried to learn about Greg and the others by asking them to record their thoughts and experiences in journals. It seemed like a good idea. And I did learn some things. But there was no way Greg could have communicated all this. This is another world. Books, work sheets, tests, even pencils seem alien here. I ask Greg to be honest with me. Did my ignorance about his way of life prevent me from being a good teacher?

"No. I learned from you," he says. "I'm being honest," he adds when he sees my face twist into a question mark. Then, as explanation, he throws out what I know

is a compliment: "You didn't always stick to the rules."

Undoubtedly, I would have been a better teacher if I had known more about my students. How would I have taught differently? I don't know. Maybe I could have been more understanding. Maybe I could have chosen books to read in English class that were more relevant to Greg and the others. Great teachers are always the ones who are able to make connections—to link literature, history, mathematics, science, art, and music to students' own experiences.

But then I stop myself. If Greg intends to live and die on this land, what does he really need to know? I ask him how he would redesign schools to better meet the needs of students like him. Would he add more

> # As she talks, I see how kids like Penny could mistakenly assume that they had failed the tests, that they were too dumb to make it in regular classes.

vocational classes? Yes, he says, but they shouldn't replace academic subjects like social studies and science. "There should be a balance. You can't learn everything through shop classes," he explains.

Greg learned the basics—a little of everything—and that is extremely important to him. I am beginning to understand why. In his world, school is the only place for book learning, and the school years are the only time to get it. "That there is your last chance," he says, referring to high school. "You better learn something there, or you're in trouble."

When it's time for me to go, I find myself wishing I had more time here. "If I ever get the chance to come back," I say, "could I tag along on one of your Friday night hunting adventures?"

"Sure!" he says amiably.

As I get into my car, I feel a pang of regret. During the two years that I taught here, I missed an incredible opportunity. Greg could have taught me a lot.

Lisa

Robert is crying. Although a box of toys has just been dumped out on the living room floor, the 2 1/2-year old wants to play with a calculator that isn't in the pile.

"Go ask pap-paw for it," Lisa says. The word pap-paw, I learned when I first started teaching in Brown County, means grandfather.

My former student Lisa, mother of Robert and 7-month-old Tina, lives with her husband, her parents, her unmarried, pregnant sister Chris, and Chris' baby daughter, Ryan, in a small, tired house.

Robert waddles back into the kitchen with the calculator, jabbing the buttons contentedly.

"I think he's gonna be good with numbers," red-haired Lisa says with her Annie Oakley smile. "More than his mother was."

Lisa was an 8th grader in 1983, so I only taught her for a year before she went on to high school. I remember her as being polite, good-natured, and energetic. Behind grade level in both math and English, she never set high academic standards but generally turned in assignments. I didn't imagine then that she would drop out of high school.

As we sit at the kitchen table sipping iced tea, Lisa tells me her story. In her junior year, she got pregnant and became ill. One day, she hemorrhaged and lost the baby. The following year, she moved in with her

---

I try to imagine myself functioning in this environment. I wouldn't know what to do, how to behave, or how to occupy my time. On his territory, I am learning disabled.

---

boyfriend, Rick, and got pregnant, and sick, again.

Getting to school during this time was a formidable task. "Lots of times I was just so dog-tired—fixing breakfast for my boyfriend, cleaning house, being pregnant," Lisa explains as she bounces Robert on her lap. "And I'd think, I can't do it. But then I'd push myself to go, thinking that if I got a good education, then I could get a good job."

After a bout of absenteeism, she remembers the vice principal calling her in. "He said, 'It's your school or your child's life,' " she recalls. Lisa quit school, but she still lost the second baby. Eventually, she married Rick—who had also quit school—and got a job as a hotel housekeeper. Over the next three years, the young couple had Robert and Tina. Lisa has worked on and off as a housekeeper; Rick, a hod carrier, has held seasonal jobs.

"It's rough," Lisa admits without a trace of self-pity. "I make about $75 a week. I pay the phone bill, and we help with the groceries." Food stamps and Medicaid for the children enable them to get by. She knows she needs a high school education to get a better job, but

working and caring for two children leave no time or energy to go back to school. She is "stuck," she says. "I'd give anything if we could get good jobs and save enough money to buy a trailer of our own."

I look around the cramped, one-level house and see only one bedroom off the living room. "Where do you sleep?" I ask.

Lisa hoists Robert to her hip and walks me through the kitchen to a utility room in the back. I poke my head inside the doorway. A double bed for Lisa and Rick, a playpen with cushions for Robert, and what looks like a doll's bed for Tina occupy the small space next to the water heater. The room hums sadly, echoing the whispered dreams, full-blown fights, cries, coughs, love songs, and lullabies of this family of four. I suddenly want to close my eyes, to give Lisa some kind of impossible privacy; but I can't even seem to blink. As a teacher, I knew that some of my kids were poor; but the word was just that—a word. As I stand in the doorway of this utility-room-turned-bedroom, the word becomes concrete.

Robert squirms in his mom's freckled arms. I look at him and blue-eyed Tina gurgling happily on the living room floor. They are clearly the light of Lisa's life and, ironically, also the reason she is stuck. Lisa, 22, is still young. It would have been so logical for her to have waited to start a family.

Unlike some teenagers, Lisa and Rick didn't have a family by accident. They knew about birth control. So, why were they in such a hurry? Didn't they get the message that it was better to wait? That life with babies in tow was going to be much harder?

"I wanted a family life, but I had it too fast," Lisa admits, unconsciously patting her son's chubby legs. I lean closer as she talks on, listening for the one statement that will explain her choice. But she isn't really offering an explanation. Instead, she talks about all the other girls she knew who either became mothers during or shortly after high school. Many of the names I recognize—more of my former students.

"Is it peer pressure?" I ask, searching for an answer.

"A lot of it has to do with peer pressure," she says, but then quickly denies that she felt pressured herself.

"If the girls could just get help, they could stay in school," she adds. And as she talks, I realize that the question on Lisa's mind is not the same as mine. My question is, why do girls get pregnant? Her question is, why can't schools serve the girls who do?

"I'm not blaming school; getting pregnant was my mistake," she states. But she wonders why her school didn't offer more candid sex education classes. (She took the school's only sex education elective, titled "Interpersonal Relations," but calls it a "joke.") She also wonders why in-school child care, comprehensive child-rearing classes, and better vocational programs for girls weren't part of the plan.

School wasn't designed with Lisas in mind. Based on what my other students have told me, there didn't seem to be much available in high school for noncollege-bound girls who weren't interested in shop classes—regardless of whether they got pregnant. A high school yearbook I borrowed from Penny illustrates this. Although only 30 percent of Brown County's graduates go on to four-year colleges, references to college dominate the pages. The message for juniors reads: "Now that you're juniors it's time for preparing for life after high school. This is the year to decide what college to attend." A few photos of vocational classes appear. But even in the caption under the photos of business classes, a college-bound bias is assumed: "There are a lot of business classes that any student would benefit from if they were going to college."

The yearbook reflects a truth so obvious that I can't believe I hadn't noticed it before: Schools are designed by people like me for people like me. I might pretend to think about Lisa, and I might even fool myself into believing that I know what Lisa needs, but I don't. It's so easy to make false assumptions. As a teacher, I never asked my students what they needed to know. I decided for them. At the time, I thought I did a pretty good job. After all, I believed that I knew my students fairly well. I was an open door kind of teacher who encouraged kids to come in and talk with me. And some of them did. I took what I learned from them and created a curriculum that I thought was relevant. In English classes, I drew up spelling lists from their own stories and used real job applications to check their reading comprehension. In math classes, we started our own business; students had to figure expenses, incomes, and their own time sheets. I required them to open and keep checking and savings accounts with me, using real banking forms.

Now, all those curricular details seem superficial. I might have been on the right track, but I was in the wrong train. I didn't really understand their needs, their feelings, their realities. Sure, learning how to balance a checkbook seems relevant to me, but in reality Lisa probably doesn't have a checking or savings account. She can't afford them.

"What would you do?" I finally ask Lisa. "What would improve education for students like yourself?"

Her answer echoes Penny's message. I will hear it

Lisa

again and again from other former students on this trip. She wishes she had had more teachers who really knew her. "I'd put in teachers who would sit down and talk to you and see what was going on in your life," Lisa says. "Teachers should take time to see how kids are doing in life and in school, to see if they understand their schoolwork. Too many teachers push kids through just to get rid of them."

She describes teachers who got so caught up in grades, rules, and details that they lost sight of the student. As I listen, I remember certain moments in my own classroom. I would be lost in a task, busily scribbling notes on the blackboard, say, or passing back papers. Suddenly, I would become aware of what I was doing and freeze. In that instant, I would picture all the other teachers in the school, scurrying around their rooms, trying to fit all these tasks into a 45-minute period. Then I would picture the students, shuffling from classroom to classroom—math in my room, science next door, geography down the hall. It all felt tragically wrong.

As educators, we were working so hard, teaching students skill after skill just as a mason lays brick upon brick. But in those moments of sudden and utter doubt, I saw that we were working without an architectural vision. I feared that instead of working together to cement a useful, strong, and beautiful structure, we were creating, in our blindness, a haphazard pile of bricks.

As Lisa articulates her idea of a good teacher, I also remember the pressure I felt every day in the classroom. I wanted to be a supportive teacher. I knew that some of my students had extraordinary needs. But getting to know 32 students, trying to individualize their work—spending evenings and weekends designing my own materials, writing my own texts, dreaming up new ways to motivate them—was exhausting. And on top of it all, I had to contend with what was happening to them in their mainstream classes. Most of the teachers graded on a bell curve, so no matter how hard my students tried or how much they improved, they still got Cs and Ds.

I remember one particularly frustrating day in 1984. It was the beginning of my second year of teaching, and the principal was evaluating my work. "Mrs. Kopkey," he began gravely (in two years, he never pronounced my last name correctly or seemed to realize that I wasn't then married), "you tend to become excessively involved in your work. And such involvement can lead to burnout."

At the time, I was appalled with his critique. Why not reward me for my dedication? But it wasn't long before I did burn out. I tried setting limits for myself—closing the door at 3:30 p.m. But cutting back didn't make me any more effective. I was still haunted by the feeling that I wasn't doing enough.

I confess some of this to Lisa. She sympathizes immediately. "I never saw a principal come into a class

---

> I knew that my kids were poor; but the word was just that—a word. As I stand in the doorway of this utility-room-turned-bedroom, the word becomes concrete.

---

and say to a teacher, 'You're doing a great job.' " she says. "They don't understand students or teachers. They just think about things like air conditioners."

I laugh as she sums it up: "Teaching is hard as hell, and the pay is shitty."

But she wishes it were different. Is it too much to expect teachers to know their students? Should a math teacher be expected to teach more than math? I don't know. All I know is that math seems unimportant right now. I want Lisa to know basic academic skills, but I want other things for her even more. I want her to have confidence, to be able to solve problems, to know how to get information. I want her to be happy.

Lisa puts the children down for a nap. While her father and sister Chris fry up some sausage for lunch, Lisa and I sit on the living room floor and continue talking. She tells me about her childhood, her marriage, what it was like when she and Rick moved away briefly, and how she cared for her mother after she had a stroke. She talks about Rick's family and the relatives her children are named after. She describes her connection to the land, the "country," as she calls it.

Buried in these stories is the answer to my earlier question. Why did she get pregnant? Because "family life" is all she knows. Her cultural tradition is to stay close—to marry and have babies. She has no real model for any other way of life.

Who am I to judge? Who am I to say that waiting to start a family is the better way? Lisa's strong family tie is beautiful—valuable. Still, there is no romance in being poor. Although Lisa is not ashamed of her chosen path, she is certainly not proud that she dropped out of high school.

"I love my kids and my husband. But I wonder a lot about what might have happened if I got my education," she confides. "Maybe I would have become an interior decorator. I always liked changing the furniture around in here."

Lisa longs for change—not a radical one, just one that will enable her and Rick to gain some financial stability and independence. But she isn't sure how to make that change happen. She is hoping when Tina is in the 1st grade that she'll have some time to get her GED. "I'd like to get it so I feel like I've accomplished something." She stops herself. "But then I think about my boss's nephew. He's been in college for years, and he flips hamburgers at McDonald's. So, what good did all that education do him?"

We both laugh. "But then I think, well, maybe it would have done something for me. I don't know," she says with a shrug. "All I know now is that I clean house here, and I go to another place and clean."

She nods at her children. "I want them to have choices I didn't have." □

From Teacher Magazine, *September 1992*

How We Will Teach

"If you don't confront students' ideas and show where they're

adequate and where they're inadequate, those ideas are going

to remain there. They're going to pounce like a Trojan horse as

soon as the children escape from the schoolroom."

—Howard Gardner, Harvard University

8.

The Mystery Of Learning

Cognitive research is shedding new light on how we learn and raising questions about how we teach.

As the industrial revolution forever altered the modern workplace, a "cognitive revolution" now holds the potential to transform America's schools. In the past 20 years, cognitive science—which includes research from such fields as computer science, anthropology, linguistics, sociology, and psychology—has emerged as a powerful source of knowledge about how the human mind works. This research has begun to illuminate the mystery of how we learn and has produced some startling and controversial conclusions.

For example, research now indicates that people of all ages actively construct meaning of their world based on constant interactions with their environment. (Indeed, some cognitive researchers suggest that the ability to solve problems cannot be separated from the cues, tools, and people that individuals have available in their environment.) The experiences and beliefs that young people bring with them to school—as well as their individual learning styles—strongly influence both what they learn and how they learn.

Such findings are in stark contrast to the theories of behavioral psychologists like B.F. Skinner who have influenced educational practice for more than half a century. These psychologists argued that all human—and animal—behaviors arise from reactions to external stimuli in the environment. Children, like pigeons, repeat actions that are rewarded and drop those that are not.

Behaviorists viewed internal thought processes as unobservable and, therefore, largely irrelevant in explaining learning. Language development, for example—like maze-running for mice—was attributed to the steady accrual of rewarded behaviors that became increasingly complicated over time.

In the behavioral approach to education, skills were decomposed into hundreds of individual subskills, and their mastery by students was carefully examined and chronicled. Such research often translated into programmed, lock-step curricula, through which students were expected to progress to ever higher levels of understanding.

The educational programs of most of the nation's schools continue to be organized and operated on the basis of such behaviorist theories.

Researchers began to challenge these views in the late 1950's, and the real breakthrough came in a 1972 publication entitled *Human Problem Solving*. In that book, Allan Newell and Herbert A. Simon, two social scientists at Carnegie-Mellon University, argued that human thought processes could be investigated with positive results. To prove it, they outlined computer models that simulated what went on inside the brain.

"I didn't accept the behaviorist premise that one shouldn't develop theories about what goes on inside the head," Simon recalls. "Cognitive theories dominant today are very much concerned with what goes on between the stimulus and the response."

Unlike the earlier research, which focused on the acquisition of discrete pieces of behavior, this new generation of research began by asking how humans solve problems, why experts perform so much better than novices in a variety of disciplines, and whether more comprehensive models of learning could be developed.

One of the most fundamental findings of this new line of research is that students do not passively absorb information like so many sponges. Instead, people of all ages acquire knowledge through regular, active explorations of their environment. Soon after they are born, children begin to form powerful theories about the world around them based on their experiences.

By the time children enter school, they have formed

robust and complex (but not always correct) theories about a variety of phenomena. In fact, the ideas that young children bring to the classroom are so powerful and entrenched, cognitive researchers have found, that they often survive years of formal education. Harvard psychologist Howard Gardner argues that the naive and misleading notions formed in childhood can greatly interfere with learning if they are allowed to go unchallenged.

For example, many students who have studied astronomy, history, and biology continue to believe that seasons are caused by the earth's distance from the sun and that evolution is an orderly progression toward perfection.

Because schools often dismiss these misconceptions and do not encourage youngsters to explore their "common sense" understandings in any meaningful context—where they can be rejected or modified—children cling to their firmly held beliefs after they leave the classroom.

Students' learning is also hampered by what they perceive as lack of relevance in their studies to their lives outside of school. Their inability to connect what they learn in school with any real-world applications leads to what cognitive scientists call "inert" knowledge—information that is stored in the head but never used. They complain that mathematics, physics, history, and other subjects—as taught in schools—bear very little resemblance to their use by practitioners.

Cognitive scientists have also concluded from their studies that what students can learn depends to some degree on what they already know. Put another way, students have to be able to make sense of a situation or a textbook or an activity in order to learn from it. This theory is what prompts some teachers to encourage students in kindergarten and primary school to write and talk about their own experiences and to move—through "research"—from those personal "stories" about things they know into new areas of knowledge.

Some cognitive researchers theorize that, in addition to bringing a unique set of experiences and beliefs to the classroom, students also bring their own particular approach to learning. Howard Gardner complains that schools often treat students as if they all learn in the same way at the same rate. On the contrary, he argues, there are different learning styles and at least seven different kinds of intelligences. Human intelligences, he says, include: language, logic-mathematical, spatial, musical, kinetic, interpersonal, and intrapersonal.

It is through these intelligences, Gardner says, that people are able to know the real world. "Where people differ," he says, "is in the strength of these intelligences . . . and in the ways in which such intelligences are invoked and combined to carry out different tasks, solve diverse problems, and progress in various domains."

One traditional school practice that may impede learning is the practice of separating "basic skills" instruction from more complex problem-solving. Recent research has found that even very young children, in their attempt to make meaning of the world, pose questions, test hypotheses, and engage in other complex reasoning skills.

Previous generations of psychologists, such as Swiss researcher Jean Piaget, focused on what children do not know. "Now we are asking what [they] can do at each stage," says Robert Glaser, co-director of the Learning Research and Development Center at the University of Pittsburgh. "We can take advantage of the wonderful skills children have, have them participate in learning, discover that they do know a lot, and be excited."

"The most important single message of this body of

> # Skillful readers tend to stop in the middle of a text to ask themselves what the author means and to conjecture about what might come next.

research," writes Lauren Resnick, co-director of the Pittsburgh center, is that "complex thinking processes—elaborating the given material, making inferences beyond what is explicitly presented, building adequate relationships, analyzing and constructing relationships—are involved in even the most elementary mental activities."

When schools force children to master "basic skills" or long lists of isolated subskills instead of engaging them in these much richer analytical processes, learning is hampered. Thinking and problem-solving and the acquisition of substantive knowledge proceed simultaneously.

Research has also found that successful thinkers of all ages actively monitor their own thinking processes. One reason that experts are able to solve problems so much more effectively than novices is because experts employ a number of sophisticated thinking strategies that novices do not. Skillful readers, for example, tend to stop in the middle of the text to ask themselves what the author means and to conjecture about what might come next. They also employ useful strategies to help them confront difficult passages—such as paraphrasing and restating passages they find puzzling or re-reading other sections that might help illuminate the passage. In contrast, poor readers simply read the passage again and again or read it "harder."

The self-questioning or self-regulating behavior of successful thinkers is often called "metacognition" because it involves keeping track of one's own thoughts. And it is now assumed to be crucial to the thinking process. Early attempts to train students in self-monitoring activities have produced promising

---

'Eventually, we should have a basic science in education that would contribute as much to education outcomes as molecular biology contributes to medicine.'

---

results. But, according to Resnick, researchers do not understand precisely why this occurs, since many of the same skills appear to be either highly automated or nonexistent in the reasoning processes of experts.

In their search for skills and strategies that might prove useful to students, cognitive researchers are exploring other "generic" thinking skills that students could transfer from one subject to another—or from the classroom to the outside world. But Carnegie-Mellon's Simon admits that it will not be easy: "Transfer is an extremely difficult, subtle area. The issue is, since each domain has its own knowledge base, is there an abstract variable that can apply across fields?"

Such variables may be hard to find. In a study of high school and college students, those taught algebra were able to notice that physics problems could be solved the same way. But those taught physics were unable to see any connections between the two sets of problems. A closer examination revealed that students were able to transfer their abilities only when the concepts involved in the problems were similar.

In looking to the future of cognitive science, many researchers call for more applied studies. Alan Schoenfeld, professor of education and mathematics at the University of California at Berkeley, says: "We need fine-grained studies of what really works. We need case studies of successful instruction, what makes them tick, the attributes of teachers that enable them to create the right kind of classroom environment." He adds: "We're talking about a very different kind of practice; we don't know enough of the dimensions of success."

For one thing, Schoenfeld notes, it is very hard to measure the effects of experiments designed to improve students' thinking. The kinds of educational assessments now available—which measure students' ability to regurgitate bits and pieces of information or to perform minute skills out of context—do not reflect the more comprehensive and applied kinds of problem solving emphasized by the new research.

Eventually, says John T. Bruer, president of the James S. McDonnell Foundation in St. Louis, which supports cognitive research, "we should be in a position to have a basic science in education that would contribute as much to education outcomes as molecular biology contributes to medicine." □

9.

Thinking About Thinking

Educators are embracing the lessons of cognitive studies and encouraging children to construct meaning from their own experiences.

By Debra Viadero

Students at the Benchmark School in Media, Pa., spend part of each day writing in journals. Their best entries are later "published" in books that are shared with the rest of the class.

At the Key School in Indianapolis, children undertake semester-long projects tied to a schoolwide theme. The results are videotaped to form part of a student portfolio that will trace each youngster's progress through the year.

In Victoria L. Bill's classes in Pittsburgh, elementary-school students draw on their intuitive understandings to develop their own mathematical "language."

And in James Minstrell's physics classrooms in Mercer Island, Wash., students arrive at formal physics equations by debating their own hypotheses and then testing them out in experiments.

Each setting looks remarkably different. But all have something in common. They are taking new findings about how the human mind works and trying to apply them in schools.

According to the psychologist Howard Gardner, one of the leading scholars in the field of cognitive science, all of the new theories about how people think and learn "are Rorschach tests, and people can come up with all different kinds of schools based on interpretations of theories." Nonetheless, the vision underlying these schools has a certain unity.

In places where educators are taking new findings about cognitive research seriously, children are taking more responsibility for their own learning and constructing meaning based on their experiences.

In many of these classes, students are encouraged to work together and to learn from each other. Rigid adherence to textbooks has been replaced with "hands on" activities and greater use of technology. Teachers lecture less and serve more as models, co-learners, and coaches. And traditional paper-and-pencil tests have been ousted in favor of student portfolios, notebooks, and projects.

Today, cognitive science is still a long way from providing blueprints for learning. But researchers say new understandings about how children think and develop can contribute markedly to education.

"We know a lot," says Lauren B. Resnick, a co-director of the Learning Research and Development Center at the University of Pittsburgh and a leading proponent of some of the newer cognitive theories. "We know what not to do in global terms."

"We just can't be terribly prescriptive yet," she adds.

But state and national efforts to rethink student testing are finally bringing ideas from cognitive research into the center of the debate over school reform.

Until now, many proponents of cognitive theory note, the education-reform debate has concentrated on issues that they view as largely peripheral to learning: new incentives for teachers, site-based management, more homework, a greater emphasis on basic skills.

"There is no question that cognition and education reform [should] go hand in hand," says John T. Bruer, president of the James S. McDonnell Foundation, one of only a handful of foundations funding research on cognition around the country.

"This romantic notion that site-managed schools are empowering teachers to come up with solutions on their own is really foolish," he asserts.

Agrees Barbara Preseissen, who helps translate scientific theory into practice as director of national networking at Research for Better Schools, a regional education laboratory: "I don't think we'll restructure anything in education unless the classroom becomes the dynamo for the kind of change we're talking about."

Encouraging Students To 'Construct' Meaning

One of the most noticeable shifts in classrooms modeled on cognitive theories is that youngsters are encouraged to "construct" knowledge for themselves—based on hands-on activities and experiences—instead of having information fed to them.

In addition, students are encouraged to draw on their previous understandings and beliefs to make sense of new information.

In his physics classroom at Mercer Island High School, for example, Mr. Minstrell routinely begins a new unit by giving students a nongraded quiz. If a one-kilogram ball and a five-kilogram ball are dropped from the ceiling at the same time, the test might ask, which would hit the ground faster and why?

He then scans the written explanations and writes the students' predictions on the blackboard. The pupils debate their ideas and then test their theories in an experiment.

Through repeated experiments, performed under varying conditions—heavy and light objects might be dropped from higher up or in a vacuum, for example—the students gradually begin to see the limits of their own understandings of the physical world.

"Then we can focus on the contexts in which that knowledge does apply," Mr. Minstrell says, "and work toward constructing the formalisms."

Magdalene Lampert, a researcher at Michigan State University, maintains her methods for teaching mathematics to 5th graders are derived more from "good mathematics teaching" than from cognitive science. But to leading researchers in cognitive science, her approach echoes the same fundamental concepts.

Ms. Lampert structures her classes to enable students to arrive on their own at key ideas about how exponents work. For example, the students might be asked to look for patterns among the squares of numbers ranging from 1 to 100. Like the high-school students in Mr. Minstrell's class, the 5th graders offer their thoughts and debate them.

"I disagree with so-and-so's hypothesis," a child might say, adhering to a conversational format he or she has been taught. In Pittsburgh, Ms. Resnick of the Learning Research and Development Center and Ms.

Bill, a local parochial-school teacher, have been working to create classrooms in which students can also "leapfrog" into the formal system of mathematics by building on their intuitive understandings.

According to Ms. Resnick, Ms. Bill never teaches any formal procedures, like computation. Instead, she poses a problem for students, discusses it with them, and then breaks them into groups to work out their own solutions. The researchers have found that, by using such an approach, children as early as kindergarten can even begin writing simple equations.

Over the past two years, the students in Ms. Bill's 1st- to 5th-grade classes have shown dramatic gains in computational skills and in problem-solving abilities, even though she does not explicitly teach such skills, Ms. Resnick says.

Another noteworthy—but still somewhat controversial—feature of many of these classrooms is the social nature of the learning process. Students are encouraged to work together, pose questions to each other, and learn from one another. According to a number of cognitive scientists, such group-based activity is much more reflective of learning in the real world.

Carl Bereiter, a researcher at the Center for Applied Cognitive Science at the Ontario Institute for Studies in Education, plans to apply the principle in a study he is conducting this year in Canada.

In his project, Mr. Bereiter will study high-school students whom he has asked to work together to construct a knowledge base about Aztec and Mayan cultures.

At the beginning of the unit, students might be asked to enter questions about these ancient cultures into a networked computer system. They might ask, Mr. Bereiter says, "Were the shamans' dreams for real, or were they just smart people?" The students will form work groups based on their interest in particular areas of inquiry and devise plans for finding answers to their questions.

The written reports resulting from their efforts can then be designated as "candidates for publication," which means that classmates will review the work and decide whether it makes a "definite contribution" to the class's growing body of knowledge.

Elementary-school children being taught by the "reciprocal teaching" method, pioneered by Annemarie Sullivan Palincsar and Ann Brown, both educational researchers, also work cooperatively to develop an interpretation of written texts.

Children read together, take turns posing questions about and summarizing the materials, and quiz one another on their understanding. They predict what will happen next or, when necessary, ask for a clarification.

Studies have found that children who participate in this teaching method exhibit improved performance—not only on tests of reading, but also on tests of science and social-studies comprehension.

According to Robert Glaser, a co-director of the

Learning Research and Development Center, "a social context for learning elevates thinking to an observable status."

"As students participate," he explains, "the details of various problem-solving procedures, strategies of reasoning, and techniques for accomplishing goals become apparent."

Classrooms based on cognitive theory are also moving away from "drill and skill" exercises and toward more meaningful, hands-on activities that are embedded in everyday experiences.

Cognitive researchers often refer to these tasks as "authentic" activities to distinguish them from the kinds of fragmented, artificial exercises often found in schools.

This shift is based on several findings from cognitive research. For example, studies have found that teaching knowledge and skills far removed from any real-world context decreases the chance that youngsters will apply such understandings outside the classroom. In addition, research suggests that attempts to separate "basic skills" from more advanced problem-solving may actually inhibit learning.

The result has been an attempt to design classrooms and lessons in which students are encouraged to engage in more holistic activities, to answer questions of their own devising, and to complete long-term projects.

In Palo Alto, Calif., for instance, high-school students are preparing video documentaries that they will use to propose to the local city council a new use for a redevelopment area in their community.

The project, part of a study being conducted under the auspices of the Institute for Research on Learning, shows how students can learn valuable lessons but still work with a genuine purpose in mind, researchers say.

'Natural Way' To Learn

In a project being conducted in elementary-school classrooms in nine states by researchers at Vanderbilt University's Learning Technology Center, teachers use entertaining video stories to pose the equivalent of complex, mathematical word problems to students.

In one such program, students must find a way to help Jasper Woodbury, a teenager on a fishing trip in a remote wilderness area, rescue a wounded eagle.

Among the questions students must answer in order to solve the problem are: How far can an ultralight plane fly on five gallons of gasoline? Can the plane carry the pilot, the eagle, and the gasoline? And where would the plane refuel?

The information needed to answer these questions is embedded in the story, much like clues in a mystery novel.

"Stories are the natural way for people to learn," says John D. Bransford, the Centennial Professor of Psychology at Vanderbilt University and a co-director

of the center. "They are much easier for people to understand because they are linked to human events."

Other researchers have argued for the creation of "cognitive apprenticeships" in schools, patterned after more traditional craft apprenticeships.

Such apprenticeships would enable students to watch teachers engaged in the kinds of real-world thinking undertaken by mathematicians, historians, or writers; work with them in solving problems; and be coached and empowered to take on increasingly complex tasks themselves.

Apprenticeships were "the predominant way education took place until the innovation of schooling," observes Allan Collins, a researcher at Bolt, Beranek,

Through experiments, performed under varying conditions, students gradually begin to see the limits of their own understanding of the physical world.

and Newman Inc., who has been largely responsible for this notion.

Mr. Collins sees the "cognitive apprenticeship" model at work, for example, in the reciprocal-teaching approach to reading pioneered by Ms. Brown and Ms. Palincsar.

The method is based on research on the kinds of questions good readers ask themselves to check their own understanding of reading material.

Under the approach, the teacher models those once-invisible strategies, aloud, for the class. Better students are called on to continue that modeling process until eventually every student can easily pore over the reading material and pose questions, make predictions, summarize, and ask for clarification.

The technique of making thinking processes visible and building an awareness of one's own thinking processes is called "metacognition." That concept, says Ms. Preseissen of Research for Better Schools, is "the real boon of the cognitive movement."

"So often we hurry and go through the thought processes ourselves and just expect students to understand," says Sue Derber, a teacher who uses the reciprocal-teaching method. "This makes it all clearer for them."

For example, Linda Flower, a professor of rhetoric at Carnegie-Mellon University and co-director of the Center for the Study of Writing there, uses tape recorders to help students become aware of the metacognitive processes involved in writing. She pairs students up for a writing task and then tape-records their conversations as they discuss how to go about it. The recordings are played back for the benefit of both students and teachers.

"It's not only a way for teachers to listen to students talking, but it's also for students looking at their own thinking—letting them in a new picture of themselves as thinkers," she adds.

Finding New Roles for Technology

In many instances, as in the Vanderbilt project, educators are also drawing more heavily on videodisks, computers, and other new technologies to provide youngsters with the kinds of rich, hands-on activities that cannot be gained through textbooks.

"I don't know that textbooks would continue to exist in the world that I'm talking about," Mr. Collins of Bolt, Beranek, and Newman says. "I think technology is going to play a big role in education in the future."

Referring to the potential of multimedia approaches, Mr. Collins says, "Hypermedia would become a major aspect of things—text, film, animation, simulation."

In contrast, he asserts, textbooks represent a passive form of learning in which minimal interaction is required of students. Most textbooks provide too much information for students, instead of focusing on true understanding, he adds.

From his classroom at Mercer Island High School, Mr. Minstrell offers a more moderate view on the usefulness of written texts. Over the course of his teaching career, he says, the role of textbooks has evolved from that of a framework for his courses to a source of "background reading" for his students.

"I might say, 'Those of you who would like to read more about it should read chapter 8,'" he says.

But Mr. Minstrell cautions that, "in looking at other schools, they're going to need a story line, something they can hang the activities on and see where they're going."

Some textbook publishers are already trying to rewrite their publications to reflect the new findings from cognitive research.

"I think any publisher is well aware these are important concepts to be capitalized on in terms of fostering learning," says John Ridley, a vice president and the editor-in-chief of the elementary division of Houghton Mifflin Publishing Company.

A 1991 reading series published by his company, for example, incorporates some of the strategies embedded in the reciprocal teaching approach—predicting, summarizing, clarifying, and questioning.

And texts published by Houghton-Mifflin and other companies are increasingly making use of what Mr. Ridley calls a "metacognitive trail"—questions placed in the white spaces of margins that are designed to help students monitor their own comprehension of the material as they are reading it.

Although some cognitive researchers think that educational technology could ultimately supplement textbooks, others question whether it needs to be an integral part of classrooms based on cognitive theory.

"The real bottleneck is not the technology, but figuring out what are the good instructional strategies and designs and materials that really come up with better ways to get students to think," says Jill H. Larkin, an associate professor of psychology at Carnegie Mellon and a senior scientist at the school's Center for the Design of Educational Computing.

In an experiment she is conducting with colleagues, for example, Ms. Larkin set out to design a computer program for teaching physics, only to abandon the idea after deciding that the technology was "irrelevant."

Instead, the scientists have designed a workbook of laboratory experiments. "When the time is right," Ms. Larkin says, 'The instructor stops the class, and they take out their equipment and do an experiment."

But in a field that has grown up in part as a result of advances in artificial intelligence, a number of researchers see technology as the essential glue binding their ideas together.

They talk about creating entire learning environments, not unlike those in Mr. Bereiter's classrooms, that are based on children's interactions with computers and among themselves. In these settings, one researcher says, "the teacher would occasionally look in to see where [the students] are."

Whatever the orientation, one point is clear: The kinds of uses to which technological innovations would be put in these new classrooms would be a far cry from the kinds of "drill and practice" exercises now found on most classroom computers.

Rather, technological innovations would be used as a "jumping-off point" and a source of motivation for students.

A few computer software programs already on the market, for example, are designed to anticipate students' preconceptions about math or science and assist them in building their own knowledge base.

One such program anticipates that students who know that congruent triangles are equal in area might also conclude incorrectly that triangles that are not congruent cannot be equal in area. The program seeks to confront that kind of misconception by randomly drawing triangles and asking students to measure them and repeat the process with triangles of varying sizes.

"It's very likely they will stumble upon a situation that's going to [challenge] their knowledge and, therefore, they will build new knowledge," says Eleanor Arita, a director at Sunburst Communications Inc., the company that produces "The Geometric Supposer" software program.

Sunburst and other companies also offer computer

databases from which students can construct their own "snapshot" of a particular period in history.

One such database, compiled from facts and figures relating to the experiences of immigrants coming to the United States, provides information on hourly wages at a particular point in time, the kinds of jobs available, and living conditions, for example. Students can draw on the information to craft their own views of what life was like for immigrants at that historical juncture, rather than hearing a lecture or reading a textbook.

Hands-On Approaches

Mr. Gardner of Harvard University also sees cause for optimism in the kinds of technologically inspired, hands-on approaches to learning commonly found in children's museums. Such experiences allow children to "see" how things work in ways that textbooks or traditional classroom media cannot, he says. And, he

---

'So often we go through the thought processes ourselves and expect students to understand,' says one teacher who uses the reciprocal-teaching method.

---

adds, "these could easily be yoked to the more formal institutions of schools."

The question, according to John Seely Brown, the Xerox Corporation vice president who helped found the Institute for Research on Learning, is: "How do you construct computer environments where the purpose is to foster a kind of collaborative learning, where what's on the screen is meant to foster conversation among students?"

In a somewhat different vein, Mr. Minstrell is collaborating with Earl Hunt of the University of Washington to develop a Hypercard program that "diagnoses" the kinds of misconceptions or preconceptions about physics that students bring to school.

"There are some things technology can do a heck of a lot better than I can, like keeping track of where all 120 of my students are in their understanding," Mr. Minstrell says. "But the pat on the shoulder, the encouragement, the 'let's work one on one'—a lot of human sorts of qualities—are what will allow us to really teach more to individuals."

But if teachers are at the heart of good instruction, as Mr. Minstrell maintains, cognitive scholars caution

that their roles will have to change markedly in classrooms based on the new research.

Rather than serving as mere conduits for information, these researchers assert, teachers of the future will have to become role models, co-learners, and coaches.

Using textbooks as more of a resource and less of a framework for the curriculum, for example, requires teachers to have a greater understanding of their subjects. In addition, teachers must understand how children think about academic disciplines and be willing to place more of the learning process into the hands of students.

"The teacher changes from an information-giver to someone who can say, 'Let's find out how to find out,'" Mr. Bransford of Vanderbilt says.

Ms. Preseissen of Research for Better Schools calls this new kind of teacher a "gadfly" or a "guide on the side."

"The teacher has to become a thinker," she adds. "If teachers can't think themselves, how are they going to teach kids how to do it?"

Finding, signing on, and cultivating these kinds of teachers, however, presents a major challenge for cognitive theorists. Few teachers come out of teacher-education programs prepared to teach in these new ways, according to researchers in the field.

"I think that the things that cognitive science imagines should be happening in the classroom will require a much more sophisticated teaching force than now exists," says Ms. Lampert, an associate professor of teacher education at Michigan State and a practicing elementary-school teacher.

Moreover, teachers themselves, faced with the prospect of turning control of learning over to their pupils, may be skeptical. As one educator put it during a January conference on thinking sponsored by the U.S. Education Department's office of educational research and improvement, "One of my concerns is that the classroom will break down into a Phil Donahue or Oprah Winfrey show."

Indeed, some of the teachers now using cognitive-based approaches to teaching concede, their classrooms may appear "unruly" as students debate possible solutions to mathematical problems or argue over a physics experiment.

But "we know we're talking about math, arguing about it," Ms. Bill of Pittsburgh says. "I have succeeded if [students] feel comfortable enough to be wrong."

The apparent familiarity of some cognitive findings also tends to inspire wariness in some teachers, researchers say. Much of what is touted as new in cognitive theory, they note, sounds much like good teaching, born of intuition and experience. Researchers call that spark of recognition in veteran teachers "tacit knowledge."

They contend that teachers may "know it when they see it," but that they may not actually be putting that intuition to work in classrooms. The problem, they say, is that teachers sometimes lack self-confidence or are constrained by school-district regulations.

"What the theorists can do is make tacit knowledge explicit," Mr. Bransford of Vanderbilt says.

Researchers concede other cognitive concepts echo successful educational programs already in place in classrooms, such as Reading Recovery, the popular remedial program imported from New Zealand, or cooperative learning, an approach in which children work in groups of peers. Neither strategy is based on cognitive theory, but both contain aspects of some of the same ideas.

"We often see stuff happening, but nobody quite sees

> ## Students can draw on the database information to craft their own views of what life was like for immigrants at that historical juncture.

why it's working," Mr. Brown of Xerox says. "What we have to have is this new perspective, to view the mind as part of a social setting, learning in context, and leveraging on content to help [students] learn."

Another cause for confusion among educators seeking to inspire their students to think more analytically has been the profusion in recent years of prepackaged programs designed to teach "higher order" or "critical thinking" skills. Researchers contend that these programs fall short of their goals because they teach thinking skills in isolation, not in the context of academic disciplines. Students tutored under such methods tend to do well on questions related to those they have already encountered, but fail to apply their newly acquired thinking skills in other areas, research has found.

"You can talk thinking skills from the central office forever," Ms. Preseissen of Research for Better Schools says. "Lots of teachers think they're teaching thinking—and that may well be—but they really need to look at it, to examine it."

Another reason for skepticism on the part of teachers, Mr. Bransford says, is that researchers have failed "to package [their theories] in a way that makes sense to" teachers. "There's still a gap between the general theoretical framework and specific implications for instruction," he says.

In addition, researchers and teachers at the forefront

of the "cognitive revolution" point out, teaching approaches based on cognitive research may be a hard sell because they require a great deal of effort on the part of teachers.

Despite the laissez-faire appearance of some classrooms and the lack of a step-by-step curriculum, many such approaches to learning require careful planning.

"The kind of teaching cognitive science is pointing to is a lot harder to do than traditional teaching," Ms. Lampert of Michigan State says. "Neither the teacher nor the learner can sustain intense engagement of the subject matter if they have only 45 minutes of math or 45 minutes of reading."

"There's no doubt about it," says Alice Gill, a 3rd-grade teacher from Cleveland who is applying cognitive theories in her classroom and training others to do the same, "this takes a lot more time."

"But whatever the time," Ms. Gill continues, "I think every one of us here would shout from the rooftop that it was worth it."

Ms. Gill is one of five mathematics teachers participating in a project sponsored by the American Federation of Teachers designed to make new research on cognition more accessible to their peers. The first product of their efforts, volume 1 of a teacher-written series, "Thinking Mathematics," is due out this fall.

At the Benchmark School, a private school for children with reading problems based almost entirely on research in cognition, Irene W. Gaskins, the school's principal and founder, requires the teachers she hires to keep abreast of educational research, attend monthly in-service sessions, and work without the aid of teachers' manuals.

Teachers applying to work at the school are requested to first work six weeks at the school's summer program.

"One year I had five applicants for one position, and all five turned down a job at the end of the summer," Ms. Gaskins says. "They all said, 'I can't work this hard all year long.' "

'Major Gridlock'

Even if teachers are sold on the research, they sometimes feel hemmed in by school district rules requiring that they follow a closely prescribed curriculum or by pressures that their students score high on standardized, multiple-choice achievement tests.

"If you expect teachers to pay attention to how children think and understand things, but you don't treat teachers as people who think and understand, you're in for a major gridlock," Ms. Lampert says.

Agrees Gaea Leinhardt, a professor of education at the University of Pittsburgh: "You can't say the learner constructs and makes meaningful knowledge, and then give a teacher a booklet and say, 'Here's what to do.' "

In contrast, Ms. Lampert says, teachers engaged in a cognitive approach to learning must be able to "move around freely" within the curriculum and to deal with fewer topics in greater depth.

In the "Thinking Mathematics" project, notes Lovely H. Billups, who oversees the program as director of educational research and dissemination for the A.F.T., "the children could talk about one word problem for 10 minutes, when 10 problems could be done in that time."

Ms. Gaskins of the Benchmark School says parents also raise questions when they learn that their children are not memorizing formulas, periodic charts, or historical facts.

"They'll tell their kids, 'I don't care what she says about constructing your own knowledge, just memorize it and get an A on the test,' " she says.

Indeed, many cognitive scholars view current forms of assessment as one of the greatest stumbling blocks to bringing about real changes in classrooms. New ways of teaching and learning call for new ways of assessing children's progress, they argue. Standardized, multiple-choice tests, which often rely on simple recall of facts and formulas, do little to foster higher-order thinking and may actually impede it, according to these researchers.

"It's not that the questions are bad," Mr. Bransford of Vanderbilt says. "It's the kinds of things they don't ask, and, if they don't ask them, they tend not to be taught."

Whether their motivations were influenced by cognitive research or by dissatisfaction with existing measures of student learning, at least 40 states are shifting from traditional, multiple-choice tests to performance-based assessments.

These new alternatives to machine-scored tests seek to take a deeper look at how students learn through the use of portfolios of student work, essay questions, and long-term projects.

Individual sites—like the Key School in Indianapolis, which is based on Mr. Gardner's theory of multiple intelligences—are also experimenting with video portfolios, student journals, and the like as an alternative to more traditional assessments.

At the national level, one of the leaders in cognitive research, Ms. Resnick of the University of Pittsburgh, is spearheading efforts to develop an examination system for all students that would focus more on "high level" skills and on the application of knowledge to real-world problems.

Under the proposal, students could complete a series of performance examinations, portfolios, and projects over a period of time in order to graduate from high school, enter college, or apply for a new job.

Although Ms. Resnick characterizes the effort as the "sum total" of her work, she says it does not represent a way to put her theories into practice.

"It is accumulated wisdom—if you want to call it wisdom rather than a direct application of any one piece of research," she says.

Mr. Collins of Bolt, Beranek, and Newman also sees an expanded role for technology in assessing student learning.

"The qualities needed for a good scientist or historian—being able to formulate questions, to listen, to explain—there's no way that paper and pencil can test those kinds of abilities," he asserts.

"But if you use other technology, like video or computers, you can have people form hypotheses, do diagnoses, give them a microworld where they're trying to design an electric circuit to do something or a system for running a government," he says.

All of these researchers view assessment as a potentially powerful "lever" for bringing about curricular change because, in the words of one scholar, "what gets tested tends to be taught."

For the same reason, however, they worry that tests, taken in isolation from other education-reform efforts, could exert undue influence on the curriculum.

"We believe exams done in certain ways are a privileged point of leverage," Ms. Resnick says. "If done alone, they can be a disaster." □

From Education Week, *Oct. 9, 1991*

10.

Madeline!

Education guru Madeline Hunter's controversial prescription for effective teaching has made her a household word.

By Daniel Gursky

What do teachers and medicine men have in common? Madeline Hunter knows. A medicine man, according to Hunter, might concoct a brew for curing malaria by mixing a gnat's eyelash with water from a magic tree and performing certain carefully prescribed incantations. While the mixture might actually cure malaria, the medicine man wouldn't understand that it was the quinine from the tree that actually produced the healing. As Hunter sees it, many teachers—like medicine men—flounder along on intuition, occasionally displaying flashes of quinine-like inspiration but lacking a sound scientific basis for their methods. "We've had wonderful teachers since the days of Christ and Plato, but they were intuitive teachers," she says. Coming from Hunter, intuition doesn't quite sound like an obscenity, but it does seem like something to avoid.

To some teachers, Hunter's insights make her an educational guru. Crusading against the intuitive, spontaneous, improvisational approach to teaching, Hunter has built a profitable enterprise by spreading her model of teaching as an "applied science." In Hunter's world, teachers aren't much different from surgeons: Education, like medicine, is based on proven research findings that link cause and effect.

"We are today where medicine was when [physicians] found that germs, not evil spirits, cause disease," Hunter tells a group of teachers and principals who have traveled from around the country to hear her message during a three-week summer workshop at the University of California at Los Angeles, her hometown. For $450 a week, Hunter will give them straightforward answers to many questions that have troubled teachers for decades. What's more, she assures the educators, these answers, when properly applied in the classroom, will help students learn more.

In her popular book *Mastery Teaching,* Hunter offers readers a guarantee of sorts: "From now on, you will know what you are doing when you teach, why you are doing what you do."

With such a positive, uncomplicated message, it's not surprising that Hunter has amassed a large, loyal following among teachers and principals. The UCLA workshop participants offer rave reviews for the woman most simply call Madeline. "Madeline makes me feel good about being a teacher," says one. Adds another: "She's an amazing woman."

Over the past two decades, Madeline Hunter has become a household word among educators. She's been called an institution, as well-known as Kleenex or Xerox. She's spoken to thousands of teachers in every state and in dozens of countries, and thousands more have been exposed to Hunter's ideas through a variety of forums. When school districts adopt a program of "effective instruction," it's probably an adaptation of her model.

But Hunter inspires as much criticism as praise. For a growing number of teachers, the idea of an externally imposed teaching model runs counter to their demands for professional autonomy. There seems to be an inherent contradiction between Hunter's model of effective teaching and education reformers' efforts to promote a more flexible, child-centered approach to learning. Teachers in many districts complain that some administrators have turned Hunter's teaching methodology into a rigid religion; nonbelievers in such schools often suffer from poor evaluations.

Other critics have condemned her work, calling it "pseudoscience" and "mechanistic behaviorism"; one leading researcher says there's no solid evidence to back up Hunter's ambitious claims that her model is effective. And some fiscal-minded skeptics question the wisdom of spending millions of dollars to train teachers and administrators in Hunter-type programs when school budgets are already strained.

An aura of science and medicine pervades Hunter's UCLA workshop. The site—the health sciences building—is surrounded by the UCLA Medical Center, medical school, and dental school; clad in white lab coats, medical professionals with stethoscopes around their necks wander hallways lined with drawings and photos of human anatomy. Even the title of her workshop—"clinical supervision"—evokes a medical tone.

Hunter, still trim and energetic at 75, comes across as the archetypal teacher: authoritative, confident, witty, and eloquent. Her manner of speaking, with concise phrases and abundant hand gestures, is a bit reminiscent of George Bush's, except Hunter speaks in complete sentences. Her catchy slogans, on the other hand—"more inspiration, less perspiration," "what is logical is not always psychological," and "thinking on your seat is easier than thinking on your feet"—bring to mind Jesse Jackson.

Hunter tells the audience she doesn't know the secret for producing virtuoso instructors, but she says her model can turn marginal teachers into effective ones. "Pedagogy is invariant just as nutrition theory is invariant," she says. "It looks very different, but a good

STEVE GOLDSTEIN

Madeline Hunter

music teacher is doing what a good calculus teacher is doing, just like it looks different if you're eating dried caribou or raw fish or peanut soup, but it's all protein."

The foundation of Hunter's pedagogy—and the thing most closely identified with her—is her "elements of successful instruction." She talks and writes about other subjects, but when districts, schools, and ultimately, teachers, implement a Hunter-type model, it usually centers on her elements of instruction.

Briefly, the model consists of:
• The anticipatory set—getting students focused on the subject, possibly by having them think about some relevant example from their own lives.
• The lesson's objective—letting students know what they are learning and why.
• Input—offering more information and stimulus to involve students in the lesson.
• Modeling—demonstrating the subject matter, sometimes with actual models, other times with relevant examples.
• Checking for understanding—having students make various hand signals or asking for individual or group responses.
• Guided practice—roaming the room to help students and correct their mistakes.
• Independent practice—giving students exercises to reinforce the lesson, after the teacher is confident they have a grasp of the subject matter.

Those seven elements, combined with positive reinforcement, Benjamin Bloom's taxonomy of thinking, and other nuggets of educational psychology, form what Hunter calls her "decisionmaking model" of teaching. "I don't tell teachers what to do," she says. "All I can tell teachers is what they better know and think about before they decide what to do."

Although it looks a lot like the traditional lecture dominated style of teaching, Hunter maintains that her model of instruction applies equally well to any situation in which someone is trying to teach, whether it's a cooperative-learning classroom, computer-assisted instruction, or a corporate training session. "I've simply taken the theory, much of which has been around for a hundred years, and translated it for classroom teachers," she says.

No one can accuse Hunter of not practicing what she preaches: Her lectures include all of her elements of successful instruction. She starts one segment by asking participants a question to get them thinking. Teachers and principals versed in Hunter lingo know she's given them an "anticipatory set." From there, Hunter states the thesis of the discussion; every minute or two, she illustrates her point with an

---

In her book *Mastery Teaching*, Hunter tells her readers: 'From now on, you will know what you are doing when you teach, why you are doing what you do.'

---

example, sometimes from her beloved field of medicine, other times from her varied experiences in and out of schools. "Examples are the most powerful thing in education," she explains.

Hunter's examples also provide a glimpse into her background and the roots of her educational philosophy. She started her career more than four decades ago as a clinical psychologist with the Los Angeles Children's Hospital and later at juvenile hall. After finding those remedial ends of psychology unsatisfying, Hunter decided to try her hand at school psychology, which she thought offered better opportunities to prevent the problems she had seen in her earlier jobs. (Her initial impression of schools: "Every teacher had taken an educational psychology course, but none of it applied to teaching.")

She has developed and refined her instructional model over the course of her long education-related career, which has included more than a dozen years as a psychologist and principal in Los Angeles-area public schools and 20 years as principal of University Elementary School, a lab school on the UCLA campus. Hunter left the lab school in 1982 but has stayed on at UCLA as an adjunct professor of education.

Of her many accomplishments, Hunter is perhaps proudest of the hand-signaling system she developed to help teachers, as she puts it, "check for understanding." A simple glance around the classroom lets a teacher employing this system know who has grasped the material and who has not. For example, a teacher might ask a series of true-or-false questions that each student must answer with a thumb up for true, a

thumb down for false, or a thumb to the side if he or she is not sure. The teacher might also ask students to show with one or two fingers if sentence one or sentence two contains, say, a dependent clause. The possibilities are endless. It's all part of Hunter's admonition to "teach smarter not harder." If teachers practice "dip-sticking," she says, they won't have to wait until test time to see whether their students really understand the material.

Naturally, every Hunter presentation includes hand signals, the seminar at UCLA being no exception. As she displays sample work sheets on an overhead projector for almost an hour, she asks the audience to respond with signals: "Raise your hand if you think this work sheet is worth doing."

Hunter acknowledges that some teachers and students think signaling is "baby stuff." But they become enthusiastic signalers, she adds, once they realize that the system offers everyone an unthreatening way to correct misconceptions.

On the surface, Hunter seems to offer teachers a helpful framework for instruction. For some of Hunter's critics, however, her model adds up to little more than an inventory of what most teachers already do. "A lot of [the model's] popularity is the fact that it's not very innovative," says Robert Slavin, an education researcher at Johns Hopkins University. "The reason it sounds sensible is because it's what teachers have been doing." Teachers who attend a Hunter presentation may leave feeling affirmed, he notes, but they return to their classrooms and practice business as usual because they think they're already teaching the right way.

"This is just a hunch," Slavin adds, "but I would guess that training in Madeline Hunter would make no difference for maybe 70 percent of teachers. Maybe 30 percent are struggling, and, for them, appropriate training and follow-up may be useful."

A different criticism comes from Richard Gibboney, who challenges Hunter's central assertion that education is "just like" medicine, nutrition, and other more traditional sciences. "She has the aura of science without the substance," argues Gibboney, a former commissioner of education in Vermont who is now an education professor at the University of Pennsylvania. "When science is applied to the human area, it comes out as pseudoscience. Teachers are told, 'research says,' and they're kind of browbeaten into believing it. They're going to think it's right; it's like arguing with the principles of physics."

Moreover, Gibboney asserts, the psychology underlying Hunter's model is the behaviorism of B.F. Skinner and E.L. Thorndike, which, by its nature, is highly mechanistic. "It's really a technique to teach without the ideas, without worrying about what you teach or the context in which teaching is done," Gibboney says. "Her method lets a social studies teacher drone through a text and present inadequate, superficial information more effectively. It's perfect for facts, but it's absolutely ineffective for teaching ideas."

Hunter disagrees and argues that her method, when used correctly, can help students understand both concrete facts and abstract concepts. It's up to teachers, she says, to take the lead in guiding students beyond the mere recitation of names and dates. Hunter offers a formula for teaching, but she cautions that teachers must apply her methods appropriately, according to the situation.

Whether a lesson involves ideas or facts, Hunter warns teachers against wandering too far from "safe" subject matter; the emotions aroused by controversial issues, she says, can sidetrack students from the lesson's objective. And, unlike many teachers who want students to become more self-directed learners, Hunter is uneasy about allowing students too much freedom. "Students," she has written, "have an absolute gift for volunteering murky or confusing examples or those which present an exception to the rule." Hunter's message coincides with her suspicion of intuition and improvisation: Teachers should stick to their plan and maintain control of the discussion.

Her method, argues one critic, 'is really a technique to teach without ideas, without worrying about what you teach or the context in which it is done.'

John Taylor Gatto, who gives his New York City students almost free reign to decide what they want to learn, considers Hunter's approach "massively ill-conceived."

"You can create geniuses without all this phony theorizing," says Gatto, the 1991 New York State Teacher of the Year. "Formal teaching is a very small and inconsequential part of learning. In truth, people teach themselves."

Probably the greatest concern from teachers about Hunter's model involves the rigid way it has been applied—and misapplied—in schools. It's a depressingly familiar story: Administrators seek set formulas that promise dramatic results. And Hunter's allusions to science and research can be seductive, especially with policymakers demanding greater "accountability" from schools. As often as not, widespread implementation results in oversimplification of complex issues, inhibiting the flexibility crucial to effective practice. In

short, many of the problems associated with Hunter's model are problems rooted in the educational system itself.

For example, Hunter says she developed her model not as a way to evaluate teachers but rather as a means for supervisors to coach teachers and "accelerate" their teaching. But stories abound of teachers who received poor evaluations because they didn't "do Madeline Hunter" properly in their classrooms.

Last January, Sylvia Amato retired from her job as a speech therapist in an urban New Jersey school district. But rather than leaving with fond memories from her 20-year career, Amato left feeling bitter because of her experience with the Program for Effective Teaching and Supervision (PETS), the district's version of the Hunter-based model of instruction.

Amato, who worked with her students once a week, recalls rehearsing a fairy tale with one group for a performance before several other classes. Observing Amato and her students on rehearsal day, the department head strongly criticized the teacher for not employing all the PETS elements. "I certainly should not have been expected to do it then," Amato says. "The kids were all excited about the play, and I was written up for not doing PETS. I had always had wonderful evaluations, and then I started to get all sorts of lousy evaluations. Coming at the end of my career, it didn't make me feel good about all the energy and enthusiasm I had put into my teaching."

In his book *Tales Out of School,* Patrick Welsh, a high school English teacher in Alexandria, Va., describes how he reacted when an associate principal began using Hunter's elements of instruction as a basis for teacher evaluations. "I'd been teaching for 18 years and received enough feedback from parents and students to know I must be doing something right," Welsh writes. "Why should I be forced to go through a set of prescribed, mechanistic procedures to satisfy the school system's need to document before the public its seriousness about improving teaching?" Welsh is even more blunt when directly asked about Hunter's model. "It's stuff for incompetent teachers teaching dumbbells," he says. "It's the antithesis of what good teaching is. Any idiot can play the Madeline Hunter game."

In response to such reports, Hunter contends that her ideas have been misinterpreted. "I have come out loud and clear that anybody who uses a checklist in observing a lesson does not understand teaching," she says. "There is nothing you should expect to see in every lesson. If somebody told me I had to do all these things in every lesson, I'd say, 'I do not; I know better.' There is no such thing as a 'Madeline Hunter' lesson. There's an effective lesson or an ineffective lesson, but not a Madeline Hunter lesson."

To their credit, many states and districts have tried to keep their Hunter programs from becoming too rigid. "I see her as non-prescriptive," says Joyce Murphy, former coordinator of the Teaching Effectiveness Network, a broad Maryland program based on Hunter's ideas. "People criticize Madeline because they take what she says and see it as one model. They don't really listen to what she's saying." Adds Bertha Stewart, an elementary instructional assistant in Maryland's Prince George's County: "It's only as rigid as the teacher makes it. You can make any program rigid and you can make any program lax. That's the teacher's choice, not Madeline Hunter's choice."

Although Hunter has often condemned the use of evaluation checklists, her books readily promote a list mentality. In *Mastery Teaching* alone, she outlines three categories of decisions in teaching, six ways to increase students' motivation, three principles to improve lectures, four characteristics of an effective model, four factors that affect what students remember, and even four principles of chalkboard use.

The workshop at UCLA offers a different sort of insight into what happens when relative newcomers to the Hunter approach try to incorporate her model into their teaching. After four days of listening to Hunter talk, the participants spend the fifth day teaching short sample lessons and receiving feedback from their colleagues. The lessons cover the gamut—everything from Eskimos to mnemonic devices—but they're remarkably similar in structure. Most start with a "think of a time when . . . " statement, followed by a declaration of the objective, a few minutes of straightforward lecturing, and some questions requiring signal responses from the listeners. Some lessons are better than others, but none of them approaches Hunter proficiency. Nevertheless, the educators are excited as they try to emulate the master. "I've taught that lesson a million times," says one participant, "but I feel much better about it now that I've analyzed it."

A nagging question keeps coming to mind: If these teachers and principals, working directly with Hunter, are inclined to distill her ideas to a few set components, how can the model remain flexible when implemented throughout an entire district? Hunter herself contends that teachers need two years of practice and regular coaching to put her theories into effective practice. But how many districts are willing to make that sort of commitment, especially if they don't see immediate results?

Hunter offers few details about her financial status, though she acknowledges that she makes a comfortable living. A 1990 article in the *Los Angeles Times Magazine* estimated that she earns $30,000 a month. That's probably not farfetched: Districts pay Hunter $2,000 to $3,000 a day for speaking and consulting, and her calendar is booked two years in advance. She also profits from the sales of her books and videos: TIP Publications—which only sells Madeline Hunter titles—offers 11 books; Special Purpose Films, another Hunter-only distributor, sells sets of her films and videotapes for as much as $3,750 for an 11-part series; and

Instructional Dynamics offers videotapes that accompany *Mastery Teaching*. In addition, UCLA's Education Extension markets many reprinted Hunter articles.

Clearly, many districts have spent large sums of money to bring Hunter and her model to their schools. Some educators who have been trained in Hunter's ideas and methods aren't convinced it was worth the expense. Kenneth Kastle, principal of William Tennent High School in Warminster, Pa., says his district allocated about $100,000 to train every teacher and administrator in the "essential elements of instruction." In the end, Kastle says, it was a waste of money: The program—which is still in effect—has done nothing to improve teaching or learning. "The amazing thing," he says, "is that millions and millions of dollars have been spent across the country, so you would think that in some place you would find some positive results."

Given Hunter's impressive claims, it seems reasonable to expect, as Kastle does, that there is evidence documenting the effectiveness of her methods. But that's not the case.

Hunter, of course, says there are many success

> **If Hunter were to stop speaking and writing tomorrow, her message would continue to spread for many years. Her followers would make certain of that.**

stories. She likes to tell one about a failing inner-city elementary school in Los Angeles that she and some colleagues overhauled in the early 1970s. Just by changing the way teachers at the school taught, Hunter says, student learning doubled and, in some instances, quadrupled, and discipline problems virtually disappeared.

Rodney Skager, a colleague of Hunter's at UCLA who studied the project, tells a different story, an ambiguous one at best. "There was improvement in achievement by kids who were in the project for a whole year," Skager acknowledges. "But those results are qualified by the fact that the poorer, more mobile kids dropped out." Skager never published his study because of this flaw; he says there was no scientific way to say if scores improved because the worst kids moved away or because Hunter's model worked. "It isn't as convincing as Madeline would like it to be," he notes.

Other, more recent, research offers similar mixed

results. One of the more detailed studies was conducted over four years in Napa County, Calif., where Hunter had consulted with district educators. That study found some positive effects on student achievement during the first two years, but those gains stopped the third year, and achievement actually dropped the fourth year. A study of a statewide Hunter-type program in South Carolina reached a similar conclusion: Teachers were enthusiastic about the training, but student achievement was basically unaffected.

"It never did anything to improve student achievement," says Slavin of Johns Hopkins, who is familiar with the various studies. "But that didn't make the slightest difference to anyone" responsible for implementing similar programs in other places.

Hunter blames the less-than-convincing results in those districts on poor implementation, not the model. "In the Napa study, they did not use the model completely," she argues. "They did not teach for transfer, which is essential in my model. And some of the consultants were working with the control school. It was a very messy piece of research." And in South Carolina? "They acknowledged that they were not doing the coaching that I said was essential to translate knowledge into practice," she says. "You find they actually do not know what I'm saying."

Furthermore, Hunter maintains that it's almost impossible to conduct a valid study in schools because it's too difficult to control the variables. She argues that her own success is proof enough that her model is effective. "Why did the model start in the 1970s, go like a dreadnought through the '80s and a hurricane in the '90s?" she asks. "You either have to say educators are so stupid that for 20 years they've continued to use something that obviously doesn't work, or else you have to say it works."

Hunter's fans seem equally unconcerned by the lack of more concrete evidence. "I'm sure it works," says Bertha Stewart, the elementary instructional assistant in Maryland. "I don't have any written research, but I really believe it helps. Not every activity inside the brick walls of schools has to have written research to support it."

It's tough to be neutral about Madeline Hunter. People love her or hate her, and no amount of evidence will change their minds. Hunter says every component of her model is based on proven psychological studies or other scientific research; her opponents cite studies showing that her model makes absolutely no difference in student performance. But as Richard Gibboney

points out, "Research findings never changed anybody's mind about anything."

Hunter is well-aware of the criticisms of her work, and she seems to relish the controversy. "They say the strength of an impact is measured by the strength of the opposition to it," she says. "If you want no criticism, you do nothing, you say nothing, you be nothing. I have learned that the criticism is inevitable."

Hunter refuses to let her critics slow her pace. Although she is well past retirement age, she has no

---

'You have to measure the love and the rapport between a teacher and a student, not just the objectives of the lesson,' says one teacher who opposes Hunter.

---

plans to close up shop. Without a doubt, additional teachers and administrators will be captivated by her engaging style and become, to use a phrase that now has many different meanings, "Hunterized." Even if Hunter were to stop speaking and writing tomorrow, her message would continue to spread for many years to come. Hunter's faithful adherents would certainly see to that.

Still, resistance to Hunter's methods is growing. Districtwide implementation of her model may become rarer as teachers gain more control over their professional lives—including their inservice training, which is how Hunter usually reaches educators.

One thing is certain: Many teachers will resist Hunter's ideas if school administrators present them as the one correct way to teach, without acknowledging the infinite variables that make every classroom unique. Teacher Sylvia Amato captures the feelings of many teachers: "You have to measure the love and the rapport and all the other things that happen between a teacher and a student, not just the objectives of the lesson." □

From Teacher Magazine, *October 1991.*

11.

After Dick And Jane

Whole language is more than a way of teaching. It's about empowering teachers and students.

By Daniel Gursky

For more than 100 years, public schools in the United States have operated on the theory that children learn by mastering the component parts of complex material before grasping the entire subject. In the current system, a carefully sequenced curriculum from kindergarten to graduation is determined largely by experts outside the schools. Within that curriculum, teachers and textbooks transmit information to students, who spend most of their time as docile recipients. They study structured textbooks containing drills and exercises that reinforce skills and knowledge they often perceive as having no relevance to the world outside the classroom. Emphasis is on the memorization of facts rather than on problem solving and creative thinking. And students are tested, drilled, and retested regularly to make sure they have learned the facts and absorbed the information.

The theory that prevails in the traditional school contends that learning is hard work and that students must be persuaded to undertake and stick with it. A system of external rewards and punishments provides the incentive for students to achieve. Learning is viewed largely as an individual activity, and students are discouraged from collaborating with each other; working together is often viewed as cheating. Since children naturally dislike hard work and would rather be playing than learning, or so the theory goes, the main challenge to the teacher in the traditional school is to maintain order and to control the students so that teaching and learning can take place.

There is a certain logic and coherence to the theory, and it has surely demonstrated a tenacity to survive and a resistance to recent research findings on how children learn. But the growing number of teachers, school administrators, and scholars who have become part of the whole language movement believe the traditional school not only doesn't encourage learning but also often obstructs it.

Proponents of whole language subscribe to the theory that children are eager to learn when they come to school, that learning is not work but rather an effortless process that goes on continuously without their even trying. Children do not learn by first mastering the smaller parts of the whole, but by constantly developing hypotheses about the world around them and testing those hypotheses. Whole language advocates point out that children arrive at school already having learned an enormous amount without the benefit of formal schooling. The average 1st grader, experts say, has already acquired a vocabulary of 10,000 words and assimilated many of the rules of grammar without trying.

Whole language is an entire philosophy about teaching, learning, and the role of language in the classroom. It stresses that language should be kept whole and uncontrived and that children should use language in ways that relate to their own lives and cultures. In the whole language classroom, the final product—the "answer"— isn't as important as the process of learning to define and solve problems.

Whole language advocates believe that the ideal classroom is a child-centered one in which students enjoy learning because they perceive that the material has meaning and relevance to their lives. The teacher is not an authoritarian but a resource, coach, and co-learner who shares power with the students and allows them to make choices. Learning in such a classroom is a social act, and children learn from and help each other. The challenge to the teacher is to adapt the curriculum and activities to the interests and talents of the children, to provide a content-rich environment, and to assure that they are constantly engaged in learning. When children are not learning, whole language teachers say, they become bored and restless, and control becomes a problem. The common techniques of whole language teaching—daily journal and letter writing, a great deal of silent and oral reading of real literature, and student cooperation, to name a few—are the philosophy in action.

It is hard to imagine two schools of thought more diametrically opposed in their view of how children learn than the behavioral psychology approach and whole language. Frank Smith, a leading authority on reading, writing, and children's literacy, finds the two views so contradictory "that they would appear to refer to two entirely different kinds of mental activity." But they share two points:

• Human learning begins with the learning of language: first, listening and speaking; then, reading and writing.

• Success in learning language is vitally important because it largely determines how well a child will do in school and in life.

The Great Reading Wars

Because children already know how to speak (and presumably to listen) when they come to school, their formal instruction in language begins with reading. As a result, the battles between the proponents of the divergent theories of learning are fought mainly over the way reading is taught in the primary grades.

These battles, known as "The Great Reading Debate," haven't been limited to intellectual jousting in obscure academic journals and at professional conferences. The war is regularly waged in the mass media and in statehouses and in school board chambers across the country. The adversaries skirmish in courtrooms as well as classrooms.

Although the debate is ostensibly over the most effective method of teaching reading, it goes much deeper, raising profound questions about pedagogy, the nature and purpose of schooling, and the role of teachers, students, parents, and administrators. It follows logically that a society will establish a pedagogy, and structure its schools, to conform to the theory of learning that it subscribes to.

In the United States, the traditional theory of learning became institutionalized with the beginning of mass schooling in the 19th century. Its intellectual rationale was later drawn from the work of experimental psychologists such as Edward Thorndike and, subsequently, behaviorists such as B.F. Skinner. The theory is based on the belief that children learn a complex skill such as reading by first making sense of the smallest components of the language (letters) and then progressing to larger components (sounds, words, and sentences). Children learn to read by learning to decode the language; understanding follows after the code is broken and the component parts are mastered.

Traditional American education, therefore, begins with lessons that focus on phonics (letters, combinations of letters, sounds, and rules), tightly controlled vocabulary, and short basal reading passages, followed by numerous skills exercises, each with only one correct answer, typically delivered by the teacher to a group of students using the same textbook.

Constance Weaver, a professor of English at Western Michigan University, calls this the "transmission" model of teaching, with teachers serving essentially as "scripted technicians" who pass on a curriculum established by people outside the classroom.

"Learning typically is broken down into small parts that can be taught, practiced, tested, retaught, and retested," Weaver says. "Some things can be transmitted, of course. But many things are likely to be forgotten because the learner hasn't necessarily connected to the material."

In other words—as assessments of student literacy point out all too clearly—we can't assume the student is learning just because the teacher is teaching. The 1988 National Assessment of Educational Progress found that about 70 percent of 17-year-olds could read well enough to get the overall message or specific information from a text, but only 42 percent could read and understand complicated passages, and fewer than 5 percent could comprehend the specialized material prevalent in business and higher education. Estimates of the number of functionally illiterate American adults, who read so poorly that they can't cope with the basics of everyday life, are even more shocking. Some figures range up to 60 million—more than one-third of the country's adult population.

But even allowing for the possibility of gross exaggeration, these figures show that the current system doesn't work for millions of students—and particularly for nonwhite and disadvantaged students. Nonetheless, inertia reinforces the dominance of the traditional model of schooling. Most people were "taught to read" that way, and most teachers have been trained to function in such a system. "It takes a revelation for teachers to even ask whether it's possible that students don't learn that way, whether language isn't acquired that way," says Patrick Shannon, head of Pennsylvania State University's language and literacy education department.

But more and more teachers are asking those questions. Sometimes with the support of their administrators, but more often on their own, teachers are embracing a holistic, meaning-first learning theory. Some do it consciously, with a solid theoretical base, while others seek new methods out of dissatisfaction with the status quo. Whole language, which has mushroomed in popularity in recent years, is by far the most widespread manifestation of this theory.

The Deep Roots of Whole Language

Although the formal label only dates back a dozen years or so, whole language has deep roots both inside and outside of education. As one leading expert puts it, there have always been whole language learners—but there haven't always been whole language teachers.

Whole language owes its intellectual heritage to John Amos Comenius, a 17th century educator who believed that learning should be pleasurable and rooted in students' real lives; to John Dewey's theories of progressive education; to Friedrich Froebel, the founder of kindergartens, which have a lot in common with ideal whole language classrooms; to Russian psychologist Lev Vygotsky, who emphasized the social aspects of learning and the role teachers and peers play in supporting or thwarting it; to Dorris Lee and Lillian Lamoreaux, whose language-experience approach encourages teachers to use students' stories as classroom reading material; and to Donald Graves, a writing scholar and pioneer of "process writing," who encourages both teachers and students to write more. Recent theories and research in the relatively new field of psycholinguistics have provided whole language with a more scientific base.

Psycholinguists argue that, almost from birth, children engage in a search for meaning, structure, and order. They reject the idea that decoding the smallest components of written language is an effective way for children to learn to read. Instead, they argue, language proceeds from meaning as the learner draws on his or her own experience, culture, and previous knowledge to understand the text and extract information from it. Learning and understanding are inseparable.

Smith, whose 1971 book, *Understanding Reading,* was a milestone in psycholinguistic theory, says that this view of learning has been accepted as common sense for at least 2,000 years—by everyone except educators. He suggests that most learning is as inconspicuous as breathing; both teacher and student barely realize it's happening. "Learning is continuous," he says. "It requires no particular effort, attention, conscious motivation, or reinforcement." People are constantly learning without even realizing it, from street signs, conversations, headlines, movies, and other hardly noticed events in their everyday lives.

Learning only becomes difficult, Smith argues, in contrived circumstances that are disconnected from a person's immediate interests and experiences, such as teaching children to read by asking them to study and memorize individual letters that have no meaning or isolated words that lack context.

In his book *Reading Without Nonsense,* Smith makes the point by inviting readers to glance at the texts in the following boxes and ask themselves which is the easiest to understand and remember:

| JLHYLPAJMRWKHMYOEZSXPESLM |
| SNEEZE FURY HORSES WHEN AGAIN |
| EARLY FROSTS HARM THE CROPS |

Smith and whole language advocates believe that the meaning is "in the head," not in the text. One cannot read (and learn) about a subject that one does not already understand to some degree. Baseball fans,

> # Baseball fans who read the paper to see how their team fared easily pick up the nuances of yesterday's game because they already understand the game.

for example, who read the morning paper to see how their team fared easily pick up the nuances of yesterday's game from the written report because they already understand the game. The same article would be almost incomprehensible to a reader who knows (or cares) nothing about baseball.

To demonstrate that meaning is in the head rather than in the surface structure of language, Smith invites the reader to determine the meaning of a number of sentences: "Visiting teachers may be boring." "The chicken was too hot to eat." "She runs through the sand and waves." "The shooting of the hunters was terrible." Obviously, all of these sentences can have more than one meaning.

The point, says Smith, is that "neither individual words, their order, nor even grammar itself can be appealed to as the source of meaning in language and thus of comprehension in reading. Nor is it possible to decode from the meaningless surface structure of writing into the sounds of speech in order to find a back route into meaning. Instead, some comprehension of the whole is required before one can say how individual words should sound, or deduce their meaning in particular utterances, and even assert their grammatical function." In short, the more one knows about, or is interested in, the subject one is reading about, the more information one is likely to glean from the text.

Furthermore, Smith sees learning as social rather than solitary. "We learn from the company we keep," he explains. "We learn from the people who interest us and help us to do the things they do." As a result, children learn to read not from methods but from people. In a sense, they apprentice themselves to people who know something that they want to learn— teachers, parents, peers, and authors. Apprenticeships were a common and successful form of learning and teaching long before the advent of formal schooling.

The Politics of Reading Instruction

For years, the debate over reading instruction focused on the relative merits of phonics vs. the "whole word" method, which holds that words, rather than letters, are the most effective unit for the teaching of reading. There were countless studies, heated arguments from supporters of both sides, and even insinuations of communist conspiracies. During the 1950s and '60s, many people came to identify phonics with political conservatives and the whole word method with liberals. The rhetoric was often malicious. Rudolph Flesch, author of the 1955 polemical bestseller *Why Johnny Can't Read,* raised the stakes by blaming whole word advocates for many of America's woes, while at the same time politicizing and oversimplifying the issue of teaching reading.

In many ways, Flesch's legacy persists today, with the past attacks on the whole word methodology now aimed at whole language, whose proponents squirm with anguish at being confused with the whole word approach. They insist that the whole word method is much like the phonic approach in that it emphasizes components rather than language as a whole, memorization of individual unconnected symbols (words), and drill and practice.

Nevertheless, deliberately or inadvertently, traditionalists' attacks on whole language echo Flesch's McCarthy-era tirades against the whole word method. Sidney Blumenfeld, for instance, in a recent edition of his "Education Letter," calls whole language "an important part of the left's social agenda. Whole language is a lot more than just a new way to teach reading. It embodies a leftist messianic vision, which may account for the fanaticism found among whole language visionaries."

In recent years, fundamentalist religious groups have latched onto phonics, with its focus on skills and literal comprehension. They denounce whole language as secular humanism, atheism, and even satanism because of its emphasis on real literature rather than value-neutral basals and because of the introspection, inquiry, and multiple interpretations of texts encouraged by whole language teachers. Not surprisingly, lobbies have sprung up around the country to influence textbook-selection committees and to persuade legislators and school boards to mandate phonics as the only acceptable method of teaching reading.

Phonics-first advocates got a boost in September 1989, when a U.S. Senate Republican Policy Committee released a document titled "Illiteracy: An Incurable Disease or Educational Malpractice?" Citing a massive study supported by the U.S. Department of Education and carried out by the Center for the Study of Reading at the University of Illinois, the document called for "the restoration of the instructional practice of intensive, systematic phonics in every primary school in America."

For whole language teachers, however, arguments about the role of phonics and other methods of reading instruction miss the point: Whole language is a theory about how people learn; phonics is a method of teaching reading based on a totally different learning theory. Whole language teachers may draw upon a number of traditional methods, including phonics, but they use them only in specific situations when they think a student would benefit; the methods are not the whole language teacher's central approach to teaching literacy. "No one's suggesting that phonics isn't involved in learning to read and write," says Kenneth Goodman, University of Arizona education professor and a leading proponent of whole language. It is the reliance on phonics as the main or sole approach to teaching literacy, he says, that whole language proponents resist.

In fact, whole language is about much more than instruction in reading and literacy. It's about empowerment and the role of teachers, students, and texts in education. In short, it's about who controls what goes

> # Fundamentalist religious groups denounce whole language as secular humanism, atheism, and even satanism because of its emphasis on real literature.

on in the classroom. Will educational decisions be made by teachers and students or by administrators, curriculum developers, textbook publishers, and policymakers?

Consequently, in addition to rethinking their attitudes about learning, many whole language teachers have found it natural—indeed necessary—to develop a broader consciousness about social and political issues. "Teachers need to think about what they're doing when they decide to teach one way or another," Penn State's Shannon says. "What does [their method of teaching] mean for teachers and their students, not just in terms of language development but in their own lives? When they ask those questions, they acknowledge the politics of their work."

John Willinsky of the University of British Columbia agrees. "To give students expression is a political move," he says. "It empowers them."

Literacy as a Threat to Kings and Popes

Literacy has always been about power. The way reading has been taught for the past 500 years has more to do with religious and secular authorities trying to preserve their power than with learning theories. When Johann Gutenberg invented movable type and printed the Bible in 1455, reading was a skill largely

> # Whole language is about empowerment and the role of teachers, students, and texts in education. It's about who controls what goes on in the classroom.

limited to the clergy, royalty, and scribes. The authorities quickly saw the dangers inherent in widespread literacy. To prevent the spread of reading to the masses, they levied special taxes on printers, regulated the production and distribution of publications, and simply banned books and broadsides.

But even kings and popes could not withstand the inevitable, so the ruling establishment switched from trying to prevent reading to controlling it. And in some ways, as Daniel Resnick of Carnegie-Mellon University points out, the educational traditions established to control literacy during the Reformation remain stubbornly intact in modern-day American schools. Catechism-style teaching, Resnick notes, with its authoritative texts, established questions and answers, and repetitive lessons, sought to produce believers rather than thinkers. And that legacy persists. Future efforts "to move literacy expectations beyond a rudimentary ability to read, write, and calculate," he writes in the scholastic journal *Daedalus,* will be "constrained by the practice of earlier centuries: modest instructional goals, textbooks in the form of religious primers, language used primarily to create a civic culture, and mass schooling mainly for the primary years."

Basal readers, designed for specific grade levels, became the modern catechism by the 1920s, as common as pencils in the hands of primary and middle school students across the country. Shannon traces the

development of the modern basal to the late 1800s, when America's growing faith in science and industry was applied to reading. Basals were intended to "rationalize" reading instruction in order to overcome the lack of good children's literature and teachers' relatively low education levels at the time. Standardized tests, which developed roughly during the same period, reinforced the use of basals.

The belief was, Shannon says, that teachers were behaving scientifically—according to psychological "laws of learning"—if they were faithfully following the directions in the manual. At the turn of the century, he notes, basal publishers apologized for 18-page teachers' manuals that accompanied all six reading levels. Today, publishers unapologetically produce manuals the size of city telephone books for each level. Textbook publishers, editors, and authors, Shannon says, have reduced teachers to managers of commercially produced materials; the best teachers are frequently considered those who explain the material well rather than those who help their students become independent learners.

In essence, the basal system has solidified into textbook form the traditional skills-based model of learning. And if the basals are something of a modern catechism, they're followed religiously by American teachers. Surveys show that more than 90 percent of teachers use basals to teach reading, and the vast majority of their students' class work and homework comes straight from the basal. In addition, many states require the use of basals, and teachers in some districts face fines for disobeying the mandate.

A system built around basal readers and standardized textbooks takes away from teachers and students key decisionmaking power about classroom materials. It's not surprising, then, that many teachers who are attempting to change the structure of their classes often start by limiting the use of textbooks or shelving them completely.

"For teachers," Shannon says, "whole language is about having the right and responsibility to choose what methods they use, the materials offered in class, the ways in which they assess students." Given the tradition of outside control, he argues, the thought of taking responsibility can be both frightening and exhilarating to teachers. "The possibility of control and choice has never really been offered to teachers," he says. "They thought they were supposed to fit into a scheme in which they apply someone else's material."

Weaver, of Western Michigan University, points out that many teachers prefer the safety of the basal to the unpredictable vagaries of whole language. "You can give some teachers all the power in the world and they will use the same old traditional curriculum," she says. And even if they decide to abandon their basals, it may not make a big difference. "If teachers haven't made the shift in models of learning," Weaver says, "they're going to take nice trade books and do all the awful things that have been done with basals," namely, use the literature to teach isolated skills.

The basal, skills-oriented approach is also easier for teachers. They are following a preset curriculum, their lessons are planned in advance, and they can reasonably anticipate how the class will proceed. Whole language teachers, on the other hand, are constantly adapting as classroom events unfold; they guide rather than control; they watch for teaching opportunities and improvise. Whole language teachers acknowledge that while their new role is far more fulfilling than the traditional role, it is also far more demanding.

Because there are so many teaching strategies associated with whole language—journal writing, book "publishing," free reading, etc.—some teachers simply implement a few strategies and call themselves whole language teachers. "A lot of different activities plucked out of whole language and put in traditional settings can seem to be the same," says Goodman of the University of Arizona. "But they lose their significance when the reasons for the activities aren't there." Smith notes that many teachers mistakenly see whole language as just another method, rather than an entirely new approach to teaching. "They still do not trust children to learn unless their attention is controlled and their progress monitored and evaluated," he says.

When Johann Gutenberg invented movable type and printed the Bible in 1455, reading was a skill largely limited to the clergy, royalty, and scribes.

Many publishing companies exploit teachers' misconceptions about whole language. "Publishers see the markets for traditional materials being eroded, so they start relabeling things and saying that if you buy their materials, you're doing whole language," Goodman says. "That's predictable, and that's a danger." Some efforts by publishers to capitalize on the movement's popularity have produced seeming anomalies—whole language basals packed with skills exercises, for example, and workbooks that are simply repackaged and billed as "journals."

There are now enough committed whole language teachers in the United States to constitute a full-fledged national movement, complete with conferences, workshops, newsletters, more than 100 support groups, and a massive whole language catalog, contain-

ing information on almost every conceivable topic related to the subject.

These whole language educators take heart from the success of their counterparts abroad, particularly in New Zealand and Australia. "Essentially, what appears as a current revolution in this country," Goodman says, "was a relatively calm evolution in other countries." In New Zealand, for example, holistic theories of learning have guided many schools since before World War II. Some whole language proponents find it more than coincidental that New Zealand and Australia rank at the top of international comparisons of literacy, while the United States barely rates a spot in the top third.

Closer to home, Canada has also become a leader in whole language, with many of the provincial educational authorities adopting the philosophy for all their schools. Extensive resources for staff development and new materials have been allocated to help with the transition.

In the United States, whole language has been a grass-roots movement, spreading classroom by classroom, as one or two teachers—rarely more than a handful—in a school change the way they teach.

Although the great debate over how children learn (and thus learn to read) seems destined to continue indefinitely, it hasn't really become a dominant issue of the current school reform movement. With a few notable exceptions, most of the efforts to improve the nation's schools seem to accept as a given the traditional theories of learning on which American public education is based. Those who would "fix" our schools have largely concentrated on issues such as increased teacher accountability, more high-stakes standardized tests, higher academic standards, more rigorous curricula, and more and better teacher training. In recent years, the emphasis has shifted somewhat to school restructuring, site-based management, and parental choice. But there has been little mention in the school reform discussion about how children learn.

Whole language advocates want to change that. They would like to focus the public discussion on classroom learning and a theory of literacy that would inevitably change the way teachers teach and the way schools are organized and operated. As Jerome Harste, professor of education at Indiana University, has written: "Whole language inquirers want the politics of literacy made explicit. Politics, they argue, is the language of priorities. They understand that not to take a position is to maintain the status quo—to keep both those who are currently well-served and those not so well-served in place. From this perspective, curriculum is not just a new set of standards to be taught, nor even an unfinished agenda, but rather a vehicle for interrogating past assumptions as well as creating a better world. There is no neutral position." □

From Teacher Magazine, *August 1991.*

12.

A Course Of Action

In a new program, students work together for weeks trying to find solutions to complex and often controversial 'real world' problems.

By David Ruenzel

The Illinois Mathematics and Science Academy in Aurora, a distant suburb of Chicago, looms over a street dotted with industrial parks. A massive concrete structure with no apparent windows, the main facility—partially burrowed in the ground—has a severe, somewhat secretive, air. Important work, one surmises, goes on here. At the doorway, a sign reads, "A Pioneering Educational Community." Inside, past a security checkpoint, looms a cavernous lobby with a flourish of artwork on the expansive white walls. Gray carpet stretches in all directions. Students in jeans and visitors in business suits pass to and fro. No matter where I stand, I can hear the hum of the brilliant lights.

Established in 1985 by the Illinois General Assembly to address a perceived shortage of outstanding science and mathematics students, the academy is a three-year residential public high school governed by an appointed board of trustees. Its 1991 class had a mean math SAT score of 714. The school's 500 students, drawn from across Illinois, represent diverse ethnic, racial, and socioeconomic backgrounds. Admission is highly competitive. Nearly 30 percent of its faculty members hold doctorates. Equipment, ranging from a ProQuest computer system to satellite telecommunications, is state of the art.

Clearly, IMSA seems a futuristic educational outpost. Yet, if Bill Stepien is right, problem-based learning, the methodology that drives much of the

school's curriculum, can help revolutionize even the most antiquated public schools. As director of the academy's Center for Problem-Based Learning—he's also a history teacher—Stepien is devoted to making sure that problem-based learning finds its way into elementary and secondary schools both in the Chicago area and across the United States.

A wiry, intense man in his mid-50s, his gray hair combed straight back and down over his collar, Stepien speaks of problem-based learning with an almost prophetic intensity. "We think," he says, "that humankind is wired, inside the brain, to pay attention to dissonance, to things that don't seem to fit. We think human beings have a mechanism that demands that they try to resolve such dissonance. If you find problems that engage that hard wiring, I don't think kids will be able to resist it."

While many American schools still proceed as if knowledge were the memorization of contextless information, practitioners of problem-based learning insist that information, if it is to be transmuted into knowledge, is best acquired in the solving of a meaningful problem. "Meaningful" is the key word here; for if the problem doesn't compel students toward a genuine if less-than-ideal resolution, or if the problem is unauthentic in the sense that it would never be encountered in the "real world," then students are merely playing at inconsequential problem solving.

Stepien makes clear the distinction between problem solving and solving problems: "Problem-solving courses are too often, like, 'Let's brainstorm today, let's talk about fallacies tomorrow.' And the problems are often dinky, like, 'How does the straw man get from behind the house to the front of the house in the least number of steps?' What does that have to do with anything? I mean, let's pose a problem and brainstorm, OK. But let's make sure it's a significant problem."

In the world of the typical American school, which emphasizes the inexorable if tedious coverage of material, problem-based learning, with its emphasis on timely discovery of information, may seem highly novel. In truth, though, problem-based learning has strong roots in the pragmatism of philosopher John Dewey, who at the turn of the century began to criticize traditional teaching and learning on several fronts.

For one thing, Dewey said, children must realize the reason for acquiring knowledge if they are truly to secure it; they must be faced with a problem they truly feel a need to solve. For another thing, information—no matter how relevant it may seem at the time—quickly becomes obsolete. Schools, therefore, must spend less time imparting information and more time helping children acquire thinking skills that will enable them to solve the problems of experience. As Dewey wrote, there is a "necessity of testing thought by action if thought is to pass into knowledge." Dewey put this into practice at his own Laboratory School by having children, for example, learn mathematics as they constructed a model farm.

Idea Borrowed From Medical Education

While Dewey's theories were much discussed, they never, with some notable exceptions, much altered the American school. Schools placed too much of a premium on control to tolerate the freedom the new pedagogy demanded. It should come as no surprise, then, that it was a medical doctor—not an educator from within the system—who resurrected Dewey's ideas and pioneered problem-based learning.

During the early 1980s, Howard Barrows, assistant director for educational affairs at Southern Illinois University School of Medicine, was becoming increasingly disturbed by what he observed in medical education. "Students," he tells me, "were given a tremendous amount to memorize in the first two years of medical school. When they got into their clinical clerkships and began caring for patients, they couldn't remember much of what they'd learned. What they could remember they couldn't appropriately apply, so they had to relearn everything."

Barrows' discouragement with the status quo led him to a development that is revolutionizing medical education: the use of standardized patients—volunteers who are so thoroughly trained to simulate real patients that medical students usually can't tell the difference. In order to diagnose and treat such patients, students must retain not isolated facts but be able to apply knowledge integrated from such fields as anatomy, physiology, and chemistry. And they are evaluated on their ability to do so successfully. They also have to learn to work together, seeing each other as resourceful allies rather than as competitors.

As I listen, all of this sounds well and good. But Barrows was, after all, working with highly motivated medical students. I tell him I can't imagine the approach working very well with ordinary students.

Without hesitation or apology, Barrows assures me

DENNIS IRWIN

that I am completely wrong. For several months, he had been traveling across the country trying to incorporate problem-based learning into the curriculums of public high schools. He says it grabbed even the poorest, most disadvantaged students. "Everyone," he insists, "is motivated by real-world problems."

Content Versus Process?

My conversation with Barrows reminds me of a seminar I recently attended at which educators continually referred to teachers as "content people" and "process people," as if they were two necessarily alien factions. "Content people" imparted information; "process people" taught thinking skills. Neither group was apparently much interested in presenting to students real-world problems. Problem-based learning seems to be trying to eliminate this dichotomy between content and process by claiming that genuine knowledge always involves thinking upon information discovered in pursuit of a solution to a problem.

When I mention this to Stepien, he grabs my notebook and sketches a pair of scissors. One blade he labels "knowledge," the other "process." "You've got to have knowledge and process working together as the blades of a scissor," he says. "I don't know why we spent so many years arguing about who was going to teach knowledge and who was going to teach process. Hell, in real-problem solving, you're going to have to teach both."

Shortly after my arrival at the Illinois Mathematics and Science Academy, I am seated in a small office off the lobby with two other visitors, scientists from Israel, listening to Stepien explain the background behind the problem we are about to watch unfold. While he and another teacher designed the problem, it's based—as are all the problems the students tackle—on an actual case. Two weeks ago, he informs us, the seniors in his "Society, Science, and the Future" course learned of an apparent August outbreak of pneumonia in the fictional town of "Centerville." Causing one death in a matter of days, the illness had not responded to treatment with antibiotics, eventually arousing suspicion that the pneumonia was in fact Legionnaires' disease. The students, acting as officials in the county Department of Public Health, must determine the best course of action.

Analysis of the problem had begun, as it always does in problem-based learning, with a blackboard divided into three columns. The first column—labeled "What do we know?"—was necessarily short, essentially a list of people who had gotten sick and their symptoms. The second column—"What do we need to know?"—was lengthy: Students knew virtually nothing about the sickness and how it was transmitted. The second column was crucial, for the third column—"What should we do?"—could not be broached until vital information was considered. Because the disease ini-

tially appeared to be so much like pneumonia, the students quickly filled the second column with questions, such as: How much pneumonia could be expected in August? What would be the expected mortality rate? Exactly what is pneumonia, and how is it transmitted? Who is most susceptible?

How the students go about answering the questions they have generated is an important part of problem-based learning. The goal is to make students probing, self-sufficient learners. In this problem, because the students were under severe time constraints—more and more people were falling ill—it was particularly essential that they gather information in a highly systematic, efficient manner. To prevent unnecessary

> # As the students ask narrowing questions, the problem acquires a rich multidimensionality that may compel students to re-examine original assumptions.

duplication of information, groups of students took responsibility for answering specific questions, later sharing the data they discovered with the rest of the class.

According to Stepien, true collaborative learning should require students to bring together disparate bits of information. "In a typical classroom," he says, "students collaborate for about 60 seconds; the rest of the time they're discussing weekend plans. The problem is that kids are all holding the same information so there's really no need to collaborate."

Of course, the critical information wasn't tidily bound up in a textbook. The students, under the tutelage of their teacher, had to become creative, persistent researchers. Seeking answers to the pneumonia questions, they searched school and local libraries, scouring through medical texts. Various groups also contacted epidemiologists as well as the county public-health officer.

A Vision of School as a Think Tank

In problem-based learning, one of the goals of requiring such extensive research is to propel students far beyond the boundaries of the classroom. Indeed, at its core is a vision of the school as a kind of think tank, inextricably linked to a community of experts who act as mentors. Because students must proceed as professionals—in this case as health officials—they had to seek out "real-world" sources: doctors, scientists, and government officials.

Once the students analyzed their pooled research and eliminated pneumonia as a cause of the epidemic, Stepien intervened, presenting the students with an "autopsy report" that clearly indicated Legionnaires' disease. Once again, in a recursive process that typifies problem-based learning, the students returned to the three columns, the items in each column shifting as the problem came into greater focus. Among the new questions were: What is the source of Legionnaires'? How is it transmitted? How is it best treated? These questions, in turn, sent students back through the cycle of research. Later, under the "What should we do?" column, the students wrote, "Survey the 22 infected subjects to see if the illness can be traced to a common source."

A well-structured problem demands that students, in striving toward a resolution, take multiple factors—social and scientific, for example—under consideration, and that was the case here. Although the students, in the aftermath of the outbreak, managed to confirm the presence of Legionnaires' and released a bulletin encouraging residents to see a doctor should symptoms occur, they have neglected, Stepien now tells us, critical public relations functions.

Earlier this morning, he released to the students a stern memo from the director of the state Department of Public Health—this actually created by Stepien—demanding to know why the county officials have neglected to communicate with his office. The memo also asked them why they have not communicated with an increasingly exasperated press, producing "an awkward and potentially panic-producing gap."

As Stepien briefs us, then, the seniors are, on very short notice, preparing for a press conference. Dave Workman, a physics teacher who will, along with the school's public relations person, play a reporter, walks in wearing a hat with a placard labeled "press" tucked into the brim. "Let's go," Stepien says. "The press is waiting."

On the stage of another corporate gray room called "The Pit," a girl, flanked by two colleagues, reads a prepared statement. She's composed, making eye contact with the "press" and a video camera sitting in a recessed area beneath the stage. So far, she says, Legionnaires' has resulted in two deaths; 15 or 16 others have come down with the disease, and 22 others have symptoms. But the public need not panic. Centerville's water supply has been deemed safe and Legionnaires', caught in its early stages, can be successfully treated with the drugs erythromycin and rifampin. Furthermore, the county is doing everything possible to locate the source of the bacteria.

The "reporters" begin to inquire. At first their questions, informational in nature, are easily handled; only when they become more interpretative do the students begin to vacillate.

"Why, if the county knows that bacteria often originate in old air-conditioning towers, has it not shut down businesses with those towers?"

"That might cause a panic," a boy says. "Furthermore, it would be unjust to penalize businesses whose towers may not be contaminated."

"Isn't it your duty, as a health officer, to consider public health above all else?"

"Yes, which is why we encourage anyone who shows symptoms to see a doctor immediately."

"Is that enough to tell, say, an 80-year-old man?"

The students look at one another and shrug.

"What specific precautions can the residents take?"

"There's nothing really specific people can do," the girl says. She thinks for a moment and adds, "Just stay healthy."

At the debriefing session that follows, the "reporters" and teachers evaluate the students' performance. Coming in for particular criticism is the "just stay healthy" remark. In the midst of what may be a burgeoning epidemic, the comment, all agree, seems superfluous and even cynical; what is needed to reassure the public is constructive action.

Here the whole class joins the discussion, trying to sort through a problem that is becoming increasingly complicated and multidimensional. Much of the debate hinges on whether it would be appropriate to close down targeted businesses or to disinfect the air conditioners, or both, raising scientific, social, and economic issues. To peremptorily close down businesses, the more vociferous students believe, may impose economic hardship and subject the board to lawsuits, and to disinfect the air conditioners may obliterate all traces of bacteria, meaning they'll never find the source. "We'd look like dorks," a boy says.

As the class ends, the students make several decisions. They'll consult with a lawyer, for one thing, to see if they have the authority to close businesses; for another, they'll see if there isn't a way to disinfect the air conditioners without extirpating the bacteria.

During the discussion, a girl has quietly made what seems a most sensible suggestion: "Perhaps [we] could simply persuade businesses to shut off the air conditioners until the bacteria is discovered." But this suggestion is passed over; the students are focused on the issue of shutting down businesses. Later, Stepien tells me that one of the things students must learn in problem-based learning is that the loudest students in a group aren't necessarily the ones who should be followed.

When 'Ill-Structured' Means 'Well-Structured'

The Legionnaires' problem is typical of those found in problem-based learning. In the parlance of problem-based learning educators, it is "ill-structured." In a strange twist of words, it is the ill-structured problem that is well-structured for learning. "Ill-structured" simply indicates a problem that changes form as it is worked on; good problems, such as those in the real world, are necessarily slippery, hard to get a handle on, and as students gather new information they must form new hypotheses to match altered conditions.

A history problem Stepien designed is indicative of this ill-structured nature. Students—acting as military, scientific, and diplomatic experts—receive a memo from Secretary of War Henry Stimson, dated July 18, 1945, informing them that President Truman would like their counsel on a strategy "to force the unconditional surrender of Japan and provide for a secure postwar world."

Initially, students may be predisposed to see the problem in absolutist moral terms: Is it right or wrong to unleash the power of the atomic bomb on innocent Japanese civilians? Such a question, asked in isolation, can only result in unwieldy, even sanctimonious, debate. But as the students ask narrowing questions, the answers to which they will spend days researching, the problem acquires a rich multidimensionality that may compel students to re-examine their original assumptions. What do we know about the Japanese mentality and the conduct of warfare? How successful has our blockade been in slowing the Japanese war effort? Does America have an invasion plan? If so, what may it cost in lives?

The answers to these questions demand a constant realignment of thought, an easing of doctrinaire positions. While dropping the bomb may seem abhorrent, students also realize that, considering Japanese intransigence, to refrain from doing so would prolong a brutal war. Finally, as is typically the case with the ill-structured problem, students must come to accept the fact that there is no ideal answer; whatever resolution they come to—launching an invasion, for example, or waiting for the Russians to join the Pacific war effort—will be tainted with ambiguities, both moral and otherwise.

Getting students to tolerate ambiguity isn't easy. "A lot of kids," Stepien says, "have the conception that when you come up with a solution, you make the problem go away, and that's untrue. We talk about making something unacceptable more acceptable. Improvement through solution, not rectification, is what we're looking for. The point is that students inevitably must act, regardless of their doubts. What they've discovered has to be put to work in resolution."

Perhaps no problem poses more difficult moral ambiguities to students than "Jane's Baby." The problem, thoroughly documented in IMSA's literature, involves a woman carrying a fetus that has just been diagnosed as anencephalic—a disorder that invariably results, the students discover, in the death of the infant soon after birth. The students, here in the position of heads of pediatrics at a large city hospital, must decide how they should advise Jane Barton and her husband,

Ralph, played by school faculty members.

The students begin by carefully structuring questions: Is the test for anencephaly highly reliable? Is abortion possible in this case? Do the personal and religious beliefs of the Bartons permit abortion? What is the law on abortion in this particular state? Further complicating the issue is the fact that tissue or organs from the fetus could be donated to research. Later, the students, cast in the role of members of Congress, will try to push legislation overturning President Reagan's executive ban on the use of fetal tissue from elective abortions.

As the students gather information, they realize, as in the case with the atomic bomb, that the problem is inherently ambiguous and even confounding. Ideally it leads, as a realistic problem, not to purely speculative debate about the rightness or wrongness of abortion but to an eventual course of action derived from a careful consideration of the many messy particulars. The hope, as the academy materials put it, is that the "ill-structured problem will lead students to a reiterative process of speculation, problem definition, hypothesis formation, information gathering, analysis, and problem redefinition several times before the problem is resolved." In short, the problem should lead to all the things that catalyze thinking and rethinking rather than rote memorization.

It seemed controversial, even risky, for the school to ask students to tackle the abortion issue. Because the problem demanded that students act as consulting doctors, they were placed in the awkward position of perhaps having to suggest a course of action that could contradict their own deeply held beliefs. Was it fair, I ask Stepien, to demand that students face such a knotty problem?

Stepien thinks for a moment. "We don't want to indoctrinate students," he finally says, "but we do want them to consider all the arguments out there—just as they must in the real world. Now, if it's a case of moral belief, we would rather have their church or philosophical system handle it. If the students want to bring their belief system to the problem, there's no way we can avoid that.

"In the 'Jane's Baby' problem, the kids each had to meet the Bartons, to do a consultation. When the patients asked, 'Are you suggesting we have an abortion?' students said, 'Talk to your clergy, to your family.' The students felt patients should make the call.

"We had one student who never mentioned the abortion option; he simply didn't believe in abortion, across the board. Other students felt they had to tell patients of the abortion option, even as they felt there were better alternatives. The point is that morality has to come in; it's part of life. But we want a rigorous discussion of morals to take place, not indoctrination."

Still, it was apparent that bringing certain problems into certain schools is a risky proposition. Stepien wouldn't want to bring an affirmative-action problem into a recession-savaged industrial city where white ethnics were being laid off, would he?

"Of course not," he says. "But you could do something else, like with the northern spotted owl in Washington State. Is it worth protecting no matter what, even though it may cost loggers their jobs and way of life?"

All Kids Have an Innate Desire To Learn

Problem-based learning advocates, like a variety of progressive educators, typically operate on the assumption that all children have an innate desire to learn. Those with a less sanguine view of human nature—those who think that even the more conscientious children must occasionally be pushed and prodded into learning—may take issue with educators who think that children simply need to be faced with challenging problems.

Still, teachers using problem-based learning with diverse groups of students seem uniformly enthusiastic about its results. Ira Rosencrantz, a teacher at DeWitt-Clinton High School in Bronx, N.Y., incorporated problem-based learning into a biology curriculum for "slow" 9th graders. Although he was initially apprehensive about giving students the freedom to explore on their own, he found that there was a lot more participation and constructive activity in class. "You can't just get up in a room and tell these students, 'This is the lecture for today: topic, infectious diseases,' Rosencrantz says. "The good thing about problem-based learning is that everyone must become actively involved."

Bill Orton, who uses problem-based learning extensively in his 2nd grade classroom at Rawls Byrd School in Chickahominy, Va., says that his students were so taken with solving problems that they even had their parents buy them chalkboards so they could visually represent the challenges. "Of course, when kids have to learn things like the multiplication tables, they just have to sit down and learn them," Orton says. "But when critical thinking is the goal, kids, not teachers, must be at the center."

The types of problems Orton uses are reminiscent of those Dewey attempted at his Laboratory School decades ago. One problem has 2nd graders learning the rudiments of algebra by designing and building a geometric dome that will act as an observatory. Another problem, designed to teach students about metamorphosis in caterpillars and butterflies, has students creating a wildflower garden that will attract butterflies. Long before the children begin to plant the garden, they must determine which flowers and geometric arrangements are most appropriate for their purpose.

Of everyone I talked to about problem-based learning, perhaps no one was more zealous about its potential than Shelagh Gallagher, who, as former associate director of the Center for Gifted Education at the College of William and Mary in Williamsburg, Va., helped develop a K-8 problem-based science curriculum that a number of schools are using.

"If we had problem-based learning from kindergarten through 6th grade, we'd have a most powerful group of learners," Gallagher says. "If, instead of hand-holding children, we expected them to be responsible learners, they'd accomplish amazing things. They'd have not only improved cognitive abilities but also an improved ability to function, to get things done."

She talks about a problem-based learning project for 2nd graders that she was involved in. "I must admit, I walked into this 2nd grade project with trepidation because both teachers and students were using a wholly new approach. Yet, I discovered that the 2nd graders were almost the best—open to the notion that they had a problem to solve. This particular problem involved the dying ecosystem of Planet X; the students were mission specialists trying to save it. They started asking questions right away. What's wrong with the planet? Can we grow plants that will thrive there? What kind of pH levels do we need? How can we transport them?

"As well as these 2nd graders did, they still had to learn and even unlearn a number of things. They had to learn not to expect that the teacher was going to answer all the questions. They had to learn not to raise their hands at every juncture. And they had to learn to take risks and to consider many ideas that aren't necessarily all right or all wrong."

If problem-based learning is going to find a permanent place in American schools, teachers as well as students will have to unlearn certain behaviors. Problem-based learning demands, for instance, that the teacher substantially relinquish the role of expert in favor of becoming a kind of metacognitive coach who helps students become attentive to how they're learning as well as to what they're learning. And, to a much greater extent, teachers must be willing to allow students to pursue their interests, even if it takes them beyond the confines of the curriculum. As Gallagher says: "If pH comes up, teach pH. You don't have to wait until the third month of the 7th grade chemistry curriculum."

Of course, there's no guarantee that schools will be willing to change even if teachers are; many will have to be pushed into providing teachers with the flexibility that problem-based learning requires. Furthermore, constructing sound problems is arduous and time-consuming; clearly teachers will have to be provided with both materials and intensive training in how to use them. Still, working to bring problem-based learning into the schools seems worthwhile, despite the many obstacles that will have to be overcome. □

From Teacher Magazine, *January 1993.*

13.

Kids Learn When It Matters

Students will take formal schooling seriously when they can see that it relates to their own lives and experiences.

Commentary By Morris J. Vogel

This spring I watched my 15-year-old son study for his final exams. In science, as in several of his other courses, studying meant memorizing lists of hundreds of words and their accompanying definitions. By the time he took the exam, he was able to spit back dictionary identifications of terms ranging from saturated carbohydrate to degrees Kelvin. This exercise reduced science to an interminable series of facts devoid of context, and struck him—and me—as pointless. Few of these words held any real meaning for him. He no more knew the workings of science or its purposes at the end of the process than he did when he began to "learn" the subject. He would have been as well served by memorizing strings of nonsense words drawn from Lewis Carroll or generated by computer failure. And yet he—like most of the students in his academically oriented suburban high school—is mastering the words and the courses.

There are lessons aplenty in why some of our nation's children succeed in high school, and go on to college, careers, and productive lives. Examining these successes may even teach us why our high schools are failing many of their students.

Those content with superficial explanations may simply note that students who work hard master whatever their schools demand. If we hold this position, we can wish away our education crisis by insisting that children apply themselves and memorize the required facts. Former Secretary of Education William J. Bennett long advocated this view, even identifying

specific facts as prerequisites for informed citizenship. Our anxious fascination with Japan's success has led us to note similarly that Japanese schools emphasize rote learning through endless, repetitive drills.

But before we impose lock-step curricula, national exams, and a back-to-basics approach on our less successful high schools, we might consider further why the children of our privileged suburbs—and Japanese children—learn and do well in school. Might it be that these children correctly understand school as a hurdle to be jumped, an obstacle whose mastery brings them parental love, social approbation, and the prospect of adult success? There is little need to examine what these schools teach, because what their students learn often has no intrinsic value; the extrinsic rewards learning brings matter most. Learning happens because students understand that it is consequential in their own lives.

To leave matters at that is to risk failing the poor and often minority children of our inner cities. To say that schools succeed and students learn if their parents are involved, if their peers are similarly engaged, and if their culture values education is to say that schools work when society works. But society doesn't work that way for many of our children. We can't provide urban high schools with a mind-numbing curriculum and then blame broken and discouraged families for not motivating children to study it. We can't tell city children that mastering high-school coursework will bring them the good life when all around them the culture of despair teaches them to minimize their expectations—and to connect few of their hopes with

FRANCIS WASHINGTON

staying in school and getting a formal education.

This is not to say that schools can't make up for some of society's shortcomings. Indeed it means we have no choice but to transform schools in order to promote student success. We can make high schools smaller so that they resemble extended families in offering students emotional support; we can link the curricula of these smaller schools-within-schools to rewarding careers, and reinforce that message by regular exposure to real-world settings in which students see adults from backgrounds similar to theirs holding meaningful and well-paying jobs. The burden of proof is on us if we are to convince disadvantaged students that learning is consequential.

We can also apply what we know about consequential learning to the very core of education. We can make learning matter—in and of itself—in the lives of our students. We have only to look at the early primary grades—in cities as well as suburbs—to see children enthusiastic about learning and about exploring their expanding intellectual skills. Most 1st and 2nd graders feel good about school—and just as importantly, about themselves—because they know that they are acquiring mastery that matters in the real world. They feel empowered as they learn to read, to add, to subtract, and to figure things out for themselves. This is learning with a consequence; this is learning that happens

because children understand that it matters in their own lives.

We ought to imagine this kind of learning in our high schools, urban and suburban alike. Why not build a curriculum that teaches essential skills by allowing students to actively explore their own worlds? Why not teach American history, for example, by focusing on questions about the society in which students live? Why not root biology courses in the life experience of human communities, in relations between recognizable organisms and familiar environments? A curriculum thus connected to the immediate and the specific can command the attention of students as it proceeds to the distant and the abstract. A curriculum that takes seriously the experience of students offers a real prospect of having otherwise unconnected students take formal schooling seriously. The alternative is a curriculum that commands students what they ought to know and national tests that tell us that they haven't learned it. □

Morris J. Vogel is professor of history at Temple University. He is working with the Philadelphia Schools Collaborative on the restructuring of that city's 22 comprehensive high schools.

From Education Week, *Sept. 25, 1991*

14.

The Unschooled Mind

Teachers need to address the flawed theories that children bring to school, argues Harvard psychologist Howard Gardner.

By Daniel Gursky

Ask a 5-year-old why it's hot in the summer, and she'll probably say it's because the Earth is closer to the sun. Ask a high school senior the same question, and the chances are good you'll get the same answer. Both are wrong; seasons result from the angle of the Earth on its axis as it orbits the sun. The high school senior, like the 5-year-old, is responding on the basis of powerful, instinctive ideas about the world that everyone develops early in life. Through experience, the child learns that the closer one gets to a source of heat, the hotter it is; using a child's logic, the same must be true of the Earth and the sun.

Such intuitive thinking is fine for a preschooler, but not for a high school senior. Hasn't more than a decade of formal instruction made any difference in the student's thinking? Not as much as most people believe, nor as much as it should have, says Harvard University psychologist Howard Gardner. In his new book, *The Unschooled Mind: How Children Think and How Schools Should Teach* (Basic Books), Gardner argues that inside every student—indeed, inside every person—there's a 5-year-old "unschooled mind" struggling to express itself.

"Just as Freud stressed the degree to which the adult personality harbors within it the complexes and strivings of the Oedipal child," Gardner writes, "I maintain that students (and non-students) continue to be strongly affected by the practices, beliefs, and understandings of the 5-year-old mind." Children, Gardner explains, come to school with robust, but often flawed, theories about themselves, about other people, and about the world. Instead of challenging and building on these theories, schools ignore them and proceed to teach a new set. Even though these theories may be contradictory, they can coexist in the child's mind. In school, the student may be able to feed back information to the teacher on request, using the theories taught in the classroom, but the flawed ideas haven't been abandoned. As a consequence, Gardner argues, once outside the school, the student reverts to the theories of the 5-year-old mind when confronting new situations.

This startling theory is the latest work in Gardner's prolific and diverse career. He's best known for his theory of multiple intelligences, but his dozen books run the gamut from a psychology textbook to works on topics as varied as children's scribbling, brain damage, and China's educational system. Whatever the subject, his work attracts attention. And *The Unschooled Mind* promises to add more variety and complexity to the growing national debate about teaching and learning.

"I think Howard's one of the freshest, most original minds working in this area," says Jerome Bruner, a psychologist at New York University and one of Gardner's former teachers at Harvard. "His contributions have been major, not only by making us aware of the different forms of intelligence but also in terms of following through with what he has learned and coming up with interesting curricular ideas."

William Damon, chairman of Brown University's education department, expects *The Unschooled Mind* to have a powerful impact on education. "The book," he says, "is very innovative but at the same time very careful and responsible. It really sets out a new direction for how to approach education."

Gardner's Harvard office is a classic academic's space: crowded, strewn with papers, and dominated by large filing cabinets. The 48-year-old psychologist is dressed in the casual attire befitting a professor: light blue shirt with sleeves rolled up, olivegreen pants, no tie.

Seated in a rocking chair in front of a computer, Gardner argues that the problems with schools are much more extensive than most educators realize. "While everybody knows there are problems with many schools," he notes, underscoring the point with broad hand gestures, "I think most people assume that our best schools are fine." Not so, he says. Even in schools with the highest test scores, students who master the material adequately enough to perform well in class and on exams don't really understand what they're being taught.

In *The Unschooled Mind*, Gardner writes about a phone conversation with his daughter, Kerith, that brought this point home. When Kerith—who had done well in high school physics—called from college, distressed about her physics class, Gardner offered some fatherly advice: Don't worry so much about the grade, he told her, just try to understand the material. "You don't get it, Dad," Kerith replied. "I've never understood it."

Kerith has plenty of company. Many top students at elite universities exhibit fragile understanding, at best. In one study Gardner cites, engineering students were asked, "What forces are acting on a coin tossed straight up that has reached the midpoint of its trajectory?" Some 70 percent of students who had taken a mechanics course answered, incorrectly, that two forces—gravity and the original force of the hand that tossed the coin—were at work. In fact, only gravity is present.

Such misconceptions about physics provide the most striking evidence of Gardner's thesis, but he spends a good deal of his new book detailing common—but incorrect—thoughts and stereotypes that show up in other academic disciplines, as well. In math classes, for example, most calculus students can competently plug numbers into equations, but even the best students flounder when problems are phrased a little differently or applied to real-life situations. In the humanities and social sciences, people tend to respond to issues on the basis of dominant images and stereotypes, even when faced with contradictory evidence. During the Persian Gulf war, Gardner points out, huge numbers of Americans saw the conflict solely in terms of good guys vs. bad guys, demonstrating the same level of sophistication as that of a young child watching a cartoon. In reality, the complex history, culture, and economics of the Middle East make such Hollywood-like analyses inadequate.

Why does this happen? Because the 5-year-old mind reasserts itself when a person confronts difficult questions outside school. "You should talk to 5-year-olds," Gardner says. "They're very smart. They've got very powerful theories about how the world works, and they've got very powerful theories about how people work. They're very serviceable theories." Unfortunately, however, they are often flawed.

The problem, Gardner says, is that schools ignore the strongly held notions of their young charges; teachers treat students as if their minds are empty and need to be filled with new information. "If you don't confront students' ideas and show where they're adequate and where they're inadequate, those ideas are going to remain there," he argues. "They're going to be ready to pounce like a Trojan horse as soon as the children escape from the schoolroom."

Every parent can cite examples of child logic. Gardner offers one from his 6-year-old son, Benjamin: "I can tell Benjamin that the Earth is round and he'll repeat that. But then, if I say, 'Where are you?' he'll say, 'I'm on the flat part.' He repeats the information, but he converts it to something that makes sense to him. The Earth doesn't look round to him."

Howard Gardner with son (left) and friend

GALE ZUCKER

Students of all ages do the same thing. They may be able to provide the expected response on homework or a test, but that rote answer offers no guarantee that they understand the material. This disparity between teaching and understanding distresses Gardner because he sees "genuine understanding"—understanding that goes beyond repetitive learning and short answers—as the fundamental goal of education. "No one ever asks the further question, 'But do you really understand?'" Gardner writes. "The gap between what passes for understanding and genuine understanding remains great."

Gardner doesn't hesitate to propose his own solutions for promoting genuine understanding. *The Un-*

Gardner is distressed by the gap between teaching and understanding; he believes 'genuine understanding' should be the goal of education.

---

schooled Mind goes beyond description and analysis; it outlines his most explicit prescription yet about how to reform schools. He proposes an education system suffused with individual and group projects, particularly apprenticeships and the hands-on experiences offered in children's museums, because he believes projects can restore the context sorely missing from students' school experience. As often as possible, Gardner asserts, students should work with and learn from adult experts in their fields.

Outside of education, people's lives basically revolve around projects. But that's still a "blind spot" in schools, Gardner explains. "I often hypothesize that people probably learn more from the few projects they do in school than from hundreds and hundreds of hours of lectures and homework assignments," he says. "I imagine that many people end up finding their vocation or avocation because they stumbled into a project and discovered they were really interested in it." By the same token, once they're immersed in a project, students might realize they're not really interested in a subject.

Schools, Gardner believes, should pay more attention to helping students discover subject areas that interest them. By focusing on basic skills, schools risk suppressing the positive aspects of children's minds—adventurousness, flexibility, creativity—as well as their natural enthusiasm for learning.

"To declare oneself against the institution of the three Rs in the school is like being against motherhood or the flag," he writes. "Beyond question, students ought to be literate and ought to revel in their literacy. Yet the essential emptiness of this goal is dramatized by the fact that young children in the United States are becoming literate in a literal sense; that is, they are mastering the rules of reading and writing, even as they are learning their addition and multiplication tables. What is missing are not the decoding skills, but two other facets: the capacity to read for understanding and the desire to read at all."

In *The Unschooled Mind*, Gardner suggests ways teachers can help students confront their misconceptions and flawed theories in order to develop deeper understanding. One way is through what he calls "Christopherian encounters," named for Christopher Columbus because Columbus challenged the conventional wisdom of his day that the Earth was flat.

In such encounters, students' intuitive ideas are validated or proved false by comparing them with more sophisticated theories about how the world works. For example, a computer simulation that allows physics students to manipulate such forces as velocity and acceleration on an image on the screen might challenge the students' assumptions about the influence of gravity. Or history students might reconsider their beliefs about the causes of World War I by examining conflicting accounts of the same event. The key, Gardner explains, is for students to contemplate and analyze material from as many different angles as possible.

"When I talk about Christopherian encounters," he says, "the point I'm trying to make is that the only way to transform our conceptions is for these things to become a major agenda of schools from the very first years. It's got to be something that's done over and over again."

These notions about the mismatch between the way schools teach and the way students learn will undoubtedly challenge people's assumptions about learning in the same way Gardner's 1983 book, *Frames of Mind*, forced people to question their assumptions about intelligence. That book stirred controversy among educators and academics and fueled many cocktail party conversations. In it, Gardner argues that instead of having one all-encompassing mental aptitude that can be measured by an IQ test, people have at least seven separate and distinct intelligences:

• Linguistic: A sensitivity to the meaning and order of words and the ability to make varied use of language; translators or poets exhibit this intelligence.

• Logical-mathematical: The ability to handle chains of reasoning and recognize patterns; mathematicians and scientists exhibit this intelligence.

• Spatial: The ability to perceive the visual world accurately and re-create or transform aspects of it based on those perceptions; sculptors and architects, for example, exhibit this intelligence.

• Musical: A sensitivity to pitch, melody, rhythm, and tone; composers and singers exhibit this intelligence.

• Bodily-kinesthetic: The ability to use the body and handle objects skillfully; athletes, dancers, and surgeons exhibit this intelligence.

• Interpersonal: The ability to notice and make distinctions among other people; politicians, salespeople, and religious leaders exhibit this intelligence.

• Intrapersonal: The ability to understand one's own feelings and emotional life; therapists and social workers exhibit this intelligence.

Gardner categorized these intelligences by reviewing studies of a range of people: prodigies, gifted people, brain-damaged patients, idiot savants, individuals from diverse cultures, and experts in various lines of work, as well as typical children and adults. Support for his belief in distinct intelligences comes in part from cases of people who lose their ability to speak but can paint beautifully, or from autistic children who can sing dozens of songs perfectly.

Gardner wrote his book *Frames of Mind* for psychologists and educated lay readers; teachers, however, provided the most enthusiastic response.

People possess every intelligence in varying strengths, giving everyone a unique "profile" of intelligences, Gardner says. Unfortunately, most schools and teachers emphasize the linguistic and logical-mathematical perspectives at the expense of other areas.

"It's important to recognize that there are many people who could make wonderful contributions to the world who don't happen to have that particular blend," Gardner says. "And if we are concerned with those individuals' lives, we cannot ignore this fact."

Not everyone buys into Gardner's theory. Some leading psychologists, including Yale University's Robert Sternberg, have argued that Gardner has merely described various talents, not intelligences. Sandra Scarr, a psychologist at the University of Virginia, has called Gardner's ideas on multiple intelligences a theory "in which everything good in human behavior is called intelligence." Other skeptics have said the that theory provides a convenient excuse for almost any poor performance by students, who can

plead inferior intelligence whenever they encounter difficulties.

Still, many teachers find the notion "immediately liberating," Gardner says. But, he adds, that doesn't automatically translate into better teaching. "To get teachers to think deeply about their strengths, their students' strengths, and how to achieve curricular goals while taking those strengths and different profiles seriously is a huge job," he says. Teachers can't be expected to become "multiple intelligence mavens," as he puts it, but they should know where to send students for help in, say, music or dance.

Furthermore, an awareness of multiple intelligences can suggest to teachers various ways to present the same material. "So long as one takes only a single perspective or tack on a concept or problem," Gardner writes, "it is virtually certain that students will understand that concept in only the most limited and rigid fashion."

Gardner's ideas about learning and intelligence aren't just the theoretical fancies of an Ivy League academic. For more than 20 years, he has put them to the test at Harvard Project Zero, an interdisciplinary research group that conducts various small-scale studies with teachers and students at different Massachusetts schools. Gardner is co-director of the project, which began in the mid-1960s with a focus on arts education. While he retains a special interest in the arts and artistic creativity, the group has expanded its focus to cover a wide range of topics relating to curriculum, teaching, and assessment.

Not surprisingly, the projects usually require teachers and students to rethink some long-held ideas. Gardner says most people, teachers included, endorse the same view of education they had when they were 5 years old: Schools are authoritarian, punitive institutions in which somebody smart stands in front of a room and tries to pass information on to large groups of students.

Project Zero's undertakings bear little resemblance to this vision of traditional schooling. One of its early childhood programs, for example, attempts to provide young children with a more rounded education than most typically experience. Preschoolers and primary students in Project Spectrum, as this study is known, explore a range of different learning areas, such as the naturalist's corner, the storytelling area, and the building corner, to name just three of the dozen or so areas that are available. Teachers at Project Spectrum form an impression of the children's strengths and weaknesses by watching them participate in the various games and activities. At the end of the year, they recommend specific activities that parents can do at home or around that community to stimulate the child's learning.

In *The Unschooled Mind*, Gardner writes about one 6-year-old boy who was doing so badly in a regular school that he seemed certain to be held back. In

Project Spectrum, the boy proved himself best in the class at assembly tasks, such as taking apart and putting together doorknobs, food grinders, and other common objects. Building on his success in this area, he went on to improve his overall school performance. Once the boy saw he could succeed and realized he had abilities valued by other people, he gained the confidence to do better in other areas, Gardner says.

Gardner's ideas have also provided the framework for the Key School, a public elementary school in Indianapolis that operates on the principle that each child should have his or her many intelligences stimulated every day. "Practically everything we do is put through the filter of multiple intelligences," says Patricia Bolanos, the magnet school's principal.

> # Only when teachers acknowledge the assumptions made by a 5-year-old mind, Gardner says, will students internalize the lessons taught in school.

All Key School students participate in computing, music, and body movement and spend part of each day in one of a dozen apprenticeship-like pods, working with peers, teachers, and other professionals on skills ranging from architecture to gardening to making money. During each 10-week term, the curriculum focuses on a theme; students complete a project dealing with some aspect of the theme, often working with other students or members of the community. They then present their projects to classmates, who ask questions and help the teacher and the presenters assess the work. The presentations are recorded on videotape, so students accumulate a video portfolio over the years.

Although Gardner has no official role at the school—he's an informal consultant—Bolanos says the school's six-year association with him has helped establish its credibility. Word of the school has circulated nationwide; as a result, Bolanos and her staff have received hundreds of requests over the past few years from educators and others wishing to visit.

Teachers at the Key School aren't the only ones flooded with requests from people who want to know more about multiple-intelligence theory and how it

applies to schools. Eight years after the publication of *Frames of Mind*, Gardner still can't keep up with all the letters and calls he receives requesting information about his theory. Gardner admits that the book received the sort of publicity most authors—and certainly most psychologists—only dream of. Still, the acclaim wasn't entirely new: In 1981, Gardner was selected as one of the first MacArthur Foundation Fellows, a distinction that included a five-year "genius" award of $196,000 and a lot of attention.

But his prominence spread far beyond academic circles with the publication of his theory of multiple intelligences two years later. Today, the theory has attained pop-culture status; *Washington Post* political reporter Lou Cannon even examined Ronald Reagan through the multiple-intelligence lens in his recent book *Ronald Reagan: The Role of a Lifetime*. Last year, Gardner's work on intelligence earned him another prestigious honor, the Grawemeyer Award in education from the University of Louisville; the award came with a $150,000 stipend.

"I could lead one life just giving workshops and speeches to people who are interested in knowing more about multiple intelligences," Gardner says. "There are about a dozen books already out on the topic and half a dozen people making a living giving workshops on it, none of whom I have anything to do with. I could lead another life just answering all the mail I get for requests for information about it."

Gardner has resisted offers from publishers who would like him to capitalize on this interest and write more "popular" books—something like *The Seven Smarts*, as he puts it. He wrote *Frames of Mind* for psychologists and educated lay readers; but, as it turned out, teachers and other educators provided the most enthusiastic response. With *The Unschooled Mind*, Gardner hopes to reach teachers again, this time with his theories about the 5-year-old mind.

"I think the new book will strike a chord among good teachers," Gardner predicts, "because good teachers will say, 'I've been assuming all along that what I teach is getting across. Here's a guy who seems to know what he's talking about saying that, in fact, what I teach has very little impact, especially after my students leave the classroom.'"

Gardner doesn't want teachers to merely read the book and put it down; he would like them to think about their teaching and embrace approaches to education that focus on genuine understanding. Only when teachers acknowledge and build on the assumptions made by the 5-year-old mind, he says, will students internalize the lessons taught in school and be able to apply them outside the classroom. □

From Teacher Magazine, *November/December 1991*

15.

Play Is Part Of Learning, Too

Play is an effective learning strategy that children use to advance their skills and make sense of their world.

Commentary By Colette Daiute

School is back in session, and children are supposed to get serious. They have had time to play during the summer, and now it is time for them to work. While such reasoning is familiar to most of us, this dichotomy between play and work is one of the greatest myths of education—a dangerous myth that often leads to leaving children out of the educational agenda and ignoring the quality of their life in school. Testing, longer school days, and parental choice all resonate with the theme of increasing the work children do in school, yet play is a powerful learning process. Clearly, there is work children have to do in school, and some structure is necessary when many people are sharing resources, but given the freedom to work on challenging tasks in the company of their peers, children devise purposeful and ingenious lessons for themselves in the context of their classroom play.

Young children do some of their most important learning through play. "peekaboo" helps them learn that the world exists independently of themselves and is often predictable. "Pat-a-cake," a cooperative game, enhances physical and social development. And children make one of the most dramatic of human accomplishments—learning language—by playing with sounds and meanings from the time they are born. After kindergarten, though, children are abruptly expected to think and to express themselves like little adults, even as they continue to make discoveries and develop their talents by playing. I have seen, in my research, how play supports children's literacy develop-ment—even up through the 5th grade, when play is all but banned from the classroom.

The transcript of a brief conversation between Andy and Russ, two 3rd graders in an urban school, shows how children do difficult work such as figuring out the spelling system of English—when they have the freedom to explore academic material on their own terms. When asked to write a report for the class newspaper on events during the Renaissance, Andy and Russ engaged in an effective spelling exercise as they played with the sounds of Christopher Columbus's name:

Andy: Yea, I spelled it right! I think.
Russ: N, no.
Andy: Oh (raspberry sounds), oops, I forgot one L. I didn't look at that. Forgot the L.
Russ: Challenged Christopher Columbus and his crew.
Andy: This was a great challenge for.
Russ: Chrissy.
Andy: Chrissy? (Laughter). This is a great challenge for Chris.
Russ: For Mr. Columbus (Laughter) . . .
Andy: It's shorter! (Laughter).
Russ: Put Mr. Columbus.
Andy: Mr. Columbus.
Russ: Columulumbus.
Andy: Colum, Columbumps (Laughter).
Russ: Colum.
Andy: Colummus? Colum, Clom, Come, Columbus?
Russ: Lumberjack (Laughter). . . .
Andy: Colombos, Columbus. Columbus . . .

Russ: Colummmmbabababababb. Ohhew. B U S. I think that's how you spell it . . .

Andy: Col-um-bus. Ya, you're right.

Russ: Christopher Columbus. Collumm.

Andy: Ya, where . . . Columbus, Columbus. The Spaniard Christopher Columbus discovered America. Now do you know how to spell the last three letters of Christopher Columbus? Oh, I already asked you. Forget it.

Russ: Actually, he rediscovered America.

Andy: No, U S.

Russ: And he even made friends with some Indians.

While this play may seem capricious, it is actually rule-governed. Breaking down the sounds of unfamiliar words, as Andy and Russ did, helps children with the task of writing about challenging material. After rejecting the temptation to shorten Columbus's name to make it easier to spell, Andy and Russ played with the name—"Columulumbus," "Columbumps," "Colum-

---

When children play, they appear to stray from the topic, but what they are doing is exploring the topic in relation to their own knowledge, needs, and talents.

---

mus" which involved analyzing the sounds of the word, testing a variety of sounds, and eventually coming up with the right spelling. Although these same students might groan when given a spelling test by the teacher, they have challenged themselves to explore the rules of spelling and to use these rules as they composed a complex piece of writing—the way that expert authors do. In fact, rather than goofing off when allowed to work together, Andy and Russ, like other children, played around material they had not yet mastered, seizing an opportunity to advance their skills.

While play may seem silly, it is children's way of making sense of the world. Just as younger children take some control over their lives by playing doctor or Mommy and Daddy, older children can take control of intellectual material by playing with it in relation to personally meaningful themes. When children play, they may appear to stray from the topic, but what they are doing is exploring the topic in relation to their own knowledge, needs, and talents. Since new knowledge is learned only when it relates to prior knowledge, playing is a sound way to create bases for new learning.

Allowing children to use their own knowledge as a springboard for learning is also a way to build the curriculum on diverse strengths. Education may be failing in our country because too little attention has been given to making sure that lessons make sense to the diverse population of children in our schools. So finding ways to support children's play around their schoolwork is worth more effort than reforms that repeat past failed attempts at telling children what is supposed to make sense.

Play is also an effective learning strategy because it allows children to take risks—which is essential when studying challenging material. Trying out a new word or using unfamiliar concepts is easier for children to do with a friend in jest than with a teacher who evaluates them and expects to see them at their most competent. In formal lessons, only the most confident children take such risks, but in the safe context of play, even low-achieving students take on intellectual challenges, examining and using academic materials as they would their toys, and they improve their performance in this process. Allowing play in the classroom means supporting children's ownership of intellectual material, and such ownership is the right of all children.

Finally, the laughter in Andy and Russ's lesson is also one of the reasons why it leads to growth. Laughter provides social and emotional support to intellectual development, providing links between the mastery of skills and the ability to use skills during the course of life. The positive feelings evoked during play give children courage to propose and test hypotheses, such as the probing ideas Andy and Russ began to explore about Columbus: Was he really the one who discovered America? What about the people who were there before him? By having the chance to say what they think rather than only what they are supposed to think, children advance their critical-thinking skills.

Through play, children spontaneously design activities that involve them in taking responsibility over their own learning. It is difficult to think of a more sound educational goal. Yet, reforms continue to propose options that put the power elsewhere—with parents, in tests, in school restructuring—not even with the teacher. Clearly, the job of becoming literate, knowledgeable, and critical does not end with exploring the logic of the English spelling system or social issues, but the kind of analysis, sense-making, and hypothesis-testing children do when they play in school sets a firm basis for their intellectual development.

Yet, even when play is properly understood as an effective learning process, several misconceptions keep it out of the classroom. One concern about play is whether it creates chaos. On the contrary, play flourishes in classrooms where teachers provide structure and guidance. For example, the teacher creates a meaningful task such as writing a class newspaper, asking children to work together and to use facts and concepts they have been studying. The collaborative process and the common goal provide the structure. And far from being chaotic, children's play in school is remarkably on-task.

Another concern raised recently is that when teachers allow children to play in school, they may be depriving students of the benefits of instruction. While this could happen, play and formal instruction work best when they work together. Teachers can offer

---

Through play, children design activities that involve them in taking responsibility over their learning. It is difficult to think of a more sound educational goal.

---

precise guidelines on spelling, vocabulary, facts, and the rules of classroom discourse. But these rules are likely to be more useful to children if they can appropriate them in their own ways. If children write reports with a classmate, for example, they can practice using school rules in their own language, lingering over aspects that interest or challenge them. In this way, children have a hand in designing the curriculum as they adapt it and introduce new elements. Creating classrooms in which children own the goals, contents, and strategies through spontaneous processes like play means providing all children with points of access and control.

There is great concern that schools in the United States are lax in comparison with those in other countries whose children score higher on achievement tests. Since a major cause of the problem is reported to be that our schools do not require children to work as hard or suffer as rigorous exams as children in other countries, allowing children to play in school might be last on the list of reforms. Yet, far from being antithetical to work, play is children's way of working. Children use play to challenge themselves, design their own lessons, and test themselves. When children in other countries do better, we should explore the culturally relevant ways of making schoolwork meaningful in those countries. Play may provide a rationale for learning that we have not otherwise conveyed to our students.

The schools and classrooms where playful learning occurs are structured with children in mind. They are schools where children are respected as special and unique and where institutional and pedagogical structures invite children to express themselves and to participate in planning—albeit in subtle ways. For young children, play is learning. Play means making sense, taking control, creating mastery. When we listen to children's play in the classroom, what we hear are their designs for education. Given a meaningful task, children as young as 8 use play as a way to stay on topic—not veer from its challenge themselves—not avoid their work—and make discoveries that are more profound than silly. Yes, learning should be fun, and finding ways to bring learning alive to children in classrooms should be on the educational agenda. □

Colette Daiute is an associate professor at the Harvard University Graduate School of Education.

From Education Week, *Oct. 2, 1991*

16.

'Full Inclusion, Not Exclusion'

A Virginia hamlet is at the forefront of a movement to bring disabled students back into the regular classroom.

By Debra Viadero

When Toni Mills started school three years ago, she rode a bus more than an hour each day to a special-education class in a nearby town. The classroom was a quiet setting where some children, like Toni, were mentally retarded, and others could not walk or talk. By the time Toni got home after another long bus ride in the evening, it was almost time for bed.

"I told her teacher, 'Well, she can't add,' and her teacher said, 'She'll probably never be able to add,' " Toni's mother, Teresa Mills, recalls. "But she wasn't doing anything."

Today, at age 9, Toni attends the same elementary school as her nondisabled neighbors and cousins. Her classroom is a bustling place with bright-colored walls and pictures and noisy 3rd graders. There are children who are willing to coax her down from the monkey bars when she balks or to help her with a classroom assignment.

She is reading at a 1st-grade level, despite psychological tests suggesting she should not be doing so well. If she still cannot add, her mother notes, she at least "knows her numbers." Ms. Mills adds: "She's learning so much more than I ever anticipated."

What has made the difference for Toni, Ms. Mills and educators at Shawsville Elementary School say, has been the opportunity to go to school with "regular kids." Toni is here because school officials in this rural Virginia county three years ago launched an ambitious effort to open up regular classrooms across the district

to all students with disabilities. Now, nine of the district's 10 elementary schools, like Shawsville, are fully integrated, and efforts are under way to do the same in the middle and high schools.

The campaign has put this tiny hamlet at the center of a national movement toward "full inclusion" of disabled students in regular classrooms. Fueled by court decisions, parental demands, new research, and the success of other educators, more schools are putting disabled children back into regular classrooms.

Some experts in the field have expressed concern that the movement could dilute special-education services and jeopardize legal protections. But others hail it as a major step forward for disabled children. "Clearly, there's a message here to students," says Douglas Biklen, a Syracuse University special-education professor and vocal full-inclusion advocate. "It says, 'I'm valued. I belong here. I have a right to be here.' "

Federal special-education law states that, to the "maximum extent appropriate," children with disabilities should be educated with nondisabled peers. But common practice, evolving from an era when people with disabilities were routinely shut away in institutions, has been to teach many such children in separate classrooms, or to pull them out of their regular classrooms for special help in nearby resource rooms. Students are typically "mainstreamed" for only a few subjects a day, such as art or physical education.

According to a recent analysis by the ARC, a national advocacy group, only 6.7 percent of students with mental retardation spend the better part of their school days in regular classrooms. In contrast, the full-inclusion movement puts the emphasis on the regular classroom. Students in fully integrated schools are not pulled out for special help elsewhere. The assistance they need comes to them in the regular classroom.

For the special-education field, the momentum the movement is now gaining marks a sea change in opinions on the issue. Just six years ago, for example, Madeleine C. Will, then the U.S. Education Department's assistant secretary for special education and rehabilitative services, proposed a "regular-education initiative" urging schools to teach all mildly disabled students in regular classrooms.

The proposal created a bitter controversy in the field. Some special educators said their students needed more intensive help, and parents and advocates worried their children would lose hard-won rights to special-education services.

While some of those feelings still exist in the field, the issue assumed a lower profile after Ms. Will left office. Her successor, Robert R. Davila, himself a product of special schools for the deaf, presented a more moderate stance on the issue. He said regular-classroom placement should be an option for all students along with other kinds of placements, such as resource rooms and special classes and schools.

The department, however, has continued to pump funds into research and demonstration projects for full inclusion across the country, awarding a total of $63-million in grants over the past three years. States and school districts, moreover, have begun experimenting on their own with the idea.

Parental Demands Have Triggered Lawsuits

At the same time, a new federal law has prodded more states to provide special-education services for disabled preschoolers. Many of those programs are housed in regular preschools. "More and more of these kids are coming up with pretty good preschool experiences," says Frank Laski, a lawyer who often handles special-education cases for the Public Interest Law Center in Philadelphia. "When they get to school age, their parents no longer automatically accept the placement

the school district recommends."

Parental demands have led to a spate of successful lawsuits around the country in recent years. The best known of those cases involved Rachel Hollan, a moderately mentally retarded girl whose parents sued the Sacramento, Calif., school system to get their daughter a place in a regular classroom. Her parents initiated the lawsuit after observing that their daughter seemed to blossom in a summer day camp with nondisabled children but did poorly in a special-education class.

Although the school district is appealing the case, similar lawsuits are also succeeding this year in New Jersey and Michigan. In the New Jersey case, which involved a young boy with severe disabilities, the federal judge who decided the case endorsed full inclusion in ringing tones. "Inclusion is a right, not a special privilege for the select few," he wrote. That decision is also on appeal.

"I'm really surprised at how well full-inclusion cases are doing in the courts now," says Diane Lipton, the lawyer for Rachel and her parents. "I think there's no stopping it."

Parents who are pressing school systems for inclusion say their efforts are born of common sense. "If a child has a speech difficulty, how can putting him in a class with six other kids with speech difficulties help him?" asks Margaret Dignoti, the executive director of the ARC of Connecticut.

Ms. Dignoti's organization and parents and other advocacy groups have filed a class action aimed at forcing Connecticut schools to serve more children with mental retardation in regular classrooms.

Full inclusion also became a potential civil-rights issue with the 1990 passage of the Americans with Disabilities Act, which bans all forms of discrimination against the disabled. Although none of the cases has cited the law, advocates say the act has raised the national consciousness about the rights of disabled people.

"It makes it hard to defend keeping a kid apart from nondisabled kids when he's going to be integrated as an adult," Mr. Laski says.

Martha Snell, a University of Virginia education professor who is studying inclusive classrooms, says

ALAN KIM

Third grade student Toni Mills reads _Castles in the Sand_ with a little help from classmate Kate Childress.

education reform also has played a role in the movement's new prominence. "Everything that's said in school reform and restructuring is very compatible with this aspect of reform," she argues. "And schools that are implementing mission statements saying all kids can learn are finding out that a lot of kids who don't have disabilities can benefit from this."

In Shawsville, however, the impetus to bring stu-

Full inclusion became a potential civil-rights issue with the passage of the Americans with Disabilities Act, which bans discrimination against the disabled.

---

dents like Toni back home to their neighborhood schools came from within the district itself. Prompted by parents and the need to plan for the future of special education, the district formed a committee to study the issue.

The task force recommended a five-year plan to phase in fully integrated schools districtwide. Special-education administrators spent the first year providing workshops on the subject for all teachers and administrators and integrating preschool programs. Then they sat back and waited for volunteers.

Dale Margheim, the principal of Shawsville Elementary, was among the first to volunteer. As a former special-education teacher, Mr. Margheim says, "I taught kids in self-contained classrooms and I thought we were being successful, and I was happy and they were happy." He adds: "But that lasted about as long as it took them to get out the doorway. I was never happy with that."

Mr. Margheim visited some of the special schools attended by children such as Toni and observed the students who lived within his school's attendance area. "I came back and told the teachers, 'I have some youngsters I'd like to bring back here and, by the way, I'd like to do away with self-contained classrooms,'" he remembers.

Now, more than 30 of the school's 300 students are children who would otherwise have been in separate schools or classes. Some have significant impairments. Jason Dudley, for example, who is legally blind and can utter only a few words, is in a regular 1st-grade class with 16 other students.

And, in the 3rd-grade classroom next door to Toni's, Billy Moss is able to remain in a regular class only with

the help of a full-time aide. Labeled developmentally disabled, he has trouble concentrating, sitting still, and forming social relationships. The aide must continually keep him on task and give him 15-minute breaks every hour to walk around and release some of his excess energy.

The school obtained waivers from state regulations to allow special-education teachers to work with wider ranges of disabled pupils and with nondisabled pupils who were having trouble in class. It closed down its special-education classrooms, converting them to computer labs and storage space.

Special-education teachers and aides were dispersed among classrooms according to the needs of the disabled students in those rooms. The teachers either team-teach classes, rotate teaching assignments, or work individually with children or small groups of students.

"We used to sit in eligibility meetings and hope a kid would come out with some kind of label so you could get help for him," says Sandra Cox, a special-education teacher. "Now I can help him anyway."

The school also began working with a special education consultant, who coaches regular-education teachers, observes the children, and suggests strategies for helping disabled pupils succeed in their regular classrooms. She also meets weekly with the teachers of significantly impaired students to review the past week's lessons and to plan for the coming week.

A 'Circle of Friends' for Less Able Children

Shawsville's parents gave a mixed reception to the idea at first. Billy's mother, Rosa Bowles, was enthusiastic because she remembered how it felt to be singled out as "different" when she was a special-education student.

Other parents, however, only reluctantly went along, voicing concern their children would be teased by classmates. But those fears were never realized. The consultant visited each classroom to talk about the special needs of the disabled classmates and the importance of forming a "circle of friends" to help the less able children.

Now, parents and educators say, nondisabled children are enthusiastic about helping their disabled classmates. Rebecca Brown, whose severely disabled granddaughter, Kathryn, attended the school for two years, recalls: "There'd be children waiting to hang up her coat for her, and they'd hang around and unpack her lunch for her."

"I've learned that she's not much different than anybody else," says Anne Ryan, one of Toni's nondisabled classmates.

Parents of nondisabled students, on the other hand, worried at first whether the new arrangement would put too much of a burden on teachers. "I felt like our school was already overcrowded, and if they were going to be including all the special-education kids, that would make the classes that much larger," says Ellen Ryan, who was the president of the P.T.A. at the time.

Ms. Ryan's concerns were allayed, however, because the new arrangement reduced the ratio of educators to children in the classroom. In Toni's class, for example, a special-education teacher was added, as well as a full-time aide who spends much of her day working with Toni.

When the rest of the class takes a 15-word spelling test, Toni will practice printing five of those words. When the class writes in journals, Toni makes sentences by working with an aide and choosing words written on index cards. When the class listens to a novel and then must predict what happens next, Toni might be asked who the main character was.

'Where These Kids Belong'

"If it looks different from what everyone else is getting, she won't do it," says Kerri Tahane, the teacher's aide.

Educators at Shawsville have found, in fact, that the motivation disabled students get from working alongside their nondisabled peers has been a powerful

---

'We used to sit in eligibility meetings and hope and pray a kid would come out with some kind of label so you could get help for him,' says one teacher.

---

learning tool. "Before, we spent a lot of time developing motivation, and we don't have to do that anymore," says one teacher. "We spent a lot of time teaching kids to take the top off the toothpaste and brush their teeth, when all we had to do was shove a grooming bag in their hand, send them off to the bathroom with another student, and say, 'Come back in 10 minutes and you'd better look good.' " In the end, educators at the school say, the new arrangement has benefited all students—disabled and nondisabled.

Outside of Montgomery County, however, fully inclusive classrooms have not worked well for everyone. In another Virginia town, Katherine Letcher Lyle removed her mentally retarded teenage daughter from a local high school because she was floundering in regular classes. "Everybody said, 'Oh, she's so cute and we love her' and she never learned a damn thing all year," Ms. Lyle complains.

Her daughter stopped receiving homework assignments after the second week of school, and her efforts to get more attention for her child failed. "It was almost as if she had disappeared," Ms. Lyle says.

The key to making inclusive programs work is providing adequate support. "I think we would be violating the spirit of the law by placing children in inclusive classrooms without plans or support," says Mr. Davila of the Education Department. Mr. Davila and other special educators have expressed concerns that some districts might see full inclusion as a way to save money.

In practice, however, properly managed inclusive programs should cost the same or slightly more than traditional programs, according to experts. Shawsville's special-education programs, for example, have been funded at a constant level for two years. The district paid for additional training by redirecting all of its training resources and grants to the full-inclusion effort.

"If you think about trying to provide the same frequency, intensity, and duration of services dispersed among all classes equally, as opposed to special classes, centers, and schools, it's got to cost more," says James Kauffman, a professor of special education at the University of Virginia. "You might save some on transportation costs."

Mr. Kauffman, who is critical of the full-inclusion movement, differs with advocates who would mandate that every child be in a regular classroom. "I think the thing the extreme advocates tend to lose sight of is individual differences," he says.

Many people who are deaf, for example, contend they are more isolated in regular classrooms because they cannot communicate with peers or teachers who do not know sign language. Mr. Kauffman also says some emotionally disturbed students may exhibit behaviors that are too trying for classroom teachers.

There is wide agreement, however, that a growing number of schools will serve more disabled students in regular classrooms in the future. President Clinton, in a letter mailed to disability-rights leaders nationwide just before his election, promised a program of "full inclusion, not exclusion" for children and adults with disabilities.

Mr. Clinton pledged to insure that "children with disabilities receive a first-rate education, tailored to their needs but provided alongside classmates who do not have disabilities."

A statement issued in October 1992 by the National Association of State Boards of Education, moreover, strongly endorsed full inclusion. "All students legally, socially, and academically deserve to be schooled in neighborhood schools with their neighborhood peers," says Ms. Snell of the University of Virginia. "I think that's the standard we should aim for." □

From Education Week, *Nov. 18, 1992*

17.

The Mother Of All Networks

A small but growing number of teachers are using a mammoth computer system to bring the world into their classrooms.

By Peter West

When Iraqi SCUD missiles fell over Israel at the height of the Gulf War, students at Vine Middle School in Knoxville, Tenn., shared firsthand the horror of the attack with young people in the Middle East.

As part of a regularly scheduled Wednesday afternoon electronic "chat session," 6th and 8th graders at the school tapped out questions about the rapidly developing military situation on a computer keyboard. Their queries appeared as text on screens in Israel by way of the Internet, a vast international "network of computer networks" that links thousands of users in more than 40 countries worldwide. And they watched in fascination as the answers scrolled in from Israeli students.

This was not the first time the students at Vine had pulled the "real world" into their classrooms. Using a channel on the system called the Internet Relay Chat, they communicated with Russian youngsters following the attempted political coup in the former Soviet Union. And they have conversed on a variety of topics with scientists as far away as Amsterdam and as close as Kalamazoo. Some of those scientists subsequently visited the school to provide demonstrations for their electronic pen pals.

The students at the predominantly black Vine Middle School may not have much experience with the high-tech gadgetry commonly found in affluent suburban districts, but the school is on the leading edge in its educational use of the Internet.

"We're a Chapter 1 school, smack dab in the middle of the inner city," says teacher Holly Towne, who helped establish the school's Internet link with the nearby Oak Ridge National Laboratory. "But we're rubbing shoulders with the elite, with the highest intellects in the world."

Most public schools in the United States are not in a position to take advantage of the enormous potential of the Internet as a real-world learning resource. But in schools that are, educators are teaching with one foot in the classroom of the future.

The genesis of the Internet can be traced to the Arpanet, an experimental U.S. Defense Department network designed in the early 1970s to survive such large-scale disasters as a nuclear attack. The system was driven by a set of rules or standards known as "protocols," which allows computers to communicate with others on a network.

In the late 1980s, the National Science Foundation developed a prototype network, based on the lessons learned from the Arpanet experiment. The objective was to enable university researchers to gain access to the National Science Foundation's system of supercomputers over telephone lines from remote locations.

The NSF eventually supported the development of an electronic network to link colleges and universities nationwide to the supercomputer sites and to each other. Known as the NSFnet, this new, high-speed network made information much more accessible to potential users and became the backbone for the Internet, serving computer users in the same way that the interstate highway system serves motorists: by providing a consistent way to get from one place to another in an efficient amount of time.

As students who were exposed to the network during their college careers have entered the work force, the number of Internet users outside of academia has grown. Ed Krol, a computer specialist at the University of Illinois and author of *The Whole Internet User's Guide and Catalog* (O'Reilly & Associates, $24.95), says the number of Internet users has increased a thousandfold during the last seven years. Others estimate that as many as 1 million people worldwide now use the network on any given day to access the 5,000 smaller networks that are connected by the system.

Only a Handful of Schools Are Using Internet

Although the majority of colleges and universities are connected in some way to the Internet, only a scattering of precollegiate schools have joined them—in part because most teachers have never heard of the network. A survey conducted by New York's Bank Street College of Education, for example, found that as many as one-third of the teachers who considered themselves "computer-using educators" didn't know whether their school had access to the Internet. And most were unaware that they could access it through state or local computer networks they were already using.

But even teachers who do know about the Internet have difficulty using it, mainly because they don't understand how it works and lack the necessary computer equipment.

In his book, Krol uses the analogy of the telephone system to explain how the Internet operates. He likens the local and regional, independently operated computer networks that make up the Internet to the local and regional telephone systems within the United States and foreign countries. Just as all of the telephone companies have agreed on a "protocol" that allows them to transfer a long-distance call from one region to another, so the Internet, through the NSFnet, allows regional computer networks to communicate with one another around the globe. In the same way that anyone with a telephone can call anyone else in the world without knowing exactly how the telephone works, anyone who is properly equipped and trained can gain access to the many networks that make up the Internet.

But the analogy with the telephone system is incomplete. While the Internet is managed by an independent contractor for the NSF, and a separate, voluntary organization called the Internet Society helps promote its use, there is no central clearing-house—no Yellow Pages—to which potential users can turn for information about the network or how to use it. And while efforts are under way to make accessing and navigating the Internet easier than it now is, the system is far from "user friendly."

It has only been in recent years—with help from the NSF, other federal agencies, universities, and regional computer networks—that some schools have acquired the technology and know-how to tap into the vast storehouse of information on the Internet. Although the information is largely free for the taking, the cost of setting up a school with the telephone and computers needed to access the network directly is still more than many school officials are willing to pay.

Access Is Getting Cheaper and Easier

Schools don't necessarily need the expensive, ultra-sophisticated, high-speed access to the Internet enjoyed by universities. New approaches, based on "off-shelf" modems and software, allow districts and schools to establish connections through a local college or university Internet node and to distribute the information to classrooms over a local computer network. Although not as technically sophisticated, such

---

Students pulled the 'real world' into their classrooms and communicated with Russian youngsters following the attempted coup in the former Soviet Union.

---

systems can bring the cost of Internet access down into the thousands of dollars per school. Use among schools may become more common as access is made even easier through public libraries and such information services as CompuServe and Prodigy.

Students at Vine Middle School are able to use the Internet through an initiative called the Oak Ridge Educational Network, or OREN. One of a variety of educational outreach programs sponsored by the Oak Ridge National Laboratory, OREN aims to provide teachers with the necessary training to use the network effectively and with individual computer accounts that allow them to access an Internet node over a toll-free telephone line. This line lets the schools log on to the Internet and exchange electronic messages with any other computer on the worldwide network.

John Wooten, coordinator for education technology at the laboratory's office of science education and external relations, says the unusual electronic experiment under way at Vine Middle School is only one very high-profile OREN project, but one that he hopes will encourage other teachers to look afresh at the use of computers in the classroom.

Too many teachers, Wooten says, have access to computers but don't know how to use them for anything other than word processing. Under the auspices of the U.S. Department of Energy, he created OREN to encourage them to use the computers to tap into the tremendous potential of the Internet. And he has had some success. So far, Wooten's project has taught some 450 students and teachers in a number of area schools to use the electronic mail and research capacities of the Internet.

Although they had no computer experience a year ago when the project began, some of the more advanced student-users taking part in the project have used the

---

'We're a Chapter 1 school, in the middle of the inner city,' says one teacher. 'But we're rubbing shoulders with the elite, with the highest intellects in the world.'

Internet to retrieve data on wetlands compiled by federal agencies and to get position papers on the abortion issue drafted by the Clinton presidential campaign and posted on the Internet. "They're becoming very excited, very motivated about things they couldn't care less about before," Wooten says.

By providing the technical access to the Internet and by showing teachers how to navigate through the quirky and complicated maze of information on the network, Wooten hopes to open the wider world of scientific knowledge and research to students in rural Tennessee, where adult illiteracy is common.

A Way of Linking Students With the Elite

The ability to communicate with the academic elite of many nations has had an immeasurably positive impact on the students at Vine Middle School, teacher Holly Towne says. On the Internet, she explains, people can't tell "whether you're rich or poor or how well-dressed you are. I would do this wherever I was, but it's just doubly meaningful here."

Many advocates of the Internet currently disagree on how schools should use the network to best promote learning. Some believe schools should use it as a library—the largest, most complex library in the world. Others see the electronic-mail capacity of the network, which allows students to converse with international

experts and peers, as its greatest educational asset. It is a debate that divides Wooten and Towne.

Wooten sides with the "super library" advocates, believing this approach will have the greatest long-term payoff. Towne, on the other hand, thinks her students get more from their Wednesday afternoon chat sessions with scientific experts and faraway peers than they ever would using the network as a tool for research assignments. These sessions, she says, give her mostly poor students contact with people they wouldn't otherwise get.

"We're using it in the way that I think is going to revolutionize education," she says. "Whenever I give a kid a computer, I look their mamma and daddy in the face and I say, 'Look, we're opening up the world here.'"

But at a time when many researchers who have used the Internet since its inception are arguing that the vastly increased use of the system may stretch the NSFnet's technological capacity to the breaking point, advocates of K-12 use of the Internet question whether electronic mail—which can, in many cases, be sent just as easily over commercial computer bulletin-board systems—may not be a wasteful use of such an advanced system.

At the NSF, supporters of wide use of the Internet endorse both options and take them a step further, arguing that the most meaningful application of the network would be to create electronically linked "learning communities" across the nation and around the world that work cooperatively to achieve a curricular goal. The NSF is already supporting at least one such endeavor, the Global Laboratory Project, through which students worldwide share ecological data on the network.

Currently, however, most of the teachers using the Internet do so in isolation, without much guidance or organized cooperation. Even so, they are putting the networking capabilities to work in some remarkable ways.

Students at Rocky Mountain High School in Fort Collins, Colo., for example, have access to the Internet through an agreement with Colorado State University and use it primarily to exchange electronic-mail messages with students across the United States and abroad. "We feel that doing E-mail is a communications skill that everybody needs to learn," says David Swartz, a science teacher and technology specialist at the school. The Internet has also become an important feature of Rocky Mountain's science curriculum by providing access to satellite images and other federal databases.

Students studying weather and climate in an environmental science class, for instance, can download images from National Oceanic and Atmospheric Administration and National Weather Service satellites to study weather patterns and track the progress of storms and hurricanes. "You can bring back the images that literally may be as little as 20 minutes old, so you can watch the storms as they develop," Swartz says. "That's really empowering for the students."

In rare cases, students using the system develop a professional relationship with researchers in the field. At Thomas Jefferson High School for Science and Technology, a school for gifted students in Fairfax County, Va., 12th grader Michael Montemerlo decided that he needed the advice of a working scientist for a research project. Logging on to the Internet with equipment that Jefferson's students won in a national competition, he began an electronic "conversation" over the network with Peter Cheeseman, a scientist at NASA's Ames Research Center in California, who is a specialist in a complex method of classifying data.

The Sky's the Limit

Some teachers are using the Internet for more unusual communication projects. Last spring, for example, Karl Kurz, a technology educator at Machias (Maine) High School, used it to help establish a VHF radio link with the Russian cosmonaut who was trapped aboard the Soviet space station Mir following the collapse of the Soviet government. Through a contact at the University of Maine at Machias, Kurz managed to download a satellite-tracking software program that allowed him to predict the brief window of opportunity when the

---

The use of the Internet among schools may become more common as access is made even easier through public libraries and information services.

---

station's orbit would place it within hailing distance of his radio equipment.

The subsequent exchanges between Kurz's students and the orbiting castaway opened new educational vistas for them and put the students into headlines around the world. "We wouldn't have been able to do that without the information and the services available on the Internet," Kurz says.

To help get more teachers on the Internet bandwagon, a handful of states—Colorado, Texas, and Virginia, among them—is beginning to make an effort to link schools to the network.

In 1991, the Texas Education Agency and the University of Texas system jointly launched the Texas Educational Network, or TENET, a statewide system

that provides teachers with access to the Internet for a $5 annual fee. So far, 16,000 of the state's 250,000 teachers and administrators have become regular users, many taking advantage of the Internet for research and electronic mail.

To ease the confusion that is common among novices when searching for information on the network, the agency developed a simplified menu system to guide users to the available offerings. The menu includes a list of areas that might have specific classroom applications, including such resources as NASA's Spacelink, which provides curriculum guides and information about space missions.

"There's really a great deal of information," says Connie Stout, the TEA's director of the TENET. "And what teachers are finding is that the data that they gather and bring in cause student interest and learning to increase." Stout also emphasizes the importance of her network in enhancing teacher professionalism. She encourages teachers to use the Internet to combat the isolation of the classroom by exchanging electronic mail messages with colleagues around the state and across the country.

A Tool for Science and Math Teaching

Certainly one of the primary uses of the Internet by teachers has been to improve mathematics and science education, a goal shared by the National Science Foundation. "One of the major obstacles to the development of really modern science curricula is the fact that the 'installed base' of equipment is, at best, a generation behind the 'state of the art,'" says Beverly Hunter, the NSF's program director for the application of advanced technologies. "With the networks," she continues, "you have access to any machine on the planet—at least theoretically."

So the NSF is supporting a nationwide series of "test bed" sites that are developing ways to incorporate the Internet into the curriculum and is making grants to districts that are developing innovative uses of the network. And some districts already have taken steps on their own to realize the vision articulated by Hunter.

The Poudre School District R-1 in Fort Collins, which is home to Rocky Mountain High, is one of only a small number of school systems nationwide that have widespread access to the Internet in all of its media centers. Two years ago, when representatives of IBM and Colorado State University first suggested establishing an Internet link in the district, "they particularly wanted to target the math and science areas," says Larry Buchanan, Poudre's educational technology specialist.

That link has already allowed students to tap into the supercomputers at the National Climate Research Center as part of a science class on climate change. "They're running their program just the way a university researcher would," Buchanan says. He notes that the technology was expected to help achieve four district goals: improving teacher training and career exploration, teaching students the value of graphic representation of data, fostering a research and information exchange, and helping students become critical thinkers. But as teachers and students have used the Internet with greater frequency, their ability to conduct research on topics across the curriculum, Buchanan says, "has probably become our most important use, although we didn't envision it as such."

Among other things, students have called up campaign position papers and speeches issued during the 1992 election, and they have held electronic conversations with an Internet user in war-torn Yugoslavia.

Buchanan asserts that the very nature of the network fosters critical thinking. "There is so much information available by way of the network that the students have to do the task of analyzing what is useful information and what is junk," he says. "Kids have to do the job of deciding 'Is this opinion?' 'Why does this person have this opinion?' 'How valid is this opinion?'"

Wooten of the Oak Ridge laboratory says he expects similar changes will take place in schools that participate in the OREN project. "We talk a lot about using computers in the classroom, but, in large part, we do not use them to change the way teaching is done," he says. "Most of the time, the computer becomes a replacement for the textbook or for the blackboard."

He hopes that, as teachers and students become more comfortable with the applications of the Internet, they will begin to probe the full potential of the computers in their classrooms.

Students Take Control of Their Own Learning

Hunter of the NSF believes that the real power of the Internet will come into play only when students are able to take control of their own learning and harness the great capabilities the network offers. "Kids can be doing real science; they can be doing original research," Hunter insists. "But, in order to do that, they have to have access to the networks. They couldn't even think about it without access to the networks."

But teachers and students generally are unequipped to use the resources of the Internet efficiently without considerable training and support. Without that support, most teachers are likely to remain locked out.

Even technically skilled and highly motivated educators must confront a discouraging problem: It is very hard for uninitiated Internet users to find their way around this great library. They have much of the world's knowledge at their fingertips but can't quite get at it.

"One of the things that has kept the K-12 out of this area was the difficulty navigating around the In-

ternet," says Poudre School District's Buchanan. He helped solve that problem in his schools by developing a locally oriented menu system. Students and staff with very little knowledge of the Internet can find the information they want by using the menus or by taking advantage of new, simpler Internet menus developed by network users at the University of Minnesota.

Others are trying to foster K-12 use of the network by creating curriculum guides based on Internet resources. The Boulder Valley School District, in cooperation with the University of Colorado at Boulder, local businesses, and regional networks, has been given an NSF grant to develop curricula based on information available on the Internet.

"One of the problems with bringing teachers on line is that there isn't any curriculum out there" for them to use once they connect with the system, says Libby Black, director of the Boulder Valley Internet Project, who is overseeing the development of the unit. By developing curriculum packages specific to the resources available on the Internet, she adds, "teachers don't have to spend hours and hours poking around. The technology is not good enough yet for people who are novices to put up with."

Widespread Use Is Still Far Off

Although more and more teachers are gaining access to the Internet through state networks, local demonstration projects, and individual initiatives, universal access for schools is still a distant goal. And that, according to Hunter of the NSF, may be all right until the technology becomes easier for educators to use. While it is important for precollegiate education that teachers should one day be able to tap into the Internet's resources, she says, not every teacher should seek to become a proficient user immediately.

"Our position is that a lot more research and development needs to be done before one would advocate that all teachers become involved in this," she says. "I think what we want is for the leading-edge teachers to be inventors, testing ideas."

As one of those "leading-edge teachers," Towne believes that, regardless of all the other sophisticated services the Internet offers, the simple link the network provides to the outside world justifies the effort she has made to learn how to use it. For her students, who live in a poor neighborhood that offers little opportunity for advancement, the Internet chat sessions provide a much-needed electronic beam of hope.

"This is a heck of a good way," Towne says, "to get the kids to understand that there is more to life than what they see in the street." □

From Teacher Magazine, *January 1993*

18

Computers Meet Classroom

Despite the past decade of technological change, computers have yet to make their mark on the school reform movement.

Commentary By Larry Cuban

Today, computers and telecommunications are a fact of life almost as basic as electricity. They have altered the daily work of businesses and industry. Yet why is it that with so much talk of school reform and information technologies over the last decade, computers are used far less on a daily basis in schools than in other organizations?

The question often generates swift objections. What about the $20 million Quince Orchard High School in Montgomery County, Md., where there are 288 computers for 1,100 students? What about the thousands of elementary and secondary school teachers who have students work together on computers to write, tally figures, draw, and think? And aren't there many experiments under way, such as Apple's Classroom of Tomorrow, and microcomputer laboratories? The answer to all of these questions is that such instances do exist but they are scattered and atypical in the roughly 80,000 public schools across the nation where over two million teachers teach over 40 million students.

As an innovation, school use of computers in the 1980's has spread swiftly, widely, and, on occasion, deeply. But the picture is clouded. A few key statistics suggest the broad outlines of the picture:

• In 1981, 18 percent of schools had computers; in 1991, 98 percent had them.

• In 1981, 16 percent of schools used computers for instructional purposes. By 1991, 98 percent did so.

• In 1981, there were, on average, 125 students per computer; in 1991, there were 18.

• In 1985, students used computers in school labs just over three hours a day; in 1989, that figure had risen to four hours a day.

These few numbers give a sense of expanding school use of computers. A closer inspection of those figures and others reveal, however, that for those individual students who use computers (and not all do), the time they spend doing it is, on average, a little more than one hour a week (or 4 percent of all instructional time). What students do with computers varies greatly. For 11th-grade computer users, as the U.S. Office of Technology Assessment found, computers seldom show up in academic subjects, and, where they are used, the purpose is often to teach about computers. The O.T.A. also found that students from high-income families have far more access to school computers than peers from low-income families. Black students use computers in schools less than white, especially in elementary schools. Pupils whose native language is not English have even less access to computers. Finally, low-achieving students are less likely to use machines to enhance reasoning and problem-solving and more likely to use them for drill and practice. The overall picture after the introduction of the personal computer a decade ago can be summed up in a one-line caption: Computers meet classroom; classroom wins.

For technology advocates with a sense of history, this good-news/bad-news picture of computer use in schools should be an old story. The introduction of film and radio into schools in the 1920's and 1930's and instructional television in the 1950's and 1960's saw a similar pattern of blue-sky promises of revolutionizing instruction and learning.

The promise of new machines has been anchored in the dream of increasing teacher and student productivity. More could be taught in less time with these machines, and students could learn more and even better than from textbooks or the teacher alone. The promise was invariably followed by limited entry of machines into classrooms, growing practitioner disillusionment with the inaccessibility of the machines, academic studies documenting small learning effects from the new technology, to a final round of teacher-bashing. With the next technological invention, this cycle of ecstasy, disappointment, and blame would begin anew.

Except for the 1980's and 1990's. With the massive technological changes in the workplace and daily life, school reformers throughout the last decade have turned increasingly to computers in schools as a solution for motivating students, reaching children with different ways of learning, and reducing reliance on teaching the whole class at the same time. The results for the 1980's, as I have indicated, are mixed.

Such good-news/bad-news statistics raise tough questions. Is the growing number of newly built schools devoted to using computers and telecommunications a sign that these are the schools of the future? Or is the apparently marginal use of computers in classrooms a sign that this technology is going to be used just like earlier ones—that is, peripherally, seldom disturbing customary ways of teaching? Or does this marginal use pattern have within it a sign of steadily growing acceptance of new technologies and a promise that, within time, schools will become more machine-friendly? I do not know the answers to these questions. What I can do is sketch out three scenarios of what might be occurring 10 years from now and pick the ones I believe are likely by 2000. Each story line is plausible and has substantial evidence to support it as a possibility. Each can be assessed for the likelihood of its materializing. Here are the three scenarios:

• The technophile's dream: electronic schools of the future now. These are schools with sufficient numbers of machines, software, assorted accessories, and wiring to accommodate varied groupings of students in classrooms, seminar rooms, and individual work spaces. The dream is to make teaching and learning far more productive than it is. Machines and software are central to this dream. They are seen as liberating tools for both teachers and students to grow, communicate, and learn from one another. Teachers are helpers, guides, and coaches to students being tutored and interacting primarily with machines.

The strategy for achieving the vision is to create total settings that have a critical mass of machines, software, and like-minded people who are serious users of the technologies. The tilt is toward making big changes swiftly rather than creating pilot programs in schools or incrementally by buying a few machines at a time. Chris Whittle's Edison Project is a recent popular instance of a technophile's scenario.

• The cautious optimist's scenario: slow growth of hybrid schools and classrooms. In this scenario, putting computers into classrooms will yield a steady but very slow movement toward fundamental changes in teaching and schooling. Advocates of this scenario see it occurring inexorably, much like a turtle crawling toward its pond. It is slow because schools, as organizations, take time to learn how to use computers to guide student learning. It is inexorable because believers in this scenario are convinced that the future school will mirror a workplace dominated by computers and telecommunications.

The evidence for this scenario is a small but growing body of research. For example, introducing a half-dozen computers into a classroom or creating microcomputer labs, over time, alters how teachers teach (that is, they move from whole-class instruction to small groups and individualized options) and how students learn (they come to rely upon one another and themselves to understand ideas and practice skills). Thus, the classroom organization might shift, albeit slowly, from one that is wholly teacher-directed to one in which students working with peers at machines begin to take responsibility for their learning.

In schools where computer-using teachers and hardware have reached a critical threshold, different organizational decisions get made. Teachers from different departments or grades move toward changing the regular time schedule. Schoolwide decisions on using technologies become a routine matter as do decisions on nontechnological matters. Hybrids of the old and the new, of teacher-centered and student-centered instruction, proliferate.

• The preservationist's scenario: maintaining while improving schools. In this scenario, policymakers and administrators put computers and telecommunication technologies into schools, but they end up largely reinforcing existing ways of teaching, learning, grouping for instruction, and curriculum. While some teachers and schools use these technologies imaginatively and end up being profiled by the media, most uses are fitted to what already occurs. New technologies become ways of tinkering toward improvement. The vision embedded in the preservationist's story is one of schools maintaining what they have historically done; providing custodial care, sorting out those who achieve academically from those who do not, and giving taxpayers as efficient a schooling as can be bought with the funds available.

There is much evidence for this scenario. Some examples: mandating a new graduation requirement on computer literacy, adding courses to the curriculum on computer science, creating a computer lab for all the school's machines, scheduling teachers once a week to bring their classes to the room where an aide helps students use software connected to their daily lessons, placing one computer in each classroom, and buying software that is part of a textbook adoption.

In this scenario, computers are seen as occasional helpers for the main business of teaching students. Adapting these tools to help teachers and students do what they are supposed to do in schools ends up with new technologies reinforcing what schools have done all century.

Which of these scenarios is most likely to occur?

The least likely is the electronic school of the future. While such schools will be built, they will remain exceptions and, in time, will probably disappear as the next generation of technology, invariably cheaper and improved, comes of age. Thus, although such schools exist now, few will spread to most other districts. Recent experiences of schools adopting instructional television, language laboratories, and programmed learning in the 1960's and 1970's have taught policymakers to be cautious. In districts that built new schools, purchased and installed the hardware and software for those technologies, administrators found in less than a decade that the machinery was either unused by teachers, became obsolete, or could not be repaired after breakdowns. The constant improvement of advanced technologies makes it risky for districts to make large capital investments in new hardware beyond a model program or demonstration school.

The cautious optimist's and preservationist's scenar-ios are basically the same story of computer use in schools interpreted differently. Each stresses different facts and derives different meanings from those facts. Preservationists argue that schools will remain largely as they are because of millennia-old cultural beliefs held by most adults about teaching, learning, and knowledge that form the core of modern American schooling: Teaching is telling, learning is listening, and knowledge is what is in books. Most taxpayers expect their schools to reflect those centuries-old beliefs. Such strongly held beliefs seldom disappear when Apples or I.B.M.'s show up in school.

Preservationists also point out that the popular age-graded school persists through reform after reform. Age-graded schools, the dominant form of school organization for over a century and a half, have self-contained classrooms that separate teachers from one another, a curriculum distributed grade by grade to students, and a time schedule that brings students and teachers together for brief moments to work. These structures profoundly influence how teachers teach,

---

For technology advocates with a sense of history, this good-news/bad-news picture of computer use in classrooms should be an old story.

---

how students learn, and the relationships between the adults and children in each classroom. They are especially difficult to change. For these reasons, preservationists argue, schools tailor technological innovations to fit the contours of prevailing cultural beliefs and the age-graded school.

Cautious optimists, however, take the same facts and give them a sunny-day spin. The optimist's version of the story displays much patience in making schools technologically modern. Conceding the many instances of technologies being used to reinforce existing practices, optimists shift their attention to the slow growth of technological hybrids, those creative mixes of the old and the new in schools and classrooms. These hybrids of teacher-centered and student-centered instruction, the optimists say, are the leading edge of a movement that will bring schools more in sync with the larger society. Thus, the current reasons for the fumbling incorporation of high-tech machines into schools—not enough money to buy machines, teacher resistance, inadequate preparation of teachers, and little administrative support—will gradually evaporate as hybrids slowly spread and take hold. It is a scenario anchored in a long-term view of decades rather than months or years. While I find the preservationist's story convincing, I lean more toward the optimist's version.

This long-term view is more compelling to me than the pessimist's view of grinding inertia and marginally adapting new technologies because of my studies of how teachers have taught over the last century. I found evidence of much continuity in teaching practices, but I

The introduction of the computer into schools can be summed up in one line: Computer meets classroom; classroom wins.

---

also found deep changes in particular ways that teachers worked in classrooms, especially in elementary schools, that resembled the hybrids that optimists identified. I found, for example, that in the 1890's, the one form of grouping for instruction was teaching the entire class at once; a century later, the practice of grouping, particularly in the elementary school, uses a mix of whole-group, small-group, and individual options. Teachers' repertoire of classroom practices has broadened over the last century. In the 1890's, lecturing, using the textbook, and tests were the primary tools of the teacher. A century later, these tools remain, of course, but in elementary schools, that array of practices has expanded with the addition of new materials and technologies. While films, videocassettes, and television may not be mainstays of most

classroom instruction, they are sparingly used, again testifying to the slow growth of hybrids in instruction. Such instances of deep changes in practice provide additional evidence for the long-term optimist's view of technological hybrids slowly changing schooling.

What happened to my initial question? I asked why with all the ballyhoo over computers in the last decade are these machines so little used in classrooms compared with large businesses and industry. My answer is that the sparing classroom use of computers is due less to inadequate funds, unprepared teachers, and indifferent administrators and more to dominant cultural beliefs about what teaching, learning, and proper knowledge are and to the age-graded school with its self-contained classrooms, time schedules, and fragmented curriculum. New technologies that fit these beliefs and organization get used often; those that don't fit get used less.

For the 1990's, I have bet on the optimist's scenario of continued slow growth of computers in schools and the spread of hybrids of teacher-centered and student-centered instruction. Computer usage within this scenario will incrementally increase but still fall well below the dreams of technophiles. Neither scenario promises major changes in schooling in this decade.

Two wild cards, however, hedge my bet. One is the current national movement for goals, standards, and testing. If the movement rolls on, it may largely confine computers to reinforcing existing patterns of teaching and learning. The other is the growing privatization of public schooling. If this continues, masses of poor children left behind in large cities will seldom experience creative uses of technology. Both of these wild cards give me pause in considering which of the scenarios will get the most play in the closing years of this century. Thus, the story of technologies in schools continues to unfold.

Larry Cuban is a professor of education at Stanford University.

From Education Week, *Nov. 11, 1992*

What We Will Teach

"The most fundamental requirement for a democracy is an educated citizenry capable of informed judgment on public issues. Participation in self-governance will require a higher standard of scientific literacy, a deeper understanding of history, and a greater capacity to think critically."

—Report of the California Commission

on Teaching as a Profession, 1985

19.

Focusing On Outcomes

A system of national standards and assessments would give teachers a much greater say in choosing what to teach.

The idea of a system of national standards and assessments is one of the most powerful and provocative to emerge from the 10-year-old school reform movement. It has become the "wedge issue" in the drive to overhaul America's schools. And its advocates see it as the crucial first step to systemic reform.

Pushed by the Bush and Clinton administrations and the National Governors' Association and widely endorsed by educational, political, and business leaders, the idea has moved to the top of the reform agenda. It has also sparked a vigorous debate and divided people who tend to see eye to eye on other educational issues.

The national standards and assessments movement begins with the assumption that all students can learn at significantly higher levels. It proposes to change the focus of the present educational system from "input" to "outcomes." At present, most states seek to accomplish their educational goals by determining what goes into the system—everything from the amount of money spent to the content of each course taught. An outcome-based system would focus on results—determining the levels of performance expected and holding schools accountable for achieving them.

The key components of a performance/outcome system are these:
• Content standards that define what students should know and be able to do—what is to be taught and what is to be learned. At their best, the standards would be specific enough to inform the curriculum, but general enough to provide a wide latitude to teachers in implementing them.
• Assessments that will measure students' progress toward the desired outcomes. Norm-referenced standardized tests are totally incompatible with a performance-based system. At the heart of such a system is the idea of setting tasks for students that will engage them, inform them, and encourage them to think and reason. The assessments must be rich enough to measure whether students are mastering the standards.
• Instructional strategies and technologies necessary for schools and teachers to enable their students to perform at high levels. The role of the teacher changes from imparting information to passive students to mentoring students who are responsible for their own education. In a standards-driven system, the gap between curriculum and assessment virtually disappears as testing becomes integrated into the teaching process. "Teaching to the test" is desirable in this kind of system because students know up front what they are expected to know, and they collaborate with their teachers and fellow students to accomplish that.
• Consequences that will undergird the standards and motivate schools and students to achieve them. Critics of the present system argue that expectations are low, and academic achievement counts for little. Students have little motivation to excel. In a performance-based system, admission to college, for example, or getting a job would be tied to mastery of standards.
• Delivery standards that will assure every student an opportunity to learn and perform at high standards. In the present system, there are gross inequities, and the quality of education is often determined by where a student lives. Advocates of a performance-based system stress that high stakes must not be attached to mastery of standards until all students are guaranteed the quality of education necessary to achieve them.
• Professional development of teachers that enables them to implement content standards and curricular frameworks and carry out newly developed performance-based assessments. A new system would radically change what goes on in classrooms and the roles and relationships of students and teacher. Most teachers

are not prepared to function effectively in such a system and will need training and assistance.

Proponents of voluntary national standards and assessments argue that their adoption will transform schools and the teaching profession. Teachers will be deeply involved in decisions that affect teaching and learning, the allocation of resources, and the uses of time and space. Students will be challenged to learn and will assume much more responsibility for their own education. The present system operates as though all children learn at the same rate and in the same way. The curriculum is divided into time slots and students move from one to the other, whether or not they have learned the material. Time is the constant and learning is the variable. In a performance-based system, learning becomes the constant and time becomes the

---

Freed from lesson plans, work sheets, and standardized tests, teachers will have both the fulfillment and the responsibility of true professionalism.

---

variable. The school schedule will be flexible so that students could take different amounts of time to master the standards.

The movement toward standards and assessments has progressed with astonishing speed. By 1994, it is almost certain that the U.S. Congress will have passed the first school reform bill in history, creating mechanisms to develop voluntary national standards and assessments and encouraging states to adopt them. A number of states, national organizations, and professional associations are already well along in the development of standards and assessments. The National Council of Teachers of Mathematics, for example, has defined content standards that states are incorporating into their standards and curriculum frameworks. The New Standards Project—a consortium of 17 states and half a dozen school districts that accounts for nearly half of the nation's students—is well along in the development of "world class" national standards in several subject areas.

Despite such widespread support for the idea, it has its critics. The issues of contention are these:

• Top-down vs. bottom-up. A significant number of prominent reformers argue that standard-setting should be left to local communities. They fear that mandates from on high will stifle creativity and lead to the kind of uniformity, rigidity, and bureaucratic constraints that hamper the present system.

• Breadth vs. depth. With various groups at work developing content standards, it is inevitable that each discipline will claim a substantial part of the curriculum. As one wag puts it: Everything will be fine as long as social studies, language arts, science, mathematics, geography, and the arts each get 30 percent of the curriculum. Something will obviously have to give, and this could lead to fierce turf battles. Multicultural tensions will also surface in the debate. Indeed, the "less is more" attitude that standards developers bring to the task is likely to intensify the multicultural issue in the arguments over what gets put into the curriculum and what gets left out.

• Quality vs. equality. Many fear that states and districts will implement content standards, performance standards, and assessments, but, because of costs, renege on delivery standards. That would put the neediest children at an even greater disadvantage.

• Administrator vs. teacher. Putting a performance-based system in place will shift power—mostly downward to the school site. Teachers and students, in particular, would be empowered. Administrators would find themselves sharing power, building consensus, facilitating.

Finally, some parents are also likely to be suspicious of an outcome-based system. Those whose children already have an advantage may be wary of leveling the playing field. Others, particularly fundamentalist Christians, are protesting the shift away from a basic-skills curriculum and arguing that efforts to foster higher-order thinking are an attack on their values.

The question of what to teach is one that will be paramount in the 1990s. It is a question made more difficult by the extraordinary accumulation of new knowledge, particularly in the sciences; the increasing diversity of the society; and the longstanding practice of calling on schools to teach mandated curriculum units that address an array of social needs—units on AIDS, drug prevention, and driver education, to name just a few.

If the performance-based system succeeds as it is now conceived, teachers will have far more freedom in designing their own classroom curricula. But they will also find that teaching is a much more demanding profession when detailed scope and sequence arrangements are gone. Freed from lesson plans, work sheets, and a plethora of standardized tests, teachers will have both the fulfillment and the enormous responsibility of true professionalism. □

20.

Voices Of Change

Educators are hard at work developing standards for what students should know and be able to do.

Marc Tucker is a traveler. Photographs from his journeys line the wall behind his desk, reminding him of trips he has taken to places as diverse as Singapore and Sweden. But he brings back more than photos; he also returns with new ideas about education. Tucker, president of the National Center on Education and the Economy, has seen how other countries run their schools, and his observations have inspired an ambitious model for education reform.

Several years ago, Tucker traveled to Western Europe and Asia, two parts of the world where students routinely outperform their American counterparts in mathematics and science. He wanted to pinpoint the causes of America's poor showing but found the systems surprisingly similar. "The curriculum other countries use in their schools, the teaching methods, did not seem that different from the ones that we use," he says.

But Tucker did note one important difference: Every country he visited had a set of official expectations for students—either a required national examination or a national curriculum, or both.

There's an unmistakable link, Tucker believes, between the poor performance of American students and the lack of national standards. "For most American kids in secondary school—save those who plan to go to a selective college—there is no incentive to take a tough course or to study hard in school," he says. "For these kids, in fact there is a disincentive. Because what you need to get a diploma—which is the ticket both to college and to jobs in this country—is simply to have a 7th grade literacy level, show up at least most of the time, and not cause much trouble. A diploma has next to nothing to do with what one knows or is able to do."

His solution: The United States should establish a national assessment system, one that builds on the best aspects of foreign schools but addresses the great diversity and large numbers of disadvantaged students in this country. "An examination system," Tucker maintains, "properly designed and embedded in the right policy system, can be an extremely powerful motivator to kids. It can elicit effort in school in a way that almost nothing else can match."

Tucker's efforts are not aimed, however, at creating another standardized test designed to measure native ability or aptitude. What Tucker and other reform leaders are advocating is a voluntary, elaborate assessment system tightly linked to curricula that are based on what we want high school students to know and be able to do.

Opponents of national standards and assessments argue that such a system is the European way of tracking students and that it does not belong in the United States, which provides educational opportunities to everyone. Tucker disagrees. "The fact is," he says, "the United States has the most vicious tracking system in the world. In some countries, it is illegal to give standardized tests to kids under 14 years old. In this country, however, based on what we take to be kids' native ability, we make judgments about them in the first grade or earlier."

In this country, Tucker continues, "we say, 'Jack, you are clearly made of good stuff and have it in you to go to the top. We will, therefore, give you challenging material, and we will grade you because that's the kind of kid you are.' On the other hand, we say to Jill, 'You clearly are never going to make it anywhere. You don't have the genes. We will give you very different and much less challenging material. And we'll give you A's and B's for showing up and being a good kid because that's all you're capable of.'"

Maintaining that on the contrary, all children are

capable of learning, Tucker and his colleagues propose that the United States create an examination system that would award a "certificate of initial mastery" to students who achieve a world-class standard of learning by age 16.

Tucker likens the idea to the system used to prepare other types of professionals for their careers: "If you're going to be a lawyer or an architect or a doctor, the question is: Do you have what it takes to do the job? You pass the bar exam, or you don't. You pass the architectural registration boards, or you don't. You get your pilot's license, or you don't. We don't ask how long it took you to do it.

"The American education system, on the other hand," Tucker continues, "is a system that uses a time-based standard—not a mastery standard. When you get your diploma, we know that you've been in school for 12 years. Beyond that, we know almost nothing about what you know and can do."

'Babble of Voices'

At the 1989 summit between President Bush and the nation's governors, the National Education Goals were set, and the United States vowed that by the year 2000, America's students would demonstrate competency in challenging subject matter and be first in the world of science and mathematics. Before this summit, many doubted that the idea of national standards and assessments would ever take root in this country. But since then, the number of groups promoting the national standards concept has soared.

Various organizations are striving to develop national standards and assessments for students, teachers, and principals. Curriculum associations are working to develop national standards in all academic subjects. Efforts are also under way nationally, as well as in state and local school districts, to develop performance-based assessments, often with the help of commercial test publishers. President Clinton has endorsed the standards movement and the U.S. Department of Education has made grants to major professional and scholarly organizations to develop voluntary national standards in different subjects.

The resulting babble of voices, which one observer describes as "characteristically American," is hard to keep straight—even for those most deeply involved in the effort. "We're a country that is trying to create a national system of education without creating a national ministry of education," Tucker says. "And what that means is that we have somehow got to come to a consensus without any one institution in our society driving it."

So far, however, the national movement has been led by the New Standards Project—a coalition of 17 states and half a dozen school districts enrolling nearly half the public school students in the United States. The John D. and Catherine T. MacArthur Foundation and the Pew Charitable Trusts made initial grants of $2.5 million to the New Standards Project.

Given the commitment and influence of the New Standards Project (which Tucker co-directs), many are viewing it as the research-and-development arm for the entire movement. Those involved in the project start from the premise that all students can learn. From there, they aim to develop a set of "content standards" for each discipline. The content standards would become the linchpin for both the students' assessment and the teachers who construct the curriculum.

In Tucker's vision, standards would be set at the national and state levels, but the means for achieving them would vary from district to district and from school to school. Assessments would also vary. They could be as non-quantitative as a portfolio of homework papers and projects accumulated over a six-month period, to essay questions measuring higher-order thinking skills. There wouldn't be one exam or one test for everyone, but many different ones. Yet a pass in one state would mean the same as a pass in another state.

In this way, a national examination system for students is also a proposal to empower teachers. Teachers would be centrally involved in setting the goals in each academic specialty; teachers (and principals) in each school would determine the most effective

> An examination system, Tucker maintains, properly designed and embedded in the right policy system, can be an extremely powerful motivator to kids.

ways to get their students to meet the national standard; teachers, not machines, would score students' performance on the assessments.

Efforts are currently under way to develop content standards in the five core subjects mentioned in the National Education Goals—math, science, history, geography, and English—as well as some of the other disciplines such as the arts and civic education. Though a confusing array of players is charting the course to reform, the "goals 2000: the educate America act," which was pending approval by Congress at press time, would establish a council to certify that academic-content standards and assessments, formulated by diverse groups, are of the highest quality across the board. Though critics of the bill feared that a national set of standards for schools could lead to a "cookie cutter" approach that might limit states' flexibility and impose costly mandates, the bill was intended to provide a broad framework for meeting the national goals, and combine the strength of bottom-up reform with coordinated reform from the top. And supporters hope that it will foster cooperation among groups working toward a common goal.

Major organizations in each of the disciplines have secured grants from the Education Department and are generally involving other professional organizations and diverse groups of business people, policymakers, and educators in developing content and performance standards. The New Standards Project is also working with these groups and expanding on their efforts by working on teacher-training programs and model assessments.

The Disciplines

So far, each discipline (except math) seems to have slightly different hurdles to clear before drafting a final model for what students should know and be able to do in that subject, but all of them are looking to have a system of standards and assessments in place within the next one to two years.

Mathematics: Concerned that mathematics teaching was not keeping pace with real-world needs, The National Council of Teachers of Mathematics surged ahead of other-subject organizations and came up with a final draft of standards, "Curriculum and Evaluation Standards for School Mathematics," as early as 1989. That document has already influenced the development of curriculum frameworks in many states, and it is guiding the development of new assessments.

Reflecting a growing consensus among math educators, the 258-page document recommends that schools shift from an emphasis on paper-and-pencil drill to use of technologies—including calculators and computers in all grades—to focus on problem solving, communications, and reasoning.

It also proposes that math courses employ actual problems, rather than those contrived for a textbook, to emphasize the subject's real-world applications and its connections to other disciplines.

Moreover, the document says, math programs should create opportunity for all students, not just those who intend to study math or science in college.

Science: A draft document released by the National Committee on Science Education Standards and Assessment rejects rote memorization and spells out four learning goals that will guide the development of national standards to foster "scientific literacy." It asserts that by the end of their precollegiate years, students should understand:

• A limited number of the basic concepts of science and the fundamental laws, principles, and theories that organize the body of scientific knowledge;

• The modes of reasoning of scientific inquiry and be able to use them;

• The nature of the scientific endeavor;

• And the history of scientific development, the relationship of science to technology, and the historical, cultural, and social contexts in which this relationship is embedded.

An effective science curriculum, it says, should also provide students with opportunities to practice their skills "outside formal education settings."

The document also includes prototypes for the specific content that students should know, and suggests activities to teach the material and ways for students to demonstrate their mastery of it.

For example, students in grades 5-8 could work in groups with minimal supervision to weigh a melting ice cube as a means of learning about the conservation of mass.

To learn about decisionmaking, high school students could work in groups, using scientific reasoning to analyze a proposal to build an industrial park in an undeveloped flood plain. Students could be expected to consult with local experts, take hydraulic and other measurements themselves, consult historical records, and weigh the economic and social impact of the development. Each group would present a seminar to the class on its findings.

The standards are designed to provide broad guidance for state and local curriculum developers and not a detailed blueprint for national control over local education policies. It further encourages teachers and

> 'If you're going to be a lawyer,' Tucker says, 'the question is: Do you have what it takes to do the job? Either you pass the bar exam, or you don't.'

school systems to "continue to construct thought-provoking, engaging lessons that build on local resources and environments, reflect their particular interests and stimulate their students."

History: At an early meeting of the National Forum for History Standards, a Vietnamese immigrant described how her son had a "terrible time" with history classes in school. The reason, she suggested, was that her son saw few Asians like himself in the history books. And the scant information he found about his culture was often mistaken or distorted.

Her remarks underscore one of the most central—

and contentious—issues facing educators and historians as they seek for the first time to develop national standards for what students should know and be able to do in history. As the United States becomes increasingly diverse and history grows day by day, educators and historians must decide whose stories to tell and how much time to devote to them.

Though the National Center for History in the Schools is only in the process of tackling that problem and expects to develop a set of standards by the spring of 1994, it has come out with a preliminary document entitled "Lessons from History: Essential Understandings and Historical Perspectives Students Should Acquire," which should influence the final product.

The guide calls for an approach to the subject that features lively storytelling and active learning. It says teaching should allow for differing interpretations. It also goes further than many traditional textbooks in discussing non-Western cultures and religions and long-ignored minorities. Members of some minority groups, however, say the document does not go far enough.

To help teachers "cut pathways to understanding through the forests of historical data, themes, and questions of enduring significance," the guide identifies four major narrative themes that run through history.

They are: the development and changing character of human societies; the economic and technological development of human societies; people's development and representation of their understandings of themselves, their moral imperatives, and their place in the universe; and the development of political theories and organizations in the quest for order, power, and justice.

And it identifies "habits of mind" that schools should seek to nurture in their students, such as a tolerance for the "complexity of human affairs" and "historical empathy," or the ability to view events through the eyes of those living at the time.

In order to understand the Salem witch trials, for example, the document says that "students should be encouraged to put themselves in the places of Massachusetts settlers, to examine the kind of religious liberty the Puritans sought—not individual freedom from religious constraints, but the freedom to establish for their community the binding religious mores and restraints they saw as scriptural imperatives for a covenant of people."

Geography: Having suffered for several years as the well-publicized neglected discipline of American education, geography received a well-deserved boost from the goals panel when it was designated as one of the select-few disciplines to be included in the National Education Goals. It is no wonder that its advocates are setting their sights high on what students should know and be able to do in that subject.

A federal panel of educators and policymakers approved in May 1992 a "rigorous" framework for the first national student-achievement testing program in geography, which will guide the development of the 1994 National Assessment for Educational Progress tests in geography for grades 4, 8, and 12.

The document attempts to dispel traditional notions of geography as a subject that largely calls upon students to memorize names of places and the natural resources of countries. Yet the framework does demand that students demonstrate a grasp of the basic knowledge of the field. At the 4th-grade level, for example, about 45 percent of the exercises would include such basic questions.

To learn about decisionmaking, high school students could work in groups and analyze a proposal to build an industrial park in an undeveloped flood plain.

Later on, students should be able to draw maps to differing scales, analyze information from satellite photographs, and use computers and computer databases to answer geographical questions. They should also understand natural systems and climate, and be able to discuss the benefits and drawbacks of the ways in which humans affect their environments and vice versa.

The content of the assessment concentrates on three areas of study: "space and place," "environment and society," and "spatial dynamics and connections." The third category refers to connections between people and places and includes factors such as communications, transportation, and cultural and economic diversity, among others.

A major focus of the framework is also on the contemporary nature of geography, and so a sample question might read: "Explain the motivations of modern-day Mexicans and Cubans for immigrating to the United States."

English: A consortium of education organizations is working together to develop standards in English—an area that encompasses reading, composition, oral communications, and literature—that are scheduled to be released in the fall of 1995.

The field, however, is among the most controversial in the school curriculum. And representatives of the groups involved in the standards-setting process acknowledge that their task will not be easy.

One of the biggest issues the group will face centers on the debate now raging over the best way to teach young children to read. Some educators favor a "whole language" approach that emphasizes the use of literature in class; others stress the teaching of phonics, or the relationship between symbols and sounds, in teaching reading.

"What we're trying to do," says one expert, "is to create something open enough so that teachers and kids can fall into the philosophy that helps them become better readers and writers."

The de facto literary canon now taught in schools, critics say, has traditionally been dominated by 'dead, white males' and has excluded other voices.

Debate is also expected over how the literary canon should be addressed in the standards. The de facto literary canon now taught in schools, critics say, has traditionally been dominated by the works of "dead, white males" and has excluded the voices of women and minority groups.

The project's co-directors say they hope to resolve such issues by providing flexibility in the structure of the standards, and by being sensitive and responsive to the needs of the local communities in which they are taught. They also intend to involve a diverse group of people to oversee the effort, including English and reading professionals, other educators, business representatives, communications professionals, and members of the general public.

The Arts: Although the arts were named as one of the core subjects in which students must demonstrate their competency by the year 2000, and are thought by some to be "frills," arts educators are determined not to be left out. They are eyeing the standards movement as an opportunity to convince educators and policymakers that the subject belongs in schools, and they are well on their way to determining what students should know and be able to do in art, dance, music, and theater.

"National standards," said one member of the national-standards committee at a recent symposium, "are one step on the road to making the arts a legitimate subject."

Funded by the Education Department, the National Endowment for the Arts, and the National Endowment for the Humanities, the arts-standards project was launched in the summer of 1992, and expected to begin circulating a draft of the standards for students in kindergarten through 12th grade by the summer of 1993.

A key issue for the standards committee thus far, says the chairman of the project, has been to determine whether to aim its efforts at all students or only at the artistically talented.

As a compromise, the draft standards have set forth one level of achievement—proficient—for students in kindergarten through 8th grade. However, in recognition that there are students who are specializing in the arts in high school, there are two levels of achievement—proficient and advanced—for students in grades 9 through 12.

The committee also has struggled to strike a balance between maintaining the integrity of the individual disciplines covered by the standards and showing students how those disciplines interconnect.

On one key point, however, committee members say they are clear: The standards will move away from the current emphasis in schools on performing or "doing" the arts to a more balanced approach that includes a significant amount of instruction in culture, history, and esthetics.

Arts educators are also hoping their standards will be bolstered by a closely aligned effort to develop national student assessments in the arts. The National Assessment Governing Board plans to begin testing students' grasp of the arts through its 1996 National Assessment of Educational Progress. □

Compiled for this book from various articles in Education Week *and* Teacher Magazine *published in 1992-93*

21.

The True Road To Equity

Standards and assessments are worthless—a cruel hoax— unless schools are able to help all students meet them.

Commentary By David W. Hornbeck

We have a miserable performance record in educating low-income, racial- and language-minority students. Given the changing demographics of our nation, we cannot succeed economically or in sustaining our democracy unless we succeed educationally with those students with whom we have historically failed. We need to create the policies and structures that result in high achievement by those students as well.

The most important question facing the nation today is whether America is really serious about pursuing educational equity. Or is it enough these days to only embrace the rhetoric that all children can learn? Many of us tend to be more delicate with the question, but for those who truly care about equity, perhaps the time has come to be blunt.

To be sure, equity will require extraordinary systemic change in the way education is delivered and governed. Different and greater capacities within the system are necessary. But those who go beyond the rhetorical must make sure that two of the essential components included in our comprehensive efforts to ensure high student achievement by all students are high national standards and a rigorous national assessment system.

Standards and assessments provide us with new arguments—moral, practical, political, and legal—that can give us the leverage we need to change the system to respond to the needs of all of America's children.

Advocating strong standards and assessments now is in sharp contrast to the traditional posture of those, including many whose first priority is the equity agenda, who come at these issues saying, "No standards and assessments until or unless . . . ." It also contrasts with others who argue for standards and assessments and "then we'll consider other features of the system."

We should be insisting instead on quality standards and assessments now as part of building the capacity to help every child reach high levels of achievement. This, for example, is the kind of "social compact" that the New Standards Project has promised with its partners, 17 states and six urban school districts.

It is not enough to have standards and examinations. They must be "done" right. To do so, the standards must first be challenging. They must be national—not federal—adopted voluntarily by states. They must be developed from the best thinking of leaders in the professional discipline areas and must include structured, significant consultation with a diverse community of perspectives, including those reflecting the interests of low-income and racial- and language-minority students.

Second, examinations should be embedded in a system of multiple exams of different types—not a single national test.

Third, these examinations must be validated for particular uses and populations. This has powerful, positive equity implications since validity criteria should revolve around students' access to good instruction and curriculum that is relevant.

Fourth, attaching high stakes such as promotion or

graduation for students should be permitted only after the school and its support system demonstrate success with a sufficient proportion of students, including those who are low-income, racial- or language-minority, to make clear "the system" knows how to educate all students.

Fifth, the primary indicator of school performance would be the proportion of successful students, broken out by income, race, and language. Success should be defined in terms of the increasing proportion of a school's successful students measured against that school's previous perform-ance. Success should not be defined through simplistic interschool or interjurisdic-tional comparisons.

Standards would be worthless without assess-ments permitting us to know whether they are being met. Similarly, standards and assessments are equally worthless—a cruel hoax—unless schools are able to succeed in helping all stu-dents meet them. Thus, the imperative of a system of standards and examinations must be accompanied by com-plete systemic change to pro-vide new capacities to serve all children well. These changes include:

• Time, not achievement, as the primary variable in the organization of each child's instructional program. High achievement as reflected by the standards must be the constant. Additional time can include instruction before and after school, on weekends, during the summer, and better use of the existing school day.

• A profound commitment to professional development that reflects school-level needs. This is analogous to the kind of commitment America's most successful corpora-tions make to the continuous training and education of their employees.

• Support for school-based staff members so they can identify or develop curriculum and practice instruc-tional strategies that result in all students meeting the new high standards.

• School staff and parents having more authority over decisions affecting the instruction of their children.

• Quality early-childhood programs for all disadvan-taged students.

• Expanded, improved, and integrated services to

FRANCIS WASHINGTON

eliminate the health and social barriers to learning.

• Technologies that enhance and individualize instruc-tion and that offer teachers and students access to the best practice and people in the world. These technolo-gies must be equitably available throughout the nation and within each state.

These are the elements of a change agenda that a number of us have been pursuing for some time. There even seems to be widespread agreement around them. So why are national standards and examinations so crucial to change and to the equity agenda? Because they provide the leverage to make it happen. They offer the leverage to affect every level of the system, from the class-room to the courtroom, from the student's house to the statehouse.

The single greatest obsta-cle faced by poor and minor-ity students is the low expec-tations most adults have for their performance. Expecta-tions are powerful, self-fulfilling prophecies. A highly visible national proc-ess of creating high stand-ards and a rigorous examina-tion system would create expectations for disadvan-taged students that are not lower than those held for others. States and communi-ties would be less likely to maintain today's system of expecting and asking less of poor and minority students and, consequently, offering them less. We must funda-mentally change the present expectation framework that holds out only failure to far too many poor and minority students.

Standards and examinations that have been devel-oped by a diverse community of interests will be a strong aid to teachers in fixing goals and assessing what they need to do at the student and classroom levels.

There are more points of leverage. The proposed system would permit fair incentive systems for teach-ers and other school and district staff. Rewards, assistance, and penalties could be based on students' performance, with the school as the unit of measure-ment. It would be wholly unfair to work toward a system of high stakes for students if there were none for the adults responsible for their education.

A system rooted in high standards and rigorous examinations could provide the political basis for significantly higher funding. The public, as shown by poll after poll, is willing to pay more taxes if it can be certain that the extra money would result in improved education results. Legislators, following that line of thinking, often say they will not "throw good money after bad." They believe that more funding for "the same old things" will not produce results. In addition, there is a widespread view that, even after large increases in funding, educators are never held accountable. Educators, on the other hand, insist that more money must precede results. A new approach is necessary. If, for example, the public were assured that either the results would be forthcoming or that educators would face penalties, including possible job loss, the stage would be set for significant increases in funding.

Where the political remedy to insufficient funding was not forthcoming, the proposed system could offer a significant new legal strategy. If schools and districts don't bring students up to the new standards, the state could be held constitutionally accountable for providing the resources districts and schools need to have their students meet the standards. Moreover, student outcomes, not just the equal distribution of money, could play a much more prominent role in remedies arising from such a legal strategy. The objective would become results, not just process and inputs.

There is at least one more compelling lever that a strong national standards and examinations system would provide. It could break the widespread complacency that now inhibits deep change. The prevalent view is that the country's schools are failing but "my school" is O.K. The fact is that a small percentage—some say as little as 5 percent—of our students perform at the levels required of an effective citizenry and an internationally competitive economy. But we now have no way of routinely sending an accurate message based on believable data. The common view arising from standardized, normed testing practice is that most students are performing at or above the "average." Many feel that is "good enough." High standards and rigorous examinations can change this perception. It will be clear that all students are at risk. Systemic change is more likely if the public knows that all children, including "my children," are in trouble.

The question we face is not standards and exams or no standards and exams. The actual choice is high standards and rich examinations in a system with enhanced capacity versus what we have now—a system of deeply embedded low standards, especially for disadvantaged students, and a heavy, sometimes exclusive reliance on multiple-choice, normed tests. The proposed system is necessary to the equity agenda. The present system demonstrably undercuts that agenda.

Many believe that some form of national standards and testing is inevitable. If so, it becomes even more urgent that those who care most about those students we persistently fail become actively engaged. Only through such engagement can we help craft a system that helps all students succeed.

Some people come to this debate with an orientation toward the quality of the work force and America's economic competitiveness. Others come with a moral imperative to succeed with all students, including, for the first time in the nation's history, low-income, racial- and language-minority students. Neither will succeed without the other. The leadership of both groups must come at these issues affirmatively.

We must ensure that the system that arises from the debate includes high standards and rigorous examinations and the capacity to educate all students. Equity and excellence are within our grasp, but only if the Bush Administration, the Congress, educators, the business community, student and child advocates, and all others who care about children and the nation's future affirm a comprehensive change agenda. It is not an either-or choice. □

David W. Hornbeck is a former Maryland state superintendent of schools. He is an adviser to the Business Roundtable and to the National Center on Education and the Economy. He is also chairman of the board of the Public Education Fund Network, chairman of the Commission on Chapter 1, and a member of the board of the Children's Defense Fund.

From Education Week, *May 6, 1992*

22.

Schools Are Not The Periphery

An accountability system that is rooted in local efforts would constitute a real national solution to our national problem.

Commentary By Joseph P. McDonald

All the proposals to develop a national assessment system for the United States assert that we have a national problem. I agree. It concerns the fact that American schooling is out of sync with the needs of democracy, and with emerging productivity demands in the workplace. By design, it aims some 30 percent of American kids toward college, and ignores the prospects of the rest. Meanwhile, it insinuates through structures and attitudes that prospects are defined by native gifts, not effort.

Nearly everywhere, an industrial pedagogy, unapprized of the emergence of a postindustrial workplace, consigns school days to a regimen of decontextualized and decomposed knowledge, and measures "achievement" in hours of exposure to it. Overall, American schooling seems more concerned with sorting and labeling kids than with challenging them all to use their minds well. For want of resources especially, it is terribly resolute in diminishing the prospects of so-called minority kids, the parents of the American majority of the 21st century. All of this occurs against an ironic rhetorical backdrop that portrays the American school as the chief engine of equity and chief guarantor of citizenship.

A national problem demands a national solution. I agree again. That is, it demands a nationally concerted effort to ratchet up standards for all kids, to transform "common sense" attitudes about what intelligence is and about how intellectual interests and practical matters relate, to tune the intimate practices of

hundreds of thousands of classrooms to new conceptions of knowledge and of learning, and to "rewire" tens of thousands of schools—that is, utterly revamp how they go about the exchange of energy and information.

But how may we best pursue such a solution? Here's where I disagree. I think the current proposals for a national assessment system—those of the National Council on Education Standards and Testing, the America 2000 strategy, the latest SCANS Report, the New Standards Project, and Educate America Inc.— represent exactly the wrong approach. That is because these proposals pursue a national solution by means of a spuriously central mechanism. They mean to drive innovation from where they are—which they take to be the center of the American educational system—to where schools are—which they take to be the periphery. In fact, in the lives of teachers and kids—and of parents and communities—schools are at the center of American education. And at this center, they filter all policies through complex cultures. Ultimately, they are responsive only in perverse ways to incentives which discount their complexity and their centrality. A national examination—even elegantly realized in regional variations and alternative formats—may well drive schools toward mindless accountability. As George Madaus has warned, no exam, however "authentic," can be considered immune from corruption when stakes rise. And as Linda Darling-Hammond has argued, an accountability system which only assesses kids, but which fails to assess the quality of the school's efforts to teach these kids, will be corrupted. Scores will rise as teachers reduce what they teach to just what the assessments assess and as principals manage to push out the kids whom they perceive as drags on their school's average. There is abundant evidence that in this fashion well-intentioned assessment hurts many kids now. Well-intentioned national assessment may enormously increase the extent of such injury.

This is not to argue that there is no good role for the National Assessment of Educational Progress, for nationally focused research and development efforts in assessment, or for nationally articulated goals and curriculum frameworks in the pursuit of higher standards for all kids. On the contrary, sensible accountability policy for the 1990's and beyond requires these initiatives. It is just that they must take care to avoid diminishing actual accountability by aiming too far and by inadvertently squelching local efforts. This will happen especially if they preempt the painstaking and difficult work of building local commitment and local capacity.

I want to see an accountability system that is rooted in local efforts to take stock—efforts that are networked with others, that are supported and audited by the states, and that are fed by perspectives on achievement and equity developed and refined on the national level. To my mind, such a system would constitute a real national solution to our national problem. It would require of each school that it open itself to inspection by stakeholders near and far; disclose what all its indicators of achievement reveal—including longitudinal and other locally constructed indicators; report annually to its community like a corporation to its stockholders; and equip itself with whatever internal systems it needs to take continuously corrective action in the interests of ensuring all its kids' achievement at genuinely higher levels. It would also require, of course, a revolution at the center of American education—that is, in each American school's sense of purpose and in each one's design.

Advocates of national assessment schemes may well

MARK ANDRESEN

regard what I call a real national solution as a romantic and unattainable one. But I hurl the charge back at them. I think it is their vision that is romantic and unattainable—a kind of Napoleonic vision, whereby an authoritarian focus blurs out a historic opportunity for democracy. Their vision presumes that most Americans cannot be trusted to discern what is good—or bad—for their own children. Chester Finn, for example, cites the evidence of polls that document most Americans' satisfaction with their own children's schools (urban parents notably excepted). You obviously can't trust bottom-up reform schemes if people's taste is that bad, he argues. But his argument—particularly curious coming from an advocate of school choice—lacks empathy for the polls' respondents. When faced with the stark question—"What do you think about the quality of your school?"—people closest to kids will color their response with an intuition: namely that kids derive much of the energy they bring to learning in school from their parents' and their teachers' investment in the value of that learning. To doubt one's own school is thus to seem to put one's own children at risk.

Yet I think most parents and teachers do harbor doubts, which then surface in their responses to the easier question: What do you think of the quality of other people's schools? That's when the fears tumble out— fears that are well warranted. That is also when the opportunity presents itself: Perhaps, after all, local commitment to genuine school reform is conceivable. In fact, I believe that many local American communities yearn for a 21st-century version of the Hoosier spelling bees, when whole prairie villages of the 19th century turned up at the schoolhouse once a year to verify that the year's school funds had been well spent. Of course, it is undeniable that many of these same communities have at best an inchoate sense of what achievement standards may be worthy of the 21st century. Some still seem to care more that their kids memorize the list of state capitals than that they acquire intellectually powerful habits of mind. It will be an exceedingly difficult task to awaken them to worthier standards than this, but to drive them there will be virtually impossible.

Meanwhile, I take heart from the recent revolution in the standards of American cuisine. Fairly recently, we had only two choices in American dining: either narrowly ethnic—red-sauce Italian, fried-rice Chinese— or else pot roast with salt and pepper. Today, however, our cuisine is among the most varied, the most inventive, the most dynamic in the world. We owe this

---

Whole prairie villages of the 19th century turned up at the schoolhouse once a year to verify that the year's school funds had been well spent.

---

result not to any effort to drive us toward the consumption of croissants and arrugula—certainly not to the influence of a national gustatory exam—but, rather, to the confluence of several diverse factors, all of them with potential analogues in the effort to improve schools. First, there was an unprecedented opportunity—product of simultaneous surges in the nation's ethnic diversity, in its health consciousness, and in its media-based connectedness. Second, there was and is national leadership—Julia Child, Craig Claiborne, the Silver Palate ladies, even C. Everett Koop. Next, a national cadre of chefs trained by a handful of restaurants and cooking schools, patronized by increasingly dispersed cosmopolitan taste, cultivated in turn by good writing and television. Finally— and perhaps most importantly—a great growth in appreciation of the value of local cuisines and of the freshness of locally available ingredients.

Like better tastes in dining, higher expectations for kids' achievement are inevitably entangled with values, and values legitimately vary somewhat from one American community to another. To ignore this preeminence of local interest in the overall effort to create change is to take a great ethical and political risk—and so to endanger a crucial mission. In the matter of transforming our tastes in schooling, I think we have no choice but to tolerate each community's painstaking effort to cultivate taste. We outsiders can play a vital role in this process—though not a decisive one— through the provision of national expectations, the provocation of richly constructed assessment models, the enhancement of communication among schools (for example, by means of the electronic network that the National Science Foundation is working on), and, of course, an insistence on the entitlement of every American child to a good education.

Happily, there is plenty of innovation in assessment and accountability that has been launched and is now proceeding well without benefit of national driving—in Vermont, California, Kentucky, San Diego, Pittsburgh, the Center for Collaborative Education in New York City, Sullivan High School in Chicago, Thayer High School in New Hampshire, English High School in Boston, to single out only a few state and local examples. In order to build a national solution to the national problem in American education, I think we need much experimentation with new accountability schemes and new kinds of assessment, and we need it at all levels of educational policy—from NAEP to Jefferson County, Ky., to Rancho San Joaquin Middle School in Southern California. We need it in such diversity and breadth as to match the enormous enterprise it seeks to serve, but we need it especially at the center of that enterprise. If we don't have it there, then all the scholarly and political talent we now have working at the periphery will be worth little. In fact, it is likely to cause a lot of trouble. □

Joseph P. McDonald is senior researcher at the Coalition of Essential Schools, Brown University.

From Education Week, *May 20, 1992*

23.

Verbal Confusion Over 'Tests'

The failure to distinguish between 'tests' and 'assessments' is muddying the debate over school reform.

Commentary By Ruth Mitchell

A verbal confusion is muddying the debate about a national system of standards and assessments: The words "tests" and "assessments" are being used as if they were synonymous. Because the word "test" fits better into headlines, the press is particularly prone to this confusion. It has to be cleared up if there is to be any clarity about what we can expect from such a system.

Briefly, tests are machine-scorable, usually multiple-choice and norm-referenced. Their essence is speed, cheapness, and psychometric respectability. Assessments, which is shorthand for "authentic," "alternative," or—my preferred term—"performance assessments," are not machine-scorable, and vary in length and in what they require students to do. Their essence is the active production of response by the student.

Almost no one concerned with the legislation that may result in a National Education Standards and Assessment Council now supports a national test. The prevailing notion envisages a system of assessments developed by states, regions, or organizations certified by a national body (possibly NESAC) to assess progress toward national standards, plus the National Assessment of Educational Progress performing the monitoring function it does now. Both the assessment system and NAEP would use performance assessments.

Although even Senator Claiborne Pell of Rhode Island has yielded as the last champion of national tests, the confusion infects the debate in the press and among educational stakeholders. It makes for strange bedfellows: In their "debate" on the front page of the *Washington Post Education Review*, both Chester E. Finn Jr., an important influence on policy in the Bush Administration, and Monty Neill of FairTest repudiated tests and endorsed assessments, although their contributions were meant to show polar opposites.

Clearing up this verbal confusion is hardly trivial in view of what is implied by the use of these words. We are talking about two incompatible models of education. The difference between the "factory" model, which uses tests, and the "community of learners" model, which uses assessments, is like the difference between the Ptolemaic and the Copernican views of the universe. As in all paradigm shifts, changed relationships rearrange the value system.

Understanding that the debate is about different systems, not merely exchanging tests for assessments, will explain why otherwise clear thinkers seem to be taking contradictory positions when they write about national standards and assessments.

I've often heard people say that the form of tests doesn't matter, that the real issue is the uses to which they are put. But the form of multiple-choice, machine-scorable tests is in itself a statement about the purposes of education, and therefore it affects the uses of testing. In the educational model that uses multiple-choice, machine-scorable tests, value is placed on ability to recognize discrete statements, to distinguish the "right" from the "wrong." "Information" is defined as what can be recognized easily and memorized.

Naturally, if what is valued is passive recognition of information, then teaching is bound to mean transmission of information in pellet-like form. The act of teaching is devalued by testing because of the vast disproportion between the hours spent acquiring facts and algorithms in strict order of difficulty and the few minutes taken up by bubbling in a few ovoids.

The purpose of this system is essentially gatekeeping, selecting and sorting students for access or denial of access to educational advantage, which, in the case of early tracking, means simply learning more interesting material than drill-and-skill. The concept of the "correct" answer at the heart of machine-scorable, multiple-choice testing is a metaphor for the purposes of the factory model: You're in, or you're out.

The demands made on students by performance assessments are quite different: active application of knowledge and skill to problems, as much as possible drawn from the world outside the school. The definition of information reflects that of Norbert Wiener, the father of cybernetics: "To live effectively is to live with adequate information. Thus, communication and control belong to the essence of man's inner life, even as they belong to his life in society."

The consequences for teaching are profound, as teachers who understand the changes are discovering. They have every reason to complain that they are being asked to do too much without adequate compensation, since their pay scales and professional duties are based on the old model's assumption that they are essentially textbook jockeys. Now they are expected to design assessments, participate in group-grading sessions, organize portfolios, read students' writing no matter what subject they teach, and recast their own classroom activity from lecturing to coaching.

The purpose of this system is the development of each student's intellectual, social, and emotional ability to function in the world. It is a noble and lofty ideal. I would be the last person to claim that any American school comes close to embodying it. But some schools, some districts, some states have begun to realize that changing from tests to assessments entails a change in purpose and attitude throughout the system.

I have drawn this contrast in models not only for its own sake, but also to make the point that using tests to measure progress in schools where change is taking place is wrong-headed. So too is the claim that accountability requires a different kind of measurement than classroom assessment. When the Arizona reformers who had rewritten their state curriculum guides looked at the state's commercial tests for accountability, they found that only 26 percent of the curriculum was covered by the tests. From that discovery arose the Arizona Student Assessment Program, which is designed specifically to perform the two functions—accountability and modeling of desired instruction—that some think incompatible.

If students keep portfolios and engage (for example) in investigations about the water quality in their community, what information can a multiple-choice, machine-scorable test provide about their abilities and experiences? For accountability, it is only necessary to sample portfolios as Vermont has done.

Furthermore, since we all agree that fewer assessments should occupy students' time (although many performance assessments are indistinguishable from ordinary classroom activities), an assessment that gives students individual grades could be calibrated to the national standards to report on progress at that level, and samples from the same assessment could be culled for state accountability.

Adopting a national system of standards and assessments—not a national test—implies a national endorsement of the "community of learners" model. Performance assessment should be seen in the context of the model: It is by no means a panacea and should not be regarded as more than a useful instrument. It is one of many factors (for example, cooperative learning, whole language, active learning, the community as classroom, the student as worker) that undermines the factory model, and provokes the asking of fundamental questions about the purposes of education. If we want to ensure that the paradigm shift happens in time to save public education, we must focus our vision on the gestalt and not oversell individual features.

To fulfill its promise as a signal of profound change, a national system of standards and assessments must be supported by resources. Otherwise, the imposition of sophisticated assessments without the means to prepare students for them is simply national cruelty. Apart from large infusions of materials into schools that now lack photocopying machines (let alone computers), the major resource needed is the professional development of teachers.

Teachers, squeezed between paradigms, need to become fully professional, to work year-round as other professionals do, with at least two months of time free from students in order to realize their place at the center of the development, administration, and scoring of national assessments. Questions about the quality of tasks—and therefore the quality of teaching—must be raised when there is time to consider them fully.

There is no guarantee that any of this will happen. With no resources to realize them, national standards and assessments could be an empty political promise. Unfunded programs, greedy test publishers, public indifference, opportunistic politicians, and business shortsightedness all threaten to abort positive change. But without it, Americans will be stuck with the educational equivalent of the flat-earth model. □

Ruth Mitchell is associate director of the Council for Basic Education in Washington.

From Education Week, *April 29, 1992*

24.

The 'Common Core'

Maine leads the way in setting standards for what students should know and be able to do.

By Debra Viadero

More than a year before a national panel of educators and business and political leaders called on the nation to define and set high standards for what every child should know and be able to do, the state of Maine had already begun to blaze the trail.

Educators and citizens came up with "Maine's Common Core of Learning," a wide-ranging, 55-page plan that establishes 151 goals for student learning. Neither as specific as a curriculum framework nor as sweeping as a vision statement, the document spells out what students should know when they leave school and the skills and attitudes they should take with them. Maine's effort resembles in some ways, but not in others, what the members of the National Council on Education Standards and Testing had in mind when they issued their final report in January 1992. A few other states, such as California, have gone farther in setting down specifics for student learning in important subject areas. The national-standards panel cited those efforts frequently and favorably in the report.

But where Maine may provide a lesson for the rest of the country is in the way it has gone about selling its blueprint for learning. In a state where residents pride themselves on being "stubborn Yankees," the Common Core is completely voluntary for school districts.

Not unlike the federal officials who may one day be pushing for widespread adoption of national curriculum standards, state education officials in Maine must depend on the willingness of local educators to "do the right thing" and the leverage of a fledgling testing system to make it work.

The foundations for the Common Core were laid in 1989, when Commissioner of Education Eve M. Bither came to Gov. John R. McKernan Jr. with an idea for a statewide panel of citizens and educators to set a vision for schooling in the state. The governor's enthusiasm for the idea was shown by his reply: "Why didn't somebody do this 200 years ago?"

"Nobody ever stepped back and said, 'What is it kids ought to know?'" Governor McKernan says. "In this state, we've been able to have an acceptable standard of living without emphasizing education as much as we could be. It was clear we needed a vision," he says.

The 45 citizens selected to draw that vision for Maine represented a wide range of opinions. They included parents, an artist, a student, legislators, businesspeople, and a museum director. Representing the education community were members of the state board of education, officials from the state education department, college presidents, school superintendents, teachers, and a principal from one of the most rural communities in the state.

The commission deliberated for 16 months, with much of that time characterized both by forceful debate and by unexpected agreement.

Interdisciplinary Focus

The biggest point of contention came over what in the end became the document's most distinguishing feature: an emphasis on interdisciplinary learning.

Rather than dividing learning into traditionally distinct academic subjects, the Common Core suggests that education is naturally interdisciplinary, and that what students learn in one subject is inextricably linked to what they learn in another. Part of educators' task, the commission decided, is to help pupils see the connections.

That idea was strongly opposed at first by some commission members, who argued that anything but a subject-by-subject approach to teaching could result in "intellectual mush" and discourage in-depth thinking in a single discipline.

"The chairman of the panel, the chancellor of the university system, and I all lined up on the side of individual disciplines, and the others favored the integrated approach," Ms. Bither recalls. "There was a kindergarten teacher on the panel who kept arguing, 'This is not how people learn,' and eventually the other side convinced me."

The final report divides learning goals into four areas: "communication," "personal and global stewardship," "reasoning and problem solving," and "the human record." The designated areas were not intended to result in four separate courses, but only to serve as guideposts for organizing the goals in the report. The goals also are listed under traditional subject headings in an appendix to the report.

Atoms and Attitudes

Students who mastered the goals outlined in the report would be, in Ms. Bither's words, modern-day "Renaissance young men and women."

Such pupils should be able to understand and apply concepts of ratio, proportion, and percent in a variety of situations, for example, while also fathoming the "historical evolution of democratic principles and components of constitutional government of the United States," according to the Common Core.

They would have a working understanding of the "concepts, processes, and systems of technology through time" and know the atomic basis of the structure of matter. They would be familiar with Shakespeare and the Bible as well as works of more "diverse literary traditions."

The pupils would also display certain attitudes, such as a willingness to "accept responsibility for personal decisions and actions" and to risk mistakes. And they would have vital skills, such as the ability to communicate effectively both orally and on paper.

The Common Core also attends to subjects not always considered basic to education. It calls on schools to prepare graduates who can ask and answer questions in a foreign language, and to instill in them an appreciation for drama, dance, music, the visual arts, and other forms of creative expression.

In addition, the plan calls strongly for abolishing the tracking of students according to ability and advocates

stronger links between schools and communities.

In most of these respects, the Common Core differs from the kinds of national standards envisioned in "Raising Standards for American Education," the report by the National Council on Education Standards and Testing. That report calls for setting national curriculum standards with greater specificity.

Such standards should not only articulate what students should know and be able to do, the framers of

---

The 45 citizens selected to draw a vision for Maine included parents, an artist, a student, legislators, businesspeople, and a museum director.

---

the NCEST report held, but also the degree to which they should know it. It divides learning into the traditional academic disciplines and focuses on the five subjects mentioned in the national education goals: English, mathematics, science, history, and geography. Moreover, it addresses content, not methodology.

"What we've identified as critically important is a much higher level of sophistication and complexity," says Richard H. Card, the executive director of the office of professional education for the University of Maine system and a former member of the commission. "But I don't think the two are incompatible."

"Any student who is able to master the goals of the Core will do extremely well on any national test," adds Ms. Bither, who also served on the national-standards panel.

Both the state and national documents endorse some of the efforts already under way to set standards in particular disciplines. The NCEST report praises the mathematics standards set by the National Council of Teachers of Mathematics, for example, while the Common Core includes them. And elements of the American Association for the Advancement of Science's recommendations for science education appear in both reports.

The documents also share a commitment to setting high academic standards for all students, as well as an emphasis on keeping the goals voluntary.

"There has to be some commitment inside the school district," says Heidi McGinley, the coordinator for the Common Core in the state education department.

"In other states, it may be possible to say, 'Here it is, the best thing since sliced bread, and we want you to have it in place by September,'" she adds. "But there's a strong tradition of local control here, and you just can't do it."

That relationship between the state and local school districts is not unlike that between the federal Education Department and the states. One of the most striking aspects of the Common Core is the widespread agreement it appears to have engendered in the 21 months since its completion in July 1990. From Guilford, a rural community, to Farmington, a university town, teachers, parents, principals, and school superintendents say they have no major philosophical differences with the Common Core.

"People said, 'Hey, this makes sense,'" says Robert Kautz, the superintendent of the Wells-Ogunquit School District, where the school board formally adopted the plan last June.

"I think there's a general perception that this is realistic, attainable, and practical," says Richard Lyons, the superintendent of a district composed of four small towns in the central part of the state.

While the document is far from a household word in the state, it has captured the attention of parents in some districts.

"When I read this, sometimes I don't understand all of it," admits Susan Tinguely, a Farmington parent. "When I come into the classroom, I really see how it applies, and I use it as a tool to begin to formulate for myself what education can be for kids."

Despite such widespread agreement, however, only 38 of 184 districts are actively working with the state to implement the Common Core, according to the state department. Only a handful of local school boards have formally endorsed it.

"There's not a stampede here," concedes Ms. McGinley, who travels more than 2,500 miles a month working with districts on the Common Core.

Far From 'Nuts and Bolts'

Part of the problem, notes Connie Goldman, the superintendent of the Cape Elizabeth schools, may be the document's lack of specificity. To avoid dictating curriculum, the framers of the Common Core consciously stuck to broad principles on what students should know and be able to do.

"It's a nice discussion piece, but it's a fair distance to nuts and bolts," says Ms. Goldman, who has used the plan to spur community discussions on reform.

"When you try to translate this into report cards and courses, you still have arguments about who ought to be in the honors course," she says. "I see it as more of a visionary statement."

State officials concede they have no one right way to show school administrators such as Ms. Goldman specifically how to implement the Common Core. "I would have to say I don't know," Ms. Bither acknowledges, "but we're working on it."

What the state has done so far is to provide copies of the report to every teacher and school administrator in the state. Last summer, state officials held workshops on the Common Core that were attended by educators from nearly 70 districts.

These days, Ms. McGinley's mission is mostly to offer tactful technical assistance to districts that seek it. Such aid is not always wanted, however. Many districts are still bristling from a raft of new requirements imposed on them under state education-reform measures of the mid-1980's, leaving relationships between the state and local districts strained.

Indeed, state officials spent the first year following release of the Common Core trying to convince local school officials that it was not a mandate. "They said, 'Ah-ha, here comes the state curriculum we never

---

Students who mastered the goals outlined in the report would be, in the words of one expert, modern-day 'Renaissance young men and women.'

---

wanted,'" says Constance Miller Manter, who works with Ms. McGinley on the Common Core projects.

But the greatest obstacle to wider implementation of the Common Core principles has been the recession of the past few years. Faced with a mounting budget deficit, the state cut aid to districts by $16.1 million for fiscal year 1992.

In fiscal '93, state education spending could be further reduced by as much as $15 million, according to Senator Stephen C. Estes, the co-chairman of the legislature's joint education committee, who noted that the cuts would come on top of an existing gap between the school costs certified by the state board and the amount actually allocated by the state.

"If we weren't going through this financial crisis, I think the Common Core would be much more visible and much more debated," says Francis McDermott, the superintendent of the Bonny Eagle School District.

Funding problems also threaten to slow down the development of the Maine Education Assessment, a state-mandated testing system for measuring students' academic progress in grades 4, 8, and 11.

The tests, another product of the mid-80's school-reform movement, now provide the state's only leverage for spurring curricular change. Although the assessments have been slowly moving to incorporate more of the kinds of performance-based questions that are reflective of the Common Core—some 40 percent of the questions on the test are now performance-based—they have been unpopular with educators because they are used in the media to compare districts.

In the future, Gov. McKernan says, he would favor changing the basic school-aid formula to reward districts that experiment with reforms. Currently, the only state funds available for innovative district efforts come from a small state grant program, which has

---

Despite such widespread agreement, only 38 of 184 districts are actively working with the state to implement the Common Core.

---

already been reduced to $300,000 from a peak of $900,000 several years ago.

Ms. Bither says she eventually hopes to add another "stick" in her campaign to foster use of the Common Core—the development of a certificate of mastery, linked to the learning goals in the Common Core, for students in the 10th and 12th grades.

Under the state's tight budget circumstances, however, even additional copies of the Common Core have become hard to get. Ms. McGinley says the state can no longer afford to fulfill large orders for the booklets.

Of the 38 districts actively working on the Common Core, those that have come the farthest tend to be districts receiving private grants or outside assistance or those that have already embarked on education reforms. The approaches they have used vary widely.

Piscataquis Community High School in rural Guilford, for example, is using a $571,000, three-year grant from RJR Nabisco's Next Century Schools grant program to underwrite a number of reforms suggested by the Common Core. In little more than a year, the school's staff has eliminated tracking in most subjects.

Teachers at the school have refocused the business, vocational-education, and health and physical-education programs, and are about a third of the way to rewriting the entire curriculum. The staff has also begun to develop mastery-based tests to gauge students' progress and success in meeting the goals defined by the Common Core.

"What we talk about is replacing the traditional clock and calendar with actual learning," says Principal Norman Higgins, who was a member of the committee that wrote the Common Core. "In the past, you had a credit or a course that was kind of a proxy for learning, except we're not sure that's valid."

In Wells-Ogunquit, where the Common Core is official district policy, teachers and administrators spent months learning how to work together and becoming more comfortable with ideas in the Common Core. "For many years, we've had the assumption that people knew how to work together," says Superintendent Kautz. "It's not true."

Two local industries provided training for teachers and administrators in corporate human-relations strategies, such as team-building and problem-solving. A third company underwrote seminars open to the community on education-reform issues.

Now, teachers are in the process of translating the Common Core into more specific learning outcomes in traditional subject areas. Later, they will refine that list and regroup the learning goals into the four areas outlined in the Common Core.

Mr. Kautz says the district is also working with the University of Southern Maine to develop authentic assessment activities to measure students' progress in meeting those curricular goals.

"You just can't take the Common Core as it's presently printed and easily translate that into a curriculum," Mr. Kautz insists. "There may be other things to learn before you can expect students to do what the Common Core says they should do."

Not Collecting Dust

Teachers at Mallett Elementary School in Farmington use the Common Core as the philosophical underpinning for a program that mixes kindergartners and 1st graders in the same classrooms and encourages their parents to take an active role. The parents and teachers on the steering committee that runs the program also are working to get other parents in the community to read the Common Core.

"To say that it's just a book and collecting dust on a bookshelf would not be accurate," says Mr. Card of the University of Maine. "This has generated a lot of activity and interest."

It is the step from "interest" to "activity," however, that is proving difficult for most districts. At Brook Cascade, for example, Principal Tom Taylor says staff members found they had hit "a roadblock" in their discussions of the Common Core. "We weren't ready to adopt the Common Core because it didn't really belong to us," he points out.

Now, the school has temporarily put the document aside and has begun working with a University of Maine education researcher to articulate its own vision for education. The next step, Mr. Taylor says, will be to look at how the two views mesh.

For now, teachers at the school agree on one important point: They want a common vision. "It's frustrating teaching sometimes, and you look at it, day to day, and you feel, 'Where am I going with this?'" says Steven Heath, a teacher at the school. "If I really had a plan to know where I was going, I could get there."

In the small town of Mexico, Superintendent of Schools William H. Richards is meeting with similar

---

State officials and supporters of the Common Core say they are approaching 'critical mass.' 'It's like a train slowly gathering speed without any obstacles in its way.'

---

difficulties working to implement the Common Core in his district. Mr. Richardson, who as a deputy associate state commissioner drafted the Common Core, says resistance in his district has come from a tradition-bound community and from teachers with no time, apart from their classes, to work on the Common Core.

"I crafted the darn thing, and I love it, but really translating it into meaningful action is difficult," he admits. "If there's a lesson here for national standard-setting efforts, it's to really understand the conditions in which we're expecting change to occur."

Despite the fits and starts, however, state officials and supporters of the Common Core say they are approaching "critical mass." "It's like a train slowly gathering speed without any obstacles in its way," Ms. Bither says.

They point out, for example, that the Maine Coalition for Excellence in Education, a group of citizen, education, and business leaders formed last year to spur education reform in the state, has made the Common Core a top priority.

Advocates also see opportunities to transform the document into practice through other education-reform efforts already taking place in the state.

For example, Maine has joined the Re:Learning network organized by the Coalition for Essential Schools and the Education Commission of the States to promote the theories of the education reformer Theodore R. Sizer of Brown University. As part of the project, the state must assist at least 10 schools in making changes "from the bottom up." Educators say much of the Common Core already reflects many of Mr. Sizer's ideas.

Several districts are also taking part in the National Education Association's Mastery in Learning project. And some branches of the state university system have begun exploring ways their teacher-education programs can reflect Common Core principles.

"I'll bet five years from now the Common Core will be implemented in over half the school districts," Governor McKernan says.

"I like to think," Ms. Bither says, "it's more like 90 percent." □

From Education Week, *April 1, 1992*

25.

A Glimpse Into The Future

New authentic assessments ask students to use their knowledge to solve problems and to think critically.

By Robert Rothman

To help her students begin working on a research project that will cap their final year at Mark Twain Elementary School in Littleton, Colo., Margie Zyzda, a 5th-grade teacher, is working with them on the topics they propose to investigate.

She takes aside one pupil, who has proposed studying the question: What are the different types of cats? "My concern," Ms. Zyzda tells the student, "is that you will come up with a list." Perhaps, she suggests, the pupil could study how the cats are different. Or, the student could compare a lion with a domestic cat.

The difference between the student's initial idea and Ms. Zyzda's suggestions is at the heart of what Twain and a rapidly growing number of schools—including nearby Littleton High School—are attempting to do.

Rather than ask students to memorize facts, these schools are designing assessments that ask them to use their knowledge to solve problems and to think critically, and to demonstrate their abilities by writing essays or performing experiments.

But while national officials anticipate that such approaches will be at the heart of a proposed nation-wide system of assessments, and a host of states and districts plan to develop them or have piloted them in some form, Twain is one of the few schools that has had the assessments in place schoolwide for some time. It offers, then, a glimpse into the future of assessment.

"My sense is that Twain is head and shoulders above most other schools I have seen in its efforts to implement performance-based assessment," says the school's new principal, Kenneth Turner, who came here from Massachusetts last July.

In the three years the system has been in place, Mr. Turner and other teachers in Littleton contend, the assessments have achieved the goal, propounded by their advocates, of driving instruction toward a focus on problem-solving, rather than rote learning.

And, they note, the assessments have also sparked valuable discussions among the staff members about what students should be expected to know and be able to do.

But, they caution, the effort is extremely time-consuming and costly, and faces resistance from more tradition-minded teachers and parents. Moreover, cautions Mr. Turner, the assessments remain "one piece of the entire picture" of student achievement. That picture, he says, should also include scores from traditional standardized tests.

"It is not our belief that this will replace everything that is out there," he adds. "What's important here is trying new things. We're building a bridge to the future and walking on it at the same time."

In many respects, Littleton is an unlikely site for an educational experiment. Located in a relatively afflu-ent suburb of Denver, the 15,300-pupil district has long been highly regarded in the area for its schools. The dropout rate in the district is only 4.4 percent; 80 percent of its graduates go on to pursue higher education.

"We were not starting from the position that this is a crappy school, and we need to fix it," says Timothy Westerberg, the principal of Littleton High School, the oldest of the district's three high schools. "We're darn good, and we want to stay this way."

The reform process began in 1987, when the school board adopted a strategic plan that focused on meeting the changing needs of students, restructuring, and assessment. But in keeping with Colorado's tradition of local control over education, the board also endorsed school-based decisionmaking and encouraged each school to go about its reforms in its own way.

"It was district policy to press the issues, but not require uniformity," says Grant Wiggins, a Rochester, N.Y.-based assessment consultant who has worked with the Littleton schools. "They see the distinction between standards and standardization better than I have ever seen it."

Although all 22 of the district's schools have moved toward the board's stated goals, Mark Twain and Littleton High School have moved the furthest with a whole-school change, according to Christine Johnson, the executive director for K-12 education of the Littleton public schools.

Twain, a 420-pupil, K-5 school—which honors its namesake by labeling the boys' rooms "Tom Sawyer" and the girls' rooms "Becky Thatcher"—began its restructuring effort by declaring as its mission: "We will facilitate student growth toward peak performance every moment of every day."

"The more we looked into it," says the school's former principal, Monte C. Moses, "the more we realized we had to change the way we did business."

The school set out toward that goal by creating an assessment system that was "basically indistinguishable from good instruction." Specifically, the assessment would ensure that students could demonstrate their performance, rather than simply soak up information from teachers. "We wanted students to be producers, not consumers," says Jan May, a 1st-grade teacher.

The faculty members also wanted to instill skills that traditional teaching omitted, such as the ability to gather information and report it in a variety of formats. "Those are skills they will use their entire lives, no matter what they do," notes Karen Quinlan, a 4th-grade teacher.

The teachers and Mr. Moses began by creating a research assessment. They launched it for 5th graders, so that the project could be a culminating activity for students about to leave the school.

In the assessment, students—like Ms. Zyzda's pupil who is interested in cats—choose a topic they want to investigate. The following week, they spend half of each day, in libraries and in class, researching their topic, writing a report on a computer, and drawing a visual representation of their report.

They then present their paper to a panel—which will include their teacher, the school's principal, and an outside observer—who will evaluate their performance. The projects are judged, on a 0-to-4 scale, according to a range of factors, including the content

and style, the use of language conventions, and their oral and visual presentations.

The topics for the assessment vary widely. On any given day, students might present papers, for example, on cancer treatments, global warming, computers, and Albert Einstein, among other subjects. Allowing students to choose their own topics ensures that they are motivated to perform well on the project, says Barbaralynn Bitzer, a 4th- and 5th-grade teacher.

Students tend to agree. "I especially liked that I got to pick my own question," says Katie Pieper, a 5th grader whose project examined what inspired great artists.

Once the 5th-grade assessment was in place, the Twain faculty expanded it to include earlier grades as well. Even 1st graders will prepare research projects, although in a modified form.

In addition to the research assessment, Twain has put in place a thinking-skills assessment, which evaluates students' ability to make predictions and determine probability; a writing assessment, which measures student responses to a text; and a mathematics assessment, which gauges students' measurement skills, use of fractions, and creativity by asking them to design a playground.

The school is also pilot-testing a cultural-literacy assessment for 5th graders, and is redesigning a science assessment that would allow them to conduct experiments and analyze data.

The students' assessments, along with other information about their school performance, are entered into a portfolio, which parents can see. The result, according to Mr. Turner, provides a much broader picture of students' achievement than simple standardized-test scores.

Not Just 'Seat Time'

Littleton High, meanwhile, began its restructuring effort by recognizing that the traditional high-school system rewarded "seat time," rather than achievement.

As a brochure produced for the school states: "If Johnny is able to sit through four years of English and a few other basic subjects, and fake his way through a few simple tests, he's got himself a diploma and a tassle for his rearview mirror."

To ensure that students excel at school, not merely get by, the school agreed to scrap coursework requirements and replace them with a set of 19 learner outcomes, which students must master in order to graduate.

Under the system, which went into effect in the fall of 1991 for freshmen, students must demonstrate proficiency in all 19 outcomes, and excellence in at least two of them, to earn a diploma.

"We want to establish habits of mind, so that when you leave here, you are good at something," Mr. Westerberg, the principal, says. "It's not adequate just to be proficient at everything."

The school has also been at work on a set of demonstration assessment tasks, along with the standards for proficiency and excellence, for each of the 19 competencies. "These will give parents a good, solid feel for what it is kids are expected to do," Mr. Westerberg says.

Many of these assessments have already been drafted and are being pilot-tested. For example, a "communications" task asks students to write a letter to a public policymaker about the official's position on a current political issue. A proficient letter is one in which the writer clearly states an opinion and uses facts to support it, uses the appropriate format and wording, and makes few grammatical errors.

An excellent letter is one in which the writer explains the writer's position and refutes an alternative position, uses interesting vocabulary and varied sentence structure, and makes essentially no errors.

People involved in the system at both of the schools

'What's important here is we're trying new things,' says one principal. 'We're building a bridge to the future and walking on it at the same time.'

---

agree that the new assessments provide a fuller picture of student achievement than do traditional tests. "We see how much they do know, instead of [how much they are] guessing," says Ms. Bitzer, the Twain teacher. "Everything they have learned up to 5th grade goes into the project."

Mr. Moses also points out that, when Twain expanded the research assessment to earlier grades, the 4th graders soon began to perform at the level 5th graders performed at in the first year of the new system. "That was an indication the assessment had the effect of elevating the performance of all kids," he says.

Deborah L. Novotny, the parent of two Littleton High students, says that her son, Josh, a 12th grader, works harder in school than he ever has because the school expects more from him. "I haven't had to ride his case," she says. "He's not normally that way."

Mr. Turner, Twain's principal, also points out that the high level of performance has generated some stimulating discussions in his school. One student's project, for example, examined who settled Colorado,

and provoked a debate on Native Americans.

Teachers say the new assessments also drive changes in curriculum and instruction, as proponents of alternative assessment had predicted. In particular, teachers at Twain have scrapped workbooks in early grades, and place a greater reliance on hands-on materials.

"We understand the textbook is not the curriculum," says Ms. May, the 1st-grade teacher. "I don't think a teacher in the building follows the book in that way."

Similarly, English classes are using more trade books, and the library is ordering more nonfiction books and news-magazines. Teachers at both levels spend less time lecturing and more time allowing students to come up with ideas.

"It's changing the way we taught for years and years and years," says Ms. Bitzer. "I'm not telling them what to do. I almost take a back seat and let them go."

"I can't go back to where I was if I wanted to," adds Glenda Miller, an English teacher at Littleton High.

The high-school teachers also say that the assessment system is encouraging them to think more about the connections among the disciplines. The school's science teachers, for example, have developed a two-year "integrated" science course, which includes material on earth, life, and physical sciences.

In addition, all teachers, in developing the course catalogue, were required to show which of the 19 outcomes the course would lead toward, says Mr. Westerberg. That way, he explains, students could see that work in one course could be related to work in another.

As an example, suggests Charles Mitchell, a history teacher, "a student might be in a debate class and do an ethics essay, which might fit the persuasion [requirement] in English."

'Much More Stimulating'

One of the most beneficial aspects of the new system is the fact that it has provoked teachers to discuss what the standards for students should be. "This place is so much more stimulating than ever before," says Daniel Brickley, a social-studies teacher. "It was a deadly place for decades."

Such discussions have permeated every department in the school, from social studies and English to music and physical education, adds Roger Whitworth, a physical-education teacher. The teachers have found it difficult to determine what proficiency in tasks such as cardiovascular fitness or strength might be, Mr. Whitworth notes. As an example, one student can perform 16 pull-ups, while another cannot do any. "The process has made our department check down to the bones," he adds.

But such efforts, teachers at both schools agree, take a great deal of time. "That's been a problem all along. There hasn't been enough time," says Jerry Cox, a technology teacher at Littleton High.

The school established a foundation to raise $1-million, primarily to pay for substitute teachers and after-hours time for teachers to write the assessments and work on the standards. But the foundation has to date raised only $200,000 in cash and $100,000 in in-kind contributions.

Standards-setting exercises can only work if teachers set the standards themselves, says Mr. Brickley, rather than having them imposed from the district or state level. By contrast, he argues, a policy adopted by the Pennsylvania Board of Education, which sets learner outcomes all students must attain in order to graduate, is doomed to failure. Teachers will resist such top-down mandates, Mr. Brickley predicts.

Some Are 'Not Comfortable'

But while most people involved in the changes consider them beneficial, a few teachers and parents have resisted them. In a letter to the Littleton *Independent*, Linda Young, a Littleton High School English teacher, expressed "grave doubts" about the school's experiment, and suggested that "the staff is sharply divided in its support of the plan."

Among her concerns were that the student outcomes will be "all but impossible to evaluate," and that "'lecture' is a dirty word as we focus more on 'cooperative learning,' a slow process of teaching where 'the blind lead the blind' as standardized-test scores fall."

Some parents at Twain also raised questions about that school's revised report card, which presented marks on dozens of student abilities, in addition to traditional grades. An editorial in the *Rocky Mountain News* called the revision "an example of the 'new age' of report cards, heavy on measurements of 'self esteem' and 'wellness' and rather short on whether Johnny knows the location of the Ukraine."

Supporters of the programs says that the criticisms reflect the views of a minority of people who are uneasy about the changes. "This is a real paradigm shift," says Ms. Bitzer of Twain. "A lot of people are not comfortable with that."

Twain faculty members were able to win over their colleagues because at least one member of each team-teaching pair was directly involved in the process. At Littleton High, meanwhile, Mr. Westerberg and the teachers held a series of coffees and have maintained an advisory board that includes representatives of local businesses.

But several teachers acknowledge that they may face additional resistance in the future. The new system, they suggest, may come as a shock to parents who are accustomed to seeing their children do well under the old system.

For example, Mr. Brickley notes that, in trying out an assessment that asked high-school students to "use the past to explain the present and anticipate the future," most of the members of his class were "almost unable to cope with it." He adds: "Eleventh graders have never been asked to use anything they've learned."

Parents may also be in for a rude awakening when their children take traditional standardized tests for accountability purposes or college admission, suggests Ms. May. "I'm not sure how well my kids will do on the Iowa Test of Basic Skills," she says. "I don't teach that way. They don't fill in answers. They don't choose from among four answers."

Perhaps the most vociferous objections will come later, when the new assessments are used as gateways to graduation, says Ms. Novotny, the parent of two high schoolers. Although parents may accept the theory that students must demonstrate competency in order to graduate, she says, they may object when their children are required to remain in high school after four years.

To build more widespread acceptance of the new assessment systems, educators at both schools say they are continuing to refine them. For example, teachers at Twain are working to ensure that the assessments are valid and reliable. Unlike traditional tests, in which all students answer the same questions and are scored by computer, the performance assessments are evaluated by judges, who may ask different questions of each student.

Littleton High School, meanwhile, received a $15,000 grant from the Denver Foundation to evaluate its program, and teachers on the program-evaluation committee say they expect to use the study to recommend changes. "Ten years from now," says Brian Letvin, a mathematics teacher, "it's not going to look exactly the same way it does now."

In addition to revising their own schools' programs, administrators from Twain and Littleton High have been meeting, along with a middle-school principal, to discuss the possibility of developing standards common across all school levels. And Mr. Moses, who is now the director for instruction and elementary education for the neighboring Cherry Creek public schools, says the idea of alternative assessment should continue to spread.

"This was just one seed out of about 1,000 other seeds that need to be planted," he says. □

From Education Week, *April 22, 1992*

26.

Reverse The Tide Of Mediocrity

A sound rationale exists behind the movement to base graduation on performance rather than seat time.

Commentary By Judy Westerberg and Tim Westerberg

The suburban Denver schools in which we work are among the first large, comprehensive public high schools in the nation to convert to a performance-based system. That is to say, to graduate from our high schools (beginning with the class of 1995 at one and the class of 1996 at the other), students must demonstrate that they know and can do those things identified in our two, somewhat different, sets of board of education approved performance-based graduation requirements. There are no Carnegie units or credits required for graduation at either school, nor are there any required courses in the traditional sense of the word. Instead, in order to demonstrate that they understand the processes of science, for example, students at our schools must be able to set up and conduct a scientific experiment. To show their command of the English language, they must be able not simply to eke out a C- in English class, but to compose a multiparagraph piece of expository writing that meets certain standards.

Given the pioneering work our two schools have done in this area, we are often asked to provide a rationale for our position. Below are 13 reasons why we believe graduation should be based on performance rather than seat time.

Performance-based graduation requirements:
• Have universal appeal; they align education with the world outside the school. Requiring students to prove that they know something in order to get a diploma makes sense to most Americans. There is a perception that much of what goes on in school is not aligned with the realities of the outside world. The global economy and this country's steadily declining share of world markets have focused the attention of the business world on performance. Employers demand performance from their employees. Educators must do the same.

• Communicate clearly what is expected of students to students, parents, and the tax-paying public; they define graduation. Go to almost any high school and ask members of the professional staff (not to mention students, parents, or members of the general public) exactly what it is that students will know and be able to do when they graduate and you will get as many different answers as people asked. Part of our recent credibility problem in education may be due to the fact that we have failed to define for the public, in concrete, specific, understandable terms, exactly what it is that we are trying to accomplish. How can we convince people outside the school that we are being productive when those of us inside the school do not know what the product is? With performance-based graduation requirements and their attendant assessments and standards, students, parents, and the public are told "up front" exactly what the school expects of its graduates.

• Make students responsible for learning. Teachers become very frustrated with students who simply put in their time, doing as little as possible but still earning credits toward graduation. In a performance-based system students are held responsible for demonstrating that they actually know and can do some specific things. In other words, four years of English with C's and D's will not get you a diploma if you cannot write the essay, read for comprehension, and speak articulately and effectively.

• Hold schools accountable. When a school states up front exactly what students must know and be able to do it is also identifying exactly what it is that the school is accepting responsibility for teaching. Schools can successfully answer the public cries for accountability when everyone in the school community is measuring the school's performance against the same set of expectations.

• Promote interdisciplinary teaching and learning. Performance-based graduation requirements (assuming that they are few in number) do not all fall neatly into subject matter or departmental categories. Understanding broad concepts and applying important skills cut across disciplines. It has been our experience that, when graduation is defined in performance-based terms, teachers begin to see the interrelatedness of the disciplines and look for ways to tie learning together across the curriculum.

• Free teachers from the impossible burden of "covering the material." Teachers in the traditional time-based system are constantly battling against the pressure to get through the book or cover the curriculum. It is a battle that we cannot win. Given the knowledge explosion that is sure to continue, covering the material is no longer a realistic option (if it ever was). We must find new ways to guide and direct our work and abandon the system that forces history teachers to cover the decades of the 50's, 60's, 70's, and 80's in the last two weeks of the school year. Using our scarce time to teach the knowledge and the skills leading to performance-based graduation requirements can focus our efforts.

• Focus the efforts of the professional staff. In a performance-based system, members of the professional staff work from a precise set of performance expectations. Consequently those requirements become the focal points for the entire school. They are so important that everything revolves around them, and all education in some way is directed toward helping

students master them. Teachers will do a better job when they know exactly what the school's educational targets are.

• Promote student involvement. Performance-based graduation requirements, by definition, require activity (performances) on the part of students. Students cannot sit through a performance-based system. Teachers in such a system approach lesson design with the realization that learning (instruction), like assessment, must include active student involvement. When the system rewards seat time, students sit. When the system rewards performance, students perform.

We must abandon the system that forces history teachers to cover the decades of the 50's, 60's, 70's, and 80's in the last two weeks of the school year.

• Allow for educational programs/progress tailored to individual student needs. In a traditional time-based system, courses are the ends of the system. Complete the required number of courses with grades of D- or higher and you get a diploma. In a performance-based system, student performance becomes the end of the system and coursework becomes the means to that end. Therefore, individualized programs of study can be designed for each student given that student's strengths, weaknesses, goals, and interests. Students can be remediated and accelerated without worrying about collecting the right number and kinds of credits needed for graduation. No longer is every student required to take 10th-grade English just because it is

THOMAS TILTON

required for graduation. For older students, seminars, internships, independent studies, community-service work, and co-enrollments with neighboring colleges and universities become viable options for learning.

• Focus on learning itself, not the artificial symbols or the "game" of learning. How many times have teachers heard a student say, "What is the lowest grade I can get on the final and still get a C in the class?" Or how about the student who refuses to take a difficult course or a non-weighted course in a weighted-grade system because it might affect his or her grade-point average by some fraction of a point? Such questions are legitimate

---

Every few years we add a semester of 'this' and reduce a semester of 'that' in response to prevailing political winds or pressure from powerful special-interest groups.

---

from a student's perspective in the system operating in most of our high schools today. A system that rewards students based on performance and not just grades can help focus students' attention on learning.

• Promote frequent, meaningful revision. In the traditional system of Carnegie units, every few years we add a semester of "this" and reduce a semester of "that" in response to prevailing political winds or pressure from powerful special-interest groups. But those changes usually do not result in meaningful changes for students because the requirements are so vague and general. Performance-based graduation requirements, assessments, and standards are specific and well-defined. Specific and well-defined requirements are unacceptable when they are misaligned with outside-of-school realities. Five credits of business education may always be appropriate. Having to perform keyboarding skills in a voice-input world may not.

• Create a system in which curriculum revision, staff development, and changes in the structure of the school (master schedule, allocation of resources, staffing, etc.) are tied together in a natural way. For years teachers have been involved in staff-development activities in which they are herded into some common area and "in-serviced" on the latest educational development.

Writing across the curriculum and cooperative learning come to mind. Teachers in these situations are polite, correct their papers, and work on their knitting. Although well-intentioned in most cases, after the in-service they go back to doing things the way they have always done them. The problem is that these staff-development activities are added on to the old system rather than made an integral part of it. Curriculum revision in most schools happens because "it's your turn," not because of a specific need. Likewise, schedule changes, staffing changes, and other changes in the way the school works are introduced without regard to the system as a whole. Adopting performance-based graduation requirements means accepting the notion of beginning with the end clearly in mind. Pedagogical, curricular, and system changes all come about in response to needs dictated by the graduation requirements. In our schools curriculum is modified when it is discovered that students lack the curricular opportunities necessary to meet the graduation requirements. Staff development arises out of the needs of teachers (the need to know more about alternative assessment, for example). And new schedules are evaluated for their effect on our ability to help students reach school goals. Performance-based graduation requirements form the foundation of systemic school change.

• Reverse the "tide of mediocrity." Performance-based education is not to be confused with the minimum-competency movement of the 1970's. Our schools have been motivated by a strong desire to increase academic standards. The graduation requirements encompass the knowledge, skills, and standards that equip students to thrive in the 21st century. Make no mistake, students will have to be truly well educated to graduate from either of our schools in the future.

Performance-based graduation requirements are not a panacea for all of society's ills. The systems in our schools are relatively new, and there remain in both schools many unanswered questions. What we do know is that the traditional time-based system is not working well for many students, and that a sound rationale exists for moving toward performance-based graduation requirements. We think that the answer to the question, "Should graduation be based on performance rather than seat time?" has become quite clear. □

Judy Westerberg is a mathematics teacher at Heritage High School, and Tim Westerberg is the principal of Littleton High School. Both schools are part of the Littleton Public School System in Littleton, Colo.

From Education Week, *Oct. 14, 1992*

27.

Enemy Of Innovation

Standardized tests dominate curriculum, shape classroom practice, sort students for tracking, and consume scarce time and money.

By Elizabeth Schulz

In 1987, a team of teachers, administrators, university faculty members, and technology gurus, bound by no tradition, gathered in St. Paul, Minn., to design a public school from scratch. Gone would be classrooms with forward-facing desks, 50-minute class periods, report cards, required textbooks, grade levels, and lengthy summer vacations.

Instead, this new school would be a place where students, working with teachers and parents, would identify their strengths, needs, and goals and create their own learning plan. Through projects that could reach into the community, students would find, organize, and make sense of information instead of just passively absorbing what the teacher and textbook presented to them. Home base for these real-world students would be nothing like the traditional school building: Instead of classrooms, students would work in labs, wired with video and computer networks, and in enormous cooperative learning spaces. Students would regularly demonstrate their progress in areas such as reading, writing, and problem solving through what they produce—written work, video presentations, speeches, and computer programs.

Dubbed the Saturn School, after General Motors' break-the-mold approach to making cars, the 4th-8th grade school opened its doors in 1989 exactly as the design team conceived it—except for one vestige of the factory-model school that it could not throw out: norm-referenced, standardized testing. As a result of

that one holdover, the true Saturn vision may not survive.

Immersed in the exciting business of learning to use their minds, Saturn students have not fared well in the trivial-pursuit world of standardized testing. Their scores in spelling and math computation declined significantly in the first two years. So, despite a shower of accolades from students, parents, and the steady stream of visitors, including President Bush, the school has been given the educational equivalent of the ultimatum, shape up or ship out: Get test scores up, teachers have been told, or the Saturn project will be terminated.

Factory-Model Schools Endure

Standardized testing and the traditional factory-model school were made for each other. In the latter half of the 19th century, the primary purpose of schooling evolved from producing an educated elite to training for industrial America the masses of immigrants and rural poor flocking to the cities. To fulfill that mission, schools were organized like assembly lines. Students would pass through grades, acquiring the nuts and bolts of knowledge as they progressed. The most basic skills would be taught first through drill and practice; material of increasing complexity would be added as students moved through school. Relying heavily on textbooks and locked into carefully sequenced curricula, teachers would efficiently transmit prepackaged information to docile students.

The public schools, Harvard University President Charles Elliot declared in 1908, should sort children according to their "evident and probable destinies." The standardized test was the scientific and effective tool for accomplishing that.

Both the factory-model school and the norm-referenced standardized test have proven remarkably durable, despite cognitive research that strongly suggests traditional schools don't teach the way children learn, and the tests don't effectively measure what students really know.

After years of study, researchers and psycholinguists have concluded that children constantly engage in a search for meaning, structure, and order and that schools should support their natural inclination to develop and test hypotheses about the world around them. The development of thinking skills does not have to wait until students have mastered the basics; in fact, higher-order thinking and the mastery of knowledge are inextricably linked and mutually supportive.

The new insights fostered by research in learning have nourished such grassroots initiatives as the whole-language movement and cooperative learning and have begun, especially during the past decade, to transform classrooms in hundreds of schools across the nation.

But, these new and more sensible approaches to teaching and learning are not likely to spread rapidly or endure for long if they are evaluated on the basis of student performance on the norm-referenced standardized tests that are dominant in American schools. Lauren Resnick, a cognitive psychologist and director of the Learning Research and Development Center at the University of Pittsburgh, says the best way to ensure the success of reform "is to attack directly what is one of the most powerful dampers to the kind of change we need: the current testing system."

"Talk to teachers who have caught on to the idea that the kind of teaching required in a 'thinking curriculum' is possible," Resnick says, "and then ask them what is the biggest barrier to it. Their answer every time is, 'Those standardized tests are coming, and I'm afraid my kids won't pass them.'"

Teachers are in a quandary: They are urged to take

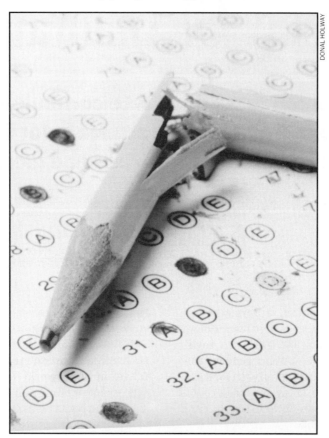

DONAL HOLWAY

risks and be innovative, but they know that their students will be judged on how well they score on tests that do not measure innovative teaching and learning. Monty Neill and Noe Medina of FairTest, a national watchdog organization, make this point in an article in *Phi Delta Kappan*. Research shows, they argue, that "teaching behaviors that are effective in raising scores on tests of lower-level cognitive skills are nearly the opposite of those behaviors that are effective in developing complex cognitive learning, problem-solving ability, and creativity."

It is not surprising that America's near obsession with standardized testing has had a chilling effect on education reform. In *Testing in American Schools*, a comprehensive 1992 report on the subject mandated by Congress, the U.S. Office of Technology warns that standardized testing is an enemy of innovation and that it threatens to undermine many promising classroom reform efforts. "Many teachers, administrators, and others attempting to redesign curricula, reform instruction, and improve learning feel stymied by tests that do not accurately reflect new education goals," the study states.

Principal Pamela Clark is one such administrator. Over the past six years, Clark transformed the program at Sunnyslope Elementary School in Phoenix. Her campaign to educate the whole child has included making sure each youngster has enough to eat, adequate medical care, and appropriate social services. She has linked the school with community service agencies, recruited a social worker for her students, and drummed up parent support in a highly transient, poor white neighborhood. As a result of the efforts, students are spending more time reading, writing, and learning from each other.

Parents are almost unanimous in their support for the school. Visitors tell Clark that Sunnyslope is on the cutting edge of school reform. Still, the principal is on the hot seat: Her students are not showing significant improvement on standardized tests. "We've taken the heat," Clark says. "People visit and say what we are doing is wonderful and developmentally appropriate, but we're sitting here with blistering fannies."

Pressure to raise test scores in groundbreaking schools comes in nerve-racking waves, observes Carole Edelsky, professor of curriculum and instruction at

Arizona State University. Every once in a while, she says, there is a "whole flurry of activity" during which teachers and principals have to defend themselves against accusations that they aren't really teaching anything because the test scores aren't going up. Things quiet down for a while, and then there is more turmoil, she says. "Then it's OK again."

This grip that standardized testing has on American education is bad enough, but what makes it even worse, many educators argue, is that the tests themselves are seriously flawed. Neill and Medina write: "The use of standardized test scores as the primary criteria for making decisions of any kind is reckless, given the erroneous assumptions that undergird standardized tests, the limited range of skills and knowledge that they measure, their limited reliability, their lack of validity, and the impact that race, ethnicity, family income, and gender exert on test results. Yet just such reckless decisions seriously damage student achievement, the curriculum, and education reform in many schools and districts."

Test Scores Treated as Magic Numbers

The nation's roughly 44 million students take a total of 127 million tests a year, for an average of three standardized tests a year per student, according to a report by the National Commission on Testing and Public Policy. A student sitting down with a No. 2 pencil in hand is most likely to encounter one of the "big four": the California Achievement Test, the Iowa Test of Basic Skills, the Metropolitan Achievement Test, or the Stanford Achievement Test.

These four, and many other smaller tests, share some common characteristics. They are standardized; that is, they ask the same questions across different populations to permit comparisons. They are norm-referenced, which means the items are chosen not to establish how much students know of what they ought to know, but rather to highlight differences in students so they can be ranked against others in their age group. And the tests are primarily multiple-choice items.

Standardized tests are marketed as scientifically developed instruments that objectively, inexpensively, and reliably measure students' skills. States and school districts are buying the pitch—and the tests. The national commission on testing estimates that test preparation and administration consumes some $100-million of tax money each year and that the nation's students spend a total of 20 million school days a year taking tests.

Although norm-referenced standardized tests came into use just after the turn of the century, they were not employed by a majority of the schools until the 1930s. And it was not until the 1960s and '70s that standardized tests began to be used widely. A position paper on the subject by the Association for Childhood Education International points out that few students who graduated before 1950 took more than three standardized tests in their entire school careers. But today's graduates will have taken up to 36 standardized tests during their 12 years of schooling.

The recent explosion in standardized testing was triggered during the 1980s by the reform movement's demand for greater accountability. To garner support for sweeping education initiatives and the bigger budgets needed to pay for them, lawmakers had to promise constituents that reforms would pay concrete dividends. Test scores, they said, would provide the proof. By 1985, two years after the publication of *A Nation at Risk*, new testing laws had been passed in 30 states. By the 1989-90 school year, 47 states had mandated standardized testing. And even in the three states that had not, many districts required standardized tests, according to the OTA report. In Pennsylvania, for example, 91 percent of districts used standardized tests though the state did not require their use.

"There has been a dramatic increase in the use of students' scores to hold school systems, administrators, and teachers accountable," the national commission on testing's report states. "Thus, not only has the volume of testing increased, but testing now looms more ominously in the lives of many educators and children, influencing what they teach and how, and what they learn and how."

Today, test scores are treated as if they were magic numbers. Newspapers rank schools and districts by their scores. Real-estate agents pitch test scores to sell houses. Some districts have even fired school administrators because of test results. The principal of the Dool School in Calexico, Calif., for instance, was fired when test scores fell the year after he implemented a whole language program.

"When you take a simple little number and elevate it to the status that it is elevated to in this particular culture, it is very destructive," says Peter Johnston, associate professor of education at State University of New York at Albany. "While people may say it's only one of a number of indicators, it happens to have a very privileged status."

One reason the public hold test results in such high esteem is that the government and education researchers routinely use them to evaluate the worth of schools and programs. Says Edelsky: "The prevailing wisdom—you have to search so hard to find someone who doesn't believe this—is that the way to evaluate the success of anything is via tests."

Federal funding—including funding for Chapter 1—is often contingent on schools meeting and maintaining specified achievement levels. Eva Baker, co-director of the National Center on Research on Evaluation, Standards, and Student Testing, says this may be the main reason so many states require testing. But even this use of tests can wreak havoc on reform. One of Arizona's top 10 schools, Granado Primary School, which has been recognized as a "Lead School" by the

National Council of Teachers of English, was forced to re-evaluate its program or lose its Chapter 1 funding, based on the result of standardized test scores.

The research community also puts a high value on standardized tests; in fact, the bulk of education research is based on test score data. When a researcher wants to know if a particular teaching method is effective, he or she usually compares test scores of students taught with the new method with those of a control group. If the students' test scores are higher, the researcher feels comfortable saying, unequivocally, that the approach is more effective. "It's such a tradition in educational research and in education," Edelsky says. "It fits so well a cultural search for and acceptance of quick answers."

Operating in a Schizophrenic World

Even some key members of the testing community believe that standardized tests have been accorded too much power. Gregory Anrig, president of the Educational Testing Service, for example, has decried the overuse and misuse of standardized testing. "When I was in the Army," he says, "the order was: 'If it moves, salute it. If it stands still, paint it.' Now if it stands still, we say, 'Test it.' "

He and others complain that tests are being used to make decisions they were never intended to make, determining the fates of students, teachers, principals, programs, and whole schools. Parents, researchers, policymakers, and the public have become almost totally reliant on test scores as a measure of achievement. Whether kids actually learn is less important than how well they do on tests.

"Do schools and policymakers ask too much of these tests?" asks H.D. Hoover, an author of the Iowa Test of Basic Skills for 25 years. "God, yes. I'm tired of seeing the tests I've worked on used for things they were never intended to do. They are using them to make policy decisions that the tests are not good at making."

The primary purpose of these tests, Hoover says, is to give parents and teachers an external view of a child's performance. Having been educated in a one-room schoolhouse in the Ozarks, Hoover knows how isolated schools can be. "Kids may be knocking the socks off the local district," Hoover explains, "but compared with other kids in the rest of the United States, how are they doing?"

But many teachers argue that standardized tests cannot provide reliable comparative data; test scores, they say, do not always give an accurate picture of students' accomplishments. "Tests measure what they were designed to measure: what goes on in a school that delivers a traditional textbook curriculum, with kids in packages of 30," says Saturn School project director Tom King. "They have limited usefulness in a school where kids are involved in activity-oriented, cooperative learning, out in the community, doing things with their hands and minds."

Saturn evaluator Hallie Preskill, a professor at nearby St. Thomas University, elaborates: "You can't test how students solve a problem with other people or by themselves, how they access resources, how they develop ideas, and so on."

Two students in Mark French's math class at Saturn illustrate the point King and Preskill are making. One, a learning-disabled student, didn't score well on standardized tests when she started with French two years ago and still doesn't. "But now," he says, "this person thinks for herself. She works in groups, she takes initiative, she is motivated, she is prepared. She is not shy and meek and afraid anymore." What's more, she can demonstrate academic achievement. "She can stand up in front of the class and give a speech," he says. "She can explain and demonstrate a computer project on geography."

The other student tests poorly but is an incredibly bright, meticulous worker. He doesn't get very far on the tests, the teacher says, because he is so careful and has difficulty with fine motor skills; he always has to go back and clean up his answer sheet. "But," French says, "he constantly challenges me as a teacher by what he can do in class, the questions he asks, and his thought processes."

Although Hoover acknowledges that tests can't reflect everything that goes on in a school, he insists that tests like the ITBS are a valid measure of a child's achievement. "People who say that you can only measure facts and low-level thinking on tests like these are just plain wrong," he insists. To bolster his argument, Hoover notes that the ITBS reflects the National Council of Teachers of Mathematics' new standards, which encourage the use of calculators, computers, and other tools to help illuminate the intricacies of mathematics rather than simply focusing on the mechanics of computation.

But when George Madaus, director of the Center for the Study of Testing, Evaluation, and Educational Policy at Boston College, looked at the leading norm-referenced tests—including the ITBS—in light of the national council's new math standards, he found that a vast majority of the test items tap lower-level knowledge. "The leading tests are peas in a pod when it comes to the standards," he says. "They don't reflect them."

And a survey of 1,000 math teachers conducted by the NCTM shows that teachers sense the dichotomy between the new math standards and the tests. Roughly half of the teachers said they emphasize rote drill and practice over problem solving and reasoning because the testing program in their state or district "dictates what they teach."

Teachers in the Westwood School in Dalton, Ga., say trying to innovate within the test-driven system has worn them out. Five years ago, while restructuring the school's curriculum, the teachers discovered "Mathematics Their Way," a program that teaches math concepts through the use of manipulatives.

At the time, Georgia had the most intensive standardized testing program in the country—starting in kindergarten. "The whole system of testing was mind-boggling," says 1st grade teacher Jimmy Nations, in a sweet southern accent that doesn't mask his anger. "The pressure on people was enormous."

Nations says he and his colleagues were operating in a schizophrenic world. "We were trying to do things that we believed as professionals were appropriate for our students," he says. "At the same time, we were being held to the very rigid state test, knowing our school's scores were going to be published and compared with other schools' scores."

Math Their Way teaches students math symbols only after they understand the concepts. Teachers at Westwood knew this approach made sense, but they didn't always use it because of the testing requirement. Nations vividly remembers one class where he drilled students on place value before they understood the concept because he knew they would need the lesson to answer questions on the test. "The little kids sat there with their eyes absolutely glazed over," he recounts. "I felt like a puppet."

The pressures Nations describes are common among teachers. A study cited in the OTA report sought to describe the effects of high-stakes testing on teaching and learning across the country. Seventy-nine percent of teachers surveyed said they felt "great" or "substantial" pressure by district administration and the media to improve test scores. Half of these teachers reported spending four or more weeks each year giving students practice exercises to prepare them for tests.

There is some evidence that tests most strongly influence the academic program in urban and predominantly minority districts. Johnston, who has been studying assessment—including standardized testing—for a number of years, has noticed that testing is most benign in the suburbs, where, by and large, the students do pretty well. "Tests in this case keep the public somewhat off teachers' backs," he says. But in urban districts, he says, the tests continually point out how things aren't going very well, so teachers feel more pressure to "teach the basics."

The same sort of thing happens within schools. Students placed in the lowest tracks are most apt to experience instruction geared only to multiple-choice tests, according to Linda Darling-Hammond, a professor of education at Teachers College at Columbia University. These students are rarely given the chance to talk about what they know, to read real books, to write, and to construct and solve problems in math. "In short," Darling-Hammond writes in an article in *The Chronicle of Higher Education*, "they are denied the opportunity to develop thinking skills that most reformers claim they will need for jobs of the future, in large part because our tests are so firmly pointed at education goals of the past."

The limitations of what standardized tests can measure in math have their parallels in language arts. For example, the advanced spelling skills of students in a whole language program in Washingtonville (N.Y.) Central School District didn't show up at all in their Stanford Achievement Test scores. Last year, students in six whole language classrooms and six traditional classrooms there scored below the 50th percentile. Yet when the children's spelling was assessed from their writing samples, three-quarters of the whole language students, but only half of the students in the traditional classes, spelled well. Many more whole language students than traditional students tried to spell words above their grade level, and they were more successful than the others when they did.

Tests can miss the mark in measuring reading ability, as well. Vivian Wallace, a teacher at Central Park East in New York City, was involved in a study with researchers at the Educational Testing Service. She says they wanted to see if students' scores on the state mandated test, "Degrees of Reading," correlated with teachers' assessments of the children's reading ability. Students who read very well do very well on the test, they found. But if a student does not do extraordinarily well on the test, there is almost no correlation between the student's score and his or her actual reading ability.

Ruth Mitchell, associate director of the Council for Basic Education, takes multiple-choice tests head on in her recent book, *Testing For Learning*. The only place multiple choice is found in the real world, she writes, is at the race track and on the driver's license test. The format promotes passivity, she argues; it asks students to recognize, not construct the correct answer. And the tests tend to measure what is easy to test rather than what is important for students to learn.

Not all educators agree with her analysis. Education professor Bob Linn of the University of Colorado has been doing research on assessment issues for more than a decade. Although he acknowledges that tests have been misused, he insists that multiple-choice questions can assess more than basic skills.

To a large extent, he says, the multiple-choice questions are fair and revealing. "If you look at the kinds of paragraphs kids are asked to read on the tests or glance through the math problems," says Linn, "you'll see that most questions are things that parents think their kids should be able to answer."

But many of the teachers who administer the tests year after year have become outraged with some of the items. Too many questions, they say, are divorced from meaning and context, unnecessarily tricky, and targeted toward the white, middle-class experience. They insist that the test items are not good examples of what a literate person can do.

Nations of Dalton, Ga., complains that the tests aren't in sync with the culture of his children and offers an example. A passage on the state-mandated test is about baking muffins—but his students don't even know what they are. So, every year he teaches an impromptu lesson on muffins. "Somewhere along the line, when I'm talking about cookies, I throw out the word 'muffin,' " he says. "When kids ask what that means, I act surprised and bring a muffin pan to school and bake muffins so that they know what muffins are when they see it on the test."

Cultural bias aside, one of the things that gall teachers most about standardized tests is the fundamental structure of norm-referencing. When creating a test, test companies choose items that will spread students out the most because that will enable them to assign percentile ranks most reliably. In effect, says Pittsburgh's Resnick, the most interesting items, the ones that everybody can do and ones almost no one can do, are thrown out.

"The worst you can imagine is throwing out those parts of the test that show kids and teachers that they can succeed," says Resnick. "You also don't want to throw out the ones that are making trouble because in a way those are setting the stars to reach for."

The end product of this sifting of multiple-choice items is a norm-referenced test on which half of the students score above the norm and half of the students perform below.

Many educators say that norm-referencing is blatantly incompatible with the belief that all students can learn. Even if all students learned everything we wanted them to, they point out, the tests assure that half the students will score below the mean. "That's an assumption that I could never accept as a teacher," says King of the Saturn School. "Why in the world would I want to devise a test where half my students were below average, condemned to failure status? Especially when the point is to teach all students; you want everyone to learn everything."

An Accident Waiting to Happen

As part of an ongoing reform project, teachers in the Hilton (N.Y.) School District defined what it means to be a good reader and writer. Good readers, they said, are people who enjoy reading, know what strategies to employ if they aren't successful, understand that the purpose of reading is for meaning, can relate things they read in different areas, know how to respond to what they read, communicate what they read, and share their perspective on what they read.

When they compared their list to the state-mandated test, they discovered that the test measures comprehension of texts, but none of the other things that they believe characterize a good reader.

They went through a similar process for writing, and only three out of their nine attributes for a good writer were even minimally addressed by the test.

When a school community decides what it values and the test doesn't look at any of these things, it is an accident waiting to happen, says Artis Tucker, language coordinator for the district.

The gap is likely to be most pronounced in schools that are heading toward reform. "Where change is being implemented," Tucker says, "often one set of values operates for instruction and another set of values operates for evaluation."

For many teachers struggling to improve their schools, this is the crux of the matter: Schools and society should decide what they value, find a way to truly assess students' progress in those areas, and then make that the criteria for whether a program is allowed to live or die.

At Saturn, these issues have not been resolved, and standardized tests are holding the program hostage. The staff has backed off from its bold vision and has devised a plan to raise test scores.

As King explains: "It's important that the school survive and become a model for change. To do that, it has to have a political base of acceptance. The community believes that standardized testing is critical, so it would be foolish not to make sure your kids do well—or the program disappears."

The Saturn staff has begun a program to familiarize students with test taking—a practice so widespread in this country that it has been given a name, "testwiseness." Students are told the test is important, given practice items, and instructed in the art of filling out bubble sheets.

The faculty is also reshaping the curriculum to match the standardized tests. For example, the school has abandoned the practice of teaching math through projects in other disciplines; now students are required to take traditional math classes that include drill and practice.

And an innovative plan to create mentorships and internships that link students with members of the community has been pushed to the back burner. What's more, teachers say that the pressure to raise test scores has discouraged them from taking their students out of the school building; they had hoped to structure their courses around the cultural, political, and business resources of St. Paul and Minneapolis.

"We've had to stifle our creativity," says one teacher, who asked not to be identified. "We haven't been able to focus on creating new and exciting learning opportunities for our students. What has taken precedence are classes that address facts and content that are going to be tested."

Saturn teachers are confident that the accommodations made to standardized testing will result in higher student scores. But some think the cost will be too high. The pity, says the teacher who asked for anonymity, is that "we are starting to look not so much like the school of the future; we are starting to look like a traditional school." □

From Teacher Magazine, *Sept., 1992*

28.

Basal 'Conspiracy'

Basal readers, along with their accompanying workbooks and worksheets, rob the nation's schools of quality education.

Commentary By Susan Harman

The publishers of elementary-school reading textbooks are engaged in what amounts to a conspiracy to deprive the nation's schools of quality education. The K-8 reading-instruction market—which is essentially the heavy, several-hundred-page textbooks (known as "basal readers") and their accompanying workbooks, worksheets, and other paraphernalia—is worth half a billion dollars a year. The big five sharers of this lucrative market are Macmillan/McGraw-Hill School Publishing Company (which owns Merrill, SRA, and Barnell Loft, who all publish basals); Harcourt Brace Jovanovich Inc. (which owns Holt Rinehart & Winston and The Psychological Corporation); Silver Burdett/ Ginn; Houghton Mifflin (which owns Riverside); and Scholastic Inc. Though Scholastic is the fourth largest of these suppliers of elementary-school materials, at the moment it does not publish a basal. Scholastic, however, has one foot in that market with a teachers' guide that "basalizes" the children's literature—real books—the company is famous for publishing, and its other foot is rumored to be poised over a basal of its own.

Whole city and county school districts, and even some states, adopt basal series for their entire districts and keep them for many years, because having once invested in a particular series, it makes fiscal sense to keep on buying the workbooks and other "consumables" that come with that series, year after year. So the choice of a basal program has a serious financial impact on both the school district and the publisher. Districts are notoriously conservative. No publisher can afford to introduce much innovation in its series because the risk of being too different from the other series and losing a large-city district or even a whole state (Texas, for instance) is too great. Therefore, each company's basals and workbooks look almost exactly like every other company's basals and workbooks.

All the series offer thick booklets containing end-of-unit tests of children's mastery of the vocabulary and skills covered in that unit. In some series, these tests are planned to be given as frequently as every two weeks. The tests are indistinguishable from the workbook exercises the children do all day as "seatwork" to keep them busy while their teacher listens to a group of seven or eight children take turns reading a paragraph each from the basal text (known as "round robin" reading).

Then, blighting the springtime of children, parents, teachers, and administrators alike, come the real tests, which are usually the sole means of holding schools "accountable" to the public. These machine-scored, norm-referenced, multiple-choice, indirect, standardized tests are held up as the "objective" check on teachers' "subjective," "soft" evaluations of their students. Teachers, after all, are said not to have the distance and detachment necessary to make these important judgments.

The tests, however, are all made by the very same

people who make the texts. The California Achievement Test (C.A.W.), the Comprehensive Test of Basic Skills (C.T.B.S.), and the S.R.A. are published by Macmillan/McGraw-Hill; the Metropolitan Achievement Test (M.A.T.) and the Stanford Achievement Test (S.A.T.) are published by Psych Corp, which is owned by Harcourt Brace; and the Iowa Test of Basic Skills is published by Riverside, which is owned by Houghton Mifflin. Of the big four basal publishers, only Silver Burdett does not publish a test. Where is the distance that supposedly sets these tests apart from the mere judgment of teachers?

Next, since the stakes riding on these tests are very high, teachers and parents naturally are under great pressure to prepare children to take them, and the publishers have come to their aid. Children as young as 3 years old are in test-preparation courses, and Macmillan/McGraw-Hill offers the two best-selling test-practice series: *Learning Materials* and *Scoring High*.

The company hasn't made the sales figures available, but 10 million *Scoring High* booklets have been sold during the last 10 years, and about 2 million students have used *Learning Materials* over the last four years. Not surprisingly, these practice workbooks resemble the tests in both format and content, up to and including some identical questions. Isn't this cheating?

Lately, of course, the publishers have read the blood on the wall, and are scrambling to stay alive by providing schools with "authentic" evaluation instruments. Both Riverside and Psych Corp have begun producing *New Tests*. Riverside's are structured like traditional reading lessons, and are scripted, like the basal teachers' guides. This shouldn't surprise us, since Houghton Mifflin owns Riverside. Psych Corp's Integrated Assessment System is just as teacher-proof as any basal reader. The company has provided us with hardware (cardboard portfolios, storage boxes, teachers' manual, training tape, and trainers' kit) and has done all the thinking for us. It has picked a few passages from real books and composed the rest; it has written the prompts; it has decided what to score and how; and—for a few dollars more—Psych Corp will score these "untests" for us. The scoring rubric reminds me of the "scoring criteria" for the family of Wechsler I.Q. tests, which are also published by Psych Corp, which is owned by Harcourt Brace.

As the publishers are well aware, these *New Tests* contain no items that the average teacher couldn't dream up on a slow day. They can't be machine-scored, and it is at least as easy to train teachers to score them reliably as it is to train publishing-company clerks.

But the *New Tests* are worse than just unnecessary. If the process of thinking up prompts that catch and hold students' attention, of deciding what is valuable enough to be taught and scored, and of establishing a "library of exemplars" has any relevance to teaching,

then it should be done by teachers. If we pay the publishers to make these important decisions for us, we will not only have forfeited the opportunity for exemplary and efficient staff development. We also will have paid in the loss of improved instruction.

So, whether the stuff that our children and their teachers spend time on is called "readers," "workbooks," "unit tests," "test preparation," "standardized tests," or "untests," it is really all the same thing, perpetrated and controlled essentially by three publishing companies.

This immensely profitable enterprise is based on a model of literacy acquisition that is pedagogically bankrupt. The result of decades of the basals' "controlled vocabulary," lists of words to be memorized out of context, artificial language, idiotic plots, trivial "comprehension" exercises, and scripted teachers' guides is generations of children who can bark at print, but don't know that what they read is supposed to sound like language and make sense.

We now know that children learn to read and write the way they learn to talk: They each invent the rules of grammar and usage; they do this in a systematic and predictable order; they do it from the top down—beginning with intention and then discovering syntax and vocabulary; and they do it within the embrace of a supportive community that responds to the meaning, rather than to the form, of their utterances.

It is the same with reading. The reading authority Frank Smith adapted the British adage "Take care of the pence and the pounds will take care of themselves" to describe literacy acquisition. His version is, "Take care of the sense and the sounds will take care of themselves." This news, however, has been slow to reach teachers, perhaps because their main source of new information (aside from the teachers' guides that accompany the basals) is the regional and local reading conferences they attend by the thousands. Many of the major speakers at these conferences are the university professors who write the basals, and whose conference expenses and honoraria are paid by their publishers. The basal companies have our teachers surrounded.

The three companies hold captive our nation's reading instruction. And since children, teachers, schools, and districts are "held accountable" essentially on the basis of test scores in reading alone, "reading" has become the curriculum that counts; so these publishers control not just reading, but the overwhelming bulk of elementary-school curriculum. Perhaps we could tolerate a benevolent conspiracy, if its attitude toward teachers were more respectful and its reading theory were sound. Since neither is the case, this conspiracy is malevolent and must be confronted. □

Susan Harman is director of evaluation for Community School District One, Lower East Side, in New York City.

From Education Week, *Nov. 13, 1991*

29

Remapping Geography

The goal of improving geographic education is to turn on the MTV generation to the dramatic change going on in the world around them.

Commentary By William B. Wood

For several years, leaders in education, government, and business have bemoaned our students' geographic illiteracy. In international comparative tests, we routinely rank at the bottom, with some students unable to locate even their own country on a world map. In response to this poor showing, geography has been designated one of five core subjects in which U.S. students must prove their competence by the year 2000.

Toward this end, a sampling of students will take geography tests in the 4th, 8th, and 12th grades beginning in 1994 as part of the National Assessment of Educational Progress. In almost every state, geographers are actively working with elementary and secondary school teachers in Geographic Alliances to develop creative resources and teacher-training programs in order to improve geography education. A National Geography Education Standards Project aims to set a high, but attainable, level of geography teaching at all grade levels across the country. Private organizations, such as the National Geographic Society and the American Express Company are sponsoring nationwide competitions designed to stimulate student interest in geography. And we have just celebrated an event called National Geography Awareness Week.

The success of this national full-court press to wipe out geographic ignorance, though, lies not with presidential proclamations, but with not-so-worldly students, their harried teachers, and their perplexed parents. Most parents remember geography as the boring recitation of state capitals; because they still remember that Pierre is the capital of South Dakota, they think they understand geography. So what is all the fuss about? We will just have a nationwide crash course on place names and country locations and, presto, we will no longer have to hang our collective heads in shame.

Unfortunately, many teachers went to the same schools as the parents and view geography with the same blinders. With many competing demands, there is little wonder that geography has tumbled down the list of daily teaching priorities. Some teachers may envision meeting the nation's geography-education goals by handing out homework assignments in which a map of the United States is filled in or the resources of some distant country are listed. Such "teaching" will fail to meet the national geography-education standards being promulgated and will assuredly condemn yet another generation of students to the scrap heap of geography.

Most students are probably unaware that a battery of geographic tests is in store for them. It's just as well; many could not care less how they compare with students in other countries. For them, a more pressing question is, "How is geography relevant to me?" If we cannot answer this reasonable question, we should resign ourselves to the continued bliss of geographic ignorance.

The goal of improving geographic teaching should

not be to ratchet up future test scores; rather, it is to turn on the MTV generation to the dramatic change going on in the world around them. Place-location drills and country reports copied from an encyclopedia will never bring a sense of excitement, discovery, and relevance that geography can offer. Here is my list of four "don'ts" for a sound and meaningful geographic education:

• Don't confuse geography with location memorization. Yes, it is important to know where places are (especially your own home), but it is even more important to understand why places are located where they are and how they got there. Some of the questions geography students should be encouraged to think and write about would include: how their parents or grandparents came to reside where they do; where items purchased on the latest trip to the grocery or department store came from and how they were produced and transported; and how land uses in their neighborhood, city, and county have changed over the past several decades. Most of these studies will transcend city, state, and national boundaries and give insight into the economic and political forces that influence our daily lives.

• Don't limit geography to map making and don't limit map making to geography. I've never met a geographer who didn't like maps, but they usually use them as a tool to help explain some issue or process. Cartography, the art and science of map making, is undergoing mind-boggling leaps with the assistance of computer-generated graphics. But more important than plugging into the latest mapping program is proper guidance on how to use a map to tell a story or solve a problem. Well-conceived and -designed maps enhance almost any social- or earth-science project, especially those dealing with environmental problems.

• Don't get hung up on defining geography. Like the blind men feeling their way around different parts of an elephant, geographers will each give a somewhat different account of what geography is or should be. Most would agree that one of geography's longstanding goals has been to bridge the schism between social and natural sciences. Long before ecology became a household word, geographers were studying the dynamic relationship between people and their environments. Geographers also tend to emphasize relationships between places and regions, which can be measured by flows of people, goods, and most important of all, ideas.

• Don't forget that geography is integrative. Of all social scientists, geographers are perhaps the most open to the theories and experiments of other disciplines. We geographers have to be more receptive because our curiosity about the world keeps leading us across the silly academic divisions that inhibit biologists from talking to historians. We'll talk to anybody who can help us better understand the complex interplay of people and places, particularly now when our world is faced with so many difficult challenges. More than any set of learned facts, this multidisciplinary perspective on issues that span from the local to the global is the most valuable geography lesson of all.

I am not a teacher, so these suggestions may be somewhat presumptuous, but as the geographer for the U.S. State Department I have a vested interest that the next generation of U.S. diplomats and businesspeople have a solid background in geography. Although improving the quality of geographic education will require a long-term commitment by parents, teachers, and students, they will find geography to be the most stimulating of subjects. And also the most fun. □

William B. Wood is the geographer for the U.S. State Department.

From Education Week, *Nov. 25, 1992*

30.

The Meaning Of 'First By 2000'

The science curriculum can no longer be isolated from the realities of our culture.

Commentary By Paul DeHart Hurd

'**B**y the year 2000, U.S. students will be first in the world in science and mathematics achievement." This is a national educational goal proposed by President Bush and 50 governors. I hope to give a glimpse of what it means for the reform of science teaching.

What's wrong with science education that needs fixing? Scientists and laymen alike have described precollege science education as a "fraud," "obsolete," "archaic," "outmoded," "dead end," and "largely irrelevant." The present curriculum is perceived as placing students and the nation at risk.

President Bush in America 2000 and in public talks described the need for a "new generation of schools" that set aside "traditional assumptions about schooling." He stated that the task will require "a quantum leap forward," with "far-reaching changes" that are "bold, complex, and long-range."

Since 1980, there have been over 350 national reports by panels, commissions, and committees lamenting the condition of education in America and calling for changes. The repeated reference to the year 2000 and the 21st century in these reports suggests that we are at the end of something in our history and entering a new era. This period is characterized by a globalized economy, a world community, and a shift from an industrial to a knowledge-based society.

The issue is not whether schools are doing well with the programs they have now, but how well they are meeting the demands of social change and life in the future. The call is for a new contract between schooling and society, one that will benefit children living in the next century as well as serve the common good and assure social progress. Schools are in bad shape only when compared with the new perspectives of schooling.

The educational-reform movement has gotten off to a misdirected start. Much of what has happened so far consists of hundreds of legislative mandates calling for structural changes in schools. Examples are lengthening of class periods and the school year, more rigor and more testing, and reorganizing existing curricula. These are actions that serve to reinforce traditional practices and can do more harm than good in terms of modernizing science education. The "radical changes" called for in America 2000 have yet to be found.

Let me return now to my main focus: the reform of science teaching within the guidelines of America 2000 and the national educational reports. Science has been a subject in the school curriculum since Colonial days. No one knows just how the goals and curriculum framework first came into being. But for 200 years it has been assumed that science can be understood only in the way scientists understand science and should be taught as science is practiced. The choice of subject matter has been that best suited to illustrate the theoretical structure of selected disciplines, including basic facts, principles, and laws. In turn, this approach requires students to learn the technical language and symbols that scientists use to communicate research findings to other researchers. As the knowledge in each field grows so does the vocabulary students are expected to memorize. The result is their understanding of science becomes more and more diluted.

Those who seek the reform of science education see the prevailing science curriculum as isolated from the realities of our culture and the lives of citizens. The charge is that the 200-year-old science curriculum is largely irrelevant and should be replaced by modern concepts of science. Although there is not a consensus on the full meaning of "modern science," there are identifiable characteristics. Since the turn of this century the old boundaries that separated astronomy, biology, physics, geology, and chemistry have faded away. Replacing them are thousands of fields of specialized research represented by more than 70,000 journals, 29,000 of them new since 1979. Old disciplines have also become hybridized: for example, biochemistry, biophysics, and biogeochemistry. Science is a singular noun, but it stands for a wide range of research fields, thought processes, and investigative procedures.

MARK ANDRESEN

During this century a marriage has taken place between science and technology. Robert Oppenheimer described the relationship as "two sides of a single coin." Today, science and technology operate as an integrated system for the production of new knowledge. Each fructifies the other. For example, research scientists conceived the laser, technologists used the discovery to develop a tool for bloodless surgery, the reading of bar codes on merchandise, and a hundred other uses. A technological achievement, the Hubble space telescope, is expected to make observations so extensive that temporarily our ignorance of astronomy will be increased by approximately 80 percent. It could take a century to determine what all the observations mean. Much of scientific research today is done by teams of scientists and technologists pooling their expertise and insights. Computers assist in recording and processing observations and in formulating interpretive models.

In this century, science and technology have become socialized. Research endeavors are now more socially than theory driven; witness the volume of research on finding ways of controlling the AIDS pandemic, improving agriculture, managing the natural environment, and maintaining a long and healthy life. Science and technology today lie at the center of our culture and economy, thus fostering enculturation as a goal of science teaching. The criticism of the present science curriculum is that it graduates students as foreigners in their own culture, unfamiliar with the influence of science/technology on social progress and public policy as well as on personal and cultural values. To meet the educational demands of a new century there is a growing conviction that the traditional purpose of school science, to educate students to be like professional scientists, is no longer tenable. The trend is to view science as public knowledge to be taught within a context of human affairs.

Although there has been little coherent progress in the reform of science teaching, new goals are being debated. One of these is the concept of scientific literacy. There are differences in how the concept is viewed. For some, scientific literacy is seen as a collection of facts everyone should know. But the essential character of science is not embedded in its facts. If one simply knew all the facts ever developed in the sciences, the person could only be rated intellectually sterile.

A different view of scientific literacy and one more in harmony with modern science relates to understanding the interactions of science and technology as they influence human experience, the quality of life, and social progress. A scientifically literate person recognizes the unique character of science knowledge and is aware of its values and limitations in cultural adaptation.

Scientific literacy is a cognitive perspective toward knowledge and includes the ability to distinguish science from pseudo-science, theory from dogma, fact from myth, folklore, and conjecture, probabilities from certainty, and data from assertions. Scientific literacy has become a cultural goal for living in a society characterized by achievements in science and technology. America 2000 describes a literate person as one possessing the knowledge and skills essential to exercising the rights and responsibilities of citizenship.

There has been a public outcry for schools to emphasize the development of higher-order thinking skills. The curriculum-reform movement of the 1960's stressed the teaching of inquiry or process skills. These are skills that have to do with how science/technology information is generated, classified, quantified, expressed, and interpreted. These processes are seen as lower-order thinking skills.

The appeal for higher-order thinking skills is related to the proper use of science knowledge in human and social affairs. These skills are for the most part qualitative. When science/technology information is brought into contexts where it is of service to people and society, elements of ethics, values, morals, bias, politics, judgment, risks, ideals, trade-offs, and aspects of uncertainty enter the thinking process. As science courses are now organized and taught in schools, higher-order thinking in the context of human experience is not an educational goal. America 2000 views these skills as essential in an era "in which citizens must be able to think for a living" and demonstrate responsible citizenship.

"Learning to learn" through one's own efforts has emerged as a primary objective for the teaching of science. America 2000 describes this goal as transforming the United States into "a nation of students." UNESCO reports that of the 141 nations now in the process of upgrading their science-education programs, "learning to learn" is the one goal common to all. This goal is particularly relevant to science education when we recognize that in the sciences all knowledge is forever tentative and new knowledge is being developed at an exponential rate. The present school science curriculum fails to recognize that science concepts have an organic quality, changing and developing as new insights and data are generated—an "endless frontier." Students are not taught how to access knowledge likely to be useful in their lives.

School science curricula as they now exist are oriented to the past, under the guise of basics. America 2000 and a host of national reports emphasize an education appropriate for the 21st century. To keep pace with changes taking place in our society as influenced by science and technology demands a future-oriented education. The purpose is not to predict but to help students shape the society where they will spend their lives. The National Committee on Education Reform in Japan states that all subject matter for schooling should be selected with the assumption that students will live to be 85 years old.

A future perspective to schooling entails providing students a sense of their place in the world and their responsibilities for human welfare and social progress. America 2000 speaks of this goal in terms of meeting the demands of living in the 21st century and assuming the obligations of responsible citizenship. It recognizes that an education viewed as preparation for the future calls for "revolutionary changes" in what is now taught and how.

A final note. Students were the first to recognize, in their own way, that the science they are learning is of little value for living and adapting in the modern world. The most common question students ask in science courses is "What good is all this going to do me?" The usual answer is: You will need to know this

---

The criticism of the present curriculum is that it graduates students as foreigners in their own culture, unfamiliar with science's influence on human affairs.

---

for the next test, or in the next grade, or in college. Rare is the teacher who answers the question in terms of human experience.

Yes, the United States can be first in the world in 2000, but not by tinkering with existing curricula and trying harder with 200-year-old teaching procedures that fail to recognize recent developments in cognition. In America 2000, the first task recommended for change is "to set aside all traditional assumptions about schooling and all the constraints that conventional schools work under." The next step calls for a "reinvention of schooling." The vision for science teaching is one of relating modern science and technology to the realities of our culture, to social progress, to life as lived, and to the values we hold. □

Paul DeHart Hurd is professor emeritus of science education at Stanford University.

From Education Week, *Sept. 16, 1992*

31.

Caught Between Two Worlds

An Indian father pleads with his son's teacher to recognize the boy's cultural tradition and personal accomplishments.

Commentary By Robert Lake (Medicine Grizzlybear)

Dear teacher,
I would like to introduce you to my son, Wind-Wolf. He is probably what you would consider a typical Indian kid. He was born and raised on the reservation. He has black hair, dark brown eyes, and an olive complexion. And like so many Indian children his age, he is shy and quiet in the classroom. He is 5 years old, in kindergarten, and I can't understand why you have already labeled him a "slow learner."

At the age of 5, he has already been through quite an education compared with his peers in Western society. As his first introduction into this world, he was bonded to his mother and to the Mother Earth in a traditional native childbirth ceremony. And he has been continuously cared for by his mother, father, sisters, cousins, aunts, uncles, grandparents, and extended tribal family since this ceremony.

From his mother's warm and loving arms, Wind-Wolf was placed in a secure and specially designed Indian baby basket. His father and the medicine elders conducted another ceremony with him that served to bond him with the essence of his genetic father, the Great Spirit, the Grandfather Sun, and the Grandmother Moon. This was all done in order to introduce him properly into the new and natural world, not the world of artificiality, and to protect his sensitive and delicate soul. It is our people's way of showing the newborn respect, ensuring that he starts his life on the path of spirituality.

The traditional Indian baby basket became his "turtle's shell" and served as the first seat for his classroom. He was strapped in for safety, protected from injury by the willow roots and hazel wood construction. The basket was made by a tribal elder who had gathered her materials with prayer and in a ceremonial way. It is the same kind of basket that our people have used for thousands of years. It is specially designed to provide the child with the kind of knowledge and experience he will need in order to survive in his culture and environment.

Wind-Wolf was strapped in snugly with a deliberate restriction upon his arms and legs. Although you in Western society may argue that such a method serves to hinder motor-skill development and abstract reasoning, we believe it forces the child to first develop his intuitive faculties, rational intellect, symbolic thinking, and five senses. Wind-Wolf was with his mother constantly, closely bonded physically, as she carried him on her back or held him in front while breastfeeding. She carried him everywhere she went, and every night he slept with both parents. Because of this, Wind-Wolf's educational setting was not only a "secure" environment, but it was also very colorful, complicated, sensitive, and diverse. He has been with his mother at the ocean at daybreak when she made her prayers and gathered fresh seaweed from the rocks, he has sat with his uncles in a rowboat on the river while they fished with gill nets, and he has watched and listened to elders as they told creation stories and animal legends and sang songs around the campfires.

He has attended the sacred and ancient White Deerskin Dance of his people and is well-acquainted with the cultures and languages of other tribes. He has been with his mother when she gathered herbs for healing and watched his tribal aunts and grandmothers gather and prepare traditional foods such as acorn, smoked salmon, eel, and deer meat. He has played with abalone shells, pine nuts, iris grass string, and leather while watching the women make beaded jewelry and traditional native regalia. He has had many opportunities to watch his father, uncles, and ceremonial leaders use different kinds of colorful feathers and sing different kinds of songs while preparing for the sacred dances and rituals.

As he grew older, Wind-Wolf began to crawl out of the baby basket, develop his motor skills, and explore the world around him. When frightened or sleepy, he could always return to the basket, as a turtle withdraws into its shell. Such an inward journey allows one to reflect in privacy on what he has learned and to carry the new knowledge deeply into the unconscious and the soul. Shapes, sizes, colors, texture, sound, smell, feeling, taste, and the learning process are therefore functionally integrated—the physical and spiritual, matter and energy, conscious and unconscious, individual and social.

This kind of learning goes beyond the basics of distinguishing the difference between rough and smooth, square and round, hard and soft, black and white, similarities and extremes.

For example, Wind-Wolf was with his mother in South Dakota while she danced for seven days straight in the hot sun, fasting, and piercing herself in the sacred Sun Dance Ceremony of a distant tribe. He has been doctored in a number of different healing ceremonies by medicine men and women from diverse places ranging from Alaska and Arizona to New York and California. He has been in more than 20 different sacred sweat-lodge rituals—used by native tribes to purify mind, body, and soul—since he was 3 years old, and he has already been exposed to many different religions of his racial brothers: Protestant, Catholic, Asian Buddhist, and Tibetan Lamaist.

It takes a long time to absorb and reflect on these kinds of experiences, so maybe that is why you think my Indian child is a slow learner. His aunts and grandmothers taught him to count and know his numbers while they sorted out the complex materials used to make the abstract designs in the native baskets. He listened to his mother count each and every bead and sort out numerically according to color while she painstakingly made complex beaded belts and necklaces. He learned his basic numbers by helping his father count and sort the rocks to be used in the sweat lodge—seven rocks for a medicine sweat, say, or 13 for the summer solstice ceremony. (The rocks are later heated and doused with water to create purifying steam.) And he was taught to learn mathematics by counting the sticks we use in our traditional native hand game. So I realize he may be slow in grasping the

methods and tools that you are now using in your classroom, ones quite familiar to his white peers, but I hope you will be patient with him. It takes time to adjust to a new cultural system and learn new things.

He is not culturally "disadvantaged," but he is culturally "different." If you ask him how many months there are in a year, he will probably tell you 13. He will respond this way not because he doesn't know how to count properly, but because he has been taught by our traditional people that there are 13 full moons in a year according to the native tribal calendar and that there are really 13 planets in our solar system and 13 tail feathers on a perfectly balanced eagle, the most powerful kind of bird to use in ceremony and healing.

But he also knows that some eagles may only have 12 tail feathers, or seven, that they do not all have the same number. He knows that the flicker has exactly 10 tail feathers; that they are red and black, representing

> # My son is not an empty glass coming into your class to be filled. He is a full basket coming into a different environment and society with something special to share.

the directions of east and west, life and death; and that this bird is considered a "fire" bird, a power used in native doctoring and healing. He can probably count more than 40 different kinds of birds, tell you and his peers what kind of bird each is and where it lives, the seasons in which it appears, and how it is used in a sacred ceremony. He may have trouble writing his name on a piece of paper, but he knows how to say it and many other things in several different Indian languages. He is not fluent yet because he is only 5 years old and required by law to attend your educational system, learn your language, your values, your ways of thinking, and your methods of teaching and learning.

So you see, all of these influences together make him somewhat shy and quiet—and perhaps "slow" according to your standards. But if Wind-Wolf was not prepared for his first tentative foray into your world, neither were you appreciative of his culture. On the first day of class, you had difficulty with his name. You wanted to call him Wind, insisting that Wolf somehow must be his middle name. The students in the class laughed at him, causing further embarrassment.

While you are trying to teach him your new methods,

helping him learn new tools for self-discovery and adapt to his new learning environment, he may be looking out the window as if daydreaming. Why? Because he has been taught to watch and study the changes in nature. It is hard for him to make the appropriate psychic switch from the right to the left hemisphere of the brain when he sees the leaves turning bright colors, the geese heading south, and the squirrels scurrying around for nuts to get ready for a harsh winter. In his heart, in his young mind, and almost by instinct, he knows that this is the time of year he is supposed to be with his people gathering and preparing fish, deer meat, and native plants and herbs, and learning his assigned tasks in this role. He is caught between two worlds, torn by two distinct cultural systems.

Yesterday, for the third time in two weeks, he came home crying and said he wanted to have his hair cut. He said he doesn't have any friends at school because they make fun of his long hair. I tried to explain to him that in our culture, long hair is a sign of masculinity and balance and is a source of power. But he remained adamant in his position.

To make matters worse, he recently encountered his first harsh case of racism. Wind-Wolf had managed to adopt at least one good school friend. On the way home from school one day, he asked his new pal if he wanted to come home to play with him until supper. That was OK with Wind-Wolf's mother, who was walking with them. When they all got to the little friend's house, the two boys ran inside to ask permission while Wind-Wolf's mother waited. But the other boy's mother lashed out: "It is OK if you have to play with him at school, but we don't allow those kind of people in our house!" When my wife asked why not, the other boy's mother answered, "Because you are Indians, and we are white, and I don't want my kids growing up with your kind of people."

So now my young Indian child does not want to go to school anymore (even though we cut his hair). He feels that he does not belong. He is the only Indian child in your class, and he is well aware of this fact. Instead of being proud of his race, heritage, and culture, he feels ashamed. When he watches television, he asks why the white people hate us so much and always kill our people in the movies and why they take everything away from us. He asks why the other kids in school are not taught about the power, beauty, and essence of nature or provided with an opportunity to experience the world around them firsthand. He says he hates living in the city and that he misses his Indian cousins and friends. He asks why one young white girl at school who is his friend always tells him, "I like you, Wind-Wolf, because you are a good Indian."

Now he refuses to sing his native songs, play with his Indian artifacts, learn his language, or participate in his sacred ceremonies. When I ask him to go to a powwow or help me with a sacred sweat-lodge ritual, he says no because "that's weird," and he doesn't want his friends at school to think he doesn't believe in God.

So, dear teacher, I want to introduce you to my son, Wind-Wolf, who is not really a "typical" little Indian kid after all. He stems from a long line of hereditary chiefs, medicine men and women, and ceremonial leaders whose accomplishments and unique forms of knowledge are still being studied and recorded in contemporary books. He has seven different tribal systems flowing through his blood; he is even part white. I want my child to succeed in school and in life. I don't want him to be a dropout or juvenile delinquent or to end up on drugs and alcohol because he is made to feel inferior or because of discrimination. I want him to be proud of his rich heritage and culture, and I would like him to develop the necessary capabilities to adapt to, and succeed in, both cultures. But I need your help.

What you say and what you do in the classroom, what you teach and how you teach it, and what you don't say and don't teach will have a significant effect on the potential success or failure of my child. Please remember that this is the primary year of his education and development. All I ask is that you work with me, not against me, to help educate my child in the best way. If you don't have the knowledge, preparation, experience, or training to effectively deal with culturally different children, I am willing to help you with the few resources I have, or direct you to such resources.

Millions of dollars have been appropriated by Congress and are being spent each year for "Indian Education." All you have to do is take advantage of it and encourage your school to make an effort to use it in the name of "equal education." My Indian child has a constitutional right to learn, retain, and maintain his heritage and culture. By the same token, I strongly believe that non-Indian children also have a constitutional right to learn about our Native American heritage and culture because Indians play a significant part in the history of Western society. Until this reality is equally understood and applied in education as a whole, there will be a lot more schoolchildren in grades K-2 identified as "slow learners."

My son is not an empty glass coming into your class to be filled. He is a full basket coming into a different environment and society with something special to share. Please let him share his knowledge, heritage, and culture with you and his peers. □

Robert Lake (Medicine Grizzlybear), a member of the Seneca and Cherokee Indian tribes, was an associate professor at Gonzaga University's School of Education in Spokane, Wash., when this was written.

From Teacher Magazine, *September 1990*

32.

Multicultural Perspectives I

Public schools should not struggle to represent every minority group in their curricula; they should reveal to students what they have in common.

Commentary By Willard L. Hogeboom

In June 1992, the New York State Department of Education made public a report by a panel of scholars and educators, calling for a revision of the state's public-school curriculum to better reflect racial and ethnic diversity. Although there were divisions among panel members, on the whole it went much better this time than it did last time.

It was in the summer of 1989 that a panel of minority educators and activists, also appointed by the state education department, issued "A Curriculum of Inclusion," which began with these words: "African-Americans, Asian-Americans, Puerto Ricans/Latinos, and Native Americans have all been the victims of an intellectual and educational oppression that has characterized the culture and institutions of the United States and the European-American world for centuries." This report was quickly denounced in newspaper editorials and columns and in television commentaries across the country.

"A Curriculum of Inclusion" was one of the opening salvos in the debate over multicultural education that has dominated the education scene in the ensuing two years. At first glance, multicultural education seems deceptively appealing: The curriculum, both at the secondary and college levels, is too "Eurocentric," too concerned with the European origins of American ideas, traditions, and people. Multiculturalists claim that the number of non-European Americans is increasing and that it is wrong to impose an alien European culture and heritage upon their children in the public schools. These children deserve a curriculum of their own culture and heritage.

Those who make these demands are ignoring some basic facts about American history and society. America has always been a multicultural society composed of diverse peoples who, willingly or not, left different cultures all over the world to come here. These people all made contributions to American history and culture. But the reality is that America has shaped its immigrants more than it has been shaped by them. The institution that has had the greatest role in that shaping has been the public school system. Public schools are the most common shared experience for most Americans, and the school system has been the key to the Americanization process. Its mission has been to preserve and transmit the common American culture to each generation of young Americans.

Many multiculturalists, historians, and educators reject the idea of a common American heritage. Yet, it is what has been taught to public-school students for generations—the story of how this country came to be; the people who came here willingly at great risk and sacrifice for a new life, and those who came here unwillingly as slaves; the people who made outstanding contributions to all areas of that society; the great domestic and foreign struggles and events.

Perhaps the most important part of that story is the uniqueness of America. Unlike other countries, it was and still is an experiment; America and its institutions were deliberately "invented" and often "re-invented" from time to time in an effort to get it right. Certainly America has had its defects, its mistakes, and, some would even claim, its crimes, but being American means being committed to keep trying to "get it right." Public schools are traditionally where young people, native and immigrant, learn what it means to be an American.

The multiculturalists are mistaken when they refer to Eurocentric culture or the white man's culture in the public-school curriculum as something alien to them. All children in the public schools, white, black, brown, or whatever color, have an equal claim to the American heritage simply by virtue of the fact that they are

> # It has long been a truism that the finest of art and learning is that which transcends 'race, class, and gender,' and touches everyone, regardless of background.

Americans. Certainly most of the American heritage derives from Europe because that's where the majority of people who settled this country came from. The early leaders were either educated there or received an education here patterned upon European education. It was therefore no accident, but neither was it a conspiracy, that our ideas and institutions derive from Europe. At the same time, in recent public-school curricula and textbooks, no secret is made of the fact that early Europeans were influenced by cultures to the east and south. Multiculturalists also make a mistake with their concern about the sources of the American heritage from a quantitative point of view. Obviously, the many different groups in America have not all contributed equally, but that does not diminish their right to an equal claim to the heritage.

This is what the Mexican-American writer Richard Rodriguez meant when he said: "I read the writings of 18th-century men who powdered their wigs and kept slaves because they were the men who shaped the country that shapes my life. I am brown and of Mexican ancestry . . . . I claim Thomas Jefferson as a cultural forefather."

This is what the African-American author Maya Angelou meant when she wrote of an incident when, as a young child, she had to give a recitation to her church congregation. She chose Portia's speech from "The Merchant of Venice" and later observed, "I know that

William Shakespeare was a black woman. This is the role of art in life."

The fallacy of the multicultural lists here is that they do not separate an idea or a work from its creator. It has long been a truism that the finest of art and learning is that which transcends "race, class, and gender," so that it touches everyone, and they can identify with it regardless of their background.

We have already had experience with the direction the multiculturalists want to take. In the 1960's, as the civil-rights movement gathered momentum, one of the issues was the missing African-American presence in the school curricula and textbooks. Other groups quickly echoed this complaint. Bernard Gifford, former deputy schools chancellor of New York City, has described his experience in trying to develop a history curriculum for the New York City schools that would satisfy the growing demands from different groups for inclusion: "We got a chapter on how blacks were systematically exploited by whites, a chapter on how Puerto Ricans were systematically exploited by whites, a chapter on how the Irish were systematically exploited by Germans, and so on. What we could not get was a chapter that said what held us together."

The path toward anything resembling comprehensive multicultural representation in the school curriculum is a dead end. Once you embark in that direction, more and more groups demand inclusion and the enterprise is doomed to defeat. More important is the fact that this approach is looking at the problem through the wrong end of the microscope. The various groups in America did not come here to bring and continue their old culture. America is not some gigantic Ellis Island in which a multitude of people are thrown together, each group to look out for itself and to carry on in its own way. Recent interracial and inter-ethnic strife in Eastern Europe, the Soviet Union, Canada, and the Third World should be lesson enough as to the consequences of the failure to get diverse people in a country to put national unity ahead of group interests.

Past experience has demonstrated that too often, programs designed for racial, ethnic, or gender identity end up setting one group against another. Students should be in public school classrooms as Americans, not African-Americans, Irish-Americans, Anglo-Americans, or any other type of what Teddy Roosevelt denounced as "hyphenated Americans." The proper function of the public schools should be to reveal to each student what he has in common with the other students in the classroom—that he is an American and that he is there to participate in the legacy of the common American heritage, as generations of students before him have. □

Willard L. Hogeboom is a freelance writer and a retired social-studies chairman from Babylon High School on Long Island, N.Y.

From Education Week, *Dec. 4, 1991*

33.

Multicultural Perspectives II

Multicultural education should focus not on whose canon to teach but on developing tools of inquiry in all children.

Commentary By Eleanor Armour-Thomas and William A. Proefriedt

The multicultural debate has generated bitter polemics within the educational community in which each side caricatures the positions taken by the other, or seizes on the most extreme formulations of the other in order to denigrate the wider position. With complex ideas, it's best to examine particular formulations and practices, rather than to argue with or blindly support slogans unhooked from any reality.

"One Nation, Many Peoples: A Declaration of Cultural Interdependence," a report of the New York State Social Studies Review and Development Committee, manages a formulation of the concept of multicultural education that is likely not only to find wide acceptance among educators but also to stimulate alterations in curriculum and teaching, and in the ways we assess students.

The committee, which included historians and practicing social-studies teachers, has accomplished this in one brilliant stroke by shifting the discussion from a crassly political emphasis to a more sophisticated educational one. The committee's conception of multicultural social-studies education is neither Afrocentric nor Eurocentric. It is learner-centric. The question is not "Whose canon to teach?" but "What competencies must students demonstrate in order to deal intelligently with the complexities of history and of contemporary society?" The committee wants to develop "multiple perspectives" in all students, helping them see historical and contemporary realities from a variety of viewpoints, helping them hear the voices of those who have previously been neglected in high-school history texts, helping them see that their own parochialism is not universal truth.

What critics such as Arthur Schlesinger and Diane Ravitch should take note of is that this particular conception of multiculturalism allies it with the best in the Western tradition of liberal education. Listen to John Stuart Mill, in his inaugural address at the University of St. Andrews, the quintessential 19th-century formulation of the purposes and practices of a liberal education:

"Look at a youth who has never been out of his family circle: He never dreams of any other opinions or ways of thinking than those he has been bred up in; or if he has heard of any such, attributes them to some moral defect or inferiority of nature or of education. What the notions and habits of a single family are to a boy who has had no intercourse beyond it, the notions and habits of his own country are to him who is ignorant of any other. . . . But since we cannot divest ourselves of preconceived notions, there is no known means of eliminating their influence but by frequently using different-colored glasses of other people: and those of other nations, as the most different are the best."

Instead of multicultural education being seen as a threat to the tradition of liberal education in the West, as it so often is, in the committee's formulation, it becomes an extension of that tradition. Defenders of liberal education over the years have offered different subjects as candidates for fulfilling its purposes. Mill, for example, in the argument quoted, was defending the teaching of ancient Greek language and of Greek culture for its capacities to free the individual from worshipping the idols of the tribe. The genius of a liberal education has resided not in its claims about the role of different subject areas, or texts within those subjects, but in its formulation of liberating educational purposes and in its insistence on the connection between those purposes and the ways in which subjects and texts are taught.

This document picks up on that tradition, insisting on the central role of the teacher and the approaches she takes to her subject matter. It identifies with John Dewey, with a number of current reform initiatives, and with more recent research on human cognition and learning in the approach it takes. The report points out the need to seek organizing principles and to sacrifice coverage of outlandish amounts of information for in-depth analysis of exemplary issues, and it calls for attention to developing the tools of inquiry in all young people.

The writers of the report, as much as they reflect theoretical ideas about educational purpose that have been a part of the discourse about teaching and learning since before Dewey, also reflect recent changes in this country brought about by the civil-rights movement and by more inclusive immigration laws enacted in the 1960's. Contemporary events have created new perspectives affecting educational policy. The report is a particularly thoughtful expression of and response to the new climate created by these events. It will not come as an idea from out of the theoretical blue to wise teachers and curriculum-makers who are already working within this kind of climate.

Attached to the report are papers by individual committee members that reflect the debate on the committee. Some of these criticisms miss the thrust of the main report. They argue, it seems to us, not with the report but with less sophisticated versions of multiculturalism. They fault the report for sacrificing the "unum" to the "pluribus." We find in the report an effort to get beyond the oppositional context of one nation, many cultures by an emphasis on increasing the inquiry skills of the learner. We see a healthier society emerging from an educational approach that encourages critical reflection on the values we share in common as well as on those that make different groups unique, from an approach that allows students to hear the voices of previously silenced groups and to incorporate the voices into their understanding of the American past from an approach that will allow them to critically examine the claims and counter-claims of textbooks of the past, and the political debates of the present. We see the need for a new understanding of American culture that recognizes its continuous re-invention, and recognizes also the many contributors to its sometimes clashing ideals. A fundamental assumption of multiculturalism is that the larger culture of the United States emerged from a synthesis of the experiences of diverse cultural groups. The report argues that the task of students learning about our society is to critically examine these experiences in their historical context.

While some of the comments on the report missed the mark, we found Nathan Glazer's balanced criticism particularly thought-provoking. He argues that we need to recognize that the various ethnic groups in this country are not "monolithic and unchanging realities." Different ethnic groups and individuals and classes within these groups have undergone different degrees of assimilation and intermarriage, taken different attitudes toward their own ethnicity and toward the American culture of which they are a part. Mr. Glazer points out that these groups are not something "hard and unchanging." But he worries that both teachers and students will want something more definite. He worries that presenting ethnicity in this oversimplified fashion might have the effect of inhibiting the processes of change that have helped us create a common society. We feel that blatant racism has been the most serious inhibitor of the creation of a common society, but that Nathan Glazer's caveat is nonetheless helpful. The silliness surrounding the attribution of different learning styles to different ethnic groups with the admonition to teach each accordingly seems to us a product of this penchant for oversimplification.

Implicit in this new educational agenda is the notion that all students, regardless of economic and cultural backgrounds, can be inducted into the habits of critical thinking. The achievement of this lofty goal will depend not only on the commitment of individual teachers, but also on the availability of curriculum resources and on extensive opportunities for teacher education. We hope that budgetary constraints will not get in the way of local districts' and colleges' offering courses to teachers that will help them teach the culturally complex history of the United States to all their students. □

Eleanor Armour-Thomas is an educational psychologist in the school of education at Queens College, City University of New York. William A. Proefriedt teaches philosophy of education at Queens College.

From Education Week, *Dec. 4, 1991*

Where We Will Teach

"The education system we have was designed to give most students only 'basic' skills. It produces a curriculum that sacrifices understanding to 'filling' in the blanks on the worksheet. It rewards those who follow rules rather than those who produce results, so it naturally generates bureaucratic behavior. Valuing efficiency more than quality, it operates by sorting students out rather than educating everyone to a high standard. Every feature of this system reinforces all the others. That is why it is so durable, so resistant to change. That is why successful schools succeed *despite* the system, not because of it. 'Breaking the mold' means breaking this system, root and branch."

—*National Alliance for Restructuring Education*

34.

Standing In The Winds Of Change

Entrenched in decades of tradition, fraught with inequities and inefficiencies, America's educational system is under assault.

The American public school system is vast and complex. In more than 80,000 schools in some 14,600 districts, more than three million teachers and administrators labor nine months a year to educate 44 million students. One out of every three Americans is directly involved in the educational system—as students, employees, parents, and policymakers. The rest of us are indirectly involved as taxpayers.

The states have the ultimate responsibility for education, and most of their constitutions guarantee children a thorough and efficient education. State departments of education, overseen by the chief state school officers and boards of education, set standards, provide funds, and regulate schools. How heavy-handed the state is in discharging its responsibility differs from place to place and from time to time.

The states delegate the day-to-day operation of schools to local boards of education, most of which are elected. There are some 97,000 local school board members—the nation's largest group of elected officials—and membership on the school board is often the entry point for a political career. The school boards hire superintendents to manage the districts, and the superintendents, in turn, appoint principals to run the schools. Because power flows from the top downward, teachers have organized into labor unions to bargain for rights and benefits.

The total operating budget for public precollegiate education totaled $252 billion for the 1992-93 school year, or about $5,800 per student. Most of the money—49 percent—comes from states; education is the largest single expenditure in state budgets. Another 45 percent comes from local communities, mostly from prop-

erty tax assessments. The federal government's share of the bill comes to about 6 percent—mostly in the form of categorical support for the poor and the handicapped.

Because the local funding for schools comes from property taxes, schools in affluent districts spend more money to educate a child than schools in poor school districts. In the state of Texas, for example, the annual per-pupil costs range from about $2,500 in the poorest districts to more than $19,000 in the wealthiest. To counter such gross inequities, states have developed complicated and arcane funding formulas, but the problem remains. Where a child lives determines, perhaps more than anything else, what quality of education she or he will get.

For the past quarter century, the war over equitable funding has been fought in courts throughout the land, from California to Kentucky, from Texas to New Jersey. In Kentucky, the state supreme court in 1989 took the ultimate step of declaring the entire educational system to be unconstitutional and ordered the legislature to rebuild it from scratch. And the battles rage on. In early 1993, school-finance litigation was under way or pending in 27 states.

Widespread funding inequities, the vastness of the public school system, and its uniquely American tradition of local governance assure that the system will be diverse and variegated. Schools meet the needs and reflect the standards of individual communities. The tiny, all-white rural school perched amid endless cornfields of Iowa is utterly different from the predominantly minority school amid the slums of Los Angeles. And neither bears much resemblance to the "shopping mall" high schools of the affluent suburbs of Baltimore.

But despite their apparent diversity, the nation's public schools are alike in profoundly important ways.

Each is part of a system shaped early in this century to prepare the rising generations for their roles as workers and citizens. The way schools are organized and operated today still largely reflects the dominant theory of that period. Industrial managers, seeking ever greater productivity, created factories in which the work was divided into a series of simple tasks and workers were assigned, in assembly-line fashion, to those tasks. Well-trained managers and supervisors oversaw the process to make sure that each worker played his assigned role quickly and efficiently. Frederic W. Taylor, the engineer and inventor known as the father of scientific management, was the architect of this method and Henry Ford made a fortune applying it to the production of his Model T's, boasting that one could buy any color one wanted as long as it was black.

The factory became the model for the school, which was expected to produce workers with the basic skills needed for the factory. The curriculum was divided into segments, the knowledge within courses was divided into components, the day was divided into periods. Students sat in rows, while teachers imparted information under the watchful eye of the principal.

That system has proved exceedingly durable in education even as it falls from favor in corporate America. In most of the nation's schools, teachers still stand before rows of students dispensing information, often culled from textbooks and fed back to them in work sheets. The day is still divided into periods, and bells ring every 50 minutes or so signaling students that the time has come to leave geography and move on to algebra. Teachers remain essentially isolated from each other, with little influence over decisions affecting curriculum and instruction. With increasing frequency, students are required to take norm-referenced, multiple-choice tests that sort them by scores along a curve. And because schools are tax-supported and thus accountable to the public, the test results are made public periodically to show how well the school is doing.

While the essence of schooling in America is much the same today as it was 70 years ago, the demands on schooling have changed to reflect the needs of a larger society in flux. To survive and succeed in the complex world of tomorrow, citizens will need higher-order thinking skills in addition to basic skills. Shopkeepers' arithmetic is not sufficient for today's high school graduate. High levels of literacy are virtually a prerequisite for success in the increasingly sophisticated workplaces of the nation. Factory assembly lines are increasingly manned by robots; tomorrow's front-line workers will need at least a high school education and will be expected to solve problems, make critical decisions, and perform at high levels.

Moreover, the society has begun to realize that it can no longer afford to waste its human resources—not if the United States is to succeed in the fierce competition of the global marketplace. We have long embraced the idea that all children have a right to all of the education they are capable of. But our definition of the pledge has evolved over the years. For a long time, "all children" did not really mean all children. The schoolhouse door opened slowly to minorities, the poor, the non-English speaking, the handicapped. And though it surely was not intended to be, the concept of "all the education they are capable of" has been a rationale for limiting educational opportunity, particularly for the disadvantaged, according to some perception—often flawed—of ability. The current system is characterized by the perverse practice of tracking.

Today, we have nearly achieved the "universal" part of universal education. Indeed, it is our success in bringing virtually all children into our schools, that exposes so painfully how far we have yet to go to fulfill the other half of the promise—the "education" part. Here, too, our definition has evolved: A central concept in the current reform movement is that almost all children have the capability to learn at a high level. That will require changes in schooling even greater than those that were necessary to open the doors to all children. And the years ahead will doubtlessly see protracted battles over quality and equality.

Launched in 1983 with the publication of the federal report *A Nation at Risk*, school reform has evolved into a concerted effort to overhaul the entire system of American education. Systemic reform involves changing every part of the educational enterprise essentially at the same time: teacher preparation and professional development, the use of time and space, the content and organization of the curriculum, student assessment, and the roles and relationships of educators and students. If systemic reformers succeed, schools will be substantially restructured, financed differently, and held accountable using a new system of rewards and penalties.

Reformers face a formidable challenge. The current system is well-entrenched; people, when surveyed, acknowledge that the system is troubled but generally believe that their own schools are doing OK. The vastness and complexity of the system pose an awesome barrier to change. The great majority of the teaching force has not been persuaded to accept, nor adequately prepared to implement, the sweeping and deep changes being proposed.

On the other hand, the reform movement has lasted longer than any in history. Much of the power structure has joined the cause: the White House, Congress, the governors, the chief state school officers, the national business leadership, and the heads of many of the nation's educational and professional associations. A number of states are well along in their efforts to reinvent their schools. And thousands of schools throughout the country are involved to one degree or another in piloting reform ideas.

The education question of the 1990s will be the outcome of the classic conflict between an irresistible force and an immovable object. □

35.

Boards Of Contention

The embodiment of democracy, school boards come under attack as defenders of the status quo.

By Lynn Olson and Ann Bradley

Last year, Massachusetts abolished the nation's first elected school board. After more than 200 years, Gov. William F. Weld replaced the popularly elected Boston School Committee with one appointed by the mayor. "The citizens of Boston will be disenfranchised by this legislation," Governor Weld acknowledged at the time. But, he said, Boston's schools are "in desperate need of fundamental change."

Rarely in American history have school boards been under such attack as they are today. A combination of forces—ranging from ever-increasing state mandates to rapidly changing demographics—is threatening an institution once considered synonymous with public education in the United States.

In districts throughout the country, radical governance ideas are taking hold. Parents can now choose from among public schools; schools have been empowered to decide whom to hire and how to spend their money; and the operation of entire school districts has been delegated to private management firms.

As the educational landscape shifts, most agree that the roles and responsibilities of school boards cannot possibly remain static. While some think the existing system of local lay governance of education is still viable, increasingly vocal critics are calling for major changes. Some would even scrap it for an entirely revamped infrastructure.

"Local school boards are not just superfluous; they are also dysfunctional," Chester E. Finn Jr., professor of education and public policy at Vanderbilt University,

has written, expressing one of the strongest views on the subject. "At a time when radical alterations are needed throughout elementary-secondary education," he argues, "school boards have become defenders of the status quo."

Far from contributing to education reform, those who agree with Mr. Finn contend, school boards have become part of the problem: mired in minutiae, prone to meddling, resistant to change, and victims of public apathy toward elected government in general. "I think a lot of school boards are taken in by the bureaucracy and fed the kind of information that would please them," says Herbert J. Walberg, professor of education at the University of Illinois at Chicago, who recently edited a book on school boards. "And since many of them are essentially amateurs and only stay on the board for two or three years, it's a way that the education establishment maintains the status quo."

Mandates From Above

School boards clearly are caught in the crossfire of rapidly changing ideas about who should control public education in America. The 1980's witnessed an unprecedented growth in state control of education, as one state after another passed comprehensive reform laws dealing with everything from who should teach to the content of the curriculum.

State financing for public education is also approaching local expenditures for the first time in history. According to the National Center for Education Statistics, the state share of K-12 schooling is now 46.4

percent; the local share is 47.6 percent.

In the midst of such changes, local school boards have been largely left out of the debate. "Local boards never, ever caught the big picture of what needs to be done in public education," says Howard M. O'Cull, the executive director of the West Virginia School Boards Association, "and because they haven't, states simply moved the policy arena to the state capital."

By 1986, a national poll of school-board members revealed high levels of anxiety about the intrusiveness of state policymaking into local affairs. The potential creation of national standards and assessments in education could undermine local control still further.

Threats From Below

Hemmed in by mandates from above, boards have also found themselves challenged from below. If schools are empowered to make decisions about everything from budgets to curricula—as many reformers now advocate—then boards of education cannot continue to exercise the same kind of direct management they have in the past.

The rapid growth of parental-choice plans that enable youngsters to attend schools outside the district in which they live has also threatened the sovereignty of school boards.

Finally, the competing demands on boards from a host of special-interest groups have resulted in what some observers describe as "policy gridlock," in which boards cannot possibly satisfy all parties. Today, argues Michael W. Kirst, a professor of education at Stanford University, education is being pushed and pulled by a "fragmented, elevated oligopoly" in which no one group has central control of the schools.

Although every state but Hawaii delegates substantial authority to local boards of education, critics charge that their role is becoming irrelevant.

Worse yet is the sense that school boards have lost their internal compass: that clarity of vision and purpose needed to steer an organization. John Carver, an expert on private and nonprofit boards, describes local lay governance of education as a "vast wasteland."

Even if board members received the best training and acquired the discipline to fulfill their roles as defined by conventional wisdom, he argues, "they would simply have learned to do the wrong things better than before." As most currently operate, Mr. Carver and others assert, school boards are collections of misguided talent that have the potential to accomplish far more for children than they do.

"It's not that many people see school boards as being damaging to the system," says Sharon Brumbaugh, a former board member in Pennsylvania, "but that they are not using the powers they have to bring about change in the system."

With 97,000 members on more than 14,500 public-school boards in the United States, it is hard to generalize about their functioning. The diversity is astounding. They range from the seven-member New York City Board of Education, whose system has more students than there are residents in the state of Rhode Island, to the five-member school board in Big Cabin, Okla., whose entire 58-student population could fit into a few New York City classrooms.

In 1990-91, 54 percent of the nation's school districts enrolled fewer than 1,000 students each. But 4 percent had enrollments exceeding 10,000—accounting for nearly half of all students nationwide. "The danger," Theodore R. Sizer, a professor of education at Brown University, cautions, "would be for policymakers to generalize about anything as diverse as school boards and, on the basis of that generalization, suggest policy."

Most of the national media attention paid to school boards in the past couple of years has focused on the turmoil and dissension on big-city boards of education. In 1990, 20 of the 25 superintendencies in the largest urban districts were vacant. And media accounts blamed the problem, at least in part, on the personal agendas, daily meddling, and inappropriate behavior of board members.

"Constructive board-superintendent relationships have collapsed almost entirely in many large cities," contends a report on school boards released this month by the Twentieth Century Fund and the Danforth Foundation. Most big-city superintendents now last less than three years on the job.

Mired in minutiae, prone to meddling, resistant to change, and victims of public apathy, school boards have become part of the problem.

Others attribute the turnover to the dwindling size and quality of the selection pool from which urban executives are chosen. They argue that some tension between school boards and their chief executive officers is inevitable, since lay boards must rely on these professionals for most of their information. When board members show any inclination to pursue data on their own, they are quickly accused of meddling. And the lack of trust on both sides can become explosive.

In some cities, evidence of patronage and the sheer inability of school boards to deliver a solid education to their charges has led to unprecedented measures. The

Jersey City and Paterson districts were taken over by the state of New Jersey, and their existing school boards were disbanded. Boston University assumed operation of the Chelsea, Mass., schools.

And in Chicago, a coalition of advocacy groups pushed through a reform law that created popularly elected councils of citizens, parents, and teachers at each school, gave them the authority to choose principals and spend discretionary funds, and significantly curtailed the powers of the central board.

The vast size of many urban school systems—combined with the daunting social problems they face—has led some scholars to suggest they are simply ungovernable. "It's not that board members are malevolent," says John E. Chubb, a senior fellow at the Brookings Institution. "It's that they're responsible for a task that is basically impossible."

But the problems with school boards are not limited to urban areas. Governance changes in the Kentucky

---

Education is being pushed and pulled by a 'fragmented, elevated oligopoly' in which no one group has central control of the schools, argues one professor.

Education Reform Act of 1990 were directed mostly at the nepotism and political agendas that characterized the state's overwhelmingly rural boards of education.

And many of the nation's suburban school boards are struggling with the same societal dilemmas as their urban neighbors: a growing population of students from racial, ethnic, and language minorities; a rising incidence of drug, alcohol, and sexual abuse; and a split and fractious community.

In many parts of rural and small-town America, however, the perception remains that school boards still work. In these relatively homogeneous communities, where most people know their board members personally, the sense of crisis is far removed.

"I'm just as happy as I can be when I go back to the Dakotas that the school board is as it's always been," says William H. Kolberg, the president of the National Alliance of Business and a vocal critic of urban boards of education.

But it is precisely the self-satisfaction of some of these suburban, rural, and small-town school boards that worries other observers. "The biggest problem in some of [these] districts is the complacency about the

quality of the educational policies they have," Mr. Kirst of Stanford says.

In a 1989 survey of 1,217 school-board presidents across the United States, the vast majority gave low marks to American public education as a whole. But four out of five awarded grades of A or B to the public schools in their own communities. Presidents in small districts and rural areas gave lower ratings to a variety of reform proposals than did their peers in urban and suburban areas.

"If our criteria are a need for risk-taking, moving away from the status quo, educating the public to understand that reform does not mean going back to what we think worked yesterday," says Jacqueline P. Danzberger, an expert on school boards at the Institute for Educational Leadership, "then I think that you find the problem in a lot of kinds of communities."

Despite such charges, there have been few systemic studies of school boards. Thomas A. Shannon, the executive director of the National School Boards Association, says "there is absolutely no substantiation" that public-school boards have stood in the way of reform. "That sort of statement is 'scapegoatism' at its ultimate."

And Susan Fuhrman, the director of the Center for Policy Research at Rutgers University, says, "I think there are many boards, maybe even a majority of boards, that function the way one would advise them to function, and that is to set general policy and delegate a great deal to the central administration."

But if school boards are supposed to focus on broad educational issues, they devote a surprising amount of time to detail. Critics charge that many boards have become so hopelessly enmeshed in the minutiae of running their districts that they fail to see the forest for the trees.

A study of board minutes from all 55 school systems in West Virginia between 1985 and 1990 found that boards spent only 3 percent of their time on decisions related to policy development and oversight. At least 54 percent was spent on administrative matters, according to Mr. Carver, who has been advising the state's legislature on governance issues. At most, 42 percent was spent on decisions that could legitimately be called "governance."

"There is no reason to expect the West Virginia data to differ substantially from that which would be obtained elsewhere in the country," Mr. Carver writes. "Recent articles in the literature suggest that the same disease afflicts all."

Mr. Carver argues that boards have become a "staff member one step removed," rather than the policymakers they claim to be. "The fact that you can't hire a janitor or a teacher without a board taking action is ludicrous," he says.

The report by the Twentieth Century Fund cites the "tendency for most boards to 'micro-manage'" as the biggest problem they face. A curriculum audit of the

District of Columbia schools last year found that board members made 181 written requests for information in 1991—many of them "frivolous."

Another indication of how bogged down boards can become in trivia is the number of times they meet. The Tucson, Ariz., school board met 172 times in one year. In such instances, superintendents spend most of their time servicing the board.

"If boards continue to involve themselves in some of the day-to-day things that should be left to the administration," warns Edward Garner, the former president of the Denver Board of Education, "I don't think boards as we know them today will exist in the future."

The tendency of boards to become immersed in fine print has also blurred the distinction between policy and administration and led to repeated charges of "meddling." In Seattle, recalls Reese Lindquist, the president of the local teachers' union, one board member decided to take the school system's budget home and analyze it in detail. "It was so large, she had to get a custodian to help carry it to her car," he laughs. "Any school-board member who thinks that's their responsibility is in serious trouble."

Other observers charge that the focus on minutiae discourages corporate executives, university presidents, and other prominent citizens from serving on school boards. "If a body is legally responsible for everything that goes on in a school district, and if the majority of people who come on a board do not have strong, broad, and deep leadership backgrounds," Ms. Danzberger of the I.E.L. says, "then the tendency is to get into everything."

'Dictated by the State'

In fairness to boards of education, much of the trivia on their agendas derives from state mandates. West Virginia requires local boards to approve all student field trips. The California education code requires boards to approve all student expulsions. "My own experience is that our board meetings are dictated almost entirely by the state," says Ms. Fuhrman, who recently completed a term as a public-school board member in New Jersey.

Such dictates, she adds, take time away from discussions about education and prevent boards from focusing on long-range planning. "We don't have the freedom to spend as much time discussing education issues as I would like to," laments Leslie Q. Giering, an 18-year board member in the 1,100-student Bloomfield Central School District in New York State.

"When I was first elected, we met once a month," she says. "Then we began having two meetings a month, with the idea of discussing education at the second. But we find that other things take up our time."

In fact, if most citizens attended an average school-board meeting, they would probably be underwhelmed by its content. But few bother. Turnouts in school-board elections typically hover between 10 percent and 15 percent of registered voters. And most board meetings are sparsely attended.

Such visible citizen apathy about a purportedly valued institution bodes ill for the future. If school boards "embody everything that everybody says they love and want in citizen-based control of a major institution," notes Neil R. Peirce, a political writer, "why is it that scarcely any of us bother to vote for any of the people who sit on these committees?"

Board watchers also describe a steady decline in the number and quality of people willing to run for election. According to Ms. Danzberger, about one-third of board members turn over each year. And it is getting harder and harder to replace them. The most noticeable drop has been among corporate executives willing to devote energy to board business.

Ward Politics

In large cities, the practice of electing board members from discrete electoral districts—rather than from the city as a whole—has helped increase the representation of minority populations. But it has also encouraged board members to focus on neighborhood constituencies and on narrow interests, rather than on the system as a whole. In some instances, critics charge, boards function more as neighborhood employment agencies than as service providers.

A 1986 study by the Institute for Educational Leadership found that board members elected by subdistrict were subjected to greater constituent pressure and voted more frequently in response to specific interest groups than did members who were elected at large.

The rise of special-interest politics and the number of socially explosive issues that boards face have further impaired their functioning. "School boards face a whole set of controversial decisions for which there is no satisfactory answer for at least half of the citizens," says Denis P. Doyle, a senior fellow at the Hudson Institute, an Indianapolis-based think tank. "Abortion and drugs and condom distribution and AIDS and alcohol and sex abuse and poor academic standards—the list is daunting. And school boards, understandably, feel some compulsion to try to step up to the plate and hit the ball. But it has produced a really dysfunctional system in many large cities."

In essence, critics assert, some boards have confused representation of the public with the public interest. "What we've really created," says Phillip C. Schlechty, the president of the Center for Leadership in School Reform, "is a situation in which the board thinks its job is to be responsive to the community." Whereas, he continues, "its job is to be accountable to the community and responsive to parents and kids."

Historically, school boards were made independent

from local government to insulate education from the corrupting influence of politics. But critics argue that school boards in many instances have become conduits for political influence. And in contemporary society, the separation is often a disadvantage.

Today, many families have health, social, and emotional problems that cannot be solved by the schools alone. Yet, the continued structural isolation of school boards has made it difficult to coordinate activities on behalf of youngsters and their families.

West Virginia requires local boards to approve all student field trips. The California education code requires boards to approve all student expulsions.

"School boards were not set up to deal with social services and linkages to outside agencies," notes Sandra Kessler Hamburg, the director of education studies at the Committee for Economic Development. "And, frankly, a lot of them just feel overwhelmed."

When school boards do try to meet their students' nonacademic needs, they can get burned. Sue Cummings, the former chairman of the Roseville, Minn., school board, was ousted by voters in the conservative, heavily Catholic community outside the Twin Cities after she supported spending $10,000 of the district's money to help a health clinic locate in the town.

"It is so hard for me to describe the tenor of the community during that time," she says. "They went wild, they were so emotional. People who were my avid supporters called me and said the Catholic priest had condemned me to hell from the pulpit by name."

The reaction also stemmed, she says, from the community's refusal to acknowledge the circumstances of its children's lives, such as teenage pregnancy. "People kept saying, 'No, no, no, this doesn't happen here,'" she recalls. "The statistics clearly show that these are not inner-city problems, that small towns in Minnesota have every bit the same problems."

The ability of 92 percent of public-school boards to raise taxes and spend money as they see fit has further strained the relationship between local boards of education and their municipalities. Some mayors and town-council members charge that this fiscal independence has produced waste and inefficiency and decreased school boards' accountability to the public.

Despite such criticisms, few think that Americans will do away with school boards entirely. The notion that local schools are the public's to run is deeply ingrained in the American psyche. "The board really is the arm of the community," says Margaret Myers, a member of the Muscatine, Iowa, school board. "I truly believe, the longer I have been involved in this, that there is real value in this kind of openness, doing business in open meetings, so that everyone in the community has the opportunity, whether they take it or not, of knowing and understanding what is going on in their school district—which is funded by their tax dollars."

Without the help of school boards and their communities, adds Mr. Shannon of the N.S.B.A., real reform will not occur. "School-board members are the gatekeepers of reality," he argues. "It's one thing to have a good idea. It's quite another to take it and put it in a form that works and that can be paid for." □

From Education Week, *April 29, 1992*

36.

Blurring The Line

Unusual new arrangements are making it harder to tell the difference between public and private schools.

By Lynn Olson

It used to be so simple: The government paid for—and provided—public education. Today, though, new approaches are challenging the government's once-unquestioned role as the direct provider of school services.

Public vouchers are being used to pay for private education, and private firms are operating public schools. Some corporations are underwriting design efforts to transform the public schools; others are investing in for-profit enterprises to compete with them. In Minnesota, a private school has even opted to become public. "The whole notion between public and private is being blurred," John Witte, a professor of political science at the University of Wisconsin at Madison, observes.

What all these new arrangements have in common is a belief that the entrenched public school bureaucracy will not change willingly or quickly. To crack it open, reformers are proposing a variety of private and quasi-private alternatives that rely on the use of market forces and competition to do what they say regulation and exhortation have not.

While such experiments are not in abundance, their acceptance is growing rapidly as policymakers become more desperate to fix the schools. Given this more congenial climate, new twists on how to deliver public education are surfacing with increased regularity.

Looking to the private sector is hardly unique to education. One of the most popular books in policymaking circles this year is *Reinventing Government: How the Entrepreneurial Spirit Is Transforming the Public Sector*. The book, written by Ted Gaebler and David Osborne, advocates making government services leaner and more effective, in part by throwing them open to competition, funding outcomes rather than inputs, and giving employees an incentive to earn money, not just spend it.

Proposals to contract out the operation of state prisons or citywide garbage collection, for instance, reflect the belief that private firms can accomplish results more quickly and efficiently than public institutions can.

"People don't think government works," says Susan Fuhrman, the director of the Consortium for Policy Research in Education at Rutgers University, "so we have to reinvent it, which to many people means making the public more private or making government more market-driven."

Private School Choice

In education, the purest reflection of this view can be found in the growing popularity of school-choice plans that employ vouchers. Vouchers would provide parents with a government subsidy to spend at public, private, or parochial institutions. Schools that failed to lure clients would shape up or lose funds.

The assumption is that competition and parental pressure—not government regulations—would spur public schools to improve. Advocates also portray vouchers as a way of empowering low-income families. "So these are our beliefs, then, that parents, not the government, should choose their children's schools," President Bush said last June in announcing a proposal to provide $1,000 scholarships to low- and moderate-income families to spend at public, private, or parochial schools.

The momentum behind vouchers has grown rapidly during the past year, in part because of the choice issue's prominence in the Presidential campaign. In addition, ballot initiatives to provide families with private school choice will go before voters in Colorado in November and in California in June 1994. And lawmakers in at least six other states are expected to consider voucher legislation this year that would include private and religious schools.

Individuals and corporations in at least half a dozen cities have forged ahead with privately funded voucher schemes of their own. The scholarships are available to a limited number of low-income families on a first-come, first-served basis.

Patricia A. Farnan, the director of education and empowerment policy for the American Legislative Exchange Council, a bipartisan organization of state lawmakers who advocate free-market principles, predicts that it is only a matter of time before a state passes a voucher law that encompasses private and parochial schools. "And when you see one go," she maintains, "you'll see four or five head right behind it."

A Common Mission?

Critics charge that vouchers would violate the constitutional separation of church and state (90 percent of private schools in the United States are religious); drain money from financially strapped public schools; and segregate children on the basis of race, ability, and income.

"What markets are best at are allocating scarce goods," argues Marc S. Tucker, the president of the National Center on Education and the Economy. "And they do it on the basis of ability to pay. Any way you look at it, the incentives for suppliers are to leave the kids with the greatest needs in the lurch."

But the more fundamental concern is that vouchers would destroy America's long-cherished notion of the "common school": a place where children from all walks of life come together to become productive, participating citizens. "The purpose of education in our schools is to get all kids in our country to learn to live with and respect each other, just as much as it is about learning algebra and Shakespeare," asserts Albert Shanker, the president of the American Federation of Teachers. "We're destroying something that is extremely important as the glue of the United States of America."

Opponents also contend that vouchers undermine the notion of education as a public good and the willingness of taxpayers to support it. In an article written for the conservative Heartland Institute, Myron Lieberman, a longtime critic of the public schools, advocates that government reconsider its role as both the funder and provider of education through a process

known as "load shedding"—"or ending government's role as funder of most or all educational services."

Unhappy with drivers' education? Mr. Lieberman asks. Stop funding it. Perhaps, he suggests, high school teachers could be offered 20 percent pay raises, contingent upon eliminating the 1st grade. If parents pay for education from their own pockets, Mr. Lieberman contends, they will be more likely to insist on performance from their children and from their schools.

Seven out of 10 Americans said they would back a government-supported voucher system that included public, private, and parochial schools.

Only those who cannot afford to pay should get government help. "Just saying that something's a public good," he says, "it doesn't follow that government should pay for it. That's just a non sequitur."

Despite the heated charges of critics—and the organized opposition of the education establishment—public support for private school choice appears to be mounting. In a Gallup Poll released by the National Catholic Educational Association last month, seven out of 10 Americans said they would back a voucher system that included public, private, and parochial schools. Sixty-one percent said they would support such a proposal even if "some of the tax money now going to public schools" was used to pay for it.

Minority and urban residents voice some of the strongest support. A poll released this summer by the Washington-based Joint Center for Political and Economic Studies found that two-thirds of black respondents were not familiar with the concept of school choice or vouchers. But, of those who were, 88 percent favored choice. "I think mobilization of the low-income community offers breathtaking possibilities," argues Clint Bolick, the litigation director of the Institute for Justice, a public-interest law firm that supports choice.

The only state-subsidized voucher program now in place is in Milwaukee, where scholarships are available to send up to 1,000 low-income children to private, nonsectarian schools. A coalition of conservative Republicans and inner-city parents, under the leadership of State Rep. Polly Williams, a black Democrat, pushed for the legislation.

The Institute for Justice has also filed lawsuits on behalf of low-income parents in Los Angeles and

Chicago, who are demanding vouchers to send their youngsters to private schools on the grounds that their public schools are unsafe, inadequate, and lacking in parental control and involvement. Mr. Bolick said at least one other lawsuit will probably be filed this year.

Whether the marketplace would enable families to purchase something better for their money—or just something different—is open to debate, research on the differences between public and private schools indicates. Mr. Shanker maintains that differences between the academic performance of public and private school students are minimal, and that neither group performs well on international comparisons of achievement. "What we're going to do is allow kids to escape from one set of schools that are lemons to go to another set of schools that are lemons, solely on the basis of phony reputation," he complains.

In contrast, many scholars have concluded that, at least on some measures, private school students substantially outperform their public school peers, even once differences in family income are taken into account.

The continued debate highlights how little is known about how an educational market would actually work and what its benefits would be. In 1990-91, the first year of operation for the Milwaukee program, seven nonsectarian private schools enrolled 341 students from low-income families. Although attendance was higher among students participating in the program than the systemwide average—and parents reported greater satisfaction with and involvement in their children's education—little progress was shown in test scores. And many of the children who enrolled in the program the first year did not return. Mr. Witte, who evaluated the Milwaukee program for the state, advocates that the experiment be continued, but not expanded.

Other studies indicate that even modest competition may produce some results. Since 1985, when Minnesota began permitting high school students to take courses at local universities at taxpayer expense, the number of Advanced Placement courses offered by area high schools has increased dramatically.

'At the Margins'

The question, many agree, is how much competition is enough to spur the system to change, without bringing it crashing down. Few think that there would ever be enough private-sector alternatives to actually replace the public schools. "Even if you doubled the capacity of private schools," notes Sandra Kessler Hamburg, the director of education programs at the Committee for Economic Development, "you'd still have 80 percent of the kids going to the public schools."

"We really are talking about movement from public to private schools at the margins, at least in the short term," Mr. Bolick of the Institute for Justice agrees.

"But that may be all that it takes to make dramatic changes in the public system."

Some think the voucher movement will fade as political power shifts in Washington. But others think the pressure for vouchers will continue. "We have tough economic times, and we're likely to have them for a while, so the public wants to save money," Mr. Shanker asserts. "And they're going to find these things very appealing." The union leader also worries about a powerful "education-industrial complex" getting behind the voucher movement.

Mr. Shanker's reference is to the Edison Project: a $2.5 billion undertaking designed to launch a nationwide chain of for-profit K-12 schools in the fall of 1995. The project is the brainchild of the media entrepreneur Christopher Whittle. And it is backed by Whittle Communications L.P., Time Warner Inc., Philips Electronics N.V., and Associated Newspapers Holdings Limited.

Mr. Whittle refers to the project as a "private mission with a public goal." The aim, he asserts, is to create schools so powerful and innovative that they will have a real influence on the structure of public education in America. As part of that pledge, he has promised to provide a significantly better education at no more than the nation's average per-pupil cost, or about $6,300 a year.

One appeal of approaches like Edison's, advocates say, is their ability to start from scratch, instead of trying to fix the schools that exist. "There are real benefits from wiping the slate clean and thinking fresh about education," says John E. Chubb, a member of the project's design team and a prominent choice advocate.

Similar thinking undergirds the work of the New American Schools Development Corporation. Business leaders launched the privately funded foundation in 1991, at Mr. Bush's request, to underwrite the development of "break the mold" schools that public educators could emulate. The 11 design teams that have received grants include both for-profit and nonprofit corporations, as well as public school systems. But one of the most striking differences between the two initiatives has been their ability to raise money.

NASDC, which relies primarily on corporate donations, has only raised $50 million of its $200 million target. The Edison Project, which its backers hope will yield a substantial return on their investment, began with $60 million just for research and development.

Market Not There?

Much of the distrust of Mr. Whittle's project centers on his motives, which many contend are chiefly pecuniary. The suspicion is that, when children's needs are weighed against the bottom line, students will suffer. The checkered history of many profit-making trade schools has fed such concerns.

Critics also allege that Mr. Whittle is counting on

government vouchers to make his project financially viable. The average parochial school in the Milwaukee area, Mr. Witte of the University of Wisconsin notes, charges slightly less than $800 a year in tuition. In contrast, the Edison Project is banking on the willingness of parents to pay up to $6,300 per student. "If you're competing at the bottom," Mr. Witte says, "you can't charge that much, unless, of course, you get vouchers. Without the public subsidies, I don't think the market is really there."

If Mr. Whittle cannot take advantage of vouchers, others suggest, he could still make a profit by contracting out his services to public school districts and educating their students for them.

Public schools have habitually contracted out the operation of such ancillary services as food delivery, transportation, and maintenance. In recent years, however, the practice has widened to encompass the very heart of the educational enterprise: educational management and instruction. The most prominent example is Education Alternatives Inc. In July, the Minneapolis-based, for-profit management firm signed a $140 million contract with the Baltimore school district to operate nine public schools. And it is conducting a feasibility study to see if it can manage several more in Palm Beach, Fla.

Education Alternatives has promised to assume day-to-day management of the Baltimore schools, train

---

'Just saying that something's a public good,' says author Myron Lieberman, 'it doesn't follow that government should pay for it. That's just a non sequitur.'

---

their teachers in new instructional methods, and produce measurable gains in student achievement, all for the same amount of money normally alloted to the schools: about $5,550 per student.

In the Midwest and Southwest, Ombudsman Educational Services has contracts with more than 60 school districts in Arizona, Illinois, and Minnesota to provide alternative education for students who are having trouble in traditional school settings. James P. Boyle, the president of the for-profit firm, is a former public school teacher and administrator. But he argues that trying to change the system from inside is "harder than changing the Vatican."

The freedom to operate outside the bureaucracy, Mr.

Boyle says, has enabled his firm to break the "course and content" gridlock in education, providing services both less expensively and more effectively. Students in Mr. Boyle's program attend school only three hours a day, enabling each teacher to work with several groups of youngsters. The program is computer-assisted, individualized, and outcome-based. The cost is between $3,000 and $4,000.

According to Mr. Boyle, the trick has been to cut out the "frills." "We don't have baseball and football and cafeteria and band and art," he says. "Particularly now, as school systems are hitting the wall in terms of funding, a cost-effective alternative becomes more attractive."

Education Alternatives is also hoping to improve education—and make a profit—by trimming wasteful expenditures in some areas up to 25 percent.

'An Extension of the District'

Such private entrepreneurs claim that they are a part of the public school system, not a threat. "We've always thought of ourselves, and still do, as an extension of the district," Mr. Boyle says. "If the district doesn't like us, they can fire us."

"Our mission," a company brochure states, "is not to replace or compete with the public schools, but to be the public schools—and to fundamentally change the dynamics of the learning environment."

In Miami Beach, where Education Alternatives is entering the third year of a contract to operate the South Pointe Elementary School, Principal Patricia Parham describes the experience as "100 percent totally positive." "People get so excited about somebody coming in that's a private group," she says. "But we buy textbooks from private companies; we have consulting services all the time from private companies. It's really no different."

That view is not shared by teachers and paraprofessionals in Baltimore, who last month boycotted the company's training sessions to protest its replacement of unionized workers with college-educated interns.

Critics warn that, as with vouchers, the cost savings from contracting out to private firms may be overstated. In its first five years, Education Alternatives has failed to turn a profit or generate a positive cash flow.

In 1990, Chelsea, Mass., turned over the operation of its school district to Boston University, a private institution. Three years later, Mr. Shanker notes, the system has lost its superintendent, the university official who was monitoring it, and many of its principals. And student performance has still not improved. "And they say, 'Well, we couldn't do much, because we haven't gotten enough money,'" he says. "They sound just like the public schools."

Others argue that, because the ultimate responsibility for contracts still rests with local school boards, the idea does not extend far enough. "If boards of education are the problem," says Phillip C. Schlechty, the president of the Center for Leadership in School Reform in Louisville, Ky., "then the fact that they contract out to someone else doesn't change the fact that you have a board of education."

In part because contracting out is less threatening, however, many predict that the practice will expand over the next few years. "Such experiments are going to become much more widespread than they are," forecasts Paul T. Hill, a senior scientist with the RAND Corporation. "Still," he adds, "it would be big news if there were 3,000 such schools in five years."

To many reformers, the private sector's allure lies in the ability of an outside agent to challenge the status quo. But some suggest that the same dynamics could be produced wholly within the public system. They advocate a third course: a new kind of school that would reflect many of the principles of high-performance businesses but that would remain public.

Under these proposals, groups of teachers or others could operate their own schools under a "charter," or contract with a school district. Unlike traditional schools, charter schools would enjoy total autonomy in budget, staffing, curriculum, and teaching methods. And they would be exempt from nearly all state and local regulations.

In return for such freedom, charter schools would have to specify the goals they want students to achieve and how they would measure progress. "It's simple," says State Sen. Ember Reichgott of Minnesota, who last year sponsored a successful measure to enact the nation's first charter-schools law. "No results; no charter. Teachers trade away regulation for results, and bureaucracy for accountability."

Although Minnesota was the first state to pass such legislation, others are close behind. Gov. Pete Wilson of California signed a charter-schools bill last month that allows for the creation of up to 100 such schools. Similar bills have either been introduced or are being considered in Colorado, Connecticut, Florida, Massachusetts, Pennsylvania, and Tennessee.

Such schools, Ms. Reichgott argues, reward innovation, empower teachers and parents, and increase choices—all within the context of public education. "I view charter schools as an incentive to enhance public education," she says. "I view vouchers as an incentive to abandon the public schools."

'A Strong Consensus'

All the talk about privatization and other new arrangements has spurred educators to think more openly about less radical options. Public school choice, an anathema in education circles a decade ago, has become widely accepted.

But the real question, many school-improvement devotees argue, is how to free most public schools to become more efficient and effective. "I don't hear much talk out there about that side of things," complains Christopher T. Cross, the director of education programs for the Business Roundtable.

Nonetheless, continued pressure from advocates of more radical approaches is forcing the public schools to diversify and to create a greater variety of options of their own. "I think over the next five or 10 years, you're going to see all these creative bursts of how you package public education," California's superintendent of public instruction, Bill Honig, predicts. "They'll still be public schools, and they'll still be subject to standards, but there'll be a lot more variety. I think that's a pretty strong consensus." □

From Education Week, *Oct. 7, 1992*

37.

Bureaucratic Gridlock?

'Entrepreneurial spirit' is the key to ending the centralization that is hamstringing schools, argues a new book.

By Lynn Olson

Forcing schools to compete for students and money holds the key to unlocking the "bureaucratic gridlock" that hamstrings public education, a newly released book argues. *Reinventing Government: How the Entrepreneurial Spirit is Transforming the Public Sector* maintains that confidence in government has fallen to record lows because top-down, centralized bureaucracies—including those that characterize public education—cannot meet the demands of a rapidly changing information society.

"They accomplished great things in their time," the authors David Osborne and Ted Gaebler write, "but somewhere along the line they got away from us. They became bloated, wasteful, ineffective." The solution, they argue, is to make fundamental changes in the way government provides services—ranging from schooling to health care—based on a new set of principles, which they dub "entrepreneurial government." Such governments are "lean, decentralized, and innovative," the authors write.

"They are flexible, adaptable, quick to learn new ways when conditions change," Mr. Osborne and Mr. Gaebler argue; they turn their employees free to pursue goals with the most effective methods they can find. And they rely on market forces—such as competition and customer choice—to get what needs to be done as inexpensively and creatively as possible, the authors contend.

Most of the education examples in the book will be familiar to educators. They range from the public school choice programs in Minnesota and East Harlem in New York City to the local school councils in Chicago. Less familiar are some of the other public-sector experiments that could also apply to education.

In Visalia, Calif., for example, the elimination of line items within departmental budgets freed managers to shift resources as needed. Departments there can also keep what they do not spend from one year to the next. And employees can keep 30 percent of any savings or earnings that result from their ideas.

What ties such experiments together, the authors suggest, are 10 principles that, taken together, can solve the "major problems we experience with bureaucratic government." According to Mr. Osborne and Mr. Gaebler, entrepreneurial governments promote competition between service providers; empower citizens by pushing control out of the bureaucracy and into the community; measure the performance of agencies by outcomes, not inputs; and are driven by their missions, not by rules and regulations.

In addition, they redefine their clients as customers and offer them choices; prevent problems before they emerge; put energy into earning money, not just spending it; decentralize authority and embrace participatory management; prefer market mechanisms to bureaucratic mechanisms; and focus not just on providing services, but on catalyzing all sectors—public, private, and voluntary—into action to solve a community's problems.

The authors' ideas are already taking hold in the policy community. Mr. Osborne, a journalist who introduced readers to some of his ideas about entrepreneurial government in an earlier book, *Laboratories of*

Democracy, is an adviser to the governors of Massachusetts and Florida and to the Presidential campaign of Gov. Bill Clinton of Arkansas. He also helped draft the comprehensive school-reform legislation put together by Massachusetts Democrats that calls for creating "charter" schools. Mr. Gaebler, a former city manager of Visalia, is the president of a public-sector management-consulting firm.

Although the authors advocate that public agencies adopt all 10 principles to increase productivity and effectiveness, they assert that the key lever for strengthening education is competition. "[O]nly competition can motivate all schools to improve," they write, "because only competition for customers creates real consequences and real pressure for change when schools fail." They propose allowing parents to choose among public schools; making it easier for parents, teachers, and others to create new schools on a contract or voucher basis with a school district; and closing schools that do not attract students.

"You can push for all the good management reforms in the world," Mr. Osborne said in an interview recently, "but if you don't have a hammer that makes it absolutely necessary that principals and teachers embrace these management reforms, it's not going to go anywhere." He added, "Competition, it seems to me, is that hammer."

Most existing choice programs have not gone far enough, he said, because inferior schools still get filled up "with kids whose parents aren't paying attention," rather than being closed down. In addition, he said, barriers that prevent new schools from emerging rapidly and easily stunt true competition. "No market is really competitive if there isn't open entry," Mr. Osborne said.

'Contract' Schools

For that reason, the authors support the creation of new kinds of public schools, including charter schools. But they reject turning all education over to the private marketplace in the form of vouchers, because of the risk that it would lead to "extreme segregation" by income. Parents who could afford the added cost would increase the value of the vouchers, Mr. Osborne predicted, while those who were poorer would not. "It's just like the auto market," he noted. "If you can afford it, you buy a Volvo. If you can't, you don't."

If their principles were applied in their purest form, Mr. Osborne and Mr. Gaebler suggest, boards of education would get out of the business of operating schools. Instead, they said, many different organizations, including teachers, colleges, or businesses, would run public schools—on something like a contract or voucher basis.

Schools would have to compete to attract students. But they would be relatively free to define and pursue their own missions, within minimum state and local regulations. Teachers would work for the school, not the school district, under the vision offered by Mr. Osborne and Mr. Gaebler. And each school would be free to set its own budget, keep any funds it did not spend, decide whom to hire and fire, how much to pay them, and whether to use performance bonuses. Tenure would be eliminated.

The result would be to separate what the authors call "steering"—or policy direction "rowing"—or the actual provision of services. "[G]overnments preoccupied with service delivery often abdicate this steering function," they note. "School boards get so busy negotiating contracts and avoiding layoffs that they forget about the quality of their schools."

Under their hypothetical scenario, state govern-

> ## 'Only competition can motivate all schools to improve,' they write, 'because only competition for customers creates real pressure for change.'

ments and school boards would set minimum standards, measure performance, enforce such goals as racial integration and social equity, and establish the financing mechanisms to ensure that their standards were met. States would also measure and publicize a much broader array of results than they do now. In addition to test scores, such measures might include evaluations of student work; satisfaction surveys of parents, students, and teachers; dropout and college-placement rates; academic and nonacademic honors won by students; and evaluations by neutral panels of expert observers.

Parents would use such information to choose their schools. And states and school boards would solve any problems that arose by changing the rules and incentives, not by meddling in administration.

According to Mr. Osborne, public education is already further along than other public sectors in implementing some of the principles he and Mr. Gaebler advocate, including participatory management and community empowerment. "We've gotten through the 'more, longer, harder' model," he said. "We've gotten through the traditional medicine—throwing money at the problem. And the debate is about how you restructure." □

From Education Week, *Feb. 19, 1992*

38.

Does 'Public' Mean 'Good'?

Has public education kept its halo of moral superiority through nostalgia, wishful thinking, and shrewd public relations?

Commentary By Chester E. Finn Jr.

As the debate over school choice heats up once again, in the halls of Congress and in many state capitals, a favorite gambit of defenders of the status quo is to damn such changes as "sure to undermine public education" or "bad for the public schools."

They always stress the word "public," for that adjective is believed to carry moral weight and political suasion. It is meant to evoke patriotism and decency, Thomas Jefferson and Horace Mann, goodness, virtue, and the American way. If "public" education is inherently good, it follows that anything apt to erode it must be bad.

The "choice" schemes that get tarred with this brush are usually designed to help poor and middle-class children attend non-government schools when their parents judge that this would result in better education. Or greater safety. Sounder values. Whatever.

Secretary of Education Lamar Alexander was savaged by the American Federation of Teachers' president Albert Shanker for suggesting that any school willing to embrace high standards, to enroll children on a nondiscriminatory basis, and to be held accountable for its results, might reasonably be deemed "public," no matter who owns and operates it. Mr. Shanker called this notion "Orwellian" and warned of schools "established by the likes of David Duke."

Other examples abound. We heard some on the floor of the U.S. Senate when Orrin Hatch sought to overturn the Kennedy bill's ban on private schools' participation in a new federal choice demonstration. But such talk is not confined to Washington. A "poison pill" for the public schools is how California's proposed voucher plan is described by Bill Honig, the state superintendent of public instruction. Some of his allies use terms like "fraud" and "evil" when discussing that initiative.

When Milwaukee's mayor, John Norquist, suggested replacing failed urban schools with a "choice or voucher system," he was sharply attacked by the press and the education establishment for disloyalty to public education. And in the closing arguments of a recent nationally-televised mock "trial" on whether the public schools are irreparably flawed, the Harvard law professor assigned to defend them asserted solemnly that our "traditions and ideals of quality public education" are responsible for the nation's evolution from a "third rate" country to a "great power." (Viewers, it seems, were not entirely persuaded. In the telephone tally that followed the show, 53 percent of callers agreed with the other attorney that the public schools are "beyond repair.")

What is it about this word "public" when it comes to schooling, and does the same moral and political alchemy occur when we meld that adjective with other nouns? Does "public" always wear a halo? Try some other combinations:

• Public welfare: Summons images of sloth, dependency, fraud, and irresponsibility. Anything but virtue.

• Public transportation: How you get around if you don't have a car, a bicycle, strong legs, or cab fare. Often unsafe, dirty, and unreliable.

• Public hospitals: Where you go if, besides ailing, you're destitute. They cost the taxpayer a pretty penny and often provide mediocre care.

• Public housing: Such bad news that virtually none of it has been built in decades. The corridors reek, you take your life in your hands on the elevator, and the maintenance people are never around when the pipes burst.

• Public radio and television: Sources of boring shows, politicized documentaries, and leaks by the likes of Nina Totenberg.

• Public parks, beaches, swimming pools, tennis courts, and golf courses: Better than none.

• Public safety: Grand idea, honored mainly in the breach. When people talk about it, watch for rising crime rates, menacing streets, and bad guys who go unpunished. Hence the surge in private security services, bodyguards, etc.

• Public colleges and universities: Often O.K., sometimes fine, but wouldn't you rather send your kid to Princeton?

• Public relations: Puts a nice face on bad situations and tries to persuade you of things that aren't entirely true.

• Public restrooms: Yuck.

The main exceptions that come to mind, places that may be enhanced (at least not diminished) by the adjective, are public libraries and—maybe—"public" utilities. As for "public" policy, it's largely responsible for all the preceding.

There are, to be sure, some domains where the only sensible way to get something done is through a single, government operated system. The armed forces. Highways. Printing money. Yellowstone National Park. These enterprises, however, have distinctive features: We seldom use the word "public" when describing them. There are fewer of them today than in the past, since many fields that once belonged to government monopolies—mail delivery, space satellites, trash collection, etc.—have privatized and diversified. Where this has occurred, moreover, the private versions usually operate more efficiently and reliably.

Elementary-secondary education is diversified, too, but not very. Its private sector consists of 27,000 schools, yet they enroll just 11 percent of all pupils. The hot policy issue, of course, is whether those numbers should be encouraged to grow. Private schools, by many measures, do a better job than government-run schools at imparting skills, knowledge, values, and character to their students. (That's not to say they do a good enough job!) They operate at lower per-pupil costs. And the vast majority of them welcome anyone who knocks on their door. They are far more open to poor and minority youngsters than the "public" schools of Bev-

erly Hills, Chappaqua, Wellesley, Evanston, and hundreds of other communities such as these.

How, then, has "public" education kept its halo of moral superiority? Mostly, I think, through nostalgia, wishful thinking, and shrewd public relations (see above). We want to believe that today's tax-supported schools are bastions of democracy and learning. That wish, however, has left us vulnerable to establishment propaganda and has helped perpetuators of the status quo lay claim to the adjective. Today they are squeezing every possible drop of political advantage from it, mostly by depicting alternatives to public schools as elitist and discriminatory.

The truth is that the emperor we know as public

The vast majority of private schools are far more open to poor and minority youngsters than the public schools of Beverly Hills, Chappaqua, and Wellesley.

---

schooling, despite an expensive wardrobe, has worn his present garments so long that most of them need cleaning if not replacing. Our solemn obligation is not to dress him up in new finery, however, but to see that American children—all of them—get access to a world-class education, no matter who provides it. Educating the public is a part of the social contract; institutions called public schools are not. Occasionally we do well to recall that it's the consumers, not the suppliers, for whose benefit we have an education system. Most Americans agree that we need a quality revolution in that system. We're a lot more likely to get one, however, if we banish from this domain—as we've done from so many others—the shibboleth that goodness and legitimacy attach only to institutions that bear the "public" label. □

Chester E. Finn Jr., a former assistant U.S. secretary of education, is a professor at Vanderbilt University and director of the Educational Excellence Network.

From Education Week, *Feb. 12, 1992*

39.

Schools Within Schools

A unique program may be the lever for radically restructuring high schools in one of the nation's largest urban districts.

By Ann Bradley

At 9:15 on a crisp, sunny fall morning, lines of students pour in through the doors of Simon Gratz High School in North Philadelphia, a formidable Gothic-style building with castle-like battlements.

As the latecomers receive passes that will admit them to class, they file into the cavernous hallway of the school, built in 1927 in what has since become one of the city's poorest neighborhoods.

At one time, Gratz was considered one of the worst of the district's 22 neighborhood high schools. But that sad distinction meant that Gratz differed from the other schools only in degree, not in kind. By almost any measure—course passage, credit accumulation, dropout and graduation rates, performance on standardized tests, and students' experiences after high school—Philadelphia's comprehensive schools are troubled institutions.

These are the schools that serve the average child in Philadelphia, those for whom there is no spot in the city's 12 special-admissions high schools. Their students are likely to be disadvantaged members of minority groups, many overage for their grade and with poor academic records.

Staffed by aging teachers and hidebound in their allegiance to academic departments, this city's neighborhood high schools "tend to be almost like a little school district unto themselves," observes Robert B. Schwartz, the director of education programs for the Pew Charitable Trusts, which is based here. "If you're looking for an entry point for structural changes," he adds, "that's typically the last place you look."

Nevertheless, the neighborhood high schools are the focus of one of the most comprehensive school-improvement efforts in the nation. The Philadelphia Schools Collaborative, with more than $16 million in funding from Pew, has been working since 1988 to break down the anonymity of the neighborhood high schools by creating "charters," or semiautonomous schools, within their walls.

'We Cannot Go Back'

Each charter serves a heterogeneous mix of 200 to 400 students and is run by a team of 10 to 12 teachers. These teachers have common planning time and develop their own instructional methods and curricula, which are often interdisciplinary. Ideally, to forge a sense of connection and commitment to the charter, the teachers and students will remain together for four years.

These smaller units also have drawn parents back into the schools. Parents are invited to participate in many of the planning and staff-development activities, and receive stipends for their attendance just as teachers do.

There are now 97 charters in the neighborhood high schools. Every school has at least two charters; 11 schools are "fully chartered," meaning that all students and faculty members are attached to a charter. By the end of this school year, the collaborative estimates that there will be 120 charters.

Some charters have ties to universities and help to

prepare new teachers. Some emphasize the humanities or multicultural studies, while others prepare students for careers in business or human services.

Despite its reputation for academic problems, Gratz is the home of what observers say is one of the most successful charters in the city. This writing-intensive program, called Crossroads, was the brainchild of veteran teachers who say that, with the collaborative's help, they were finally able to create a school that made sense to them.

Crossroads "has made a remarkable difference in the lives of some adults and children," says Marsha Pincus, an English teacher who founded the charter with two colleagues. Talking with a reporter, she and Bob Fecho, another English teacher and a co-founder of the program, interrupt each other in their eagerness to talk about Crossroads. "You're always cautious and cynical" about new programs, Mr. Fecho says. "We'd plan and then say, 'If it doesn't work out, we can go back in the room and close the door.'"

"Never having tasted this, we could do that," he continues, "but having tasted this autonomy, and sharing with other people, the continuity . . ."

"Or that I could know these kids . . ." Ms. Pincus interjects.

"We cannot go back," he says.

"If this is taken away from me," she warns, "then, personally, I am out of here."

Aside from teachers' enthusiasm, there is evidence that the more personalized approach is paying off for students. The collaborative reports that students who are attached to charters have better attendance records and lower dropout rates, and pass more courses than students who are not. The number of students who repeat 9th grade has also increased, meaning that they are returning to school for another year instead of dropping out.

The concept of creating "schools within a school" is a familiar one in education, but the charters are not ends in themselves. Michelle Fine, a senior consultant to the collaborative and a professor of education at the City University of New York, makes no secret of her disdain for what she calls "precious" programs that serve only the "creamy slice" of the most able students.

Instead, the charters are seen as a lever for radically restructuring each high school and for decentralizing the district. "Decisions and money should be at the site of practice," Ms. Fine asserts. "Schools should become autonomous sites for teacher work, student work, and parent involvement."

In setting as its goal the realignment of the district's bureaucracy to support these small, personal units, the Philadelphia Schools Collaborative "has adopted a much more encompassing view of restructuring than that typically espoused by reform initiatives in other communities," concludes an assessment of the P.S.C.'s first three years.

Janis I. Somerville, the executive director of the collaborative, and Ms. Fine have designed a multifaceted approach to school reform. The collaborative has played a lead role in establishing shared decisionmaking and school-based management in the district. Nineteen of the comprehensive high schools have governance councils that are charged with developing educational plans for the schools that include provisions for planning charters. More than 60 parents serve on the councils. Teachers in 12 charters are exploring the use of performance assessments for their students, also under the P.S.C.'s guidance.

The collaborative encompasses a College Access project to help inner-city students continue their studies, and the Algebra Transition Program, which is working to improve students' access to and passage of higher-level mathematics courses.

One of the collaborative's most difficult challenges is to identify the administrative and procedural hurdles that interfere with high school restructuring and to work with district officials to remove them. The nonprofit organization occupies a prime spot for doing so: just down the hallway from Superintendent Constance E. Clayton's office in the district's massive Art Deco headquarters.

A $8.3 million grant from Pew paid for the P.S.C.'s first three years. Last summer, the foundation approved a $7.8 million grant for another three years. The gifts were the largest ever made to a district by a single philanthropy, Pew says.

Ms. Fine, explaining why she believes big-city school bureaucracies need to be broken down, compares the work here with the massive decentralization of the Chicago schools mandated by the Illinois legislature. "Chicago is the best test of what the law can do," she says, "and we're the best test of what money can do."

'Creeping Academics'

What Pew's money has purchased, collaborative officials say, is enriching professional opportunities for seasoned teachers who have spiced the charters with academically rich programs. The charters receive some discretionary money from the district for materials and "release time" for the charter coordinators to plan the program.

In the earliest days of the collaborative's work, Ms. Fine has written, teachers who were asked to dream about what schools "could be" envisioned very traditional improvements: more teachers and counselors, more tracking, and more special-education placements. The collaborative's task became to help teachers broaden their ideas, an approach she calls "neither top-down nor naively bottom-up." The result of the emphasis on including special-education students in charters and broadening all students' access to college-preparatory courses, she says, has been a phenomenon she calls "creeping academics."

Schools were given a set of broad guidelines for

creating charters, specifying that they should have "substantive themes" to which teachers and students would commit for several years, teams of teachers, rigorous and integrated academic curricula, and varied instructional strategies.

The planning teams began their work by focusing on the 9th grade, a difficult transition year for many students. In Philadelphia, it is particularly so, because the district's promotion policies have resulted in as many as 25 percent of 9th graders being overage for their grade.

Through travel to national conferences, contact with teachers from around the nation who visited Philadelphia, and summer institutes and curriculum-planning

---

The collaborative's task became to help teachers broaden their ideas, an approach one consultant calls 'neither top-down nor naively bottom-up.'

---

seminars, the teachers began creating the new charters. Last summer, 1,300 parents and teachers registered for the summer institute.

The charters have provided a fertile environment for teachers whose intellects have been stimulated by such professional opportunities. In the past, teachers who developed new approaches were "sent back into institutions that were defeating," notes Morris J. Vogel, a professor of history at Temple University who helps teachers develop interdisciplinary curricula. "In all of the charters, it's the same principle," he says. "You don't separate the person who designs the curriculum from the person who implements it."

Teachers have seen immediate results from their efforts. Zachary Rubin, a history teacher at Lincoln High, which has a charter with a professional-development emphasis that is affiliated with Temple University, says his students' grasp of the subject has increased markedly since teachers at his school organized their instruction around such themes as "creation." Before the charter began, he says, "there was absolutely no retention. I realized I was not getting the materials across."

Jacqueline Burton, a mathematics teacher who works with Mr. Rubin, recalls overhearing a student saying how he heard about nothing but creation in his math, English, and history classes. She knew then that the interdisciplinary message was getting through.

Working as a team with other teachers also has cut down on attendance and discipline problems, Ms. Burton adds, because students know that their teachers are in close contact with each other. "If something happens in Mr. Rubin's room, I will know about it," Ms. Burton says. "It helps a lot, it really does."

Ultimately, collaborative officials say, the success of the restructuring effort rests with teachers like Mr. Rubin and Ms. Burton. "We are trying," says Ms. Somerville of the collaborative, "to build a constituency for change from within the ranks of teachers."

In doing so, and in pursuing the kinds of policy changes at the district level that will support the charters, the collaborative and leaders of the charters have begun to run up against some of the formidable barriers to urban school reform. "A whole lot of dynamics are involved when it becomes a school full of charters, as opposed to an isolated program from the rest of the building," Ms. Somerville explained. "When the whole building is involved, there is this tremendous energy and questioning everything."

At Gratz, a "fully chartered" school, teachers in the Crossroads program have begun questioning some of the traditional high school staffing positions. They wonder, for example, whether it still makes sense to have a full-time "roster chairman" to schedule students and teachers, since charters are devising their own schedules. The role of department heads—who teach a reduced load, order supplies, discipline some students, and observe but do not formally evaluate teachers—also has come into question.

The average high school class size is 33, a number that many teachers would like to see reduced. "There are ways we could do it," Mr. Fecho says, "but not just with Crossroads. The whole school would have to buy in, and there are real turf problems. You don't talk about department heads teaching four classes."

At Kensington High, says Shirley Farmer, a teacher in a charter there, "we have charter meetings instead of departmental meetings. It's clear to me that [system] is pretty obsolete."

But these positions, the teachers note, have provided some of the few perquisites available to teachers and have spawned a number of union leaders who are loyal to the jobs. There has been a great deal of reluctance, in general, to rethinking the organization and mission of the high schools, Ms. Fine says. She calls the lack of faith in change and suspicion that has grown up in some schools "communitarian damage," and frankly admits that the collaborative had underestimated it when the restructuring work began.

Teacher Mobility

Such attitudes have meant, not surprisingly, that the quality of the charters varies. Ms. Fine estimates that 15 are "really interesting," 30 to 40 are "pretty good and getting better," and that the rest are "not so good, but no worse than the high schools they came out of."

The wariness that has greeted the collaborative's initiatives is easy to understand, says Mr. Schwartz of Pew, because there has been so little new blood in the comprehensive high schools. Special education has been one of the few exceptions to that rule. "Particularly in high school English and social studies," he says, "there hasn't been anybody new hired for 20 years. You're dealing overwhelmingly with a veteran teaching force in these schools that has seen highly touted innovations come and go."

Even though few new teachers have been hired, teachers themselves are highly mobile. Fluctuations in the student population, caused by such factors as mobile families and dropouts, mean that teachers must be reassigned. The mobility of students and teachers, in fact, has emerged as one of the central challenges for the charters. Without finding a way to reduce it, teachers here warn, the goal of having teams of students and teachers stay together for more than a year will be impossible to attain.

Essie Abrahams, an English teacher at Lincoln High School and a charter coordinator, recalls the time during the end of her charter's first year when it was announced that the school could lose 17 teachers. "I walked into our charter meeting, and it meant that the only person who would be there was me," she says. "We certainly can't do everything they want us to do if they are constantly throwing away our people."

The losses at Lincoln were prevented, but teachers say they are mindful that teacher turnover could undermine their best efforts to create cooperative faculties. The problem is particularly acute given the fact that the charters began with the 9th grade, the level at which high school teachers with the least seniority are clustered, according to the evaluation of the P.S.C. "The collaborative, district, and Philadelphia Federation of Teachers must examine policies related to teacher assignment and staff allocation to insure that charters are not jeopardized," it warns.

The concern about teacher mobility was highlighted this fall, when the teachers' union and the district announced an agreement on a two-year contract that will move the district from a yearlong schedule into a

The Crossroads charter "has made a remarkable difference in the lives of some adults and children," says Marsha Pincus, center, an English teacher who developed the program with two other teachers at Simon Gratz High.

two-semester calendar. The motive for the switch was to give students who were failing courses the opportunity to have a fresh start during the second semester, explains Ted Kirsch, the president of the union.

But some teachers involved with charters express fear that the district will have to realign teacher assignments during the middle of the school year, which could disrupt their programs. The outcry of concern after the contract was signed was loud enough that Superintendent Clayton sent teachers a letter noting that they could ask for a policy waiver if they believed transfers would harm their charters.

The new schedule "has nothing to do with breaking up the continuity of instruction in the charter or in any other school," Ms. Clayton says. "I tried to put that to rest."

The concern over how systemwide or schoolwide policies affect charters has raised a deeper question about whether charters might someday be completely autonomous units. Ms. Fine is enthusiastic about that possibility.

But Dick Clark, a consultant to the Pew Charitable Trusts, warned that a school cannot simply be a collection of charters because the overall environment must be a "healthy setting" for students and teachers. "The piece that hasn't been worked out," he says, "is what is the role of the schoolwide leadership? Is it a confederation or a republic?"

Over lunch with Mr. Kirsch and an associate, Ms. Somerville and Ms. Fine throw out the question of whether teachers might be allowed to transfer into charters, rather than simply moving from school to school. They argue that the option would help create a better match between teachers' interests and the charters' themes. Some teachers say they would like to go a step further and have the authority to hire their colleagues to work with them in the charters. Others, however, adamantly oppose that idea, arguing that it would create an "elitist" system that would discriminate against some teachers.

The teachers' union, Mr. Kirsch says, takes a "firm and consistent" position that teachers should not start hiring other teachers. "I don't see the need to hire their own teachers," he says. Focusing on the teachers sends the message that the program would be more successful with different teachers, he explains, which means that teachers are to blame for the current conditions. "I don't believe that," he adds.

In schools where the topic has come up, says Jerald Hairston, a union official who assists restructuring schools, teachers have decided that "they shouldn't be about getting teachers to come in," but should concentrate on helping existing teachers "buy into it."

'In Constant Discourse'

The answers to some of the larger questions posed by restructuring the high schools ultimately will have to come from district officials and not classroom teachers. Some teachers remain skeptical of the extent of the administration's commitment to the charters. "The district hasn't moved much," Mr. Fecho of Gratz's Crossroads charter says. "We are like a big person in a small room. We have pushed this district as far as it has moved. Unless downtown changes, this whole school is going to be stuck."

At this point, observers say, the district and teachers' union are considered to be generally supportive of the high school restructuring, but each side appears to be keeping a close eye on the other to make the first move toward radical change. They note that the new teachers' contract was reached through traditional bargaining and contains little to advance the high school initiatives.

The problem of teacher mobility, Ms. Clayton asserted, is a "union issue." "We stay in constant discourse with the union on issues of that nature," she says. "I am trying to negotiate with the federation without having them feel that there's an erosion of what they worked so hard for and what they feel are the rights of their constituents. It doesn't happen overnight."

Mr. Kirsch believes that, while the superintendent is supportive, "middle management gets in the way."

The assessment of the collaborative's first three years concludes that its efforts to create an environment in the central administration that is "conducive to restructuring" have been "stymied." But Ms. Clayton insisted that she has sent a strong message in favor of reform to her subordinates. "We have tangibly and honestly taken a much stronger position of being of service to the field rather than issuing directives," she says.

Over the past 10 years under the superintendent's leadership, the district has achieved a remarkable degree of stability for an urban system, Mr. Schwartz of Pew noted. Ms. Clayton has balanced the budget, achieved labor peace, standardized the curriculum, and established a good working relationship with the board of education. "The flip side of that continuity and stability also means that when you're talking about change of the magnitude that is contemplated in this restructuring effort, it makes it more difficult," Mr. Schwartz observed. "The key players have been in place for a long time, and they are accustomed to a certain way of doing business."

As the larger questions raised by the reform effort are debated, hundreds of teachers throughout the city are pressing on with their programs. At Horace H. Furness High on the city's south end, the creation of charters has "bred nothing but professionalism," says Bill Tomasco, a department head. Before the charters were created, he says, the school was "languishing. It was a sleepy hollow with no direction." Now its students, many of whom are Southeast Asian immigrants, are using the city as their classroom to study immigration, planning trips abroad, and writing books about resettling in America.

The investment in their professionalism, says Valerie Nelsen, the coordinator of the school's multicultural charter, "makes teachers rise to the occasion." She adds: "Their creativity is at such a high; plus, there's the enthusiasm of the kids." □

From Education Week, _Nov. 18, 1992_

40.

Who's In Charge?

The movement to decentralize and empower individual schools is colliding with the teacher unions' most cherished protections.

By Ann Bradley

As urban districts move to grant individual schools greater autonomy, teachers' unions are confronting challenges to some of collective bargaining's most cherished protections and procedures. In particular, the push to decentralize big-city school systems often calls into question the centralized personnel policies that were created when teachers were regarded as interchangeable laborers in a factory-like system.

In recent months, attempts to give schools greater control over their budgets, staffs, and programs in such cities as Boston and Detroit have run headlong into the desires of unions to protect the tenure and seniority policies, centralized hiring, and common work rules that have traditionally been key features of teaching contracts.

And at the same time that reformers are pushing for greater authority at the school site, the American Federation of Teachers, which once led the charge for schools to govern themselves, is downplaying school-based management as its primary reform strategy. Without clear curriculum goals, better assessments, and incentives for students and teachers, such initiatives often flounder, says Albert Shanker, the president of the A.F.T. "We're convinced that school-based management, in and of itself, does not lead anywhere," he says.

Union leaders acknowledge that school autonomy calls traditional labor practices into question. Some

union presidents, such as John Elliott, who heads the Detroit Federation of Teachers, insist that teachers should not and do not want to take on the responsibility of managing schools. Others, such as Adam Urbanski, the president of the Rochester (N.Y.) Teachers Association, contend that unions could give up some of their traditional roles and become "service centers" for their members. "It would mean a different kind of union," Mr. Urbanski says, "not lesser, just different."

Researchers have found that the most successful schools are those in which teachers, principals, and students feel a sense of ownership, have created a distinctive culture, and have the freedom to go about achieving their goals. Many reformers are now suggesting that principals and teachers be given greater control over who works in their buildings as a way to build such school cultures.

But in many big-city districts where such devolution of authority may seem most critical, teachers are hired and assigned to jobs in a centralized way that allows individual schools little leeway in choosing and managing their own teachers. These procedures, many experts now believe, eventually could undermine efforts across the nation to give schools more autonomy.

"If teachers continue to be assigned on the basis of seniority or other general criteria," says a RAND Corporation report on decentralization, "staff assignment could become a serious barrier to the continuation of healthy site-managed schools."

Decentralization efforts are under way in a number

of urban school districts. Unlike the movement of the late 1960's and early 1970's that resulted in the creation of community school boards in New York City and subdistrict offices in Detroit, the focus of the current activity is on devolving power and authority to schools themselves.

The best example is Chicago, where local school councils that include administrators and teachers along with parents and community members now hire and fire school principals and make critical decisions about a school's budget and programs.

School reformers in other cities, while advocating a variety of approaches, also believe that the best strategy for addressing the problems that plague their schools lies with the people who work in them. In Los Angeles, a diverse civic coalition has drafted a plan for moving decisionmaking and budget authority to the schools. In Detroit, the school board has been locked in a struggle with the teachers' union over a proposal to "empower" schools to run their own affairs. In Philadelphia, the comprehensive high schools are being broken down into smaller units that are viewed as a step toward eventually decentralizing the district.

And in Boston, the school committee has proposed creating deregulated "demonstration schools" that would be free to hire and manage their own staffs. The committee and the Boston Teachers Union are now negotiating a new contract.

Whether these efforts will be successful is unclear. Three members of the Detroit Board of Education who were most closely associated with the empowerment effort there lost their bids for re-election last month, in large part because they had alienated the district's labor unions.

Because the historical trend has been toward more, not less, centralization, experts believe that these efforts face formidable obstacles. The issue of what to decentralize and what to maintain as the province of the central office is not a simple one, says Susan Moore Johnson, a professor of administration, planning, and social policy at Harvard University's graduate school of education. "People are totally unrealistic about how complicated these organizations are, how difficult it is to bring about change, and how long it takes," she says.

But the unmistakable trend toward breaking down the centralized administration of big districts has important implications for teachers' unions. As districts move decisions about what to teach and how to teach it, grading and attendance policies, and the like down to schools, observes Charles T. Kerchner, a professor at the Claremont Graduate School in California and the editor of a new book on urban school reform, "you tear big hunks out of the notion of the existing bureaucracy."

"We are talking about departures from industrial-style organizations that are strongly hierarchical, relatively formalized, and relatively differentiated between levels," he says, "where teachers are real

different than managers." Mr. Kerchner adds, "Once you depart from that mode of operation, the existing mode of organizing teachers doesn't work very well."

Some union leaders have thought about new ways of serving their members that break with existing practices. "My whole thrust has been that the bargaining agent has to play a minimal role: Bargain and get the hell out of the way," says Patrick O'Rourke, the president of the Hammond (Ind.) Federation of Teachers. "Practitioner power, not bargaining-agent power."

"That is controversial within the A.F.T.," he adds. "There has always been a minority who wants to really increase the role of practitioners at the expense of traditional roles for the unions."

The "logical consequence" of school-based management, write the RAND researchers in their decentralization study, would be a "districtwide teacher labor market in which teachers and schools choose one another on the basis of affinity to school mission and culture."

How to create such a system—while still protecting teachers' rights and guarding against inequity—is a subject of intense debate. Union leaders insist that, for a number of reasons, it cannot and should not be done. For one thing, school-site hiring would create imbalances among experienced and inexperienced teachers, Mr. Shanker, the A.F.T. president, argues.

"In New York City," he says, "if you didn't have a central-assignment and central-transfer plan, then teachers would be distributed according to the racial composition of the school and the socioeconomic status."

"It's also true right now that when New York City teachers are centrally hired and sent to the school that probably about 30 percent of the teachers quit because they do not want to work at the school that they are sent to," he adds. "So this is not a simple issue."

In addition to concerns about equity, union leaders point out that districts have to guard against undue political pressures in teacher hiring. And some, most notably Boston, are under centrally administered school-desegregation orders that regulate the racial composition of their teaching forces.

"In the 1950's," recalls Jack Steinberg, the director of education issues for the Philadelphia Federation of Teachers, "we had ward schools, where a teacher had to go to a ward leader, pay the ward leader, and work for that person on election day [to get a job]. That's not so far back in our history."

The notion of schools choosing teachers on the basis of their adherence to a certain philosophy or approach to education also runs counter to the egalitarian norms that influence teachers' relationships with one another.

In Philadelphia, some of the teachers who have created "charter" schools in the comprehensive high schools have expressed interest in hiring the other teachers who will work with them. The teachers' union opposes the idea, arguing that it would create divisions in the ranks. Some teachers, Mr. Steinberg argues, tend to become "dictatorial" in their views.

"The thought of only having people in your school who agree with our philosophy is one that we reject," he says, "because the whole purpose of restructuring is to give an opportunity to all ideas to come out and be discussed."

In addition to personnel policies, the centralized work rules contained in teaching contracts have come under fire in some cities. Critics argue that it no longer makes sense to negotiate a specific set of regulations that apply to all teachers, because schools are being encouraged to find the practices that suit their communities and students best.

Steven F. Wilson, the co-director of the Pioneer Institute for Public Policy Research in Boston and the author of a book about reforming the Boston schools, writes that the detailed contract "overpowers" anyone who wants to undertake change.

"The teachers' union demeans its own membership by insisting that everything about the workplace be prescribed," he writes, "from the length of lunch breaks, to the length and schedule of the workday, to the maximum number of minutes per week that teachers are permitted to meet with one another." The rules in the Boston contract governing staffing, he reports, are spelled out in 221 single-spaced pages.

Edward Doherty, the president of the Boston Teachers Union, says it was unfair to criticize his union's contract as unduly restrictive, noting that with its clause on school-based management it is more "educationally flavored" than most such agreements.

Other union leaders point out that work rules have grown up over time to protect teachers from poor managers. "Most are in there because of some real or perceived abuse," says Edward McElroy, the secretary-treasurer of the American Federation of Teachers. "The unions also become a bureaucracy, because they are dealing with a bureaucracy."

The frustration with the Boston procedures is one reason the school committee wants to create demonstration schools, according to Robert Culver, the senior vice president and treasurer of Northeastern University and a member of the Boston school committee. "We've got to focus on outcomes," he says, "as opposed to processes."

In Chicago, a group of teachers, principals, and members of local school councils that convened last spring to brainstorm about how to further decentralize the system proposed that teachers be hired and given annual contracts by individual schools. Teachers whose contracts were not renewed at a particular school, they suggested, could have their names returned to a citywide eligibility list maintained by the central office.

Chicago principals now work directly for schools on four-year performance contracts. But in what is widely regarded as a political compromise to secure the support of the Chicago Teachers Union for the reform legislation, teachers continue to work for the school

system under a central contract.

The reform law did give principals the authority to hire teachers for vacant or newly created positions without regard to seniority; it also shortened the remediation period for teachers who are judged to be performing below par. In addition, schools can ask for waivers from the teaching contract.

Paul T. Hill, a senior social scientist at the RAND Corporation who was present during the Chicago brainstorming discussions, says the tone was not hostile to teachers. "The desire was to make it clear that the real employer of the teacher was the school," he says. "It isn't like the teachers become helpless pawns—they are involved in collaborative activities at the local level in ways that are not constrained by other loyalties they might have."

But the proposal for individual school contracts was denounced by the C.T.U. as the equivalent of having "600 superintendents." "That would do more to destroy the profession in this city than anything else I've heard of," Jackie Gallagher, a spokeswoman for the union, says. "No one in their right mind would walk into a situation that you could be asked to walk out of in a year."

G. Alfred Hess Jr., the executive director of the Chicago Panel on Public School Policy and Finance, noted that the political power of Chicago's unions makes it highly unlikely that labor-protection laws there could be relaxed. "A lot of people are riding the anti-unionist wave at the moment," he says. "With the political structures bending over backward to make the unions happy, as has recently happened with the settling of the budget in Chicago, I don't see how anybody thinks there's going to be any relaxation of the labor-protection laws for Chicago."

Both Mr. Hill and Mr. Wilson have given some thought to how a teacher labor market could work. If teachers were hired by schools, those who did not make a good match with a school could have the right to a paid period to search for another position, Mr. Hill suggested in an interview. Teachers with more seniority could be given a longer job-hunting opportunity. At some point, however, teachers who were not hired by any school would no longer be employed in the system. The union contract would set salaries, qualifications for employment, and standards for promotion in such a system.

Mr. Wilson, in his book *Reinventing the Schools: A Radical Plan for Boston,* proposes that the teachers' union in that city "serve as a placement agency" for teachers contracting individually with schools. "The Boston Teachers Union could come to protect the right of teachers to enter into such contracts," he writes, "rather than constrain it through collective-bargaining agreements that limit autonomy and choice for both teachers and principals."

Mr. Wilson's book, which has influenced the school committee in its negotiations with the union, outlines an "entrepreneurial model" that would allow any teacher or principal in Boston to come up with a plan for creating a school. These plans would be reviewed by several "sponsoring councils" whose members had been approved by the superintendent. The councils would decide which schools the system should "invest in."

The new schools would receive funds based solely on the number of students they enrolled, with special-needs students carrying greater amounts of money. But the schools would have great flexibility in spending that money.

Mr. Doherty, the president of the Boston Teachers Union, summarizes the proposal as: "Pick a principal, and let him operate in a union-free environment with no work rules."

"I think it's almost all political," he says of discussions of Mr. Wilson's proposals. The new, mayorally appointed school committee, Mr. Doherty charges, is "out to kill the union."

The Boston teaching contract that ushered in school-based management gave school councils the right to pick teachers transferring into their schools without regard to seniority, the union president notes. In schools that do not have councils that can serve that function, principals pick from any one of the three most senior teachers.

"We have gone a long way in the area of staffing," Mr. Doherty says. "I think we've shown a willingness to be flexible and innovative at the bargaining table."

Giving schools their money on a per-pupil basis, Mr. Hill believes, is the key to creating a labor market for teachers. Most school systems now give schools resources, but not their own budgets to manage. Although the cost of teachers' salaries in a big-city high school might be between $4 million and $5 million, Mr. Hill points out, the school might only have about $85,000 to spend on its own.

If schools were given lump sums based on their enrollment and told to live within their means, a district could create a labor market. Schools with concentrations of highly paid teachers would find themselves over budget, while those with lesser-paid teachers would have a surplus, Mr. Hill says.

The teachers' union could then become a broker, recommending teachers to schools, Mr. Hill suggests. "In the old days, and still in a lot of trades," he says, "that's the brokerage role the union plays."

Although such a scenario might seem far-fetched, the Los Angeles Unified School District has entered into a consent decree requiring it to distribute money to schools for salaries and supplies on a per-pupil basis. Schools will be given broad discretion over how to spend the money. The agreement is intended to equalize the distribution of experienced teachers and resources throughout the district. The order comes in a lawsuit brought by advocates for disadvantaged, non-English-speaking children, who were found to be commonly and disproportionately taught by inexperi-

enced teachers or those who were unlicensed.

The court order contains provisions sought by the United Teachers of Los Angeles to mitigate its effects on the current teaching force. In general, says Mr. McElroy, the A.F.T. secretary-treasurer, a teacher labor market could drive down salaries. Schools would replace retiring senior teachers with lower-salaried teachers, he argues. Principals in other schools would want to transfer senior teachers to free up some salary money for other uses. "Then it becomes a business decision," he says, "not an educational one."

These debates go far beyond the celebrated teachers' contracts of the 1980's, when school-based management, peer-evaluation plans, and other reforms were negotiated. During that time, Mr. Kerchner of Claremont Graduate School observes, unions, management, and members of the public coalesced to bring about a "renaissance around the schools" in such places as Dade County, Fla.; Jefferson County, Ky.; Pittsburgh; and Rochester, N.Y.

As the cry for radical change in big-city districts has continued, he adds, "powerful external actors" have gotten involved in education, changing the terms of the debate. These actors include the Chicago reform coalition and Gov. Roy Romer of Colorado, who stepped into a labor stalemate in Denver to create a sweeping plan to give the city's schools more autonomy.

William Ayers, an associate professor of education at the University of Illinois at Chicago and the author of a chapter about that city's reforms in Mr. Kerchner's book, says he believes that the city's teachers' union is in "deep crisis, deep pain" about the implications of school reform. "This puts them in a situation of chaos and confusion, not because they're sitting on their hands," he says, "but because who knows how this will turn out? Teachers hiring teachers is the least of it. Where's my contract going to come from if the end of a big-city school system is also the end of negotiations and unionism as we've known it?"

Other observers say that it is simply unfair to focus too much attention on the unions, since management has a critical role to play in bringing about reforms. The administration often does not "courageously try to renegotiate things," Ms. Johnson of Harvard University says, "or really exercise the discretion that they have."

In the end, says John Kotsakis, the assistant to the president of the Chicago Teachers Union for educational issues, the teachers' union represents the only stability urban districts have. "Future contracts will reflect flexibility for local-site initiatives more and more," Mr. Kotsakis says. "Wouldn't it be much better to have the union driving the change, being significant partners in it, accepting accountability, and identifying with success or failure, than having them simply sitting on the side?" □

From Education Week, *Dec. 9, 1992*

41.

Taking Flight

A winner in the 'Break-the-Mold Schools' contest hopes to become the breeding ground for new elementary schools.

By Lynn Olson

St. Mary's County, Md., juts into the Chesapeake Bay between the Potomac and Patuxent rivers, a place better known for its annual oyster festival than for its schools. But in the next five years, this rural community hopes to become the breeding ground for a new generation of elementary schools that will be so visibly superior to what now exists that they will be replicated across the United States.

The project is known as "Roots and Wings," and it is the collective brainchild of a team of researchers at Johns Hopkins University, officials at the Maryland Department of Education, and local teachers and administrators.

In August 1992, their design was one of only 11 selected nationally for funding by the New American Schools Development Corporation, out of nearly 700 proposals. American business leaders launched the multi-million-dollar nonprofit corporation in 1991, at the request of President Bush, to help foment a "revolution" in education by financing the design and replication of a group of "break the mold" schools.

"Their mission," the corporation proclaimed in an advertisement announcing the award winners, "is not merely to reform what already exists, but to start with a clean sheet of paper and rethink everything about American education and how it must work in the 21st century." But the leaders of the St. Mary's County project, like most members of the design teams recognized by NASDC elsewhere, cannot start from scratch. They must work with the schools they have. This is the story of that effort.

When Elfreda Mathis, the principal of Lexington Park Elementary School, heard that Roots and Wings had been awarded a NASDC contract for nearly a million dollars, "I had to go outside and get some air," she recalls. "I thought I had died and gone to heaven," she chuckles. But these days, she admits, "I'm kind of overwhelmed."

A large woman who attracts children like a magnet as she sails through the halls of her building, Ms. Mathis had begun drafting a New American Schools submission on her own before being approached by the St. Mary's County school district about joining the Roots and Wings team.

The project's genesis dates back to several phone calls between Robert C. Embry Jr., the chairman of the Maryland state board of education; Nancy S. Grasmick, the state superintendent of schools; and Robert E. Slavin of Johns Hopkins, one of the nation's most prominent educational researchers. It was Ms. Grasmick who identified St. Mary's County as one of the more progressive districts in the state and one that might be willing to work with the researchers from Johns Hopkins, a private university in Baltimore. The district had already planned to submit a NASDC proposal of its own and had an energetic new superintendent of schools. For Ms. Mathis, it was the appeal of working with a major research university that finally won her over.

Lexington Park Elementary is a one-story brick building with three mobile classrooms on the side to cope with overcrowding. Fully half of its 516 students turn over each year, in part because of the military bases and low-income neighborhoods from which the school draws its students. Approximately 40 percent are from minority groups, primarily African-American. "When you're in a school where kids are floating in and out," Ms. Mathis explains, "you need a strategy to hold on to."

The strategy that Roots and Wings offers is grounded, in part, on more than two decades of research by Mr. Slavin and his colleagues at Johns Hopkins University's Center for Research on Effective Schooling for Disadvantaged Students. Working in some of the most poverty-stricken schools in the United States, they have demonstrated that early reading failures among children can be virtually eliminated by applying a high-quality curriculum that enables children to work in teams and that provides aggressive one-on-one tutoring, family-support services, and other assistance to children who are falling behind.

Until now, most of Mr. Slavin's efforts have focused on equipping children with the basic skills needed to succeed in elementary school, or what

At Lexington Park Elementary School in St. Mary's County, Md., kindergartners match up vocabulary words from a chart with a book they have been reading.

he refers to as the "roots" of the Roots and Wings program. But the NASDC project will also provide children with "wings," by redesigning curriculum and instruction so that every child is expected to meet world-class standards in English, mathematics, science, history, and geography.

This agenda, which requires reconstituting whole schools around new and more ambitious standards, is far more demanding than anything that the research center has previously undertaken.

Reaching Out to Families

In Roots and Wings schools, children will work in groups based on their abilities and interests, not their age. The schools will reach out to students and their families from birth to identify youngsters who need special assistance before they begin school. Starting at age 4, the project organizers say, every child will have the opportunity to participate in a "language rich" preschool and kindergarten program built around thematic units.

Students will not be retained in a grade. If children are having trouble keeping up, they will be given tutoring, family-support services, and other assistance

to help them master the content. They may also take more time to finish a learning block. But the same high standards will be held for everyone, the organizers stress, with the resources and time needed to meet them—rather than outcomes—allowed to vary by child. To secure this vision, every school will operate as a "family-development center," combining federal, state, and local resources to serve families in need.

One of the most ambitious features of the design is a project known as "WorldLab": a series of elaborate simulations that will enable students to work in teams to solve problems that are rooted in "real world" contexts. In WorldLab, explains Yael Sharan, an expert on group investigations who is co-directing its development with her husband, Shlomo, "the kids get the chance to investigate issues that they are interested in investigating."

"The point," she says, "is to lead them to the stage where they can say, 'This is what we'd like to learn. This is the question we'd like to investigate.'" Rather than having students answer questions by rote, WorldLab will encourage them to solve problems creatively and flexibly and to apply the knowledge they have gained from a variety of subject areas.

For example, teams of students might collect data on the contamination of a nearby stream that is contributing to the pollution of the Chesapeake Bay. Their report, presented in both graphic and narrative form, might be based on water samples from the stream, interviews with area residents, telephone calls to local environmental experts, and library research using CD-ROM disk-based encyclopedias and computer databases on the bay and its tributaries. Back in the classroom, the students might present their findings in the form of "testimony" to an elected "town council" of their peers.

The children might also identify imaginary families and businesses that could be affected by the stream's pollution. While completing their research, they might learn songs about the bay and read a novel describing how the pollution of the bay affects the 11-year-old son of a waterman.

These kinds of long-range, multidisciplinary projects, which will draw heavily on the use of computers and other technologies, will replace the existing science and social-studies curricula in the four participating elementary schools. "We want to make real changes in the style of instruction and in what kids are involved in for the bulk of the day," explains Nancy A. Madden, a senior research scientist at the Johns Hopkins center.

Teachers and researchers plan to pilot a small segment of WorldLab in some 5th-grade classrooms in the Roots and Wings schools.

Roots and Wings schools are also revamping their math curricula to bring them in line with the standards of the National Council of Teachers of Mathematics, which emphasize problem-solving, hands-on learning, and teamwork.

In some ways, St. Mary's County provides fertile ground in which to sow such schools. When it comes to family support and integrated services, says Lawrence J. Dolan, a research scientist at Johns Hopkins, "we have as much to learn from St. Mary's County and the state as we can probably provide them."

Under state law, every school in the county already has a "pupil-services team" that meets regularly to provide case management for students who are having trouble in school. Several of the schools are also located near publicly or privately funded family-support centers that provide one-stop shopping for parents and children in need of social services.

At the state level, Gov. William Donald Schaefer has

Much of the fall was spent in a delicate courtship between teachers in this rural community and researchers from the university.

---

made the integration of services for children and their families one of his top priorities through the creation of a subcabinet for children, youths, and families. The subcabinet is headed by Ms. Grasmick, the state superintendent.

But a walk through the halls of any of the four Roots and Wings elementary schools—Lexington Park, Green Holly, Ridge, and George Washington Carver—suggests that for many teachers, the project will require difficult, even wrenching, changes in how they do their jobs.

Although some teachers are experimenting with team teaching, cooperative learning, and multi-age grouping, others can be seen lecturing in the front of the room or working with small groups of children while the other students fill out worksheets, chat with

their neighbors, or gaze into space.

The huge amount of time that students typically spend on such inefficient and often uninspiring "seat work" is one of the primary reasons that Mr. Slavin developed his cooperative-learning strategies. Much of the fall was spent in a delicate courtship between teachers in this rural community, who are proud of their schools, and researchers from the university, who are trying to understand what they have to build on.

At a meeting with teachers earlier this school year, Anna Marie Farnish, one of the university's principal liaisons with the district, tried to reassure educators. "We saw some wonderful things at your school that we're not planning to do away with," Ms. Farnish told them.

But some teachers remain skeptical—including several of those who have been seen as the most innovative in the past. One teacher, who asks not to be identified, says: "I deal with gifted kids. I'm not sure this answers their needs."

"For those kids who are already doing well," this teacher states, "I can see that, in cooperative learning, they're going to be a great help to other children. But are they going to learn at their own level? That's just a concern to me, as a parent and as a teacher."

Ann Shumaker, a Chapter 1 remedial-education teacher at Ridge Elementary School, says: "Part of me is in that grant. I wrote sentences, and it's exciting to me. I want to see change, but I want to take the best of St. Mary's County also. That's the frustration that we are feeling right now: how to fit in what [the researchers] have proven successful to what we already have."

Some of that integration is beginning to take place at schools like Lexington Park Elementary. In Chris Jensen's reading class recently, 4th- and 5th-grade students paired up with a partner to alternate reading paragraphs aloud from a text. There was a constant hum of activity as students quietly read an excerpt and corrected each other's mistakes. When they finished, the partners began a "treasure hunt"—looking for the answers to questions and making predictions based on the text and discussing them with each other.

Each student then wrote down his answers individually. When one team was stymied, the partners turned to another pair of students working nearby for assistance before going to the teacher. By working in teams, every student had a chance to speak and to participate most of the time. And the process was one that the class seemed to enjoy.

After his partner attempted to answer a question on the treasure hunt, one boy retorted: "That ain't got nothing to do with the question. You don't have to get it from the book. You have to think about it."

Another student corrected a teammate's spelling of the word H-U-N-D-E-R-D: "Nope, because 'red' is R-E-D. Just listen."

According to Mr. Jensen, the students like the structure provided by the Johns Hopkins exercises.

And the discipline of having to listen to others' views and defend their own has resulted in sharper thinking. "Their oral reading is a lot better, because they're correcting one another," Mr. Jensen says. "Their comprehension, I think, has improved by 80 percent, because they're into this game of challenging each other."

"They're asking critical questions," the teacher continues. "They're asking the 'why' questions. And I think that will transfer to other subjects."

Structure Worries Some

One initial source of tension between the university scholars and some teachers was whether the Johns Hopkins approach might be too structured and rigid. In the area of beginning reading, some teachers also worried that the program was too phonetically based—stressing the sounds of individual letters and syllables as a key component of reading instruction. In a series of meetings last fall, Johns Hopkins researchers and St. Mary's educators tried to work out how to mesh their two approaches.

The university has also provided teachers with training, so that they can try out new instructional strategies "risk free" this year and adapt them to their schools' needs. According to Ms. Madden of Johns Hopkins, some of the teachers who were most concerned initially about the researchers' approach to reading instruction have become "strong advocates" after trying it out in their own classrooms. "They found that kids are proceeding very well," she says, "and that the phonics core has filled a gap." That view is seconded by teachers like Mr. Jensen, who says, "I think teachers are a lot more comfortable with it, because you see the results."

Beginning in mid-October, Lexington Park revamped its reading instruction in grades 1-5. Students are now grouped and regrouped by reading level—rather than age—every eight weeks, and no teacher has more than two reading levels in a classroom.

The time set aside for language arts has been expanded from 60 to 90 minutes. And children who are having the most difficulty receive 20 additional minutes of tutoring a day. Kindergarten and pre-kindergarten teachers are also making efforts to incorporate some of the Johns Hopkins methodologies into their approach in the classroom.

Christin Berryman, a Chapter 1 teacher at the school and a facilitator for the project, says, "We actually had children that jumped a year's reading level on paper—from pre-primer to primer to 1st grade—in just eight weeks."

In addition, says Ms. Mathis, the Lexington Park principal, behavioral problems and referrals at the school have decreased, because students are more engaged and are placed more appropriately.

Janice Walthour, the principal of the George Wash-

ington Carver Elementary School, who supports the new approach, says: "We cannot run our school on one or two master teachers. I want to see teachers have a structure that they can pull from that is sound."

Like Lexington Park, Carver has a highly transient student population. Last year, it had a 60 percent mobility rate—the highest in the county. Nearly half of its students are eligible to receive free or reduced-price lunches; some 42 percent are from minority groups, primarily African-American. The neighborhood school, built in 1960, was originally one of two all-black high schools in the county. Lockers still line the walls in one wing of the red-brick building.

In contrast, Green Holly Elementary School is a brand-new building with more than 600 students that draws from a mixture of upper-middle-class and

> # Five years from now, says the superintendent, 'I don't expect people to look at St. Mary's County and see four schools that have spotlights on them.'

low-income communities. Teachers half-jokingly comment that they run a mile every day just to navigate around the school building. The school also houses the district's program for the severely and profoundly handicapped, which draws students from across the county.

Teachers at Green Holly decided to pilot the Johns Hopkins approach to beginning reading in only one classroom this year, with students who were having the most difficulty with traditional reading instruction. "This school is taking a more cautious approach than the other three," Principal Mary Blakely says. "We're not totally sure that Johns Hopkins has the answer in this area; but if they do, we want to use it."

To Ms. Blakely, a former special-education teacher, the primary attraction of Roots and Wings was to get away from labeling too many students as "slow" or "handicapped" and pulling them out of mainstream classrooms. "I saw a lot of kids in high school who had been steeped in failure," she says.

Technically, this year was supposed to be a planning year for the project. But teachers and researchers have found themselves operating on two tracks at once. With assistance from Johns Hopkins faculty members, many teachers, such as those at Lexington Park, have begun trying out new approaches to cooperative learning and literacy instruction.

The majority of teachers at the four schools also have volunteered to participate in work groups that meet monthly to develop specific aspects of the Roots and Wings design. At Johns Hopkins, separate committees that correspond to these groups are working feverishly to develop more detailed prototypes and plans.

Next summer, a large number of the schools' teachers will be hired to work at Johns Hopkins full time to flesh out the final curriculum materials and strategies. In addition, the state education department has assigned a full-time liaison to provide technical assistance and brokering for the project.

In part to allay teachers' fears, all of the school principals involved, as well as Joan Kozlovsky, the superintendent of the county school district, have emphasized that participation in the project is purely voluntary this year. By next year, both teachers and students will attend the four schools by choice; those who disagree with the approach will be free to transfer elsewhere in the district.

"This is almost a no-fault year," says Michael Metz, the principal of Ridge Elementary School, a small neighborhood school with 260 students and 11 teachers. "We're going to put [Roots and Wings] into practice as much as we can, and kinks are going to come up."

"Our goal is not to wipe out the progress we've made," Ms. Kozlovsky adds, "but to inculcate the good things and merge our programs and their programs."

'Walking to Kansas'

For now, the question is: How much change, how quickly, can the four schools accommodate? "We confidently expect that many of the things we try will fail," Mr. Slavin told teachers and parents during a ceremony to launch the project in September. "If we didn't, we wouldn't be pushing the envelope."

"But there's a unique opportunity to do things here without having to worry about the way things have always been," he added.

Five years from now, Ms. Kozlovsky says, "I don't expect people to look at St. Mary's County and see four schools that have spotlights on them." Instead, the superintendent is hoping to use school-improvement teams at each school, combined with the state's new performance-based assessments, to push for changes throughout the system.

Similarly, state officials are hoping that, in subsequent years, some of the money that the new-schools corporation raises for replication will flow Maryland's way to help spread the design to other parts of the state.

"It's not like climbing Mount Everest, where you're not sure if you'll get to the summit," Mr. Slavin says about the project. "It's more like walking to Kansas," he says. "You know you'll get there, but it's a long way." □

From Education Week, *Jan. 20, 1993*

42.

Crossing The Tracks

Massachusetts leads a nationwide charge against ability grouping, but the resistance is formidable.

By Peter Schmidt

When school districts in this state group students according to their academic ability, Daniel V. French in turn groups the districts, separating those that agree to abandon the practice from those that face losing some state funds for declining to do so. As the Massachusetts Department of Education's director for student development, Mr. French is leading his agency's effort to discourage public schools from putting children in different classrooms based on their perceived ability.

The agency lacks the authority to forbid ability grouping outright. But it uses the award or denial of state dropout-prevention and remedial-education money as leverage to get schools to "rethink traditional notions of grouping students," in the words of a 1990 department advisory statement that strongly criticized the use of homogeneous grouping.

With the backing of Gov. William F. Weld and Commissioner of Education Robert V. Antonucci, the department has put Massachusetts in the forefront of a growing offensive against ability grouping and tracking in public schools. Here and elsewhere around the nation, increasing numbers of educators, educational researchers, and civil-rights advocates are aggressively promoting an end to such practices.

Many of these critics base their efforts on a long-held conviction that ability grouping contributes to segregation of students by race, ethnic group, economic background, and other nonacademic characteristics. Just last December, the Amherst, Mass.-area chapter

of the National Association for the Advancement of Colored People filed a federal lawsuit charging that the Amherst-Pelham Regional School District had violated the civil rights of minority students by grouping them disproportionately in low-ability classes.

But many of the newest attacks on ability grouping are based not only on concerns for insuring integration and equity. Advocates of heterogeneous grouping have also begun to frame their arguments in terms of a broader movement for educational reform. They argue that it is not enough simply to mix together students of different ability levels; a commitment to a stimulating curriculum and to methods such as cooperative learning, they say, is central to insuring that heterogeneously grouped classrooms succeed.

"If you just implement heterogeneous grouping without any thought, it doesn't help," Mr. French acknowledges. "It does not help high-achieving kids and it does not help low-achieving kids."

Unless its proponents can demonstrate that heterogeneous grouping improves the education of all students, including the brightest, it is likely to continue to meet staunch resistance, especially from many parents and advocates for children deemed high-achieving or gifted and talented, experts from both sides of the debate say.

"By totally doing away with ability grouping, you are clearly preventing children from reaching their full potential," argues Peter D. Rosenstein, the executive director of the National Association for Gifted Children. Educators of the gifted have increasingly seen their programs under attack by both budget cutters and education reformers. Mr. Rosenstein contends that the elimination of higher-ability classes in Massachusetts and other states has been inspired by a desire to trim budgets and is being carried out by "politically misguided educators who are looking not at what is good for children, but what is politically correct."

In Massachusetts, 21 percent of all public middle schools now group all students heterogeneously, compared with only a handful a decade ago, and an additional 69 percent have adopted more heterogeneous grouping during the past three years, according to the Massachusetts education department.

Some schools and school districts in the state undertook heterogeneous grouping well before the state began promoting it, and are seen as models for others that are considering such a change. Among the districts is the Pioneer Valley Regional School District in northwestern Massachusetts. Kevin J. Courtney, the superintendent of the rural, virtually all-white district, says pedagogic concerns, rather than civil-rights considerations, inspired the heterogeneous-grouping effort that they undertook eight years ago.

The so-called "detracking" effort there was initiated by teachers who questioned the educational value of ability grouping, Mr. Courtney says. The move probably would have been "doomed" if it had been imposed on teachers by school officials or the state, he says.

John D'Auria, the principal of the Wellesley (Mass.) Middle School in the suburbs of Boston, credits a long list of experiences for his decision to push for mixed-ability grouping soon after taking his school's helm in 1988.

He notes his stint as a teacher in a heterogeneously grouped Catholic school, which impressed him with its "sense of community." And he cites his experience as a guidance counselor in public schools, where he came to see young adolescents as "molting," or experiencing a key formative stage, during which they are especially vulnerable to negative messages that may be conveyed by grouping practices.

Thus, Mr. D'Auria says, he was distressed when he came to Wellesley and found the 7th and 8th grades divided into three levels each. "We really had some hidden belief that kids who learned things the first time and quickly were the bright ones," he says.

Mr. D'Auria set out to heterogeneously group the

At Pioneer Valley, John C. Lepore teaches a class in which students of different skill levels learn together.

school's classrooms and to have all children taught the honors-level curriculum. He endeavored to create a culture within the school that constantly reminds all children they can succeed, and he established an after-school study center for students who got low marks for effort.

At about the same time that Mr. D'Auria was undertaking his changes in Wellesley, officials at the Massachusetts education department were attempting to identify the obstacles that seemed to be limiting the impact of its discretionary grants for dropout prevention and remedial education.

State officials were frustrated because, although dropout rates had dropped slightly, grade retention and in-school suspensions apparently were rising in a number of districts where the state-funded programs were in place, Mr. French says.

The state began to encourage systemic change in schools to improve student achievement and, in 1990, targeted ability grouping as one of the biggest obstacles to improvement for low achievers. The education department's statement issued that year is one of the most strongly worded state advisories on ability grouping to date.

"There is little evidence that ability grouping or tracking improves academic achievement," it says, "while overwhelming evidence exists that ability grouping retards the academic progress of students in low- and middle-ability groupings."

The advisory blamed ability grouping for widening the gap between high and low achievers and for segregating students by race, income, language background, and disability. Gender also skewed the grouping process, it says, with girls being more likely than boys to be placed in low-level science and mathematics classes.

The education department offered schools technical assistance and training to implement heterogeneous grouping. Agency leaders asked the department's staff to work with educators, other state agencies, and various child-advocacy groups to promote an end to ability grouping and tracking.

Lacking authority under the Massachusetts constitution to require heterogeneous grouping, the department opted to use as its "carrot and stick" the awarding or denial of grants for dropout prevention and remedial education. For example, one school that embraced heterogeneous grouping, the Bartlett School in Lowell, received an additional $150,000 in state money over a year, which it used to fund professional development to prepare teachers for heterogeneous classrooms. Other districts had state grants revoked if they refused after a year to abandon ability grouping, Mr. French says.

Depriving the Gifted?

Some local newspapers responded to the state's initiative with editorials charging that the education department was trying to water down the curriculum used in public schools. And some educators criticized the state advisory as ignoring the fact that the research appears inconclusive on the value of ability grouping for high achievers, especially those deemed gifted and talented.

Many parents of gifted and talented children, meanwhile, have continued to oppose some districts' efforts to act on the state advisory. Some parents have removed their children from public schools over the issue, according to Joseph F. Harrington, the president of the Massachusetts Association for the Advancement of Individual Potential. "The bottom line," Mr. Harrington says, "is that bright kids, while they can learn cooperatively, at the same time learn better with other bright kids."

Although a small minority, the parents of gifted and talented and other higher-track children tend to be among the most well-to-do, influential, and heavily involved parents in schools. Such parents have proved to be formidable opponents when they feel the welfare of their children is threatened, according to many educators and administrators who have tried to implement mixed-ability grouping.

Many educators also have reservations about heterogeneous grouping, and getting them to implement such programs remains "an enormous struggle," says Maria Garza-Lubeck, the director of the Middle Grade State Policy Initiative. That program, with the oversight of the Council of Chief State School Officers and funding from the Carnegie Corporation of New York, has targeted grouping by achievement level as a practice it wishes to eliminate.

Many teacher-training programs continue to prepare their graduates only for ability-grouped classrooms, and the use of ability grouping and tracking remains "deeply entrenched in the junior high model," Ms. Garza-Lubeck says.

Elizabeth J. Bryant, the principal of the Bartlett School in Lowell, says teachers there "still have some serious concerns" about the heterogeneous grouping undertaken by the school five years ago. Bartlett's enrollment is about 40 percent white, 30 percent Cambodian, 25 percent Hispanic, and 2 percent black; 77 percent are economically disadvantaged.

"Teachers still are wondering if the brightest kids are getting sufficient attention," Ms. Bryant says. "They worry sometimes about whether to gear their instruction to the top or the middle."

Nevertheless, Ms. Bryant says, most teachers in her school have given an "overwhelmingly positive" response to heterogeneous grouping, largely because they still remember the "horror show" each had encountered in teaching the lowest of four tracks in the school's 7th and 8th grades.

The students who had been in Bartlett's lowest tracks "had no role models" under that system, Ms. Bryant says. In contrast, she says, their behavior improved dramatically once they were placed with higher achievers.

Although Wellesley Middle School did not face the same disciplinary problems as Bartlett, teachers there had been uncomfortable with ability grouping because they felt it encouraged students to focus on grades rather than learning, or discouraged them from taking risks out of fear their placement would be questioned, Mr. D'Auria says.

In her book *Crossing the Tracks,* released last December, Anne Wheelock, a former policy analyst for the Massachusetts Advocacy Center, a child-advocacy group, examines dozens of efforts to heterogeneously group students undertaken by schools in Massachusetts and elsewhere.

Heterogeneous grouping, Ms. Wheelock concludes, requires a profound shift in a school's basic mission and culture. Existing emphases on quantifying intelligence, defining ability, and identifying weaknesses must give way to emphases on releasing intelligence,

---

'By totally doing away with ability grouping, you are clearly preventing children from reaching their full potential,' argues one advocate.

---

nurturing effort, and building on strengths, she writes.

Mr. D'Auria of Wellesley Middle School echoes that view. "What people believe really, truly influences the outcomes that you see," he says. To help reinforce that message, Mr. D'Auria has decorated his school's hallways with street signs bearing the names of triumphant underdogs, such as Jim Abbott, a professional baseball player who was born with one hand.

Schools that undertake heterogeneous grouping, Ms. Wheelock writes, also need to provide their teachers with staff development so they can learn to use mastery learning, cooperative learning, curriculum-embedded assessment strategies, and other pedagogic tools that have proved useful in working with diverse groups of students.

Phasing In Changes

An updated version of the Massachusetts education department's advisory on ability grouping maintains that all students, including the gifted and talented, benefit from a change to mixed-ability grouping as long as it is accompanied by appropriate changes in curriculum, instruction, and testing. The updated advisory cautions, however, that such changes should be phased in. It recommends that schools spend a year on staff development and planning before they implement heterogeneous grouping.

"I have to really think about the concepts I want to teach, and I have to think: What is a really student-centered way for them to learn this?" observes John C. Lepore, who teaches science at Pioneer Valley High School.

One recent morning, Mr. Lepore was teaching a class of heterogeneously grouped 7th graders, some of whom had special needs. Working cooperatively in groups of four, the students dipped thermometers into various-sized containers of water to determine which would lose heat faster—a mountain lion or a mouse.

Watching the class, one could not tell the brightest children from those with special needs. Working in one of the groups was a child with autism, a beneficiary of the complementary relationship between heterogeneous grouping and the mainstreaming of students with disabilities.

Mr. Lepore says his task of teaching a mixed classroom was being helped by "an explosion of new textbooks that are using an integrated approach to science education," as well as newly available interactive laser disks and hands-on activities. Noting that he had taught in both homogeneously and heterogeneously grouped classrooms, he calls teaching the latter "more fun."

Largely due to the efforts of the state education department, only about 10 percent of public middle schools in Massachusetts continue to separate their students into at least two groups based on ability, Mr. French says. However, he adds, ability grouping remains prevalent at the high school level, which the state so far has given a lower priority in its campaign to promote heterogeneous grouping.

"If you are really going to talk about all kids graduating from high school with a high-quality academic preparation, then you need to look at some of the rigid tracking that goes on in the high schools," Mr. French says. He says he plans to give high schools "a bit more of a friendly push" to reconsider their grouping practices.

Heterogeneous grouping appears, ironically, to meet the most acceptance and success in schools that are relatively homogeneous to begin with. In such schools, proponents of mixed-ability classes acknowledge, the prospect of lumping all children together appears less threatening to parents and faculty members.

Ms. Bryant of the Bartlett School in Lowell says that she received virtually no unfavorable reaction from parents when she implemented heterogeneous grouping. But she says she probably would have run into more resistance if more of her students were from wealthier socioeconomic backgrounds.

"There is no question that it is easier if you are more homogeneous to start with," Ms. Wheelock says. "But I don't think it is fair to say it is impossible when you are extremely diverse."

School leaders in the Amherst-Pelham district strongly defend their ability-grouping policy, which is the target of the federal suit filed last month. John E. Heffley, the principal of Amherst-Pelham Regional High School, argued that grouping students by ability is a necessity in his district, which serves both the

---

Although a small minority, the parents of gifted and talented children tend to be among the most influential and heavily involved parents in schools.

---

children of recent Southeast Asian refugees and of University of Massachusetts faculty members. The enrollment is 72 percent white, 10 percent Asian, 9 percent Hispanic, and 9 percent black, and it is disproportionately limited-English-proficient.

Mr. Heffley says the vast majority of parents and staff members at his school endorses its grouping system, which provides three tiers of instruction in most courses and involves parents by asking them to approve or reject a teacher's recommendation about where their children should be placed. "I believe that school systems should develop their institutional pattern of grouping students to fit their own system," Mr. Heffley says.

The Amherst-Pelham grouping system, Mr. Heffley says, produces large crops of National Merit Scholarship finalists and college-bound students, as well as low dropout rates among limited-English-proficient students who get the extra help they need.

William A. Norris, a lawyer for the Amherst-area chapter of the N.A.A.C.P., believes otherwise. He contends that the chief product of the Amherst-Pelham grouping system is "permanent, irrevocable scarring, low self-esteem, underperformance, and boredom" inflicted on minority students who are disproportionately represented in the lower tiers.

"This is a racial issue," Mr. Norris says. "Within the same schoolhouse, we have two groups being treated differently. We have in-house segregation." The district's policy of involving parents in the grouping process "is no defense," Mr. Norris adds. Many parents may be unwilling, unable, or afraid to challenge a teacher's recommendation, he says.

The suit Mr. Norris filed in U.S. District Court argues that Amherst-Pelham should be denied federal funds because its grouping system deprives minority students of full access to the school curriculum, and thus violates their rights under the 14th Amendment to the U.S. Constitution and various federal civil-rights laws. "We want to choke off funds," Mr. Norris says. "That is the ultimate sanction."

On a recent Friday afternoon in Lowell, meanwhile, Ms. Bryant celebrated the success of the Bartlett School's heterogeneous-grouping efforts by treating her faculty to ice cream. Last year's 8th graders surpassed those in comparable schools in all four areas of the Massachusetts Assessment Test, Ms. Bryant points out, and "we celebrate when we can."

Ms. Bryant concedes, however, that she puts little stock in standardized-test scores and that she probably would have barely mentioned the test results if they had not been good. Mr. Courtney, the superintendent of the Pioneer Valley district, takes an even dimmer view of the state's standardized tests, which he describes as "so full of holes they are not worth talking about." The tests, he asserts, are incapable of measuring the positive impact of heterogeneous grouping on higher-level thinking skills and in other areas.

Unless educators in Massachusetts and elsewhere can agree on what constitutes a valid measurement of student achievement, the debate over the relative merits of homogeneous and heterogeneous grouping appears unlikely to be resolved. In the meantime, many proponents of heterogeneous grouping base their arguments on personal observations, ideals, and faith.

"When kids are forced to explain and answer questions, they are learning that material in much greater depth," Mr. Courtney declares as he gives a tour of Pioneer Valley High School.

Mr. Lepore, the science teacher, says, "I have never had a parent come back to me and say their son or daughter is not challenged." □

From Education Week, *Jan. 13, 1993*

43.

Rear-Guard Reaction

What happens when a radical state reform law bumps into the entrenched local establishment of eastern Kentucky?

By Lonnie Harp

When Kentucky lawmakers designed their landmark education-reform law in 1990, their most controversial provisions were meant to erase chronic political influence and patronage. The anti-nepotism section of the law clearly spells out that spouses, parents, children, and close cousins are not allowed to hire one another for school jobs or to work together as administrators. But in tackling the stubbornly independent spirit of this close-knit, insular area, legislators forgot about Castle Whitaker.

Mr. Whitaker, a veteran educator and part of one of the state's best-known local education dynasties, was narrowly elected last month to the Magoffin County school board after pointing out to state officials that the law does not specifically disallow election of a superintendent's uncle, which he is to the local schools chief, Carter Whitaker.

Castle Whitaker's success in exploiting the legislature's unwitting avuncular exemption has been seen in the state either as the last hurrah for the old-time politics targeted by the reform act or as one of the first chinks in yet another doomed plan forced on these poor Appalachian counties in the name of progress.

In several counties near here, the clash between state and local political forces over school-governance reform has recently become more heated. Although Castle Whitaker, who declined to be interviewed for this story, can claim a personal victory, the battle elsewhere goes on and has been bruising to both sides.

As conflicts in the courts and the legislature inten-sify, impatience on both sides is threatening to break up the broad consensus that swept the reform measure into law. Reform activists want stronger state action and greater support, while opponents complain that state officials have become political bullies trampling on the deeply ingrained tradition of local school control.

Jobs, Power, and Money

A trip along the winding mountain roads east of Salyersville provides a vivid picture of the economic and social forces at work behind the battle over the schools. In the occasional clearings among the ancient mountains, families have claimed level plots by anchoring trailers, raising garages and sheds, building modest houses, grazing goats and cattle, and fencing off small cemeteries. The residential lots usually sit alone, surrounded by walls of rock and trees that permit little space for the sky.

The natural and man-made features alike testify to a long-established way of life in the coal-fields region, which stretches to the Virginia and Tennessee borders. Appalachian experts describe a desperate economy where steady jobs are hard to find, family ties are precious, and outsiders are welcomed as visitors but viewed warily as settlers.

Analysts say the forces have for decades shifted the focus of school administrators away from student achievement to a preoccupation with awarding jobs, doling out contracts, and maintaining political power.

In response to abuses in eastern Kentucky and throughout the state, lawmakers in 1990 moved to reduce the hiring authority of board members and administrators, force competitive bidding and other common business practices, and remove corrupt administrators. While many have welcomed the new system, in recent months the state has found itself in a contest of political hardball against local officials determined to protect both their personal prerogatives and their regional independence.

"This is the acid test," says John B. Stephenson, the president of Berea College and an expert on Appalachian culture. "School systems have become the engine of countywide political machines that are relatively stable and relatively impenetrable, but a lot of these folks will be passed by to the extent that these reforms are successful. It's pretty easy to see why there is a ructious situation in certain places."

The resistance, which in some places has spread from disenchanted administrators to parents and others, has left top reformers feeling besieged and frustrated. "There are some people who don't believe the state can enforce the law in their area, and they don't want it to," explains Robert F. Sexton, the executive director of the Prichard Committee for Academic Excellence, a citizens' advocacy group. "In some places the engine that drives the civic process is busted—it has thrown a rod—and we may have to look again at how to reinvent it."

The Rev. Timothy D. Jessen says he and other school reformers "thought we were on the edge of the promised land, but now we may be back in the wilderness."

At Prestonsburg, the seat of Floyd County and the next major crossroads east of Salyersville, John David Caudill offers a brief lesson in survival and local politics. "What you've got is confrontation from both sides and no cooperation. It's all mandates and reactions," the lawyer says. "If you put me back in a corner, I'm going to bite you."

Mr. Caudill has been a visible force among the school-reform critics, having represented a principal who was removed by the state board of education and a school board member charged with improperly suggesting a hiring during a meeting. He faults the state's tactics more than the substance of the changes it has enacted.

"I'm not here to defend our board or school system; we've got all kinds of problems," he says. "But I think the state needs to change its attitude about how it conducts its investigations and how it comes at us. There are some people that deserve credit here."

Mr. Caudill's appeal of the principal's removal is intended to force the state to reconsider the role of the office of education accountability, which was established by the 1990 law as the watchdog of reform. He and others charge that while the office has the power to effectively prosecute local school officials before the state board, it does not abide by common legal procedures needed to insure a competent defense.

Noting that an earlier investigation ousted the district's superintendent, critics also contend that the state has come down too hard on local leaders. At the same time, some people in the district's central office have taken steps to sour teachers and citizens on the intent of the school reforms. An anonymous letter mailed from the district's headquarters and traced back to administrators there urges an all-out fight against the law's changes.

The six-page letter points to earlier reforms, such as educational television, open classrooms, standardized testing, and new teaching techniques. "Our heroes . . . managed to overcome this myriad of threats to their classroom and school operation and independence," it says.

The letter implores educators who were "bought" by pay raises in the first two years of the reform program to resist changes. "We must join together to reclaim our classrooms, our schools, and our kids' education from the San Diego megalomaniacs, the out-of-state philosophers, and the New Hampshire test-makers," the writers urge.

Reform critics have been particularly resentful of the role of Commissioner of Education Thomas C. Boysen, who came from the San Diego schools to become the state's first appointed schools chief.

Local observers and state officials agree that scrutiny of the reform law—which also mandates governance by school councils, ungraded primary programs, expanded pre-school and after-school programs, new assessments, and the increased use of technology—is growing outside of Floyd County as well. While the law's substantial increase in education funding initially won it acceptance, the recent state administrative crackdown and the autonomous role played by Mr. Boysen have begun to frustrate school leaders. Resentment also seems to be growing at the grassroots.

In Harlan County, where the Appalachian Mountains rise to their highest reaches, the state has taken its strongest action to date. After targeting the entire school board and superintendent, the state succeeded in ousting three of the five board members. One was cleared and another resigned, as did the superintendent. Since then, the state has issued a lengthy improvement plan calling for a host of changes in the district, whose policies it labeled "outdated, incomplete, and inadequate."

Last month, about 100 people gathered at Cawood High School to applaud speakers demanding that the state "get out." The demonstration frustrated Rep. Roger Noe, a Harlan County resident who as chairman of the House Education Committee was one of the architects of the reform law. Mr. Noe was defeated for re-election this year in part because of the board upheaval.

"What we had was a rally against good government and standard business practices," Mr. Noe says. "Many people around here believe that we have crooks, but they are our crooks and we should deal with them with our own measures."

Harlan County residents apparently are still undecided on whether the ouster of the board members was justified. A local judge reinstated the three members, although that move was blocked by another court and is due to be reviewed by the state supreme court this month.

Ronnie G. Ball, one of the ousted board members, was narrowly re-elected last month in a four-person race, while another ousted board member was easily defeated. Mr. Ball declined an interview, citing his ongoing court case. But, in written responses for a pre-election story in the *Harlan Daily Enterprise*, he complained that the state had stepped in despite improvements under way in the district.

"My top priority is to see the control of our schools returned to the local people who care about them," Mr. Ball wrote. "The way I see it, the O.E.A. and Boysen's office chose Harlan County to make an example of for all the state to see."

Some analysts contend that the state has itself stirred up some of the opposition by charging ahead without regard for local considerations and traditions.

State Errors Seen

The state moved quickly into Harlan County in its attempt to remove the board and superintendent, who resigned only to be appointed to an advisory post by his temporary replacement. The state then acted to foil that effort.

In Floyd County, where a local committee was appointed to screen applicants for the superintendent's post, Mr. Boysen effectively eliminated all of the finalists, including one local candidate. That left only a school administrator from central Kentucky who had served on an advisory panel with the commissioner. "If

that's not political, what the hell is political?" Mr. Caudill asks.

Most observers agree that state officials erred badly in interceding in the Floyd County search and, in many ways, started the avalanche of open hostility in the Appalachian counties. But they add that the state has had a difficult task in being forceful enough to bring about real change without unnecessarily antagonizing local officials and residents.

Beyond the dramas that have unfolded in Harlan and Floyd counties, observers say, efforts to thwart the reform law are rampant in the region.

Moreover, the pressure to move strongly to clean up poorly managed Kentucky districts comes not only from lawmakers and educators from elsewhere in the state, but also from the 1989 supreme court ruling that struck down the state's entire education system and led to the reform law. "The perception was that a lot of money was being wasted in districts that were highly political and badly managed," says Mr. Sexton of the Prichard Committee. "The dilemma is that you get sucked into a fight over governance issues at the local level, and that lessens the energy and time you have to deal with the rest of the reforms and weakens your political base."

Mr. Boysen acknowledges the fragile balancing act. As a result of some of the uproar from eastern Kentucky, the state has looked again at its management-assistance program, which was designed to move into troubled districts. Political considerations make it more important that the program seek to guide and support improvement efforts at the local level, Mr. Boysen says, rather than imposing them from outside.

"The criticism goes with the territory, because when one gets assertive, the people who are getting squeezed start to fight back," Mr. Boysen says. "What I've been surprised with is how much good stuff is going on even though there is corruption and incompetence at the top. There are some teachers out there doing great work, and we're trying to get them all of the policy support and resources they need."

Local residents who have been involved with education say the state is sorely out of touch when it comes to understanding the local system and how best to change it. The Rev. Timothy D. Jessen has been waiting for 12 years for help from officials in Frankfort, the state capital. As chairman of the Floyd County Education Forum, the Presbyterian pastor is a veteran of battles with the school bureaucracy. But, Mr. Jessen laments, "I don't think they have a ghost of an idea of what it's like here, and that's where the state has made its errors."

"Right now we're experiencing a number of setbacks," he adds. "It's not going to wipe out the reform act, but if citizens don't fight back, the legislature may become inclined to say that the people don't support this."

Others emphasize the obstacles posed by the deep

web of self-interests within the school administration, or portray the current backlash as a natural part of the reform program. But almost everyone agrees that the state has miscalculated the forces at work here.

"The state should have gone in and built upon what had already taken place," says Tom Gish, the publisher of *The Mountain Eagle newspaper* in Letcher County for 35 years and a first-term member of the state school board. "Instead, it has wound up almost making the reform people its enemies."

Mr. Gish fired off a heated letter to Mr. Boysen for his part in the Floyd County superintendent search. While describing Mr. Boysen's performance as improving, he predicts that recovery will be "a long process."

Like others who have followed the school-reform effort, Mr. Gish says that a stronger state presence may be needed. "The state is putting money into the hands of people of dubious ability who have historically produced an educational product that is second rate," he explains. "There is nothing to indicate that if you give them money and leave them alone, anything will be any different except that they will be spending more money."

"Sure the state's hand is heavy at times," he continues, "but I think it has been established that the state's hand needs to be heavy and may indeed be too light."

During the 1990 debate over the reform law, many lawmakers viewed Representative Noe as an extremist when he called for dismantling local school boards. In retrospect, though, many on the front lines of the reform battles in eastern Kentucky say they now view his position with newfound respect.

Mr. Noe predicts that the reform law will work through its current difficulties, despite state officials' lack of understanding. "Many people had no idea how deep the network was and how entrenched the economic and social forces of the school system were. They didn't see that they were involved in a major social change, and they don't realize it today," Mr. Noe says. "A level of education has to occur here before the people who are screaming and hollering and raising hell will appreciate this."

"It is going according to plan, but it ought not to have to be this way," he says. "I am hoping that the remaining members of the legislature will have enough grit to get through this period."

Questions about lawmakers' resolve to back the reforms these days call to mind Rep. Gregory D. Stumbo, a Floyd County lawyer who serves as the leader of the Democratic majority in the House. Although he was an important backer of the reform law, Mr. Stumbo has become increasingly critical as the local struggle has grown. Given Mr. Noe's fate, observers suggest that Mr. Stumbo is under pressure to express the frustrations of Floyd County voters.

Far from retreating, though, Mr. Stumbo continues to proclaim firm support for the law, if not Mr. Boysen's execution of it. He says his frustrations have resulted both from the continued publicity about his district and from concerns about Mr. Boysen's performance in such areas as the restructuring of the state education department and the implementation of technology programs.

"I'm maybe more supportive of the reform law now than I ever was," Mr. Stumbo says. "What I'm upset about is accepting mediocrity. People are criticizing the law when it isn't the law's fault."

To that end, Mr. Stumbo was a leading force behind the creation of a task force that will tour the state to discuss implementation of the law. In some quarters, the panel is seen as an effort by lawmakers to take more control of the pace and direction of reforms. "People in Kentucky want a better education system, and my district wants better schools. What people don't want is to hear that all this is wrong and you all are crooks," Mr. Stumbo says. "For years we governed by crisis, and the reform act was designed to alleviate that. The significant part of the law is that we have a game plan now and we're not going to drop it."

"In fact, things on the whole are improving in central Appalachia," says Ron D. Eller, the director of the Appalachian Center at the University of Kentucky. "While there is still a strong resistance to change, we are seeing communities where the old structures of power are breaking down."

"There are very, very strong pockets of resistance, but for each of those there are also places where the reform law is working very well," Mr. Eller adds.

"We've come right down to the life-and-death struggle with those who have been in power," says Mr. Jessen, the Floyd County minister. "Some big strides have been made," he adds. "In 1990 we thought we were on the edge of the promised land, but now we may be back in the wilderness and in for a protracted period of strife." □

From Education Week, *Dec. 9, 1992*

44.

A Perilous Odyssey

Citing 'satanism' and 'secular humanism,' angry Christian activists are out to sink an award-winning reform project in North Carolina.

By Meg Sommerfeld

School officials in Gastonia, N.C., who last summer were celebrating winning a grant to create "break the mold" public schools find themselves now under fire from hundreds of conservative Christian activists who are questioning the project's academic integrity and saying it would undermine their children's religious beliefs.

In recent weeks, the "Odyssey Project"—an effort to restructure three of the district's 54 schools with a longer school day and year, coordinated education, health, and social services, and early-childhood schooling—has run into growing opposition.

A letter to the editor of the local newspaper speaks of the project as the work of the "Antichrist." A hand-out making its way around town links the project to "secular humanism" and "new age" teaching. The project has even come under fire for its use of Greek terms, which one opponent decried because "the Greeks practiced sodomy," according to a project organizer. One project planner has heard herself described by an irate parent as a Nazi, a Satanist, and a communist.

While leaders of the formal opposition have distanced themselves from some of the more inflammatory rhetoric, they have vowed that, if the district does not abandon the project, they will demand the ouster of the superintendent and seek the defeat of several school board members who face re-election next year.

To compound the project's problems, its director was found dead in his garage Feb. 19, a victim of accidental carbon-monoxide poisoning. A county medical examiner say Joseph F. Miller, the assistant superintendent of the county schools, had started his truck on a cold morning with the garage doors closed and was overcome by the fumes.

In the wake of Mr. Miller's death, Melinda Ratchford, the district's media and technology director, says that "with the massive . . . concerns of the 'religious right,' we felt we were under attack, and all of a sudden what we thought was such a bright spot for Gaston County had been turned against us."

The Opposition Forms

Educators in Gaston County, a blue-collar, textile-manufacturing region outside Charlotte, had high hopes that the $2.1 million they received from the New American Schools Development Corporation for the first year of a five-year project would revolutionize county schools. Their Odyssey Project was one of 11 proposals selected to receive a grant from the private, nonprofit corporation created at the behest of former President Bush to raise $200 million to create innovative schools.

The project plans to abandon traditional grade levels, introduce older students to weekly seminars on multiculturalism and current events, require community service of all students, and use an outcome-based assessment that focuses not on the number of courses taken, but on the knowledge, skills, and attitudes students must have before graduation.

Ironically, while one of the project's primary goals is to enhance parental and community involvement, the unprecedented involvement of some community members now poses a challenge to its implementation.

Leaders of Concerned Citizens for Public Education, an organization formed to fight the project, have a long list of objections, but most of their ire is directed toward its outcome-based approach—often a target of conservatives, who say it forces schools to teach values at the expense of core subjects.

Some 400 community members met Feb. 28 at Catawba Heights Baptist Church in nearby Belmont, N.C., to hear the group's leaders criticize the project. Organizers distributed bumper stickers and literature critical of the program.

Standing under a banner reading "Being Who God Wants Me To Be," the Rev. Gregory A. Dry Sr., a local Baptist minister and one of the group's leaders, urged the audience to fight the program so their children "do not become the guinea pigs in a failed experiment."

Mr. Dry says he did not object to the academic aspects of the project, but felt that the overall philosophy behind it was designed to "teach in opposition to Christianity."

Concerned Citizens has considered more formal ties with Citizens for Excellence in Education, a conservative Christian advocacy group that has worked to elect its sympathizers to school boards nationwide.

NASDC's Role

Much of the furor over the project erupted the week before Mr. Miller died, as the school board selected the three pilot schools for the project. Although the district's receipt of the NASDC grant was widely publicized last summer, several area residents say most people knew little about the program until the board announced its plan to vote on the sites.

The board decided to choose the sites before consulting parents so project officials could involve the parents of children in participating schools, according to Superintendent Edwin L. West Jr. He notes that students and teachers who object to the plan can apply to transfer to other schools. Critics say the district should first have asked parents at each school if they wanted the program, or set it up as a voluntary magnet school.

Despite protests by several hundred individuals urging a delay in the vote, the board approved the three sites on Feb. 15. Over the next few days, debate over the issue intensified, each day bringing new rumors about the program, the design team, and NASDC itself. Mr. Miller's death four days after the vote fueled further speculation about the fate of the program.

Calling Mr. Miller's death "a terrible blow," Robin Murphy, a NASDC spokesman, says the organization was working with the design team to regroup in the wake of his death and the community opposition.

Although the recent events in Gaston County are "clearly a barrier," NASDC is "not alarmed" about the controversy, says Paige Cassidy, another NASDC official, because some level of resistance to change was expected at all of the project sites. As of last week, Ms. Cassidy says the organization was receiving about 20

The Reverend urged the audience to fight the program so their children 'do not become the guinea pigs in a failed experiment.'

---

calls a day about the Odyssey Project, about evenly split on the issue.

In the days since the sites were chosen, senior school administrators have attended meetings at the three schools to answer parents' questions and have distributed material explaining some of the project's controversial components, says Sandra G. Frye, the superintendent's executive assistant.

She and Mr. West also note that extensive efforts had been made to inform the community about the program last fall through a regular weekly column by the superintendent in two area newspapers and numerous presentations to elected officials and business and civic groups.

But Saul Cooperman, the chairman of NASDC's education-advisory panel, observed that such outreach efforts to prepare communities for reform often go unheeded until changes are about to be implemented. "When you have massive change, you can talk and you can explain and really do a fairly competent job, but many people don't really pay attention," says Mr. Cooperman, a former state education commissioner for New Jersey.

"But," he adds, "then when you say in four weeks the training is going to start, and the bus routes are going to change, and your kids are going to have new books, then people wake up."

In Gaston County, people also seem to be waking up to the fact that the project's outcome-based approach could affect their children's chances of being accepted into college. Ashley Hartley, the wife of a high school teacher and a member of Concerned Citizens, says she called two higher-education officials in the state to ask what impact not having a grade-point average would have on college admissions.

One official she spoke to was Anthony R. Strickland,

the associate director of undergraduate admissions at the University of North Carolina at Chapel Hill. Mr. Strickland acknowledges that such a system could put applicants at a disadvantage. "It forces us to place more emphasis on standardized tests," he says. However, he also cautioned that he was unfamiliar with specifics of the Gaston project and that, as more schools adopt outcome-based models, universities "will deal with whatever system they come up with."

The state legislature has also mandated that higher-education institutions in the state develop mechanisms for accepting proficiency certificates in lieu of Carnegie units. In addition, students will initially receive both traditional grades and outcome-based measures of progress.

Meanwhile, a noted academic whose research is cited in the literature distributed by the Concerned Citizens group says that his work has been distorted to reach false conclusions regarding outcome-based education. "I think it's way out of context," says Robert E. Slavin, a researcher at Johns Hopkins University, of several references to a 1987 report he described as a narrow study of "a particular way of using mastery learning in the classroom." "It does not at all apply to the situation they're relating to," he adds.

Next Steps

But beyond the disagreements over the merits of outcome-based education, opponents say that they have been unfairly tagged as religious extremists, and, as a result, their concerns have not been addressed. In addition, Ms. Hartley and Brenda White, another member of Concerned Citizens' steering committee, both say they no longer trust school officials because they feel the district deliberately misrepresented the program and failed to provide adequate information.

District officials reply that they have gone out of their way to answer questions during a difficult period. Ron Hovis, the school board chairman, issued a statement last week supporting the project. "The board of education is solidly behind the Odyssey project and has been since the beginning," the statement says. "I believe once it is presented to the public in the comprehensive manner we are planning that they will support it also."

School officials attribute much of the conflict to confusion over the language used to describe the program. "Every profession has its jargon," Mr. West says. "However, because a lay person doesn't deal with those terms on a day-to-day basis, it is understandable . . . that some individuals will experience those kinds of emotions."

The district has planned a series of meetings for parents of children in the three Odyssey schools as well as seven town meetings for the general public. "I think the opposition is basically based on lack of information about the program," agrees Tony Giacobbe, the president of the local affiliate of the North Carolina Association of Educators. "I would say the majority of teachers are in support of the program and the change it represents."

NASDC officials say they do not anticipate ending the project's funding. "To assume 100 percent support of anything is pretty unrealistic," Ms. Cassidy of NASDC says. "We're not concerned to the point that we are worried about [the design team's] ability to make this design work." □

From Education Week, *March 10, 1993*

45.

Under The Surface

An unusual study looks at schools from the inside and finds a set of problems that reformers aren't dealing with.

By Robert Rothman

An unusual study that examined schools "from the inside" has concluded that the policy remedies offered by most education reformers bear little relation to the problems identified by students, teachers, and parents. The study, based on 18 months of in-depth conversations in four Southern California schools, found that such issues as low student achievement and problems in the teaching profession, which many reforms are aimed at addressing, are in fact consequences of what the authors see as the real problems in schools.

These underlying issues include unsatisfactory relationships between and among students and staff members, differences of race and class, and deep concerns about school safety. Perhaps as a result of such factors, the schools studied exhibited a "pervasive sense of despair," the authors write.

"If the relationships are wrong between teachers and students, for whatever reason," John Maguire, the president of the Claremont University Center and Graduate School, which conducted the study, said at a New York City press briefing late last November, "you can restructure until the cows come home, but transformation won't take place."

"If that is right, the national conversation about restructuring schools has to change," he said. "You can't get the answer right if you don't ask the right questions."

Marc S. Tucker, the president of the National Center on Education and the Economy and a prominent leader in national school-reform efforts, noted that the Clare-

mont report is consistent with his group's analysis of the need for reform. "Any effort to restructure schools for high performance has got to take into account the realities they report on," Mr. Tucker said.

The report does not offer specific recommendations for change. But the authors said that the participatory process they undertook in conducting the study could serve as a way of allowing schools to change themselves. They also said that they plan to spend the next few years identifying policies and practices that impede schools from addressing the problems identified in the study, with an eye toward dismantling them.

"We can't afford to spend any more money or time trying to enact changes that will not increase the ability of practitioners to relate and spend their energies and talents with students," said Mary Poplin, the director of Claremont's Institute for Education in Transformation and the study's director.

'Surprising' Findings

The study differs markedly from most of the 300 or more reports on school reform issued in the past decade, according to Mr. Maguire. Unlike most such studies, which examined schools "from the outside in or from the top down," he said, the new study went inside schools to find out what the problems are.

The John W. Kluge Foundation funded the study by Claremont, an independent, exclusively graduate-level institution in Claremont, Calif. The research team chose four schools in the area surrounding Claremont, which is 35 miles east of Los Angeles. The schools—two elementary schools, one middle school, and one high school—are made up of low-income urban populations as well as affluent suburban students. They are representative of the schools of California and the nation, according to the study directors.

The researchers spent over a year in the schools, held more than 160 meetings with members of the school communities, and received written comments from them. In all, they heard from 4,000 students, 1,000 parents, and 200 teachers, administrators, and other employees. The meetings generated 24,000 pages of transcriptions, essays, drawings, journal entries, and notes, as well as 18 hours of videotapes and 80 hours of audio tapes.

Culling through the data, the researchers—along with members of the school communities, who contributed as part of an unusual "participatory" form of research—found a surprising amount of agreement around a set of themes that differed sharply from those that usually pervade reports on schooling.

"No one was more surprised by the results of this report than those of us on the outside," the authors write. "We, like the authors of previous reports on schooling and teacher education, would have predicted issues such as what to teach, how to measure it, how much a teacher knows, and choice of school would have surfaced; they did not."

Rather, the report states, the most commonly cited problem identified by the people in the four schools was the issue of "relationships." "The typical school day is nothing more than a series of relationships," said William Bertrand, the principal of Montclair High School, one of the participating schools.

But the study found that most relationships within schools leave something to be desired. Students reported that, although one of the best aspects of school for them was "seeing their friends," they often had a very narrow circle of friends. They also said that they liked teachers who cared about them, but they complained that they were often ignored or received negative treatment. These attitudes had a direct effect on how well they performed in the classroom, Ms. Poplin noted. "Kids said, 'I do well in classes where the teacher respects me, and I do poorly where the teachers don't like me,'" she said.

Teachers, for their part, said that they often did not understand students who were ethnically different from themselves. They also complained that they were isolated from other teachers and that their relationships with administrators were often strained. "We have to put relationships at the core of what we're doing," one middle school teacher is quoted in the report as saying.

In addition to relationships, questions of race, culture, and class ran through every other issue, the report says. Many students, both white and minority, perceive schools to be racist, it states. These perceptions, it says, reflect incidents of racism on campus as well as a curriculum that they say is heavily weighted toward white Europeans.

"Students from various races and occasionally young women doubt the very veracity of the content of the curriculum," the report states. "Students of color rarely see their histories or their literatures adequately addressed in schools." One high school student is quoted in the report as saying: "One thing that should be done is to change the history books. Our history books show Hannibal, a man coming from Africa on elephants, as white. It shows Egyptians as tan, and we don't even teach about the Zulu Nation, but we teach about the Roman Empire—what's the difference?"

These problems are exacerbated by the fact that most teachers are white, Ms. Poplin said. She noted that several schools issued edicts not to talk about the controversial verdicts last spring in the Rodney King police brutality case, despite students' strong interest in it.

In a more encouraging finding, the study contradicts the popular view that members of different cultures hold different values. "Different groups and people may express particular values in different ways," the report states. "However, in our data, participants across race and class express values of honesty, hard work, beauty, justice, democracy, freedom, decency, and the need and desire for a good education."

'Pervasive Sense of Despair'

The study also found that many teachers and students held strong views on teaching and learning, and their concerns echo those found in other reform reports. Many students, it found, consider schoolwork boring and irrelevant to their lives, and teachers find themselves under pressure to cover mandated material so that students can pass tests.

It also found, like previous studies, that students and teachers consider schools unsafe and complain about the physical environment. But such concerns go beyond the surface-level threats of physical harm and crumbling buildings, noted Mr. Bertrand, the high school principal. "When students speak of safety, they are talking about psychological safety more than physical safety," he said. "That's more at risk."

It may be due to all of these factors, the report suggests, that there is a "pervasive sense of despair" in the schools included in the study. "Teachers and staff have a sense that some students do not perform because they feel hopeless," it states.

But it also says that the study itself offered hope by allowing students and teachers to discuss issues of mutual concern. "All of us agree change is absolutely necessary," said Patricia Ortiz, a 6th-grade teacher at Vejar Elementary School and one of the project's participants. □

From Education Week, *Dec. 2, 1992*

46.

Clock Watching

A federal commission on time and learning is rethinking the calendar and schedule of schools.

By Mark Pitsch

Tears well up in the eyes of Marilyn Davenport, the principal of Governor Bent Elementary School in Albuquerque, N.M., as she reads a series of poems to visitors. With titles like "Divorce," "Daddy Went Bye-Bye," "My Mom's Boyfriend," and "Four Years Ago It Happened," the poems by the 10- and 11-year-olds are filled with pain, honesty, and catharsis.

"You talk about rearranging the schedule," Ms. Davenport says, "but I don't care when I have the children as long as wonderful things are happening."

Ms. Davenport's visitors are members of the National Education Commission on Time and Learning, a federally chartered panel assigned the task of examining the use of time in schools. While for Ms. Davenport the paramount concern lies in what goes on during regular school hours, many educators testifying before the commission over a two-day period indicated support for longer school days and school years, as well as for a more creative use of time in schools.

As it analyzes how the use of time affects schooling and development, and whether more time—or more efficient use of it—is needed to improve student performance, the commission is conducting a series of site visits and hearings across the country. Each is devoted to a particular theme, such as how time affects curriculum, professional development, or learning and student motivation—the subject at hand here.

Created in 1991, the panel has nine members, three each appointed by former Secretary of Education Lamar Alexander, the House leadership, and the

Senate leadership. With a current budget of $975,000, the panel is slated to present a report on its findings to Congress next year. Sen. Jeff Bingaman, D-N.M., the sponsor of the legislation that created the commission, said its study of time issues is as important as the efforts to set national education goals and create curricular and performance standards. "The kind of changes that we're talking about here are systemic changes that are going to occur over a period of years," Mr. Bingaman said. "If we're serious about it, we've got to address the issue of time."

A similar view was offered by John Hodge Jones, the chairman of the commission and the superintendent of the Murfreesboro, Tenn., school district, which has pioneered the use of extended-day schools. "If we can do a good job with our work," Mr. Jones said, "we can have a lasting impact on education into the next century."

It's About Time

Under its Congressional charter, the commission's job is to analyze and make recommendations on:
• The length of the academic year and day in the United States and elsewhere;
• The time in school that students devote to mathematics, history, English, science, and geography;
• The use of incentives for students to improve their academic performance in available learning time;
• How children use their time outside of school, including doing homework, and whether those hours can be considered learning time;
• How teachers can make use of their available time for

professional development;

• How schools are used for extended learning or social services; and

• The funding and state or federal legislation needed to implement its proposals.

"I'm convinced the timing is right for this," said Milton Goldberg, the time panel's executive director. "A lot of issues have been addressed by the education-reform movement, but none will have been addressed like this one." Mr. Goldberg should know. He was the executive director of the National Commission on Excellence in Education, which produced the landmark 1983 report, *A Nation at Risk.*

Formidable Obstacles

Although *A Nation at Risk* has had a profound impact on education over the past decade, its call for a seven-hour school day and an academic year of up to 220 days met with little response from states or districts. Efforts to lengthen the school day or year ran into formidable political and fiscal obstacles, which may also bedevil the coming recommendations of the time panel.

But Mr. Goldberg said he expects the new panel's report on time to be broader than the time recommendations contained in *A Nation at Risk.* "If you radicalize what you think about time, it makes you think about everything," Mr. Goldberg said. Moreover, by holding hearings across the nation and issuing a report solely on how time is used, he said, the panel hopes that its report will succeed in reaching a wide audience.

Mr. Bingaman also intends to insure that Congress hears what the commissioners have to say. He indicated that the commission's report could serve as the basis for federal legislation, and suggested that the report arrive on Congressional desks as members debate reauthorization of the Elementary and Secondary Education Act over the next two years.

"There are ways the federal government can facilitate and provide incentives for schools to expand their hours of instruction," Mr. Bingaman said.

In Albuquerque, commission members saw a range of activities developed out of the creative use of time and a creative definition of the function of school. Commission members visited Emerson Elementary School, one of 26 schools here that operate on a year-round basis.

Principal Anna Marie Ullibari led commission members on a short tour of the school. The early childhood-literacy program, she explained, provides an extra hour of instruction each day for kindergarten and 1st-grade students who have been identified by their teachers as needing extra help with reading, writing, or other skills. Six such team-taught sessions are conducted each day, with as many as 76 children participating, she said.

In addition, a child-development center on school grounds provides day care and a learning environment for 3- to 5-year-olds. Administered and staffed by the city, the center's space and food is paid for by the Albuquerque school district.

Emerson also offers students a place to go when they are out of school—typically 15 days for every 60 days on campus. During these "intersessions," student teachers provide 2 1/2 hours of low-pressure instruction in a relaxed atmosphere for 10 of the 15 days.

Ms. Ullibari said the year-round schedule, the special programs, and an effort to involve parents more in school operations contribute both to better learning for students and to helping the school survive an overcrowding problem. "For our children, what it offers are some additional opportunities in learning," Ms. Ullibari said. "After three weeks, students come back, and it's as if they've never gone."

At Governor Bent Elementary, commission members find that Ms. Davenport has taken a different approach. Foregoing such special interventions as after-school clubs, she has sought to make better use of the school day by implementing learning techniques involving the concept of "multiple intelligences."

While members were impressed by Ms. Davenport's students, they were unsure whether an approach that works with children from the school's relatively affluent attendance area could be applied to schools that must contend with a host of pressing social problems. "I have no problem with her philosophy, but she's looking at her isolated situation," said Mr. Jones, noting that Governor Bent serves far fewer poor families than does Emerson. "Schools are public entities and paid for by the public. They need to integrate more with public needs."

At its hearing, the commission also heard from other local educators and administrators, including a school official who said the year-round effort has "probably caused the most bitter disagreement" in the community in regard to the schools.

Other witnesses, including university researchers who specialize in student motivation and learning, urged that the creation of more time in schools be used for ongoing teacher training and student learning. ☐

From Education Week, *Jan. 27, 1993*

47.

More Time, More Learning?

Advocates of year-round schooling are shifting their focus from budget and space concerns to educational benefits.

By Lonnie Harp

The presence of Kathy Phillips, a parent from Kansas City, Mo., at meetings in Las Vegas, marks an important change under way in the movement for year-round schools. Squeezing more out of tight budgets and stretching the uses of cramped school buildings—the twin crises that long-time year-round schools were founded on—are not overriding concerns for the mother of three school-age children.

Instead, Ms. Phillips came to this desert town in search of evidence that doing away with the customary nine-months-on, three-months-off school calendar could lead to fundamental improvements in her children's education.

The local P.T.A. representative is part of a growing tide of parents, educators, and school administrators who surmise that a school year with shorter, more frequent vacations and supplemental activities during the break time would better serve most students.

Still, Ms. Phillips and others taking time to attend a meeting of the National Association for Year-Round Education to consider a year-round calendar found a striking contrast. On one side are glowing reviews from educators who have converted to the new calendars. They report benefits ranging from higher attendance by students and teachers to more innovative curriculum and teaching strategies. On the other side, however, are reports of staunch community opposition to the idea and only modest research that testifies to its benefits.

Ms. Phillips said she likes the idea of shorter breaks

in which young children could enroll in "intersession" education programs and not have to be put in child care for months during the summer. But she also acknowledged the shockwaves created by such a change. "We need to see the evidence of the benefits if we're going to consider this," Ms. Phillips observed. "I'm not sure it's the right thing to do because there are traditional families out there that want the summertime with their children and don't need day-care options, and we don't have a pressing need for it."

For long-time leaders of the movement, who were forced to adopt year-round calendars by escalating enrollments, failed bond elections, and tight finances, the meetings of the N.A.Y.R.E. in the past have been swap shops for ideas about the mechanics of calendars, staffing, and ties to community programs.

That operational emphasis, however, was eclipsed at this year's meeting by larger doses of salesmanship for year-round schools as a way of achieving such reform goals as longer school years and new instructional and management schemes.

For the first time in the organization's 24 years, an annual survey of school districts on a year-round schedule found that a majority were operating on a single track—which, by keeping all students on the same schedule, saves neither space nor money.

Just three years ago, the survey found only about 25 percent of year-round schools were on the single-track calendar. Unlike overlapping multi-track schedules, which are normally used to save money, single-track calendars are usually adopted to boost achievement.

In his annual address to the conference, Charles

Ballinger, the executive director of the association, used sharp rhetoric to underscore his call for a focus on educational results rather than housing and financial benefits. "Year-round education is an idea whose time has come," Mr. Ballinger said. "Increasingly, educators are questioning the traditional school calendar. It must give way to something better."

"What do the opponents have in return for their attempt to block calendar change?" he asked. "Not much: only a non-educational calendar, a poor way to educate children, adherence to the status quo, and an inability to move toward the 21st century."

But that stern stance may offer little assurance to educators and parents who are confronting skeptical and sometimes hostile communities. Even year-round-school supporters admit that there is scant research confirming substantial learning gains from a shift to a 12-month school calendar.

A review released by the N.A.Y.R.E. of 13 studies of year-round-education performance since 1985 found 10 that favored the year-round system over traditional schools. Of those, seven found statistically significant learning gains by the year-round students.

But association officials and conference participants said the review offered evidence more of a lack of research over the past decade than of the proven success of year-round calendars. The studies that are available generally provide mixed results and no overwhelming learning gains. A recent study by researchers at Texas A & M University for a state legislative-policy group showed growing public support but no measurable achievement gains for year-round students.

In a presentation at the N.A.Y.R.E. meeting, Douglas Roby, a school administrator from West Carrollton, Ohio, said his recent research showed some modest math and reading gains by elementary students in the district's lone year-round school.

Even for local champions of the movement, proving results is a tough job. Norman R. Brekke, the superintendent of the Oxnard (Calif.) Elementary School District, said the year-round calendar in place for 17 years in his district has reduced teacher and student burnout, sparked an expansion of staff-development efforts, and led to innovative between-session programs that challenge students and help address learning problems.

But achievement scores have not skyrocketed, although officials are pleased with their upward direction, Mr. Brekke said. Over the past nine years, Oxnard students have made steady gains but have yet to reach the average state-achievement-test scores in most categories.

Administrators of the Orange County, Fla., school district also are focusing on educational benefits as they prepare the Orlando-area public for their plan to move all elementary schools to the new calendar by 1995. The move actually was forced by space and budget concerns, however. Surveys in the district so far have shown that many of the benefits associated with the year-round schedule have been more perceived than realized.

While teachers and parents believe attendance at schools that have already made the transition is better, for example, in fact it is not much different. The same has been observed about the quality of instruction, leaving officials wary about claiming significant achievement gains.

"People want you to prove that test scores are going to go up, but that's a very difficult thing to do," advised L. Dianne Locker, the district's year-round-education specialist. "We don't go out and tell the community we're going to have higher achievement because that's just digging yourself a hole," Ms. Locker said. "We're saying it is better delivery of instruction."

Peggy Sorensen, an elementary school principal in the year-round Jordan, Utah, district, pointed to the uncertain relationship between educational improvement and year-round calendars adopted to ease overcrowding or budget problems.

In many areas where overcrowding was the inspiration for year-round schools, Ms. Sorensen contended, school officials have yet to see clear of that problem in order to begin focusing on achievement. In other schools, instruction has not been overhauled to take into account the fact that time no longer needs to be set aside at the beginning of the year to review topics that students may have forgotten over the summer.

"I've thoroughly read the literature, and, unfortunately, it's very skimpy as to whether this is educationally beneficial," Ms. Sorensen added.

But Mr. Ballinger said he would stick with his bold claims. "Even in the very worst reports, there's no one anywhere who has shown that year-round education hurts kids, so I say with confidence your students will do as well as or better than they've been doing," he said in an interview. "Even if you only make modest gains each year for 12 years, you have a significant gain in the end, and sometimes people, including researchers, forget that."

As they wait for more forceful research, leaders of the movement also express confidence that the benefits provided by existing programs will be strong enough and obvious enough to begin winning converts. "We'll be in this position for a while," said Mr. Ballinger, pointing to statistics showing that about 4 percent of the nation's students currently attend schools on a year-round calendar.

"In one sense, we are in front of reforms, and, in another, we've got a long way to go," he said. "We're going to be on the cutting edge for 15 years before the changeover occurs in a big way, because we're not just changing the school calendar, we're changing the whole rhythm of American life." □

From Education Week, _Feb. 24, 1993_

48.

Where The Dollars Go

For the first time, a major study analyzes school budgets and shows how districts divvy up the money.

By Lonnie Harp

The first detailed statistical analysis of how school districts spend their money reveals wide disparities in spending on individual schools within districts. Tackling an increasingly important political issue for many districts, the study, issued by the U.S. Chamber of Commerce, also documents levels of spending for central offices and administration. The research found that between 80 percent and 95 percent of the districts' operating budgets was reaching local schools.

Architects of the study said the results have taught local administrators and educators new lessons about their own districts, while giving the public its first good look at how tax dollars are spent locally.

The study examined a range of urban, suburban, and small-city districts: Alameda, Calif.; Bartlesville, Okla.; Cambridge, Mass.; Charlotte/Mecklenburg, N.C.; Great Falls, Mont.; Jefferson County, Colo.; Nashville; and Spartanburg, S.C.

Study authors emphasized that the districts, which were chosen from among 240 applicants, were considered to be well-managed systems and had volunteered for the detailed financial analysis. "We now can break through the facade and come up with the information that is needed to make the decisions that are going to have to be made at the local level," said Robert L. Martin, who guided the Chamber study. "We've never asked these questions before," added Mr. Martin, who currently serves as the director of adult-business development for the Jostens Learning Corporation.

The study breaks down local spending into the categories of administration; operations; teacher support, including professional development; student support, including extracurricular activities and counseling; and instruction. Each of those categories shows spending at the school level and central office.

Among the study's findings:
• Central-office spending ranged from 20.4 percent of the local operating budget in Alameda to 5.9 percent in Great Falls.
• Administrative spending in both schools and central offices ranged from 17 percent in Alameda to 8 percent in Nashville. Instructional spending held more constant, varying between 58 percent in Alameda and 63 percent in Great Falls.
• Teacher support, the smallest category, ranged from 0.9 percent of the overall budget in Nashville to 5 percent in Alameda.

In addition to the cost breakdowns, which present spending profiles for all 422 schools in the eight districts studied, the study also compares patterns of spending on elementary, middle, and high schools. In Bartlesville, for example, where the overall per-pupil spending average was $3,024, the study found that $2,439 was spent on elementary pupils, $2,626 on middle school students, and $3,338 on high school students.

The study also examines spending disparities within the different types of schools in each district. While one Bartlesville elementary school spent $3,125 per student, another spent only $2,121.

Leaders of the project said their goal was less to provide comparisons among districts than to give local education leaders new information about their schools and encourage educators and parents to become involved in management decisions. "This is not about pointing fingers," Mr. Martin said. "What is important is that people start to look at the variables and analyze the costs. When local administrators have the ability to know the high and low costs, they can start making better decisions."

The study was based on a cost-analysis formula developed by Bruce S. Cooper, a professor of educational administration and urban policy at Fordham University. It simplifies local school spending into an easily understandable format for the first time. "The nature of the way districts report to the state doesn't give the country the information it needs," argued Mr. Cooper, who so far has examined 30 districts. "The state just cares that no one is putting the money in their own pockets."

The first version of the model was used to track central-office and school-site expenses in the New York City schools. The current model, funded through the Chamber by the Lilly Endowment, follows money into much more specific areas. School costs for instruction, for example, are made up of teacher salaries and benefits, classroom equipment and supplies, and partial teacher salaries for instructors who spend only a portion of their time at a given school. The school-level-operations category, which includes maintenance and building costs, is sensitive enough to show variations for buildings that depend on electrical rather than gas or oil heat.

"If you like averages and the kind of information education departments produce, you're not going to like this study," Mr. Martin said. "This is going to tell you how much money really gets there."

Bond-Issue Support

Jefferson County, the largest district included in the study, spent an average of $4,074 per pupil. Of that amount, administrative spending accounted for $441, with more than two-thirds of the total devoted to school-level administration tied to the principal's office. Operations took $470, and teacher support cost $62, with both categories being spent entirely from the central office.

Student support was $542, with most of the money being spent in school buildings. Classroom instruction, which accounted for 63 percent of the overall budget, cost $2,559 per child. All but $69 of that amount went for expenses at the school.

District officials said that while the study echoed much of their own information about spending, the independent verification has helped win greater community support. "Your really hard-line critics would discount any study, but the general public and business community were very impressed by this," said Lew Finch, the superintendent of the 76,000-student district. "This helped to dispel some of the rumors about how the money gets garnered at the central office."

Local officials said the analysis was a key factor in the victory last fall of a $325 million bond referendum, the largest ever in Colorado. "I don't think it unmasked anything we weren't generally aware of," Mr. Finch said, noting that since the Jefferson County study, a number of Colorado districts have volunteered to go under Mr. Cooper's microscope.

Intradistrict Differences

Most startling to school officials was the study's finding of wide inequalities among local schools. In Jefferson County, for example, where average elementary school spending was $3,606, the district's highest-spending school received $5,352 per student, compared with $2,328 for the lowest.

Mr. Finch said the seniority of each school's teaching

> **In Jefferson County, the district's highest-spending school received $5,352 per student, compared with $2,328 for the lowest.**

staff, which largely determines salary levels, made a big difference in the figures.

The Chamber study concludes over all that the age and experience of teachers had a powerful impact on the spending level of local schools. Other factors that commonly caused variations included the age, condition, and location of school buildings; the concentration of special-education students; specialized programs within certain schools; and the number of students attending classes in the building. Small schools, the report notes, bring higher costs.

Beyond the intradistrict-equity issue, the findings also raise questions about spending at different grade levels. At a time when many education reformers and experts are calling for a focus on the early grades, the study suggests that school administrators could do more to build up services for the youngest students. "Elementary schools are getting systematically and, in some cases, dramatically less money," Mr. Cooper said. "We found tremendous differences."

Except for Charlotte/Mecklenburg, where per-pupil spending showed only slight differences between elementary and secondary schools, the more common experience was that of Spartanburg, where elementary schools averaged $4,016 per pupil, compared with $5,530 for high schools.

'We Wanted To Know'

Spartanburg officials said they would use the document in drafting a new strategic plan. "We went into this thinking that if the study pointed out we were doing something drastically wrong, we wanted to know it," said Wayne M. Chamblee, the director of finance for the Spartanburg County School District # 7.

The information will not only help the district as it considers a school-based-management plan, he said, but may also force administrators to work toward greater parity among schools.

In Nashville, local school officials held their own press conference last week to release the results of the study. Noting that their central-office expenses were ranked the lowest among the districts studied, they said the report should help them move beyond past debates to turn attention to program reforms and greater efficiency. "We needed a hook to hang our hat onto, something that would show the public what we were doing," said Edward M. Taylor, the assistant superintendent for business and personnel services. Despite a previous efficiency study by local business leaders that praised the district's management, many residents had called for more concrete data.

Nashville officials said the report's finding that the district spent 25 percent of its budget on building operations—twice as much as most of the other districts—will spur greater efforts at preventive-maintenance projects and physical improvements.

Officials said they hope to push even more money to the classroom by repeating the analysis every year. "We're beginning to build a school system based on goals of equity and excellence," Mr. Taylor said. "Decisions have to be made by those people that are affected by them, and this study has given us the data to analyze and determine exactly what course of action we might want to take." □

From Education Week, _March 17, 1993_

49.

Savage Inequalities

Jonathan Kozol's slashing book goes beyond arcane finance formulas to put a human face on fiscal inequities.

By Lynn Olson

'We have a school in East St. Louis named for Dr. King," the author Jonathan Kozol quotes a 14-year-old girl saying toward the beginning of his new book, *Savage Inequalities: Children in America's Schools.* "The school is full of sewer water and the doors are locked with chains. Every student in that school is black. It's like a terrible joke on history."

Such humor is bitter indeed, according to Mr. Kozol. He places most of the blame for such conditions on the "arcane machinery," based heavily on local property taxes, that is used to finance public education.

Drawing on visits to inner-city and suburban classrooms in some 30 neighborhoods around the country, the prominent social activist and former teacher concludes that American schools are more racially and economically segregated today than they were at the height of the civil-rights era.

This "dual society seems in general to be unquestioned," he writes in the book, released by Crown Publishers. "The nation, for all practice and intent, has turned its back upon the moral implications, if not yet the legal ramifications, of the *Brown* [v. *Board of Education]* decision."

Mr. Kozol established his reputation as an impassioned commentator on inequities in education with his first book, *Death at an Early Age,* published in 1967. That book was a first-person account of his experience as a 4th-grade teacher in inner-city Boston. Since then, he has written about school desegregation, illiterate Americans, and, most recently, the plight of the homeless.

Savage Inequalities marks a return to the classroom for the 55-year-old writer. His latest, highly personalized reportage comes at a time when school finance has re-emerged as one of the central issues in education. More than 20 suits seeking reform of state systems of financing K-12 education are now pending.

The author's firsthand account describes schools that are 95 percent to 99 percent nonwhite—where "desegregation," as one principal told him, "means combining black kids and Hispanics."

Mr. Kozol depicts buildings that are literally collapsing around children's heads; teachers who only bother to attend school three days a week; principals forced to ration books, crayons, and toilet paper; and programs where little effort is made to teach failing students.

The insult, he maintains, is that such paucity exists within shouting distance of richly endowed public schools attended almost exclusively by the children of the prosperous.

'On Their Side'?

One school the author visited in the South Bronx in New York City operates in a former ice-skating rink, where four kindergarten classes and a 6th-grade class of Spanish-speaking students share a windowless room. The school has no playground; the library contains 700 books.

Minutes away, in Riverdale, a more affluent part of the Bronx, a public school—surrounded by dogwoods, two playing fields, and a playground—houses a planetarium and a library of almost 8,000 volumes.

In many ways, Mr. Kozol says in an interview, the situation has become worse since he left teaching 25 years ago. "I think it was better in 1965," he said, "because at that point, although the schools were, of course, segregated and unequal, there was at least the conviction among poor black kids that the government was on their side . . . and the vast majority of white people were on their side." "I don't think they feel that any longer," he adds. "And I think they're correct."

Mr. Kozol attributes the shift he sees in the attitudes of the public and the federal government toward disadvantaged students to the "powerful effectiveness of Ronald Reagan" and conservative think tanks. But he identifies the property-tax-based system of paying for schooling as the leading culprit in perpetuating inequalities.

The system enables wealthier districts to raise more money for their schools at a lower tax rate, he points out. At the same time, the richest homeowners get back a substantial portion of their money in the form of federal income-tax deductions that, in effect, promote and subsidize inequality.

In cities like Chicago, such disparities are made worse by the disproportionate number of tax-free institutions that reside in urban areas, and by the large portion of tax revenues that must be spent on such needs as law enforcement and health care.

Total yearly spending in Illinois, Mr. Kozol reports, ranges from $2,100 for a child in the poorest district to above $10,000 in the richest. When the relative needs of students are factored in, he contends, the disparities in funding are "enormous."

"Equity, after all, does not mean simply equal funding," Mr. Kozol argues. "Equal funding for unequal needs is not equality."

Income-Tax-Based System

In the long run, the author maintains, if Americans are serious about providing a level playing field in educa-

tion, "we will abolish the property tax altogether as the primary, initial source of school funding in America."

Instead, Mr. Kozol proposes that three-quarters of public-school funding come from the state in the form of a steeply graduated income tax. The remaining one-quarter would come from the federal government. "That should be our peace dividend, at long last, at the end of the Cold War," he adds.

But the book is not primarily about public policy, according to Kozol. "I was never a political person," he says. "I went to Harvard in the 1950's; I studied English literature. It was about as apolitical as it could be . . . I went into the Boston schools because I liked children."

Rather, the book is a stark depiction of the lives of children affected by what public policy has wrought. "The problem is that [most people] don't see that child," Mr. Kozol says. "I want to put that child in front of them and say to them, 'Look, this child is as precious as your child. And if you believe that, then fight for some decent policies.' "

"[W]hat struck me most, apart from the inequity and racial isolation [in inner-city schools]," he says, "is that most of these kids are having such rotten lives in these schools, that schools are so unhappy."

Mr. Kozol suggests that a special kind of despair characterizes the education of inner-city youngsters. The proximity of urban districts to some of the wealthiest school systems, he writes, "adds a heightened bitterness to the experience of children. The ugliness of racial segregation adds its special injuries as well."

"It is this killing combination, I believe," he continues, "that renders life within these urban schools not merely grim but also desperate and often pathological."

"Kids see an unmistakable message in the degree that white people and affluent people have fled their school systems," he adds. "In the inner city, the children suffer not only the injury of caste, which is primarily an economic injury, but they also have the visceral experience of being shunned, of feeling themselves the object of despisal."

Jonathan Kozol

THOMAS VICTOR

In such bleak and destitute environments, Mr. Kozol maintains, it is not surprising that students drop out. What is frightening, he argues, is that so many black school administrators appear to have accepted the idea of separate and not-quite-equal education.

"It is the promise of American public education that no matter what other factors exist in a child's life, the school can make a difference," Mr. Kozol says. But, he writes, "[d]enial of the 'means of competition' is perhaps the single most consistent outcome of the education offered to poor children in the schools of our large cities."

'Two Separate Schools'

Even in "integrated" schools, the author found, there was little integration in classrooms. At P.S. 24, the school in Riverdale, for example, the vast majority of black and Hispanic students were in classes for the educable or trainable mentally retarded.

There were, in effect, "two separate schools," he writes, "one of about 130 children, most of whom are poor, Hispanic, black, assigned to one of the 12 special classes; the other of some 700 mainstream students, almost all of whom are white or Asian." Rooms for the former group were half the size of mainstream class-rooms and equipped with far fewer materials.

Mr. Kozol sharply disputes the argument that money makes no difference in education. "There is no doubt in my mind that a good teacher with 20 children is twice as good as a good teacher with 40 children," he says. "There's absolutely no question that, regardless of what happens in the home or in the streets, a school that has a French teacher teaches more French than a school that can't afford a French teacher."

The author is also highly critical of school-choice proposals, which he maintains will widen the gap between the haves and the have-nots. People "can only choose the things they think they have a right to and the things they have some reason to believe they will receive," he writes. "What reason have the black and poor to lend their credence to a market system that has proved so obdurate and so resistant to their pleas at every turn?"

And while Mr. Kozol is not against "restructuring" public education, he questions the efficacy of such efforts. "What are they trying to do?" he asks in an interview. "A restructured ghetto school? A ghetto school with more participation by ghetto parents?"

What is saddest, Mr. Kozol argues, is that America has the wealth to "give a wonderful childhood to every child, and the great pity is that we don't believe this."

"It was a despairing experience for me to find that all those years of work had come to nothing," he says about researching the book. "I do feel that this book was written less in anger than in sorrow," he says. "There's a very black feeling in the book, and it does not end with any real hope. It ends with longing." □

From Education Week, *Sept. 25, 1991*

50.

Shortchanging Girls

The 'glass ceiling' that keeps females from realizing their full potential in society begins in the classroom.

By Millicent Lawton

Girls face pervasive barriers to achievement throughout their precollegiate schooling and are "systematically discouraged" from pursuing studies that would enhance their prospects for well-paying jobs, according to a study commissioned by the American Association of University Women. Described as the first synthesis of the existing research on girls in public education, the report lists 40 recommendations for bringing about more equitable treatment of girls by schools, ranging from strengthened enforcement of federal laws prohibiting sex discrimination to the adoption of "gender fair" curricula. The recommendations will be the basis for discussion at a national summit of education organizations to be held in conjunction with the report's release.

"Construction of the glass ceiling begins not in the executive suite but in the classroom," said Alice McKee, the president of the A.A.U.W. Educational Foundation. "It starts in preschool. . . . By the time girls reach high school," she said, "they have been systematically tracked toward traditional, sex-segregated jobs, and away from areas of study that lead to high-paying jobs in science, technology, and engineering."

In her foreword to the report, Ms. McKee calls its implications "enormous." She refers to the growing ranks of women and children among the poor and chides education policymakers for failing to address the relationship between poverty and inadequate education. By not properly educating girls, "we are losing an extraordinary amount of talent," Anne Bryant, the executive director of the A.A.U.W. Educational Foundation, added in a later interview. "We are losing the talent that creates management-level and greater-than-poverty-level-wage jobs," she argued.

The research review, entitled "The A.A.U.W. Report: How Schools Shortchange Girls," was conducted last year by the Wellesley College Center for Research on Women with a $100,000 grant from the A.A.U.W. Educational Foundation. It draws on research showing, for example, that girls do not receive the same attention from teachers that boys do, that they learn lessons from gender-biased textbooks, and that they are not encouraged to pursue the same curricula or careers as their male peers. Such findings provide the basis for dozens of specific recommendations. Among other suggestions, the report calls for:

• Tougher enforcement of Title IX of the Education Amendments of 1972, which bars discrimination on the basis of sex by schools receiving federal funds. The report urges that school districts be required to conduct regular reviews of their compliance with the law and to report their findings to the U.S. Education Department. Saying that many schools still discriminate against pregnant girls and teenage parents, the report calls for greater scrutiny of Title IX violations affecting such students.

• The provision of teacher training and staff development in gender issues. The report says that state-certification standards should require course work in this area.

• The adoption of "gender fair" and multicultural curricula that avoid sex stereotypes and reflect natural differences in learning styles.

• Increased efforts by schools, business, and government to involve girls in the study of mathematics and science and to promote career choices in those fields as appropriate for women.
• Greater attention to gender equity in vocational-education programs.
• The reform of standardized tests to eliminate sex bias, and a decreased emphasis on test scores in awarding scholarships.
• A more central role for girls and women in educational reform, including equitable representation on reform committees. The report also advocates national standards for data collection including breaking down statistics by sex and other characteristics that permit more accurate comparisons of states and districts.
• Improved programs in health and sexuality, including tough policies against sexual harassment.

The messages sent by both the formal school curriculum and informal classroom interaction are "discouraging" for women and girls, according to the report. A 1989 study, it notes, found that of the 10 books most frequently assigned in public high school English courses, only one was written by a woman and none by a minority group member.

In addition, the report cites studies showing that academic achievement for all students was linked to use of nonsexist and multicultural materials, and that a curriculum portraying the sexes in nonstereotypical roles prompted less stereotyping among students.

The report also discusses what it calls the "evaded" curriculum—topics of concern to girls that are not taught, or are only touched on briefly, in school. Adequate sex and health education to help prevent pregnancy and the spread of venereal diseases and AIDS "is the exception rather than the rule," the report says. It also says topics such as incest, rape, and other physical violence are rarely discussed.

But the "most evaded of all topics" are those related to gender and power, the report contends. School curricula, it argues, must deal with the fact that girls "confront a culture that both idealizes and exploits the sexuality of young women while assigning them roles that are clearly less valued than male roles."

The A.A.U.W. review also cites research indicating disparities in how teachers treat boys and girls in the classroom, as well as differences in teacher behavior toward black girls and other students. Teachers pay more attention to boys, give them more encouragement, and coax answers from them more often, according to the report. One study quoted showed that boys in elementary and middle school called out answers eight times more often than girls did; when the boys did so, teachers listened. But when girls called out, they were told to "raise your hand and speak."

Other research indicates that black girls have less interaction with teachers than white girls do, even though black girls try to initiate such interaction much more often than white girls or than boys of either race.

Black girls also receive less reinforcement from teachers on their academic achievements, even though their performance is often better than that of boys.

While the report sees reason for concern about disparities between the sexes in achievement and participation in both math and science, it suggests that the differences are markedly more worrisome in science. In math, it says, gender disparities in achievement seem to be small and declining, and differences in participation appear to be small and only in higher-level courses.

In science, however, gender differences in achievement are significant and may be increasing, it notes. While the disparity between the number of science courses taken by boys and girls is small, the two sexes take different types of courses, the study found. Girls are more apt to take advanced biology, and boys are more likely to enroll in advanced chemistry or physics.

The physical sciences are also the area in which boys have the greatest advantage over girls in achievement, the report says. Even when girls take science and math, it says, they do not receive the same encouragement to pursue scientific careers.

Still, Ms. Bryant of the A.A.U.W. Educational Foundation said, the report's findings about girls and math are heartening, because they seem to show that efforts made by educators in recent years to alter math instruction and tests to better serve female students have paid off. "To me, that is a very powerful statement," she said.

One of the aspects of schooling in which gender bias is most evident, according to the report, is in standardized testing. The "most obvious" source of such bias, it says, is in the disparate numbers of references to women and men in test items and in the stereotypical portrayals of the sexes.

Despite efforts begun in the 1970's by test companies to balance references to men and women and to screen out items deemed offensive to women, the report says, a 1984 analysis of standardized tests found twice as many references to men as to women, and more pictures of and references to boys than girls. A subsequent study of reading comprehension passages in the four 1984-85 versions of the Scholastic Aptitude Test turned up references to 42 men and only 3 women.

Such bias, the report argues, makes the test a poor measure of both boys' and girls' abilities and can skew the awarding of financial aid when S.A.T. scores are the main criterion. When college scholarships are based on S.A.T. scores, it says, boys are more apt to receive scholarships than are girls who get equal or slightly better high school grades.

The report recommends that such factors as grades, portfolios of student work, and extracurricular activities be considered along with test scores to make more accurate assessments of student abilities. □

From Education Week, *Feb. 12, 1992*

51.

Forging Policy For Harassment

Sexual harassment of students by students is on the rise, and schools and teachers may be liable.

By Millicent Lawton

What happened to Johna Mennone in her environmental-science class in the fall of 1990 left her feeling "humiliated, terrorized, and distraught." In the presence of her teacher and a roomful of classmates, Ms. Mennone says, a male peer grabbed her hair, legs, breasts, and buttocks nearly every day. He repeatedly made remarks about her breasts and told her that he was going to rape her. The student allegedly continued the behavior in a later course.

In the past, what happened to Ms. Mennone might well have been chalked up to "high school" behavior or "boys being boys." Today, it is the subject of a federal lawsuit filed by Ms. Mennone against the district superintendent, the school board, and her teacher at Amity Regional High School in Woodbridge, Conn.

Like Ms. Mennone, students across the nation—together with their parents, teachers, and school officials—are beginning to deal with the thorny issues of how to define, prevent, and punish sexual harassment among students.

In recent months, experts in the field say, inquiries on the topic have increased markedly. In fact, the National School Boards Association has received so many requests for information that it created a "fax pack" of information to be sent out via facsimile machine, says Karen Powe, the director of policy services for the association.

Many factors appear to have contributed to the heightened interest, experts agree, including a chang-ing social climate that is less tolerant of sex discrimination of all kinds, the 1991 Clarence Thomas-Anita Hill hearings on Capitol Hill, and a U.S. Supreme Court decision nearly a year ago that says school districts could be held liable for sexual harassment in school.

Although sexual misconduct by teachers involving students seems to have garnered more attention and has been the subject of more school-district policies, sexual harassment exclusively involving students is actually much more prevalent, according to Nan D. Stein, who in 1980-81 conducted the first study of peer harassment in schools for the Massachusetts Department of Education.

Most of the harassment in schools is inflicted on girls by boys and often takes place in the classroom, as in Ms. Mennone's case, according to Ms. Stein, who now directs a project on school sexual harassment at the Center for Research on Women at Wellesley College.

But the subject remains an unfamiliar one full of gray areas for school districts that are trying to codify prohibited student behavior and educate pupils and staff members in how to handle harassment.

Most experts agree that sexual harassment is defined by the victim: If an individual finds the comments or physical contact to be unwelcome, then it is harassment. But others acknowledge that what might not feel like harassment to the victim might appear to be harassment to, say, an administrator—and vice versa. Then, too, what may be acceptable in a social setting or among some racial or ethnic groups—teasing, joking, or flirting in a sexual manner—is not acceptable in an educational setting, experts say.

Because sexual harassment is a continuum that can range from spoken or written comments and stares to physical assault and attempted rape, some of it may also be actionable as criminal activity, depending on local laws, Ms. Stein notes.

Policymakers also face a difficult task in wording guidelines banning such behavior, according to Robert Peck, the legislative counsel for the American Civil Liberties Union in Washington. "The key is that it cannot be regarded as harassment just because someone takes offense at an utterance," such as the word "bitch," Mr. Peck says.

However, a "personally directed threat that makes it impossible for a person" to learn is something that a school has a right to regulate, he says.

Notion of Trust Undermined

As the issue has grown in public prominence, students have begun seeking school policies, legislation, and court decisions to protect themselves from the unwelcome verbal taunts and jokes, bathroom graffiti, pinching, groping, and other assaults that girls and women have been subjected to for generations.

"I think this is a dirty little secret that's been around for a long time . . . something we've kind of accepted," State Sen. Gary Hart of California says of peer sexual harassment in school.

Senator Hart sponsored a state law that took effect last month that makes sexual harassment by students in grades 4 to 12 an offense punishable by suspension or expulsion. "We're just serving notice to the principals and teachers . . . that they need to pay attention to this," Mr. Hart says.

If sexual harassment is allowed to go unchecked, "the whole notion of trust or school as a safe and democratic place is vastly undermined," Ms. Stein, of the Wellesley center, says.

The issue is also receiving national attention. Nineteen of the 40 sexual-harassment cases currently being investigated by the U.S. Education Department's office for civil rights involve elementary or secondary education. Of those, at least two involve harassment by students, a department official says.

Both of those cases—one in Eden Prairie, Minn., and the other in Sherman, Tex.—allege harassment on school buses of elementary-age girls by their male peers. In addition, two separate attempts are under way to document the prevalence and develop a profile of in-school sexual harassment.

This month, the results are expected from a national survey on sexual harassment in school designed by Ms. Stein and another researcher at the Wellesley center and printed in *Seventeen* magazine last fall. And the American Association of University Women will also try to find out from a national random survey this year what both girls and boys have to say about their experiences and thoughts about sexual harassment.

The survey, the results of which are expected in June, will "hopefully raise the level of debate beyond anecdotal evidence," says Pamela Hughes, a spokeswoman for the A.A.U.W.

Sometimes it is a specific incident in a school district that prompts officials to address the issue. Ana Sol Gutierrez, a member of the Montgomery County, Md., school board, says she knew her district needed rules about sexual harassment after a high school girl harassed by a male peer finally turned around one day on the school bus and slapped him. The incident earned both students a suspension for fighting because that was the only policy that applied. The board has since enacted a sexual-harassment policy for students to give them a better line of defense.

Educators often cite the October 1991 allegations of sexual harassment against then-Supreme Court nominee Clarence Thomas by Anita Hill, a law professor, and the High Court's February 1992 decision in *Franklin* v. *Gwinnett County Public Schools* allowing a

> # If sexual harassment is allowed to go unchecked, says one researcher, 'the whole notion of trust or school as a safe place is vastly undermined.'

student to sue a district for monetary damages in a sexual-harassment case as helping shape their thinking on harassment.

In Indiana, for example, before the Thomas-Hill hearings, many school administrators were not willing to acknowledge that sexual harassment of any kind was a problem in their schools, says Beverly Peoples, an equity consultant with the state department of education. Only a tiny number of administrators attended the voluntary in-service awareness sessions on sexual harassment offered by the state, Ms. Peoples says. But in recent months, such sessions have drawn a total of about 50 administrators. Still, there are 296 school districts in Indiana, she says, and "systemic change is very slow."

In the High Court's unanimous decision in *Franklin*, the Justices ruled that victims of sexual harassment and other forms of sex discrimination in schools may sue for monetary damages under Title IX of the Education Amendments of 1972. The law bars sexual discrimination in federally funded schools and colleges. While the *Franklin* case concerned harassment and abuse of a student by a teacher, many observers attach great significance to the decision and its expansion of students' ability to obtain redress from school districts for discriminatory acts.

Others, however, say that it is not clear whether the protections of Title IX extend to sexual harassment by a student's peers. That issue, and the potential for damage awards against school districts, must still be decided in the federal courts, they say, although some expect that such guarantees will be extended to students.

On a related topic, the U.S. Supreme Court last January refused to consider the issue of whether the U.S. Constitution obliges public school officials to protect students from sexual assaults by teachers or other students.

"An employer is responsible for the conduct of employees," says Gwendolyn H. Gregory, the deputy general counsel of the National School Boards Association. "Is [a school district] responsible for the conduct of students? I don't think you can necessarily say [that]," she says.

The lawyer for Ms. Mennone, the former Connecticut student who alleges harassment in class, says she did not think the case would have been filed if it had not been for the precedent set by *Franklin*.

That case "certainly opens the door to students enforcing their rights under Title IX," Maureen M. Murphy says. "I really think we're going to see a lot of litigation in this area."

Becoming Less Vulnerable

Lawyers and others say that school districts with established policies on sexual harassment may stand in better legal stead should a lawsuit arise. In two states, districts have no choice but to confront the issue.

In Minnesota, and now in California, schools are required by law to adopt sexual-harassment policies that cover students. Unlike the new California law, Minnesota's statute also requires each school to develop a process for discussing the policy with students and employees.

And State Commissioner of Education Betty Castor of Florida last year "strongly" urged the state's 67 school districts to adopt procedures for dealing with sexual misconduct in school, including student-initiated sexual harassment, which she termed a "serious problem."

"The safest thing for a school district to do is to adopt policies that provide remedies for students who believe they are victims . . . and to build an awareness of the problem," says David S. Tatel, a Washington lawyer who is a former head of the office for civil rights at the U.S. Education Department.

Ms. Stein at the Wellesley center agrees. "If we don't believe those kids, then get ready for a lawsuit," she says. "Because the kids that speak up, and write and tell me about sexual harassment—the descriptions are parallel to the descriptions that come out in the lawsuits," she says.

But Ms. Stein says officials also need to think about how to resolve complaints through both formal and informal, nonlitigious procedures. One approach, she says, is to have the accuser—who may be satisfied simply to have the harassment cease—write a letter to

---

An employer is responsible for the conduct of employees. Does it follow, asks one official, that a school district is responsible for the conduct of students?

---

the perpetrator, under the supervision of an adult trained in the procedure, asking him or her to stop the harassment.

Other educators use parent conferences or even have a police officer present during a discussion with the harasser to strengthen the message.

Even punishment under harassment policies can be a learning experience if an offending student must, for example, write a report on the subject of sexual harassment, officials say.

Teachers and counselors must also be intensively trained beyond basic awareness to discuss these issues in the classroom, Ms. Stein says, so that they can "impart not just knowledge, but the subjectivity and difficulty of this subject to the kids."

Lesson plans and pamphlets exist for junior high and high school students, who are able to grasp the meaning of sexual harassment when it is compared with its benign counterpart, flirting, experts say. But conveying the concept to elementary-age students—for whom curricula are still in the works—is more of a challenge and calls for comparisons to bullying, they say.

And the youngest student should not be left out of policies or education, educators say. Susan F. Sattel, a sex-equity specialist for the Minnesota Department of Education, says she knows of an incident in which two 6-year-old boys who were 1st graders at a private school sexually assaulted another 6-year-old child at knifepoint.

"The earlier you intervene [with kids on sexual harassment], the better results you have in the long run," says Cynthia Chestnut, the director of student and community services for the Alachua County, Fla., schools who headed up the effort to draft that district's policy last year. "If you make them aware of this in schools," she says, "you break the cycle and they're not growing up to be sexually harassing adults."

Students Push for Policy

Efforts to educate students can pay off, school officials say. Central High School in St. Paul is planning to reinstate two-day awareness lessons with its students that were successful several years ago in addressing sexual harassment, says Franklin Wharton, a social worker at the school.

The presentations—which included discussion of typical harassment situations—provided a "real dramatic impact on redefining what some youngsters thought were fun and games," Mr. Wharton says. "Many of them don't even know what constitutes sexual harassment."

In one district, the students gave the educators a policy lesson. The Sequoia Union High School District in Redwood City, Calif., credits the existence of its peer sexual-harassment policy to the activism of students. Prompted by the Thomas-Hill hearings as well as by an incident in the district, a 23-member student advisory council decided to draw up the policy as its annual project, says Susan Bendix, the administrative liaison to the student group.

The panel, about evenly divided between high school boys and girls who are appointed by school officials, got administrators as well as students in the 6,400-student, ethnically diverse district to sign on to the idea. They saw their efforts result in the adoption of the policy last April by the school board, which had one eye on the possibility that the legislature would mandate such policies, Ms. Bendix says.

Policy Road Problematic

For some districts, the road to drawing up and implementing a policy against peer sexual harassment has been full of controversy and legal potholes. The school board in Montgomery County, Md., of which Ms. Gutierrez is a member, had just adopted its policy on student harassment in November when it found itself threatened with legal action, in part because training and educational materials were not yet in place.

Superintendent Paul L. Vance determined that one school had handled poorly a harassment complaint brought under the new policy. In addition, he says, the school's printed information on the policy, which students had assailed as "sexist," has also been withdrawn.

Last year, another district, the Petaluma Joint Union High School District in northern California, found itself on the losing end of a lawsuit even as it was developing a peer sexual-harassment policy. Displeased

with the way the district handled her complaint about boys who "mooed" and commented on her breasts, Tawnya Brawdy, then a student at Kenilworth Junior High, and her mother filed suit. Last year, they settled out of court with the school district's insurance company for $20,000.

However, "the district feels that it did act appropriately," says Kim Jamieson, Petaluma's deputy superintendent.

A committee, which includes Tawnya's mother, Louise, is expected to submit a "model, state-of-the-art" student-harassment policy to the school board within a couple of months.

Yet, even when a school district has a policy in place, it may face legal challenges. In what is considered the first case of a student's winning monetary damages from a district because of a peer harassment case, Katherine Lyle, a former student at Central High

---

As part of the settlement, custodians in the district must check daily for graffiti, remove it, and report its existence to school officials.

School in Duluth, Minn., received a $15,000 settlement in September 1991 from the state human-rights department for "alleged mental anguish and suffering."

The award came after an investigation by the state office found that the district had failed to act appropriately after sexually offensive graffiti about Katy, as she is known, appeared in a boys' bathroom at the school in 1987 and was not removed despite repeated requests from the Lyles.

Duluth has had a sexual-harassment policy that covered students since 1982, officials say. Unfortunately, says Katy's mother, Carol Lyle—who is a teacher in the district—graffiti was not considered sexual harassment at the time.

As part of the settlement, custodians in the district must check daily for graffiti, remove it, and report its existence to officials. And the district now instructs students about sexual harassment in grade-level appropriate curriculum, and Katy herself has led lessons on the subject.

"It seems," Carol Lyle says of the policy change, "to be taken seriously." □

From Education Week, *Feb. 10, 1993*

52.

The 'Radical Middle'

Fed up with promises from the left and right, Americans take a common-sense, middle-of-the-road approach to education reform.

Commentary By Bruce S. Cooper

The apparent failure in the United States of both liberal-left and neoconservative policies and programs has given rise to what has been variously called the "radical middle," the "extreme center," the "snarling mainstream." The terms have been used before. Canada's former prime minister, Pierre Trudeau, described his Liberal Party's turn to the right in 1978 with these words: "We are a party of the extreme center, the radical middle." This year, a frustrated U.S. electorate turned to a radical-centrist, third-party candidate, Ross Perot. The plain-speaking Texas businessman, a political novice, shot to the top of presidential-preference polls before opting out of the race in July. He may yet be the kingmaker in the general election, determining the swing votes that give victory to either George Bush or Bill Clinton.

Similar developments are detectable in efforts to reform the nation's schools. There is general consternation about both the liberal desire for higher government spending, more regulation, and greater equity and, equally, about the right wing's programs for privatizing, marketizing, and radically decentralizing the schools. In response to these conflicting ideological positions, we see a generalized rage about some 35 years of failed attempts to use schools to improve and equalize society. The modern liberal school agenda began with the *Brown* decisions in 1954 and 1955 and continued in a national effort to end segregation. Next

came a wave of *Serrano*-type cases after 1971 to equalize education spending across districts. Then policies were designed to improve bilingual education, the education of all handicapped children, and laws about equality between the sexes in school.

Behind these policies stood a growing system of "accountability" and "control" that reached from Washington to the classroom. That program is now being abandoned, as some school districts use, instead of forced busing, for example, voluntary school choice through magnet schools to achieve racial balance. We also see separate programs for special-needs students being replaced by mainstreaming such students in the "regular" classroom. Even non-English-speaking children are being taught in immersion English classes instead of more isolated bilingual programs.

In the 1980's and early 1990's, neoconservative remedies have been in the ascendancy. School choice, education markets, decentralized decisionmaking, site-based management, empowerment of teachers and parents, and even vouchers have been proposed. But the nation has seemed slow, too, to embrace many of these remedies, expressing an unwillingness to make schools into free-flowing "markets," to fund private and parochial schools with tax dollars, or to "sell" schools to the highest bidder through various privatization schemes. This rejection of radical decentralization and privatization has come from an allegiance to the public system and a nervousness that such a course of action might very well destroy what little education was left for students living in poor, urban areas.

Instead, the center has been radicalized, refusing in state after state, district after district, to raise taxes another cent or to pass even small bond issues for schools. Like Ross Perot supporters, these neo-centrists want to see some results before they ante up more money. The average taxpayer is tired of the "bully pulpit" in education, the constant flow of negative commission reports, "new" ideas, promises from candidates for high office to be the next Education President, and new kinds of American schools that have not yet materialized. Most of all, citizens are fed up with the apparent inability of the national government to act, the stand-off between a Republican White House and a reactive Democratic Congress. Many voters, the extreme center, were willing to entertain the election of an unknown political figure as a dramatic way of breaking the gridlock and doing something—any-thing—to improve government policies.

The average person would like to see schools do better at the simple things: helping students acquire some manners; learn to read, write, and compute; and work hard and succeed. While they reject radical policies of the left and right, these average citizens want a radical-center program, including choice (but within the public system); more

accountability and better information on school and pupil progress (hence, the interest in national standards and assessments); more work and less complaining from teachers (hence, the emphasis on teacher productivity before big pay raises). The sympathy that the average American felt for the overworked, under-paid teacher has diminished now that teachers work, on average, only 900 hours in the classroom per year (though preparation and grading papers certainly take hours longer) and earn, on average, $38,000 plus fringe benefits. While the cost of education has doubled in nine years, test scores have dropped on many indicators or have remained stubbornly flat in others.

A radicalized center wants to know: Where have all the increased money, higher salaries, better benefits, and shorter workweeks led? Save the rhetoric about equity, choice, empowerment, and shared governance, citizens are saying, and try teaching students more vocabulary, civics, deportment, and willingness to work hard. While "radical center" may seem an oxymoron, this movement is radical to the extent that

it is a clear and different political position, one that rejects the ideology of the two major parties and upsets the status quo in both politics and education. Thus, to the extent that Ross Perot captured the mood of this nation as a whole, he also typified what educators and policymakers from the White House to the schoolhouse are seeing:

• Fatigue from the voting public with ideologies of left and right, promises about equal education for all, the one best system, and the importance of education.

• An unwillingness on the part of voters to keep opening their pockets and funding ineffective schools and expensive reforms that show few real results.

• A neo-centrism and anti-government bias based on anger with the establishment and a deep desire for something new.

• Skepticism about both a new-left radical egalitarianism and the new-right effort to sell the schools.

The public wants a new reality about making schools work better through moderate, "rad-mid" plans to let parents choose schools from among the public schools; to require students to work harder, do more homework, take real tests that assess what schools are really doing; and to provide an accounting of where scarce public funds are going.

John Chubb and Terry Moe were right about the hyper-controls built up since the mid-1950's: They have strangled some schools. The radical center wants less government-imposed "equity," fewer requirements for equal treatment and, instead, much better treatment for all. The Democratic "lefty" Jerry Brown and the right-wing Republican Pat Buchanan were both soundly rejected in the primaries, and the Rev. Jesse Jackson and Senator Edward Kennedy were pushed carefully out of sight by Democrats intent at their convention on appealing to the middle-class, middle-America, middle-of-the-road majority. Similarly in education, voters have rejected pleas for more funds, more buildings, more special programs, more regulation, and more talk, in favor of solid education.

Educators need to read the trends, just as the presidential, gubernatorial, and legislative candidates do. America has apparently "had it up to here" with promises from right and left. It is tired, jaundiced, and skeptical. It is waiting for the educational community to begin proving that money, trust, and programs work, that students are faithfully attending school and learning, and are graduating with usable skills and positive work attitudes. The mad-as-hell frustration is being felt by school boards, superintendents, and teachers.

The quick fix is not attracting much support. Instead, some real results are awaited. Perhaps a few states and localities will try vouchers or other such plans, but these reforms will more than likely be of a moderate cast, including middle-ground changes such as "controlled choice" or public "within-the-system options." Why not let public schools compete, within and across school districts, by letting families choose from a range of local and regional options? This kind of retreat to the center occurs when the extremes are unworkable or unattractive. The changes are sometimes hard to detect because they draw support, as Mr. Perot did, from both the left and right, from both traditional Democratic and Republican ranks, and in all parts of the nation.

Regional loyalties to party and candidates, then, have broken down as the center seeks a radically middle solution. In education, this discontentment is most difficult to grasp, since local public schools have had, until very recently, such broad, bipartisan support. Now people are increasingly questioning the enterprise, and their frustration, exacerbated by poor economic times, results in low turnouts for school-board elections; communities that have not passed a bond issue for school construction in over a decade; cutbacks in school funding from federal, state, and local governments; and budgets being scrutinized and rejected.

Included, too, are: high turnover rates in school superintendencies, as school boards fire their chief executives; less and less sympathy for the "plight" of teachers with little-to-no pay increases; and demands that some bottom-line results be forthcoming. Requiring higher standards has not improved outcomes. More testing has not provided more useful information about how all students are doing. More technology in schools has not demonstrably improved learning, attendance, promotion, graduation rates, or test scores.

The new "rad-mid" reforms are radical in that they are new and outside the education establishment. They are not based on liberal or neoconservative ideologies as much as on deep concern and good common sense. Mr. Perot, for example, talked about cleaning house, "taking out the garbage," "making things work better." Whether much substance lay behind this hard-hitting, uncluttered rhetoric was difficult to tell. But what it apparently produced was the adoption in both the Democratic and Republican platforms of a moderate, centrist, common-sense approach to education, one reflecting the directness, the clarity, and the middle-of-the-road philosophy of the extreme center.

This non-ideological language, a Perot trademark, appeals to Americans because they perceive the government, and our schools, as failing—not always their own child's school, but schools in general. Thus, the public is going to be less easily persuaded. Educators and politicians, whether liberal, conservative, or radical-middle, must produce results with what they've got, seeing how to make money, staff, and materials go further. Sympathy is low, new funds scarce, and expectations high.

Overregulated, inefficient, and ineffective schools are no longer to be tolerated. Radical-centrists idealistically seek to fix education without new categorical or entitlement aid, without vouchers or radical deregulation, and without much new staff and equipment. For the first time since the 1960's, the school system must look to its own resources: to reduce waste, raise standards, make demands on teachers and students, and show results—or face the firing of superintendents, the defeat of bond referendums and tax measures, and less public sympathy.

Just as Governor Clinton and President Bush are feeling the force of the Noisy Majority, competing for Perot-ites of the Irate Middle, so, too, are our schools. Educational leaders will have little choice other than to respond to these new realities. □

Bruce S. Cooper is a professor at the Fordham University Graduate School of Education.

From Education Week, *Aug. 5, 1992*

Who We Are

"We are close to a fundamental rethinking of the way teaching works in America. We are ready to build on the tough standards we have created in the past three years. With an expanded pool of talented teachers, we can explore ways to empower teachers to do their jobs better. We can get teachers more involved in professional decisions within the school. We can help teachers better share their talents and knowledge with their colleagues."

—Thomas H. Kean, President, Drew University

53.

A Profession Evolving

Reformers envision more demanding and more gratifying new roles for teachers in the restructured schools of the future.

For as long as anyone can remember, teaching has been more of an occupation than a profession. The emergence of teachers' unions in the 1960s was tacit acceptance of that fact. Traditionally, all important decisions affecting teachers' classrooms have been made by administrators and policymakers at the state and district levels. They largely have determined the content of the curriculum and how it should be taught, selected textbooks and teaching materials, and decided which standardized tests would be administered on what schedule. The objective, in part, was to make schools "teacher-proof." Only when the classroom door was closed could teachers exercise a modicum of autonomy—and then at some risk.

To some degree, this situation has prevailed because teaching has largely been women's work. Before the feminist movement of the 1960s, a woman aspiring to a career had essentially two choices: nursing or teaching. Public schools had no trouble staffing their classrooms with women who were willing to work in unappealing working conditions for low wages. It used to be called the "hidden subsidy of women's work." The situation has changed over the past three decades, and women have many more career options. But 8 out of 10 beginning teachers today are women. Working conditions haven't changed much, and the average beginning salary for teachers is just over $22,000—not much higher in 1960 dollars than it was 30 years ago. And minority teachers are in short supply. Despite the widening diversity of the student body, only 5 percent of beginning teachers are African-American and only 2 percent are Hispanic.

Although teaching is often referred to as a profession, teachers' working conditions and career patterns reflect the characteristics of a blue-collar occupation. Teachers rarely have their own offices, lack the services that professionals have access to (secretary, telephone, typewriter, fax machine, copier), and, in large urban districts, must punch in and out on time clocks. The teacher's workday is highly structured, with little or no time for reading, reflection, or intellectual interaction with colleagues. Salary schedules are so rigid and precise that teachers can see immediately where they will be on the salary scale at any given point in their careers. The labor contract spells out their rights and responsibilities, their rewards and punishments.

Not surprisingly, the current school reform movement's early initiatives reflected the view of teacher as laborer. Administrators and policymakers believed that student achievement could be increased by improving teaching—and that could be done by ratcheting up the present system. So in the early and mid-1980s, many states raised requirements and standards in schools of education, required teachers to pass minimum competency tests, provided highly structured curricula for them to follow, and increased teachers' salaries. These actions had no noticeable effect on classroom practice or on student learning.

As reformers probed more deeply into the structure and content of schooling in America during the late 1980s, they became convinced that the entire system of schooling had to be overhauled. The emphasis, they argued, should be on learning rather than teaching, on understanding and thinking rather than on acquisition and memorization, on cooperation rather than competition. In this scenario, reminiscent of John Dewey, teachers would be mentors and coaches rather than dispensers of facts; students would take more responsibility for their own education, and teachers would collaborate with them in a search for knowledge and understanding. The school structure would be substantially changed: within broad curricular frameworks, teachers would decide how best to meet content standards; they would participate in the development of new performance-based assessments; they would be empowered to make decisions that affect instruction, budget, personnel, practice, scheduling, and student/teacher assignments.

Such a radically changed system would drastically alter the role of teachers. As one major report put it: "Teachers must think for themselves if they are to help others think for themselves, be able to act independently and collaborate with others, and render critical judgments. They must be people whose knowledge is wide-ranging and whose understanding runs deep."

In short, "teaching for understanding" would require restructured schools and truly professional teachers.

Sociologists who have studied professions such as medicine, law, and architecture, note that they share several common characteristics. A true profession:
• Possesses a body of specialized knowledge to be mastered by the practitioner;
• Recruits able people to its ranks, requires rigorous preparation for its members, and controls who is admitted;
• Sets high standards of practice and holds its members to those standards; in return, the professional is freed of undue regulation and bureaucratic supervision;
• Recognizes its responsibility to those it serves and places their interests above its own.

Although it has a long way to go, the movement toward professionalization has been gaining momentum. In many "restructured schools," teachers are deeply involved in decisionmaking. States are waiving regulations for innovative schools. School schedules are being revised to provide teachers with more time for preparation and opportunities to work together. Teachers are playing central roles in national and state efforts to develop standards and assessments for students. There is growing recognition that teachers, like physicians, need continuing professional development—rich programs that go well beyond earning college credits in night-school courses.

A major step toward the professionalization of teaching was the establishment in 1987 of the National Board for Professional Teaching Standards. Dominated by teachers, the board seeks to define what expert teachers of a variety of academic subjects and grade levels should know and be able to do, to develop assessments to evaluate them, and to award national certification to those who meet these high standards. The approach is analogous to the medical profession's board-certification system. The hope is that board-certified teachers will be in demand and will be compensated accordingly, that districts will compete for their services and rely on them to be leaders among their colleagues in schools. The first teachers are expected to "take the boards" in 1993-94.

In addition to this effort, a newly established consortium of state policymakers and representatives of the teaching profession has developed a model set of standards for beginning teachers that identifies for the first time the "common core" of knowledge and skills that all new teachers should possess.

Defining what teachers should know and be able to do is an important step forward, but it will not automatically result in a supply of teachers who are capable of teaching for understanding. Nor is it likely that even the most rigorous teacher education programs will produce such teachers. At best, pre-service programs can help students acquire a deep understanding of their subject matter and of the pedagogies that are essential in this new kind of teaching.

If good professional practice is to spread through the nation's classrooms, it must be made visible to teachers. They must have opportunities to see it, reflect on it, and discuss it. They must have opportunities to connect with other teachers in professional communities or networks of like-minded colleagues. One of the startling and important findings of a major study described in this chapter is that such connections have a powerful effect on how successful teachers are in adapting their instructional strategies to meet their students' needs.

Unfortunately, role models for teaching understanding are relatively rare in schools today. The present system discourages it; it is more difficult than conventional teaching because it is more improvisational and less planned. Only the most exceptional teachers (a few of whom are portrayed in the following pages) have mastered the practice. They have done so through years of observing, questioning, and researching how their students learn and how they learn different things differently. And they have experimented with their craft and modified their practice to meet changing circumstances. That is what professionals do.

It is hard to imagine any social endeavor more worthy of being a profession than teaching. No one questions that those who treat the sick, promote justice, and design structures are professionals and should be treated as such. Why should there be questions about those to whom society entrusts the minds of its children—the people who are charged with interpreting and transmitting to each new generation our collective memory, our cultural heritage, and our accumulated knowledge?

Physicians, lawyers, and architects can leave tangible and lasting records of their important contributions—a pioneering new surgical procedure, a precedent-setting judicial decision, a soaring skyscraper. The contribution of the teacher is not so evident and breathtaking. It is intangible, immeasurable, invisible—given to children, one by one. But, as Henry Adams wrote, it "affects eternity." □

54.

By The Numbers

Percentage of beginning teachers who are female: **81**

Percentage who are white: **92**   Black: **5**   Hispanic: **2**

Percentage who are married: **33**

Average college grade: **B plus**

Average combined SAT score: **955 out of 1600**

Proportion who attended college within 100 miles of home: **3 in 5**

Within 500 miles of home: **9 in 10**

Proportion who commuted daily: **Half**

Percentage who hope to teach in or near their hometown: **80**

Who would seek a job nationally: **30**

Percentage who grew up in rural areas or small towns: **50**

In suburbs: **28**   In cities: **20**

Percentage who plan to teach in suburbs or small towns: **76**

In rural areas: **9**   In cities: **15**

Percentage who plan to teach elementary grades: **58**

Secondary: **42**

Percentage who want to teach in middle-class schools: **75**

In culturally diverse schools: **14**

In low-income schools: **6**

Proportion who prefer to teach in traditional vs. experimental schools: **3 in 4**

Percentage who feel very positive about a teaching career: **90**

Who plan to teach 5 years or more: **90**   20 years or more: **34**

Percentage who would consider or seek principalship: **51**

Superintendency: **48**

Average public school teacher's salary in 1991-92: **$34,213**

In 1960: **$4,999**

Sources: the American Association of Colleges for Teacher Education,
the American Federation of Teachers, National Center for Education Statistics

55.

Forging A Profession

A pioneering national board faces challenges in defining what expert teachers should know and be able to do.

For the first time in history, a national body with a teacher majority is undertaking to define what every classroom teacher should know and be able to do. The National Board for Professional Teaching Standards is setting standards for excellence in teaching and expects to spend $50 million developing a voluntary national certification system.

The teacher-assessment system is being created under a very tight deadline. Initially, the standards board announced that it would begin assessing the first candidates for certification in 1993. "What we have always said was, we will be ready to offer the first assessments in 1993-94," said James Kelly, president of the board, "and we will be ready."

The first assessments will be administered to a limited number of teachers in a field test. In the fall of 1993, Mr. Kelly said, the national board will set the "ground rules" for whether to actually certify the teachers who participate in the field tests. "We will follow 'Kelly's law,' " he said. "We will move as fast as we can, but only as fast as it can be done right."

Teachers who meet the standards may earn higher pay and have greater autonomy. At least that is the hope of the national board. All teachers who hold valid state teaching licenses and have completed "three full-time-equivalent" years of teaching will be eligible for national certification.

The board's primary goal is ambitious: to raise the status of teaching to that of other professions such as architecture, medicine, and law. Many argue that this effort is critical to the future of American education, and that dramatic improvement in the nation's schools will only occur through the "professionalization of teaching."

"Other professions, such as medicine and law, took decades to set their standards," said Mr. Kelly. "Our board will attempt to compress this arduous process into one half of one decade, because we want to influence the quality of the enormous influx of new teachers needed during the 1990's."

The 63-member board, established in 1987, plans to offer national certification in 29 fields, ranging from early childhood education to vocational education. The fields are clustered under five age-group categories. Within two of those categories, teachers will receive general credentials; within the others, teachers may choose a specialty.

Currently, 12 committees are working to set standards for accomplished teaching. In determining what expert teachers should know and be able to do, the committees consider both the subject they teach and the age of the children with whom they work. The committee members, who are not members of the national board, are nominated by its staff. The majority of the dozen or so members on each panel are classroom teachers.

The first four committees, named in 1990, are setting standards for "generalists" and English-language-arts teachers working with "early adolescents"; mathematics teachers who work with adolescents and young adults; and art teachers who work with children in early adolescence through young adulthood.

The board also has contracted with two university-based "assessment-development laboratories" to produce materials to evaluate the English-language-arts and generalist teachers.

None of the first four committees has issued a final report yet. Draft reports from the committees have been reviewed by a "working group" of national-board members who oversee the standards-development process. Some also have been shared with members of subject-matter organizations.

The creation of the national board was the key recommendation of *A Nation Prepared: Teachers for the 21st Century*, the widely publicized report of the Carnegie Forum on Education and the Economy.

Traditionally, teachers have been subject to examinations only for state licensing, which is often mistakenly referred to as certification. A license guarantees the public that a teacher has met a minimum standard of competency set by the state. Generally, these standards reflect a specified number of credits in

---

The board's primary goal is ambitious: to raise the status of teaching to that of other professions such as architecture, medicine, and law.

---

required college courses and a passing score on an examination like the National Teacher Examination.

By contrast, the national board proposes to set standards for what teachers actually should know and be able to do and plans to develop assessments to evaluate them. The national certification would be voluntary and is seen as complementing, not replacing, state licensing.

"For once in this country, we are working out standards for excellence rather than minimum competency," said James Hunt Jr., the governor of North Carolina who has served as chairman of the board since its inception. "The certification process has the potential to transform the current educational system, leverage current investment in teaching, and build a national consensus for increased support of schools," he added.

At the direction of the national board, all of the standards committees have framed their work in terms of the board's five core propositions about what accomplished teachers know and can do.

Such teachers, the principles state, are committed to students and their learning; know the subjects they teach and how to teach them to students; are responsible for managing and monitoring their students' learning; think systematically about their practice and learn from experience; and are members of learning communities.

The decision to use the five principles as a guide for setting standards was made because they have gained wide acceptance among educators, said David R. Mandel, the board's vice president for policy develop-

ment. "As we began the process," he said, "it seemed to us a sensible way to organize their work." The principles also were used "for reasons of comparability," he added. "We wanted to design a system where all teachers feel they are being treated fairly, and no one has the sense that 'My field's standards are tougher than someone else's.' "

Using such a framework, however, has produced a more "atomistic" picture of teaching than the "holistic" view the board had hoped to capture, he acknowledged. Both the working group and board staff members also want the reports to be more explicit about the goals and expectations that teachers have for their students, Mr. Mandel said, and to portray more clearly the difference between highly accomplished practice and less expert teaching.

By including these aspects, board officials said, the reports could serve as "teaching documents" that would communicate expectations throughout the profession.

By this fall the standards committees for English-language-arts and generalist teachers of children in early adolescence will probably have completed "75 to 80 percent" of their work. In addition, the standards working group is scheduled to consider the reports on art and mathematics standards at the national board's next meeting. "We are a little nervous about the first ones," said James R. Smith, the board's senior vice president in charge of standards and assessments. "If we can get a couple that everyone likes, the rest will come along much more quickly. The learning curve then gets very steep."

Already, Mr. Mandel pointed out, lessons learned from the experiences of the first committees are being applied to later groups. For example, the three panels setting standards for science teachers who work with children in middle childhood, early adolescence, and adolescence and young adulthood will collaborate on some aspects of their work.

Committees working in fields in which there have been previous attempts to define standards—for either students or teachers—have had a leg up on panels that have to start from scratch, standards-panel members note. "We've had an immense advantage over other committees," said Gail Burrill, a high-school mathematics teacher who chairs the mathematics committee. Her group, she said, was able to draw heavily on the work of the National Council of Teachers of Mathematics, which has been in the vanguard of national standards-setting efforts.

On the other hand, the committee setting standards for generalists working with children in early adolescence has struggled to define exactly how much teachers should be expected to know.

Some of the committee members think of themselves as generalists, along the model of elementary teachers, said Deborah Meier, a national-board member who serves as a liaison to the generalist committee. Others see themselves as "specialists who integrate other curriculum areas," said Ms. Meier, who is the principal of the nationally recognized Central Park East Secondary School in New York City.

Some education-reform efforts, she pointed out, have urged that secondary-school teachers become more like generalists. In setting standards, Ms. Meier said, the generalist committee is trying not to "straitjacket a very fluid picture of education in this country."

"We are sort of under pressure," she said, "to get something out in usable form, that we are not too embarrassed by, at the same time that we are treading very nervously into difficult terrain."

Mr. Smith said "major headway" was made with the emergence of an analogy of a generalist teacher to a pediatrician, who knows the whole baby and can refer its parents to a specialist if necessary. "That still begs the question as to how much is enough in every subject," he said, "but it does get past the notion the committee had that a generalist is a specialist in one area, who knows a little bit about everything else."

Since its inception, the board has pledged to fully involve a variety of "stakeholders" in the development of the teacher-certification system. But it is coming under pressure to more closely involve members of the teaching profession, through various organizations, in the actual creation of its standards and assessments.

Drawing in a broad range of teachers is the only way to ensure that the board's work is a "professionalization project" and not just another test, argued Mr. Myers, of the National Council of Teachers of English.

Board officials say complaints that the N.B.P.T.S. is operating like a testing operation are simply unfounded. "Our mentality is based on the belief that there's no sense doing this unless it is a serious professional-development activity," said Joan Baratz Snowden, the board's vice president for assessment development. In defining standards for teachers, the national board realizes that it must not lose sight of the first constituency teachers serve: their students. What teachers should know and be able to do, they say, should be intimately related to the expectations for students. The board's work has implications for separate projects to create national standards and assessments for student learning.

"If the work is to continue on both fronts," said Adam Urbanski, a member of the national board and the president of the Rochester (N.Y.) Teachers Association, "then there is a dire need for coordinating, or inevitably the risk is that the two will end up incompatible."

"There is a need for more conversations" with those now engaged in a multitude of parallel efforts to draw up national standards and assessments for students, Mr. Urbanski added.

Senior staff members of the national board say they have close contact with the educators working on student standards and assessments. While the various groups already engage in frequent conversations on an informal basis, the national board is seeking a grant that would enable the efforts to establish formal ties.

Mr. Kelly, the N.B.P.T.S. president, emphasized, though, that he does not believe the emerging effort on behalf of students should delay the board's work. The momentum for establishing certification for outstanding teachers is too great to risk losing, he said. "We feel the teaching profession is capable of developing this system in a decade and assuming a leadership position in the reform debate by defining high standards for itself," Mr. Kelly said.

"We think it's doable," he added. "We are making an authentic commitment to try our damnedest to do it right." □

Compiled for this book from various articles in Education Week *and* Teacher Magazine *published in 1992*

56.

Standards For New Teachers

A new consortium is defining a common core of knowledge and skills novices must demonstrate to get licensed.

By Ann Bradley

Aconsortium of state policymakers and representatives of the teaching profession has developed a model set of standards for beginning teachers that identifies for the first time the "common core" of knowledge and skills that all new teachers should possess.

The Interstate New Teacher Assessment and Support Consortium, a project sponsored by the Council of Chief State School Officers, is now seeking comment on the model standards for licensing teachers. The consortium also plans to develop standards for new teachers in specific subject areas and to create prototypes of assessments that states could use to evaluate candidates for licensure.

Rather than focus on what courses teachers should have completed as most current state requirements for teacher licensure do, the model standards describe what novice teachers should know and be able to do in order to practice.

In devising the common core of standards for new teachers, the interstate consortium drew heavily on the work of the National Board for Professional Teaching Standards, a privately incorporated group that is developing a system of voluntary national certification to recognize outstanding teachers. The consortium will identify how state policies should be changed to make requirements for initial licensure compatible with the work of the national board.

The consortium decided to undertake the project because a number of states are in the process of overhauling their licensure standards and because various subject-matter groups are setting standards for what students should know and be able to do. Linda Darling-Hammond, the chairwoman of the consortium's standards-drafting committee, said in an interview, "Given that we now have a goal of learning on the part of all students, rather than merely 'offering instruction,' the standards [for teachers] have to rise." She added, "We aren't going to be able to achieve our goals if we only prepare teachers to cover the book."

Members of the consortium hope that the model standards, which have begun circulating over the past few weeks, will be used as a guide by states interested in revising their licensure procedures and by professional organizations concerned with teacher education and development. Currently, said Ms. Darling-Hammond, a professor of curriculum and teaching at Teachers College, Columbia University, there is "a huge disparity across the states in terms of the nature of standards for teacher licensure and in terms of the rigorousness of those standards."

The level of interest in the consortium's standards-setting project—40 states are involved—could mean that such gaps will close.

Organized Into 10 Principles

The draft standards for beginning teachers are organized into 10 principles. Each includes an explanation of the knowledge, dispositions, and performances that characterize the principle.

The principles state that new teachers:

• Understand the discipline they teach and how to

teach it to students;
- Know how children learn and develop and can provide learning opportunities that support that development;
- Understand that students learn differently, and adapt their instruction to diverse learners;
- Use a variety of instructional strategies to encourage critical thinking, problem-solving, and performance skills;
- Create environments that encourage positive social interaction, active learning, and self-motivation;
- Understand effective communication techniques and use them in the classroom;
- Plan instruction based on knowledge of subject, students, the community, and curriculum goals;
- Use formal and informal assessment strategies to evaluate and insure the continuous development of the learner;
- Continually evaluate their own practice and seek opportunities to grow professionally; and
- Foster relationships with colleagues, parents, and community agencies to support students' learning and well-being.

Mary Diez, the president-elect of the American Association of Colleges for Teacher Education and a member of the drafting committee, said the panel had little trouble in devising the standards. "It's like there's an emerging national consensus" about good teaching, she said. "We were arguing about the emphasis on some things, but not about the specifics."

The committee drafted the standards over the past year and a half. It includes representatives of 18 states and a number of professional associations, including both national teachers' unions, AACTE, and the National Council on Accreditation of Teacher Education. Another 22 states have formed a "networking committee" to help the consortium gather public comment on the draft standards.

M. Jean Miller, the director of the interstate consortium, said the group expects to issue a final set of standards in June, after gathering feedback from focus groups and written comments from a mailing of 1,500 copies of the draft standards.

Several states—including California, Kentucky, Minnesota, New York, and Texas—are developing licensure systems that focus on what teachers know and can do, rather than on what coursework they have completed. These "outcome based" systems would place a heavy burden on assessments to identify whether candidates possess the necessary knowledge and skills to teach, Carol Smith, the senior director for professional issues for AACTE, pointed out. "But this is the direction that most of us feel is the right one to move in," said Ms. Smith, who is a member of the standards committee.

Focusing on the knowledge and skills that teachers must possess to enter the classroom also mirrors the national emphasis on identifying what students should know and be able to do, Ms. Smith added.

Eventually, members of the consortium's standards-setting committee said, such a focus on the outcomes of teacher preparation also would have profound effects on the way colleges prepare teachers and on the way such programs are accredited. "We've got a lot of work to do to come up with having higher education be in sync with the standards and be training toward the standards," Ms. Miller said. "That in itself would be a major revolution."

Sample Assessments Planned

The next step for the consortium will be to come up with some sample assessments that can measure the qualities described in the standards. That effort is still in the planning stages. Like the assessments being developed for the national board, Ms. Miller said, the consortium's prototypes would provide evidence about a teacher-candidate's knowledge and skills through portfolios, videotaped samples of teaching, and structured interviews. Such prototypes would differ markedly from the standardized tests typically used by states in licensing teachers.

The consortium also plans to examine the technical issues involved in performance assessment, including the cost and legal considerations, and to develop guidelines for states that are considering using such assessments.

The consortium, which was formed by California and Connecticut officials in 1987, was created so that states could share information about such issues. Funded by the Carnegie Corporation of New York, the group also has a grant from the U.S. Education Department's office of educational research and improvement for setting standards in subject areas.

To develop the prototype assessments, the consortium probably will draw up guidelines and specifications, but not actually develop the exercises, Ms. Miller said. The consortium is not seeking to duplicate the national board's work, Ms. Miller pointed out. "We're just trying to draw from their experience and structure [assessments] for a beginning teacher," she said.

The state of Connecticut, a founding member of the consortium, has developed some of the national board's assessments.

In setting standards for teaching particular subjects, the consortium will work closely with the subject-area groups that are developing standards for what students should know and be able to do, Ms. Miller said. For each subject, subcommittees will use the same core materials to set standards for initial licensure: the work of the national board's standards committees, the standards for students developed by various subject-matter groups, and the consortium's own common-core standards. □

From Education Week, *Feb. 10, 1993*

57.

Assessing Teachers

The National Board for Professional Teaching Standards pilots a new kind of assessment for teachers.

By Ann Bradley

In an annex of a downtown Methodist church in Austin, Tex., across the street from the state Capitol, three teachers are comfortably seated at a table with piles of paperback books in front of them. Across from them sits an interviewer, ready with a stack of prepared questions to ask. A video camera is trained on the entire group.

This is the new face of teacher assessment. There are no paper-and-pencil tests in sight. In this exercise, the teachers are judged on their ability to hold a productive discussion about the books with their peers.

The activity is one of a series the National Board for Professional Teaching Standards has developed to assess middle school teachers of English language arts. The board plans to launch its system of voluntary certification for accomplished teachers on a limited basis next fall.

All told, the N.B.P.T.S. plans to set standards for excellence in about 30 subject areas for students of all ages and to spend $50 million developing its certification system. The developers of the first assessment have now created and field-tested three components: a written examination of candidates' knowledge of their field; a portfolio showing their own and students' work from their schools; and performance exercises completed at an "assessment center."

From the results, the national board will decide which exercises to administer to the first candidates for certification. In the two days the Texas teachers spent at the assessment center, each completed four exercises. Before arriving, each teacher also had taken the written test and prepared a portfolio. The process proved to be draining for many teachers, who put in an estimated 150 hours of work to finish the three components.

During a roundtable discussion about the assessments, one woman joked that, by the time she had finished, she felt like she "deserved another degree." "It's been a great deal of work," Ivey Mossell, who teaches in San Angelo, Tex., acknowledged. "But it has been interesting and enlightening."

'Cooperative Discussion'

The developers of the assessments—who are based at the University of Pittsburgh and the Connecticut Department of Education—tried to capture the essence of teachers' work through a variety of exercises. While the written examination and the portfolio drew directly on teachers' knowledge and experiences in their own schools, the assessment-center exercises were designed to examine their broader understanding of teaching.

For the "cooperative group discussion" exercise, for example, the teachers were told to imagine that they had been named to a curriculum-development committee in a mythical school. They were told that the school was in a metropolitan area and served a diverse group of students. They were also given a specific grade level and a theme for the unit of instruction they were to plan.

Each teacher had received eight novels ahead of time to read. To begin the exercise, they were given about an hour to prepare to discuss the books with other teachers. Their task was to decide which four of the books would be most suitable for the students in the fictional school, to justify why they had chosen or rejected each book, and to talk about how the books fit together.

The teachers then came together to talk about their recommendations, with the help of questions from the interviewer. It was clear from the discussion, which had a relaxed and friendly tone, that some of the teachers were thinking of their own students and not necessarily those described in the assignment. One teacher said, for example, that she thought a book would appeal to her rural students because it was laced with Biblical language.

Diversity Issues a Challenge

Removing themselves from their own classrooms and drawing on their general knowledge of how to teach language arts to early adolescents proved to be a challenge for most of the teachers here, in fact. One of the qualities that the assessments seek to identify in teachers is their ability to take students' genders, races, ethnicities, cultures, and socioeconomic levels into consideration in designing instruction.

The developers of the assessments have found that teachers either have "a real command of those areas, or they don't," said Raymond Pecheone, a Connecticut education department official who is developing the assessment package. "There is not an even distribution across all of the candidates."

In the essays, "we found that those topics were very difficult to try to assess," he said, "because many teachers haven't had a lot of experience with those types of activities. The answers didn't go into great depth."

As troublesome as they may be, multicultural issues were included in the board's vision of accomplished teaching because teachers think they are important, Mr. Pecheone noted. Part of the rationale for creating the board was to improve teachers' preparation and continuing professional development, he explained, so information from the certification process could be used to provide a new focus for training.

One of the most difficult exercises that teachers were asked to do here was the "instructional planning" activity, which focused on teachers' knowledge of language diversity. The teachers were given time to review a variety of materials that could be used to teach the topic to 7th graders. With those materials, they were directed to select a focus for instruction and to design three activities for the students.

The interview was designed to explore the teachers' reasoning and to examine such issues as what difficulties might arise for the students and how the teacher would adjust for them. Although the activity was designed to tap teachers' knowledge of diversity and how it could be used to enrich students' understanding

of themselves and others, two teachers who were observed downplayed the role of diversity in their interviews.

Instead, they appeared to interpret the exercise as an opportunity to highlight the similarities among people and to teach students not to be "prejudiced," as one teacher said.

In a third exercise, the teachers were provided with batches of students' writing to analyze. They were told to assume that they were 8th-grade teachers at the beginning of a school year, perusing the papers for clues about the students they would now be teaching.

In the interview, the teachers were asked to talk about how they would instruct these students and develop their writing skills. They were asked to identify patterns that were characteristic of the papers in their entirety, and also patterns of specific language elements, such as grammar, usage, and spelling.

The interviewers then asked the teachers a series of questions about these patterns and how they would

> **As troublesome as they may be, multicultural issues were included in the board's vision of accomplished teaching because teachers think they are important.**

help the students improve. The wording used in the exercise to distinguish between features common to the entire paper and those specific to language usage appeared to confuse some teachers.

Most teachers he interviewed, said Cliff Coan, a high school English teacher in DeLeon, Tex., realized what was being asked of them during the course of the interview. But, he noted, some confusion appeared to stem from different terms that educators around the nation use for the same concepts. "I had to spend a lot of time saying, 'Could you clarify that?' because the terms we use may not be used everywhere," he said.

Mr. Coan said he found the exercise interesting because it simulated what teachers have to do during the first days of school to make decisions about what their students know and what they need to learn. "Different people keep coming up with different ideas to work on," he said of the teachers he had interviewed, "and most of them seem to have some validity."

The final activity required teachers to step outside their own experience perhaps more than the others. It was designed to gauge their ability to analyze instruction and offer solutions to a beginning teacher. For the exercise, the teachers were given a written commentary prepared by the new teacher that described what she was trying to accomplish in her classroom. They were then shown a videotape of a scene from her classroom and given time to prepare written feedback on her instructional approach, her performance in the classroom, and her ability to meet her stated goals.

In the essays, the teachers were instructed to make recommendations about what the teacher still needed to learn and how she could improve her instruction.

In addition to completing the four exercises, each teacher who came to the assessment center here also participated in a roundtable discussion to talk about their experience with compiling portfolios and with the assessment process in general.

Although the teachers had spent dozens and dozens of hours working on the assessments, they still expressed skepticism about the concept of national teacher certification. Texas teachers are particularly leery of another type of test, they said, because they have been subjected to so many of them in their state.

Maria Teague, a 6th-grade reading teacher in San Antonio, praised the group-discussion exercise, noting that it "teaches the need for teachers to get together and plan."

But she cautioned that she has "mixed feelings" about national certification, worrying that teachers might price themselves out of jobs if they receive bonuses for becoming certified. Other teachers worried that, without a financial reward, teachers would be unlikely to subject themselves to the work required to obtain certification.

In Texas, the distinction that is made between teaching reading and teaching English could be problematic, some teachers here said, because the assessments place a great deal of emphasis on student writing.

Judy Gasser, a language-arts coordinator for a regional service center who acted as an interviewer, said the Texas curriculum "doesn't always lend itself to as much writing as is indicated" in the assessments. "It's a bit of a challenge for the ones who are straight reading teachers," she observed.

A Catalyst for Change

A 6th-grade teacher also mentioned during the group discussion that her primary emphasis in class is grammar, while the assessments drew heavily on teaching literature.

Teachers of English as a second language and special education also expressed concern that the types of activities they do in their classrooms were not reflected in the assessments' emphasis on reading and writing. For some teachers, however, the assessments' emphasis on writing caused them to take a second look at what they expect of their students.

Ms. Mossell, the San Angelo teacher, said her participation with the assessment field test made her realize that her students, who have limited proficiency in English, were not writing at all. Compiling her portfolio, she said, "caused me to reassess the writing portion of my program. And I realized I did not have one."

Since that time, Ms. Mossell said she has been doing research to identify techniques to help her students understand the rudiments of sentence structure with an eye toward writing in the future.

That kind of realization and effort to improve is what the national board is looking for, Mr. Pecheone of the Connecticut education department said. "One of the major reasons why we do performance assessment is that it can really be a catalyst for professional development and a way in which teachers can share their practice," he said. "If all it was was getting a certificate of accomplishment, and we didn't inform the profession," he added, "I'm not sure whether the national board really would meet its goals. It has got to do both." □

From Education Week, *Nov. 11, 1992*

58.

The Spoils Of Success

Teachers of the Year are often lured from classrooms by more money and the chance to reach a wider audience.

By Joanna Richardson

Last summer, the syndicated columnist Colman McCarthy wrote an editorial imploring Rae Ellen McKee, the 1991 national Teacher of the Year, to shun corporate job offers—and a spot on the lecture circuit—and remain in the classroom. "Please, stay put," wrote Mr. McCarthy. "You're more needed by your children at Slanesville Elementary than in front of a microphone or behind a corporate desk."

Soon after the column was published, says Ms. McKee, she was bombarded with hundreds of letters of advice. Many of those with careers outside education agreed with the columnist and urged the West Virginia native to continue teaching. But "most of the letters I received from teachers," she says with surprise, "encouraged me not to stay in the classroom."

She says she believes the teachers, in a nod to the power of celebrity, thought Ms. McKee could "use her influence to make changes." And a few acknowledged that the six-digit salaries she had been offered would be a welcome fringe benefit. So despite Mr. McCarthy's pleas, Ms. McKee took the teachers' advice and accepted offers to speak on behalf of teachers and teaching.

She is not alone. Although most Teachers of the Year remain in the classroom, many decide to pursue other activities in administration, in higher education, and—like Ms. McKee—on the lecture circuit. "They go to other areas, perhaps, but they never leave education," says John Quam, the director of the Teacher of the Year Program for the Council of Chief State School Officers.

"They just broaden their activities."

Ms. McKee says that her new career has enabled her to make more of a difference in education by spreading her message beyond her students. But she acknowledges that the added income—a considerable boost over her $20,000 salary as a remedial-reading teacher in a rural school—has helped ease the pain of the transition.

"At the heart, I think [Mr. McCarthy] very much understood how I felt" about teaching, she says now. "But I don't think he realized how little money I've made. I've been the first one not afraid to admit that."

Like many Teachers of the Year, Ms. McKee says that her life began to change when she won her award in April 1991. The offers from educational associations, universities, state governments, and corporations were overwhelming.

But it was not the money or the fame that lured her away from Slanesville Elementary School, in the northwestern corner of West Virginia, she contends. "I wanted to be involved in changing instructional tactics," she says.

To that end, Ms. McKee has been travelling around the country speaking to groups about what she knows best: teaching. "I had always been kind of worldly, trying to bring ideas back into my school," she says. But now she is exporting her knowledge to the outside world.

Ms. McKee hopes to bring to teachers the message that their work is significant. And she says she aims to shatter stereotypes about the profession. "I think it's important for society to see me as articulate and professional . . . not as a schoolmarm," she adds.

On leave from her teaching job since she won her award, Ms. McKee commands $2,000 an appearance for her speaking engagements. While she is still based in West Virginia, by all accounts the former teacher is leading a corporate life. Her community, in the heart of Appalachia and just 10 miles from where she was raised, is amazed that "I'm riding on airplanes and I have a fax machine," she remarks.

Now, she has two publishing contracts to develop stories she used as teaching tools. And a national book tour could be imminent.

Despite all the excitement, she says she has not considered leaving Slanesville. "My heart is in West Virginia, so I feel like I want to try to bring about change [here]," she says. "We need to retrain and reinvigorate our teachers."

Ms. McKee says she has considered looking for a county-level position in educational policy. And she has not ruled out going back to the classroom. "It's a shame I can't be paid more for what I like to do and what I do

Rae Ellen McKee, Teacher of the Year for 1991

well," she observes. "But I think I will eventually go back to the classroom, or I'll run out of things to talk about."

Terry Weeks taught social studies at Central Middle School in Murfreesboro, Tenn., just south of Nashville, when he was named the 1988 Teacher of the Year. But he has since moved on to other pursuits. Now, Mr. Weeks is "four or five blocks away" from the middle school, at the department of educational leadership at Middle Tennessee State University. He teaches a course in social-studies methods there and is working toward a doctorate in curriculum and supervision.

"During my travels [as Teacher of the Year], I had the opportunity to speak to several college classes," Mr. Weeks says. "In my interaction with them, I saw their readiness to learn, and I came to the realization that maybe I had something to give" them. "Now the spark inside me burns a little brighter because of the freshness" of a new career, he adds.

Though Mr. Weeks says he was "desiring a challenge" even before he won the award, he says being Teacher of the Year "cast a light" on some hidden strengths. And "if you have talents that extend beyond the four walls of the classroom," Mr. Weeks says, "you might want more."

As a teacher, "you tend to think you have very little to offer . . . but the desire to reach for the stars and advance is always there," he adds.

In teacher education, there is the opportunity to create a "ripple effect," Mr. Weeks explains. "My influence extends out further than it did before. And if I have an impact on these teachers-in-training, then they will go out and make a difference with even more people," he reasons.

Donna Oliver has a similar philosophy toward education. She got involved in teacher training at a local college in 1988, the year after she was recognized as Teacher of the Year. "I was convinced that I had a greater effect there," says Ms. Oliver, who was a biology teacher at Hugh M. Cummings High School in Burlington, N.C., when she was tapped for the national award.

Now she is working on her doctorate in curriculum and teaching at the University of North Carolina at Greensboro and is directing the teacher education program at nearby Bennett College. She says she was reluctant to leave her classroom to accept a short-term post in higher education. But once the switch was complete, "I knew immediately this was the area I needed to be in," she says.

Bennett is "historically African-American and all female," adds Ms. Oliver, "so I had a unique opportunity to train this group as teachers." And "every time I touch one life there, I can multiply that by 20," she remarks.

Ms. Oliver, like her successors, says she did not look at the teaching honor as "a way out," but rather an "invigorating experience." "I'd say 99 percent of those [named Teacher of the Year] would stay in the classroom," she adds. "I think they just get into other areas of the field."

A handful of former Teachers of the Year have tackled careers as college instructors, educational consultants, or administrators, according to the Council of Chief State School Officers. And some choose to continue on a speaking circuit while they are teaching part time.

"I encourage the teachers the year after [the award] not to do anything drastic," says Mr. Quam, the program's director. But "what makes many of them so special is they can move among so many worlds." And, says Mr. Quam, there is no reason for the teachers to feel divided by that freedom. "They are not just teachers or administrators or trainers of teachers," he remarks. "They're educators." □

From Education Week, *Dec. 2, 1992*

59.

Dynamic Duo

Two teachers start a feisty newspaper, an experimental school, and a reform movement to change their schools.

By Karen Diegmueller

It's a late winter day in Milwaukee, and a brilliant sun has elevated the temperature to a balmy 50 degrees—a rarity for these climes. All along Lake Drive, the road that hugs the Lake Michigan shoreline, people are bicycling, tossing Frisbees, walking, and celebrating the golden weather. But holed up inside a two-story red brick building several miles from the lake, a dozen men and women resist the promise of spring and concentrate on the task at hand.

They are volunteers, dressed in the casual uniform of the day—jeans, flannel shirts, sweatshirts, and sneakers. Some wear buttons touting a particular cause. A 3-month-old boy naps cozily atop a formica conference table while his mother works. In these cramped quarters, haphazardly decorated with mismatched furniture, posters, and plants suspended in macramé hangers, they pass the afternoon proofreading copy, writing, and typing corrections into a computer.

Were it two decades ago, this could easily be a conclave of anti-war activists. Despite the wrinkles and graying hair, these men and women are clearly agitators. But unlike their counterparts from the 1960s, the people gathered here are not outsiders. They agitate within the system. Their cause: to reform the Milwaukee public schools. They are the editors and publishers of a first-of-its-kind newspaper, a periodical produced by an independent group of educators. Collectively, they spend hundreds of hours each month getting out their message of reform to colleagues and the community at large.

Two among them—Bob Peterson and Rita Tenorio—

exemplify the passion and energy that has driven *Rethinking Schools* since the quarterly tabloid was started six years ago.

Peterson and Tenorio have been at the forefront of school reform in Milwaukee for nearly a decade. They co-founded *Rethinking Schools* in 1986 and a year later helped establish a nationwide organization for educators and parents seeking to change public education. Then in 1988, the two helped create the experimental Fratney Street School, where they are putting the principles and ideas they preach into practice. And last year, they headed a reform slate that gained control of the local teachers' union.

Says Anita Simansky, a volunteer proofreader for *Rethinking Schools* and a guidance counselor in the nearby Kenosha public school system: "These are people who, when they were very young, decided on a lifetime conviction of putting a lot of time and energy into trying to change the world."

People who have known Peterson for a long time say it's only natural that he grew up to be some sort of reformer. That he did so as a school teacher is another matter entirely.

Peterson was raised in Madison, Wis., in the late 1960s and early 1970s when it was the heartland's hotbed of student activism. At Madison West High School, he worked for student rights and against the Vietnam War. Peterson thought of high school itself as an infringement of his rights, and he rebelled by participating in sit-ins and walkouts over the dress code and other issues. "For the most part," he says, "I really despised school."

Nonetheless, after high school, Peterson took a job as a teacher's aide in Milwaukee. His first day on the job did little to improve his opinion of public schools. It happened to coincide with the first day of busing to desegregate the school system. Black students were being bused to his predominantly white high school. The bus arrived late, and as the wary students emerged, a physical education teacher stood at the school door noisily demanding that they go get tardy slips. "I couldn't believe it," Peterson says. "Here are these kids, they're scared, and this gym teacher is yelling at them."

Surprising even himself, Peterson subsequently enrolled in the University of Wisconsin at Milwaukee, got a degree, and began teaching in a city school in 1980.

Like Peterson, Tenorio had not set her sights on a career in teaching while growing up in the Milwaukee suburbs. But as a young woman coming of age on the verge of the women's movement, it was one of three career options suggested by her high school counselors. "They told me I could be a teacher, a social worker, or a nurse," she recalls. She chose social work. But during her field experience at the University of Wisconsin in Milwaukee, she discovered how much she enjoyed children. So, Tenorio switched majors and in the early 1970s, took her first full-time teaching job at an all-black, inner-city parochial school.

She liked the work. Her students' parents had high expectations for them and were actively involved in their education. But the pay was bad; after eight years at the school, she was only making $8,000 a year. To gain some financial security and to get involved in a new bilingual education program, Tenorio decided to move to the public schools.

The switch, however, was not all positive. She was surprised to find that parental expectations and involvement in her new school were both disappointingly low. And she was soon disenchanted with the curriculum and pedagogy the district imposed. At the parochial school, she had been free to use components of what is now known as the whole language approach to instruction. But not at her new public school. It seemed that each year, the district added another basal reader to get through. "I really resisted having to do some of the things public schools said we had to do," says Tenorio, whose principal gave her some leeway. "At times, it really did feel like I was a subversive. If there was a choice between painting on an easel or [completing] two workbook pages, in my mind, there was no choice."

Peterson and Tenorio met in 1980 at a meeting of the city's human relations committee and quickly realized they shared many of the same educational philosophies

and concerns, including an unhappiness with the city's public school system. "We sort of connected at that point," Tenorio says. Strengthened by their mini-alliance, both plunged into more civic and school activities.

In the mid-1980s, Peterson and Tenorio began meeting regularly with a group of educators who shared their frustrations—both with the school system and with the lack of leadership in the teachers' union. The Milwaukee school district was plagued with all the

Rita Tenorio says *Rethinking Schools* was created to challenge every teacher in the school system, including the union leadership. In the publication, she says, "we try to offer a vision of what we think should take place in public schools."

problems of major urban districts: rampant truancy; a severe dropout problem; declining test scores; low grade-point averages; and a growing minority enrollment coupled with a lack of minority teachers. The central office and the school board were formulating reform plans, but without much input from teachers or their union.

Peterson, Tenorio, and their colleagues decided they needed to find a way to stir up the waters and get more people involved—some sort of sustained way to promote their ideas. So, the idea for *Rethinking Schools* was born.

As one member of the group would later write: "*Rethinking Schools* is the child of our frustration with how little voice teachers are allowed in the debates over what is and what should be happening in the schools. In Milwaukee, as elsewhere, the public schools are in deep trouble. But most of the people authoritatively offering solutions to the public have been central office officials, legislators, and businesspeople. When the blue ribbon commissions are established to investigate the schools and offer reforms, they usually include only one or two classroom teachers, often invited as an afterthought. As pawns rather than respected colleagues in the search for school reform, teachers often feel isolated and powerless."

The newspaper was created to end the sense of isolation and impotence and make teachers central players in reform. "We no longer wanted to be on the defensive all the time on school issues," says Peterson. "We wanted to have a vehicle in which we could begin to address in a pro-active way issues that affect teachers and parents."

The first idea was to produce something like an academic journal. But that idea soon gave way to a newspaper format, which seemed more appropriate for their mission and more accessible to teachers and the community. Moreover, the availability of desktop publishing software would enable them to do much of the work themselves.

Once a format was established, the group developed a statement of purpose, which still appears in essentially its original form in every issue under the headline "Who We Are." The educators vigorously debated whether their publication would incorporate a cross section of viewpoints or speak with one voice. In the end, they decided that unity would be more powerful.

They chose not to shy away from confrontation. Tenorio's "Confessions of a Kindergarten Teacher," the lead article in the first issue, set the rebellious tone for the publication. In it, she revealed her pedagogical transgression—forsaking the basal reader.

In the early days, the editors didn't know if *Rethinking Schools* would survive. When the newspaper first went to press in the 1986-87 school year, the group didn't even have enough money to pay the printer. What little they had was scrounged up from house parties, donations, and $10 voluntary subscriptions.

When most of the writing was completed for each issue, the educators, who had but a fleeting knowledge of journalism and the production process, would set up shop in one of the editors' apartments.

David Levine, a former Milwaukee teacher and a member of the original group, recalls one of the early deadline periods: "For the next four days, my small Milwaukee flat would cease being a home in any normal sense of the word. Every flat surface— kitchen table, study desk, borrowed card table—was covered with layout paper. Extra lamps had been imported to augment my dim lighting and an ugly brown filing cabinet had displaced my living room rocking chair. I would have no place to cook dinner, no privacy, and little rest. I was entering a temporary throwback to my early days of political activism, when we cheerfully let the greater cause jostle and shove personal life into the corner."

The lack of money and amenities were not the only obstacles. Initially, the teachers were also concerned about repercussions from administrators who might take umbrage at the hard-edged copy. After the second issue was published, Peterson was summoned to his principal's office. Although personally supportive of the endeavor, the principal warned him to be cautious. As Peterson recalls, the principal said: "It's like the McCarthy era down at central office. Just tell your people to be very careful."

But nothing untoward occurred. In fact, a member of the original group, Cynthia Ellwood, was later moved, under a new district administration, into the central office as coordinator of a K-12 curriculum reform project. She subsequently became the school system's curriculum director, resigning from the newspaper's staff to avoid any potential conflict of interest.

Many who know the teachers doubt that political repercussions would have quieted them anyway. Says Erin Krause, a newspaper volunteer who teaches with Peterson and Tenorio: "They aren't afraid to step on people's toes."

Nothing was immune from scrutiny. Even the Milwaukee Teachers' Education Association became the target of their criticism, which produced cries of

> ## Peterson and Tenorio decided they needed to find a way to stir up the waters and get more people involved—some sort of sustained way to promote their ideas.

alarm from within the union. According to Tenorio, many union officials were convinced that *Rethinking Schools* had been created as a vehicle to attack and undermine the MTEA. Some union members, Peterson says, even thought the newspaper was being underwritten by another union.

Undermining MTEA "certainly was not the purpose," Tenorio says. But, she adds, the publication was created to challenge every teacher in the school system, including the union leadership. "We can no longer run the union as we have in the past 25 years," she says.

In 1989, the teacher-editors' financial plight was eased temporarily thanks to the first of several small grants from the New World Foundation of New York City. Says Ann Bastian, a senior program officer at the foundation: "We became interested in *Rethinking Schools* not only because of the quality but also because we thought the paper provided a forum in a way that teachers could really connect to the community. *Rethinking Schools* was very crucial in getting teachers actively and independently thinking about school change themselves." And because the ideas were not being generated by outsiders, she adds, teachers "were not stuck in a defensive position and could help set the agenda, which they should be doing."

The content of *Rethinking Schools* focuses on many of the crucial issues facing urban educators and parents today, as well as societal issues and teaching methods. The editors pay particular attention to multicultural issues. The paper has run in-depth articles about tracking, whole language, school choice, standardized testing, and teacher evaluation, among other topics.

The front page of the March/April 1992 issue offers: "The Illusion of Choice" and "Examining Proposals for Improving [Milwaukee's Public Schools]: Reform vs. Scapegoating." Inside stories include: "Teachers Evaluating Teachers," "Recession Goes to the Head of the Class," and "Experimenting with Assessment."

Most of the articles are written by the core group of editors, although a small stable of correspondents from school systems elsewhere in the country also contribute stories. The writing style is a blend of reportage, analysis, and advocacy. It is the rare article that leaves the reader wondering on what side of the issue the writer falls. The editors have a number of firmly held opinions. They oppose, for example, choice and the creation of so-called "charter schools." And they are critical of standardized testing.

The newspaper also excerpts articles and books by prominent education writers and researchers such as Jonathan Kozol and Linda Darling-Hammond, a professor of education at Teachers College at Columbia University. Parents and politicians occasionally contribute articles to *Rethinking Schools*, as well. The back page is reserved for the art, prose, and poetry of schoolchildren.

Linda Christensen, a high school teacher in Port-

land, Ore., is one of the regular contributors. "The thing that I really find exciting about *Rethinking Schools* is that it is a collection of teachers who are putting it together," Christensen says. "Most publications that I've seen are specific toward a content area or issues in education. But *Rethinking Schools* really combines all of those. It's about classroom practice, but also about the large issues and struggles in education. And it comes from a perspective that is both pro-teacher and pro-student and, at the same time, pro-parent and pro-community."

The paper has grown from a 6,000 circulation periodical to one nearing 40,000, with an audience as far flung as New Jersey, Kentucky, and California. While the publication is free to Milwaukee teachers, it also has 2,000 paid subscribers, most from outside the metropolitan area. This latter group includes a number of teacher educators who use the newspaper in their classrooms. After seeing an issue for the first time, Joyce Penfield, an associate professor of education at Rutgers University, ordered back issues for her students. "It raises very important topics," says Penfield, noting that it tends to be ahead of most other educational journals. "It's very applicable to what I see as good teaching, good learning, and good education."

Even though its budget has nearly doubled over the past few years to about $64,000, the paper is by no means a flush operation. Its founders have been able to raise enough money to hire two part-time employees, including a managing editor, and rent modest office space, but it still is mainly produced by volunteers. Dozens show up to unload the printed copies and sort them for distribution to schools, churches, libraries, and other area locales.

The editors have published a few advertisements but generally eschew them because of the potential conflict between the ads and the paper's rebellious philosophy. They also acknowledge that this same philosophy has hindered efforts to score additional foundation support.

One observer describes Bob Peterson as having a strong behind-the-scenes leadership style. "He has a way of making things work and keeping things going," she says. "He can do five things at once and still be nice to everybody."

Consequently, they are putting their energies into expanding the paid subscriber list to 6,000. And the publishers have launched a fund-raising campaign, asking readers to make an annual pledge to the publication.

To help the newspaper broaden its outlook as its national audience widens, the editors recently established a national advisory board. Their hope is that it will help critique the newspaper, identify prospective writers with differing perspectives, and raise funds.

Although the focus of *Rethinking Schools* has been on Milwaukee, its tone and message clearly have struck a chord with teachers elsewhere. Christina Brinkley, a member of the advisory board, says the paper has had a serendipitous effect. About three years ago, letters started arriving from grateful teachers relieved to learn that they were not alone in their attempts to improve their schools. "The letters were almost heart wrenching," says Brinkley, an associate professor of sociology and women's studies at Bates College in Maine. Until they started reading the newspaper, she says, "those lone teachers had been isolated."

Adds Christensen of Portland: "*Rethinking Schools* enables us to look at our local issues in terms of a national picture."

But its editors intend to keep *Rethinking Schools'* emphasis on Milwaukee. "We pick articles that we think are going to move things ahead," Peterson says. If the overall perspective shifts to a national audience, Peterson and Tenorio fear the newspaper will become abstract.

What's more, many articles have a hometown political flavor that might be lost if the emphasis shifts. This past spring, for example, the paper ran a piece knocking various community and school leaders— school board members, the mayor, a mayoral aide, and a local radio and television station—for taking whacks at the schools. "Criticizing [Milwaukee Public Schools] is not the problem; this newspaper has never been shy about criticizing MPS," Peterson wrote. "What is disturbing is the lack of analysis behind many of the current criticisms and the potential dangers in several of the proposed 'solutions.' "

The periodical's Milwaukee focus has made it a must read for local policymakers. Even those who are the occasional targets of criticism appreciate the paper's overall high quality. "The publication is well-written; its thinking is supported by background data, interviews, good writing," says Milwaukee Mayor John Norquist. "It's really an important part of Milwaukee's political culture now."

The paper's main flaw, he says, is that it is too much a part of the establishment. "Their reform is within the system; they don't threaten the basic premise of the system," he says, citing the newspaper's opposition to parental choice. "If we are going to keep the basic system we have, then *Rethinking Schools* has all kinds of great ideas."

Because they want to be taken seriously by everyone from fellow teachers to inner-city parents and state lawmakers, the editors take great pains to produce a top-notch product. They reject roughly two-thirds of the articles submitted by outside writers. But they are equally tough, if not tougher, on their own work. They spiked their premier edition, slated for mid-1986 publication, because it did not meet the standards they had set for themselves.

Peterson and Tenorio's schedules are particularly dizzying. They both generally arrive at school at about 7:15 a.m. and put in a full day there. After school, they attend union, newspaper, or district committee meet-

---

The paper has grown from a 6,000 circulation periodical to one nearing 40,000, with an audience as far flung as New Jersey, Kentucky, and California.

---

ings about four days a week. And then there are the night meetings. Tenorio says she often doesn't get home until after 9:30 p.m.

Weekends, too, are frequently taken up with business. On one Saturday, for example, Tenorio spent the entire day in union meetings while Peterson revised several newspaper stories. They both worked on the newspaper on Sunday from 1 o'clock in the afternoon until 9:30 that night, and then they had to get up bright and early the next morning for a 6:30 meeting.

Their growing celebrity has also made them hot commodities on the conference circuit. This is particularly true for Tenorio, who last year was named Wisconsin Teacher of the Year. One friend marvels that Tenorio is able to attend "30 meetings a day but still knows somehow about Bart Simpson or a [news] report."

But Peterson and Tenorio, neither of whom is married, insist that the long hours and the wrangling are necessary if they are to fulfill their mission. A quick glance at some of their recent accomplishments shows that their efforts aren't for naught.

A series the paper ran helped persuade former Milwaukee Superintendent Robert Peterkin to spend $100,000 that had been earmarked for basal textbooks on other materials instead. Articles convinced the district to form a council to help schools adopt the whole language approach. And the publication played a role in swaying the school board to block an outcome-based education approach and a consultant's student-assignment plan.

The district's assessment task force, which Peterson co-chairs, successfully persuaded the district to replace a 3rd grade standardized test with a 4th grade holistic assessment—a move that *Rethinking Schools* had advocated.

Says Mary Bills, a district school board member and former chair of the board's curriculum committee: "Many of [the newspaper's] board members were instrumental in helping us change our curriculum. They showed the same dedication to developing our curriculum process as they do to putting out a very timely and useful publication. I'm generally very supportive of the role they play. They make us think, they occasionally make us change what we do, and they bring something to the table."

Peterson and Tenorio attribute their successes to hard work, a proven track record in the classroom, and a tested political strategy. "We have been able to criticize and take issue with policy, but at the same time we have been willing to get involved in the traditional mode of things," Tenorio says.

Peterson and Tenorio's juggling act also includes the MTEA, the largest unaffiliated local teachers' union in the country. Both were elected to the executive board five years ago but, according to Peterson, they represented such a minority voice that they were virtually ineffective.

Last year, however, the two of them ran as part of a reform slate, and a majority of the progressive candidates were elected; Tenorio was elected vice president and Peterson was re-elected to the union's executive board.

Mayor Norquist believes the new leadership from *Rethinking Schools* has an opportunity to open up the union to fresh ideas. "The previous [leaders] felt threatened by their own elections," he says. "You had a lot of sclerosis of the arteries."

Says Peterson: "I want our union to be an advocate,

not a barrier, to reform." He notes that there are already signs of progress: The MTEA is promoting a mentor program and supporting curriculum reform.

But Tenorio says the election has not eliminated tensions within the MTEA. Tenorio, for example, wants the union to retreat from its traditional adversarial approach to doing business, a stance that some within the organization argue is the equivalent to "giving away the store." That assertion, she says, is untrue. "I am an advocate of teachers," she declares. "I think we have to look at new ways of interacting."

As a result of all their labor, Tenorio and Peterson have come to be seen by many as the leaders of school reform in Milwaukee. But Christensen describes them another way. "Organizers would be the term that I would use," she says. "They are really trying to organize the community around the school people in a way that is not around cookies and teas."

Tenorio agrees that organizer is the more accurate assessment. One of their main goals, she says, is to involve others in school reform. "Every person working on a small piece can accomplish something," she says. She points to Erin Krause, who volunteers for each issue of *Rethinking Schools* despite having a young child and a full-time job. "That is a big sacrifice for her," she says.

Besides, Tenorio declares, "I'm not going to be able to continue at this pace forever. There are days when I want it to all go away." She pauses for a moment, and then adds, almost as an afterthought: "I'm a driven person; I need to be challenged all the time."

Both Peterson and Tenorio have been urged to turn their leadership and organizational talents to a principalship or some other administrative post. But they believe the only people who can really turn schools around are teachers—working primarily through the union. "We can't do that once we become part of the administration," Peterson says. "Plus," he adds, a grin spreading across his face, "we love to teach." □

From Teacher Magazine, *August 1992*

60.

Consummate Professional

Throughout her teaching career, Nancie Atwell has been the constant questioner, the constant learner.

By Elizabeth Schulz

Down a snowy lane in Edgecomb, Maine, a town with more steeples than stoplights, the blanket of white is interrupted only by spruce trees and the occasional house with a snake of smoke escaping from the chimney. Fences of stacked, weathered rails zigzag across the frozen New England countryside.

Just off the road stands a two-story, clapboard structure with an addition jutting off one side. It looks like any other house—except for the bell on the roof. Inside, a sea of children are seated on pillows in a large carpeted room. Facing them, with sun pouring through three windows behind her, is a woman with thick, dark hair pulled back in a headband, Hillary Clinton style. Dressed in a maroon sweater that covers a flower-print blouse and a long gray-green skirt, she sits—legs crossed—in a rocking chair, leaning forward with elbows resting on her knee like a mother reading to her children.

The woman is Nancie Atwell, renowned teacher, author, and researcher. The building is the Center for Teaching and Learning, the K-6 private school she built with royalties from her popular book, *In the Middle*—and with her own sweat and blood.

In the back of the bookshelf-lined room, three women furiously take notes. Teachers at Fayette Central School, a little over an hour away, the visitors don't want to miss a thing. Atwell doesn't want them to miss anything either—they are, after all, the main reason she built this school.

The center represents Atwell's vision for school reform in the United States: give thoughtful teachers real and practical models of good classroom practice— what she calls "primary sources"—so they can go back to their schools and be agents for change. Atwell admits it's a "slow growth" model; only a handful of teachers at a time can visit her center. But those who do are able to immerse themselves in a school that's organized very differently from their own. They can watch as students do real-life work; they can see how the children talk to each other and interact with teachers, how parents are involved, and what the tools of teaching actually look like.

Atwell's own experience has taught her to be respectful of the time one needs to change. It was a long and painstaking journey that led her to this quaint New England building. Years of reading, thinking, talking, observing, and experimenting spurred her to reshape her classroom. Then she tried to entice other teachers to re-examine their teaching. The school was born of the frustration Atwell felt when earlier efforts— speeches, workshops, and classroom demonstrations— fell short. But she believes she may have hit on a solution.

"It's the problem of trying to imagine teaching in a different way," she explains. "How do you do that when you went to traditional school for 13 years, went to college for six more years, and then went into a school that's always been organized one way? The only way to break the lock step and mindset is to put people into a situation that is organized completely differently. Let them learn the rhythm and incorporate it into their heartbeat."

The only books that Nancie Atwell had easy access to as a child growing up in Clarence, N.Y., a semirural bedroom community near Buffalo, were a set of encyclopedias. Her parents, a mailman and a waitress, worked hard to make ends meet. "Books," she says, "were just not something people could afford."

In high school, Atwell was a tough kid who traveled with a tough crowd. "She was smart as hell but not necessarily playing the school game," says her long-time friend and well-known educator Donald Graves.

"Education was really not where my ambitions lay at all," Atwell recalls. "I just wanted to get out of high school, marry my boyfriend, live in a trailer, and party."

Her school days may not have turned her on to education, but they had an impact. "I've always found her an enormous champion for the underdog," Graves says, "for kids who have known what it is to struggle—because she has known it, too."

Atwell and her brother were the first members of their extended family to attend college, but even that was mostly by happenstance. She won a New York Regents scholarship to the State University College at Buffalo. She remembers her mother saying: "This is too good to pass up. Go for a year; if you don't like it, you don't like it. At least give it a try."

She started out majoring in art, a subject she loved in high school. But after a year of taking only art courses, she realized that she missed reading and writing, so she signed up for some English classes. In the fall term of 1970, Atwell landed in a seminar taught by a professor named Toby McLeod. "It completely turned my head around," she says. "It was a course where people talked passionately about ideas that were represented in literature, argued, acted out scenes from plays, and debated. It wasn't just people flapping their gums; we had strong personal opinions that were rooted in text. I had never heard this kind of discourse, certainly never in an English class in high school."

After receiving her bachelor's degree in English, Atwell stayed around the area for another semester to get certified to teach. "Teaching was something to do until I figured out what I really wanted to do," she says.

But in the classroom, she understood for the first time what it means to have an aptitude for something. "What happened, even during my student-teaching, is that I discovered I loved it," she says. "I had never done anything that I loved as much as teaching.

"It just seemed to be miraculous that you could have this kind of dialogue with kids," she adds, still with a note of incredulity in her voice. "That this would be a *job* and that you would be *paid* to do it. It gave me extraordinary pleasure." She pauses. "It still does."

Atwell says Tonawanda Middle School, where she did her student-teaching and later landed a full-time job, was an extraordinary place to begin her career. At the time, her methods were mostly traditional, but her principal, "an enlightened instructional leader," ex-pected teachers to be learners, constantly questioning their practice.

The wild beauty of the Maine coast, however, lured her away just a year and a half later. While on vacation with her new husband, Toby McLeod, the professor who brought literature to life for her, Atwell interviewed for an opening as an English teacher at Boothbay Harbor Grammar School. The superintendent there asked her if she would focus on teaching grammar. She said no; she had trained to teach kids to write, and that would be her first priority. As she left, she was certain that she wouldn't get the job.

Days before the start of the school year, Atwell got a call from the Boothbay superintendent. The other job candidate had seen the classroom where she'd be teaching and backed out. The superintendent asked Atwell if she still wanted the job.

So the couple put a new muffler on their beat-up Valiant, tranquilized the dog, and headed back to Maine. The day before school was to start, Atwell saw for herself why the other candidate had jumped ship. The school building, a Civil War-era structure, should have been condemned. There were rats, and raw sewage was seeping into some of the classrooms. Her own classroom was half of a big room, separated from another class by massive sheets of plywood. The tile floor was half gone, and bare light bulbs hung from the ceiling.

But it was in these shabby surroundings that Nancie Atwell gave birth to "thoughtfulness" in her classroom. The story of how she came out from behind her desk to sit with her students and understand better how they learn has reached more than 200,000 teachers through her book *In the Middle* (Boynton/Cook, 1987). In it, Atwell describes how she puzzled over students' behavior, invited researchers to observe and comment on her class, and looked critically at her practice. Deep analysis of what she does when she writes spurred her to experiment with structures that would help, rather than hinder, students' writing. "I saw the choices I made as a writer—deciding how, when, what, and for whom I'd write—weren't options available to writers in my classroom," she recounts in the book.

In the process, she reached out to other teachers in her school—not with answers but with questions. With a two-year grant from the federal government, she launched the Boothbay Writing Project to study the writing process. The 23 teachers involved read research papers, attended professional conferences together, kept detailed logs of observations of students, and discussed their own writing.

The teachers met formally and informally. Many of the conversations took place at the Thistle Inn, a bar they frequented. "We were madly talking all of the time about what we were finding," she remembers, "thinking about how the whole system of writing instruction in the school needed to be changed based on what we were learning."

"The process worked," she writes in *In the Middle*. "It worked because it was so complex. Layer upon layer of experience accumulated to form a body of shared knowledge and expertise. No one handed us a program from on high; in intense and personally meaningful collaboration, we invented our own wheel. Together, we learned from ourselves, each other, and our students."

They created a model for a "writing workshop" for students that later spread throughout Boothbay Region Elementary School, the new consolidated school they taught at. Students were given regular chunks of time to write. They chose their own topics and genres and were given feedback during—not just after—the writing process. Teachers covered the mechanics of writing in mini-lessons and when issues came up during individual writing conferences. The teachers wrote themselves and talked to students about their own writing.

Donald Graves, then a professor at the University of New Hampshire, remembers his first encounter with Atwell's 8th graders' work. "We were just amazed at what her students wrote," he says. "It wasn't just single pieces; she showed us whole collections where you could see how students first started and what they could do toward the end. I've seen very few situations where students changed so dramatically." In 1985, her students scored the second highest in Maine's writing assessment; a fifth of her students were in the 99th percentile.

Atwell soon began to wonder how all she'd learned about writing applied to her reading program. Her talks with Toby around the dinner table became the yardstick by which she measured her reading class. "It is a literate environment," she says of her dinner table in *In the Middle*. "Around it, people talk in all the ways literate people discourse. We don't need assignments, lesson plans, teacher's manuals, or handbooks. We need only another literate person. And our talk isn't sterile or grudging or perfunctory. It's filled with jokes, arguments, exchanges of bits of information, descriptions of what we loved and hated and why. The way Toby and I chat most evenings at that table were ways

DANUTA OTFINOWSKI

Nancie Atwell

that my kids and I could chat, entering literature together. Somehow, I had to get that table into my classroom and invite my 8th graders to pull up their chairs."

The "table" she developed for her classroom was the "reading workshop." The idea behind it was that students learn to read by reading. She let students choose what to read just as real readers do and gave them opportunities to discuss what they were reading. Atwell flooded her room with books—both recognized literature and popular novels, such as S.E. Hinton's *The Outsiders*. She required students to read all period long and regularly write letters about what they were reading to her and other students. Students who had never voluntarily read a book were reading an average of 35 a year.

Throughout *In the Middle*, Nancie Atwell shows in painstaking detail that thoughtful change happens only through careful observation of how kids learn to read and write. She became an avid data collector. Her students' writing stayed in school all year; she scoured the material, looking for growth and changes. Every day, she filled out a "status of the class" chart, so she could look for patterns over time. She did some number crunching, keeping track of how many books students read and what genres were represented, what punctuation they used in writing, and what students chose to write about and why. She even interviewed her students about their own learning. "My experience as a teacher who observed her students—as a teacher-researcher—has changed me forever. Everywhere I look I see data," Atwell writes in a later book, *Side By Side*. "As I filled my notebooks, my teaching became more patient and more sensible."

Still, she needed a structure for all this information. "*In the Middle* became a story of me and my students and our struggles to make sense of school," she writes, "and I became the rueful, insightful, cheerful first person that my husband sometimes wishes he were married to when he finishes reading a manuscript with my name on it."

In the Middle, which struck a chord among teachers

because it presents teaching as an intellectual activity but in a practical way, won her a loyal following and critical acclaim. She was the first classroom teacher to receive the David H. Russell Award for outstanding research in the teaching of English from the National Council of Teachers of English and the prestigious Mina P. Shaughnessy Prize from the Modern Language Association.

The awards were a welcome affirmation but didn't really change how she felt about herself and her work. "I have such an ego," she says with a self-deprecating laugh, "that I really believed I had something to say." Still, the attention was not for naught. She believes that the recognition she received lends credibility to other teachers who want to conduct research in their own classrooms.

The acclaim also made her a hot commodity on the lecture and consulting circuit. Atwell had left the Boothbay school system after her daughter was born in 1986, the year before *In the Middle* was published. Over the next few years, she conducted independent research and directed a writing-across-the-curriculum project for elementary schools through the Breadloaf School of English in Middlebury, Vt. But between 1987 and 1990, she also accepted more than 30 speaking engagements. She welcomed the opportunities, hoping she would be able to reach other teachers with her discoveries and challenge them to re-envision their classrooms.

She found the process of writing speeches rewarding; it forced her again to sit down and think about what went on in her classroom. "I've never written anything where I wasn't surprised in the act of writing," she says. "I'm always amazed by what turns up." She remembers one speech-writing epiphany in particular. She was writing about two very different students who had been lagging but gradually became successful in her class. "I can remember almost falling off my chair when, as I was sitting there with my data in my dining room, I figured out what was going on with these two kids," she says. "There is no other feeling like that, finding the connection and then trying to find the language for it before you lose it." Many of these speeches later evolved into articles for publication.

Although she enjoyed preparing the speeches, Atwell found that giving them wasn't a very effective way to reach teachers. She felt like "a talking head." And delivering them, she remembers, was often a letdown. "The unfortunate thing about speaking is that the learning part was over by the time I left my house," she says. "Then I had to go deliver the speech. By then, it was dead on the page."

She was further dismayed to see that a kind of cult movement had formed around her work. After giving a speech, she would find herself hounded by teachers, who said things like: "Your book is my bible, and you're my guide."

"It's one thing to have people say in a letter, 'I admire your work,' but it's another for people to take work that is serious and intellectual and turn it into a charismatic movement," she says. "*In the Middle* offers a model of a teacher who found her own problems and used every resource available, especially her own students, to solve the problems. I want teachers to be professional enough to respect the genesis of the story."

Traveling around the country, leading teachers in inservice training, Atwell saw some other trends that disturbed her. "Everywhere I went, I would be sandwiched between the Madeline Hunter person and the thinking-skills person," she says. The programs these people were touting seemed to force artificial frameworks on teaching and learning and missed the crux of the problem and the solution: the relationship between teacher and student. "There was always some obstacle between us and kids, some prism through which you have to look at kids, something that will make teaching more efficient, easier, cleaner, neater, less emotional."

To break through this barrier, Atwell began looking for opportunities to teach teachers in situations where they could witness and experience a different kind of interaction between teacher and students. In graduate courses she taught through Northeastern University, she ran half of each class as a writing workshop, treating the student-teachers like her 8th graders, so they could feel how it worked. And she took up demonstration teaching, where she would take on a class and invite other teachers to observe. Atwell's friend Donald Graves watched her teach a class of students in Atlanta that she had never seen before. "She has that knack of making almost instant contact at a student's level," he says. "She doesn't do it by coming down to the student. She is able to produce this incredible invitation to the student to go where she is going."

Atwell recalls those experiences with mixed feelings. "That was closer to what I wanted because at least teachers could see it happening with real kids," she says. "But in some ways it was still artificial because they weren't my students. I had no idea what had happened before I came in; I had no idea what was going to happen after. So the context was strange."

Atwell was ready for the next step. She wanted to continue teaching and working with teachers, but she wanted to do it right, without staying in a Holiday Inn every weekend. She also wanted to remain in Maine, an area that she and her husband love. And she needed a place for her daughter, Anne, to go to school.

So on Aug. 2, 1990, a grueling year after Atwell decided to start her own school, builders broke ground on the Center for Teaching and Learning in nearby Edgecomb. By Aug. 29, they had fit together two pieces of the prefab house and secured the roof. On Sept. 10, Nancie Atwell cried; the movers had brought the furniture, and, for the first time, the center looked like a real school. On Sept. 12, she and four other teachers opened their doors to 30 students.

In a part of the country that is run by town meetings, the students at the Center for Teaching and Learning have a distinct advantage: They are learning to speak out. When they are taken on field trips, the guide inevitably asks: "Who *are* these kids?" It's not because they are brilliant or particularly articulate; it's because they have a voice. They ask questions and want to know things.

One reason is that the school day starts and ends with a meeting attended by all 58 students, kindergartners to 6th graders, who sit side by side with their teachers in one room. On this bright winter's morning, Nancie Atwell leads the group from her rocking chair, peppering the talk with Spanish phrases the students have learned.

The meeting starts simply enough, with children raising hands to tell their news from the weekend. One describes a ride on a snowmobile sled; another tells how she spotted a fox. Atwell asks if anyone has heard any national news. "Arthur Ashe died of AIDS," one offers. Teachers and students alike talk about who this man was, the disease, and the loss.

Then Atwell leads them in reciting a poem; students clap and snap their fingers in rhythm. After that, Atwell reads aloud an excerpt from an interview with Eloise Greenfield, a poet they have read. According to the article, Greenfield does her best writing from about midnight to 4 a.m. The children gasp. Greenfield's advice to young writers: If you read a book you like, read it again to see how the author puts the words together.

Atwell then reads from a book about the Underground Railroad, and the group discusses it. Following the discussion, the students sing a song that they wrote about the work of the school.

This rich exchange takes about 15 minutes.

The only people who remain silent through the meeting are the three teachers from Fayette Central School. One of eight teams of teachers invited to spend a week at the school this year, the "interns" are asked not to speak to the children or teachers during class. This way, Atwell says, they can concentrate on observing and reflecting without interfering with the dynamics of the school. In fact, to minimize the disruption, no other visitors are allowed in the school.

"The great thing about the center is that these are real kids in a real school," Atwell explains. "We have a stake in what happens to them."

The interns are encouraged to take detailed notes and jot down questions to ask the teachers during meetings that are scheduled throughout their stay. As the week progresses, these women sometimes sit shoulder to shoulder with a teacher as she confers with a student; they scrawl notes but say nothing.

The application process for the intern program is rigorous. The teachers in each team must write essays about their professional development and their educational philosophy. The team application must include a letter from the school administrator stating that the teachers will be allowed to make changes based on what they learn during the visit. Each team leaves at the end of the week with a long- and short-term plan and three graduate credits.

When the morning meeting adjourns, most of the students scramble off to their work; a few stay behind to put the pillows back into an oversized closet.

Unlike at most schools, the students at the center don't have assigned desks. Instead, they move among four major rooms—the reading room, writing room, math and science room, and projects room. The rooms are plentifully stocked with the tools that real readers, writers, scientists, mathematicians, and artists would use. Students are broken into four groups by grade levels—kindergarten, 1-2, 3-4, 5-6—so most students stay with the same teacher for two years.

This morning, Atwell joins teacher Susan Benedict and her 5th and 6th graders in the writing room, an open space with wooden tables of different sizes to accommodate different size children. Strategically placed around the room are folders, papers, pencils, pens, scissors, books on writing, a dictionary, and a thesaurus. Atwell joins the students in a circle of chairs. A quotation by the poet Rainer Maria Rilke posted on the wall behind her captures the essence of the mini-lesson Atwell is about to teach: "Be patient toward all that is unsolved in your heart, and try to love the questions themselves."

Atwell tells them about an experience her friend Donald Graves had recently on a flight to Atlanta. Graves found himself sitting next to someone from Boothbay, a man named Barry Sherman, whose 23-year-old son, B.J., had died in a car accident a few weeks earlier. Graves asked Sherman if he knew Nancie Atwell. "Yes," he replied, "She was the best teacher B.J. ever had." Sherman went on to tell Graves how he cherishes the piece of B.J.'s writing that Atwell excerpted in her book. When he reads it, Sherman says, he can hear B.J.'s voice and understand his feelings.

Atwell hands out copies of B.J.'s story about moving out of his mother's house to live with his dad. "We've been talking about narrative voice," she says. "This is in the third person. I call this fiction. Some of it is real; some is made up."

As she reads aloud, the students follow along, gripped by the tale. She finishes, and, after a long period of silence, she asks quietly, "Why did Barry Sherman remember this piece of writing?"

"Because it was an important incident," one student offers.

"Because B.J. was trying to work out his feelings in it," another adds.

Atwell lets other ideas emerge before she adds her own: "Because it was something that *mattered* to B.J. I call it *authentic* fiction. These are the things that last. When you sit down to write, ask yourself: Is it a real need I have? Is there some tension or problem I want to work out? Otherwise, all you're doing is an exercise to fill time."

She ends with a quotation from playwright Neil Simon: "I can't write anything unless my character wants something *dearly*."

Although Atwell does not have a class of her own in the center, she thinks of herself as the instructional leader. When Atwell and Benedict noticed that students in Benedict's class were turning out a lot of beautiful but voiceless writing, Atwell offered to teach a series of mini-lessons on the purpose of writing. Donna Maxim, a teacher at the center who knows Atwell from Boothbay Writing Project days, says: "To watch her do a mini-lesson is one of the greatest pleasures in my life. She's such a great writer, and she can just talk to kids and make them aspire to be great writers, too."

As the writer's workshop continues, the students move off to tables to work. Some meet with Benedict for a writing conference during which they pose questions about their work in progress, read the piece aloud, and ask for comments and suggestions.

(Even the kindergartners at the center learn this process; they, for example, have written a parody of the popular children's book *Bread and Jam for Francis*, a piece called *Bagels and Salsa for Nancy*, about how their teacher eats bagels and salsa for lunch every day.)

Later in the day, Benedict's students gather, sprawled comfortably on the floor of the reading room, to hear her read aloud from *Roll of Thunder, Hear My Cry*, a book by Mildred Taylor set in the 1930s. In the chapter, a black man who has gone into town with his son is attacked by white men on his way home. After the reading, Benedict asks the students what they think. The conversation that ensues is easygoing but firmly rooted in the text.

"She describes too much . . . that part about the cracking bones," one girl says with a shudder.

"I predict Papa's going to die," a boy adds.

"What does Mildred Taylor care about?" asks the teacher.

After a moment, Curt, who is reclined on the floor, says: "She wants to tell us what really went on at that time, to really feel it. Not like the history books. She wants to show us the human side of history."

Nathaniel, obviously troubled by the events in the book, asks, "Could a white person get arrested for shooting a black person?"

In virtual unison, the kids say: "No. Now, but not back then."

Kristin expounds on the idea: "I think she's against racism. She's showing how wrong it is for a white person to shoot a black person."

Benedict pushes: "Is she promoting integration?"

When the students answer no, she asks, "What in the book leads you to believe that?"

They point out that the blacks and whites in the book live separately and that one of the most prominent characters, a black gentleman whom readers grow to respect, is against his son's becoming friends with a white boy.

All of the students at the center spend half an hour to an hour reading independently each day, but there is also ample opportunity to hear good literature read aloud. Like most teaching at the center, the decision to read aloud to the students was based on research. It has been shown, Atwell points out, that listening to someone read builds students' long-term memory. "Reading aloud isn't just charming," Maxim tells one of the Fayette teachers. "It is essential."

Since the opening of the Center for Teaching and Learning, the dinner-table talk at the Atwell-McLeod house has not been confined to books. Recently, their daughter, Anne, who is now a 1st grader at the center, cleared off a space at the table after dinner to draw electronic circuits in series and in parallel on paper napkins. She wondered which kind of circuit would conduct more power. Anne was still thinking about her science class, where she'd learned about circuits by making them. Students at the center investigate science as real scientists do, by asking real questions and setting up small experiments to prove or disprove a theory.

Recently, when teachers at the center talked about how they were going to have children write formally about the work they were doing in science, Atwell dug up a series of papers that a rain forest biologist who visited the school had presented at a scholarly conference. The teachers studied them and decided to use them as a model.

Today, in keeping with this real-world philosophy, Donna Maxim starts a conversation about magnets with her 3rd and 4th graders by passing out magnets and asking students what they know about them. On a piece of chart paper, she writes their ideas: "Magnets attract and repel." "They have poles."

A student named Meghan interrupts with a question: "Do magnets attract all metals?" Maxim writes down Meghan's question—it is, after all, the point of the lesson—and asks her what made her think of it. Meghan explains that she has a butterfly magnet at home that doesn't stick to all surfaces.

Maxim hands a nail to each student and poses a question: "What will happen to the nail if it is kept near the magnet for a while?" The students think out loud: "It will make the nail lighter?" "It will make it rust?" "The magnet will 'magnetify' the nail."

"Is a nail a magnet?" Maxim asks. Most of the students say no, but one boy says yes. Maxim asks him: "Will this nail pick up a paper clip like our magnet?" The boy says no.

"Is it a magnet?" she pushes.

The boy doesn't budge; he says yes. Another student postulates that maybe all things are magnets, but in different degrees. With that, the class launches into a discussion about electricity, conductors, and insulators—all aspects of one of the school's themes this year, energy.

It is just this kind of rigorous exchange that Patricia Dickinson, one of the teachers from Fayette Central School, says really shakes up her thinking. "Everything they do is a meaningful learning experience for the children," she says. "They never ask the students to do anything unless it is authentic and has a reason. This is something I will think about constantly now. Is this really an authentic activity? Could I make it more so? How could I do it?"

The center's teachers and the interns probe the issues surrounding thoughtful teaching in a series of meetings, often held in the teachers' upstairs office. (The space is comfortable. The teachers each have their own desks, but they are grouped together to promote collegiality.) They first discuss some of the surface details the interns have noticed about the school. The way teachers and students remove their shoes when they enter the building, so the floors stay clean enough for students to sit and lie on. The way there are no chalkboards so there is less dust. The way students call their teachers by their first names so they realize the teachers are real people.

Then the talk turns to bigger issues. How to create a rigorous intellectual atmosphere in which students still feel safe enough to take risks. How to give students real choices in a structured way. As they get into the nitty gritty, the teachers quote liberally from research on teaching and from reading they've done in the subject areas.

As the week draws to a close, the conversation at these meetings focuses on the most pressing issue: How will these three teachers be able to go back to their public school and create a more thoughtful learning environment? Although their classrooms are housed in a trailer, the Fayette teachers hope to create a kind of ghetto for real learning next year. Among other things, they decide to meet weekly to talk about their practice, to make presentations to parents and administrators about their experience and ideas, to begin reshaping their classes, and to work to get doors installed between their classrooms.

But Atwell insists that this group will go away with something even more important. "They began to understand that they could be brave together," she says, "that there was real power in the coherence of their theory. There was a new sense of what was possible when teachers who shared beliefs got together and tried to forge some common ground."

Nancie Atwell calls the time she spent preparing to open the Center for Teaching and Learning "the nightmare part" of her life. When she went looking for a place to house the school, the first three sites fell through. Her decision to build a new school gave her more control over its layout but also filled the following months with hundreds of details she had to work out. Even after the land was purchased and a blueprint drafted, it took four months to get approval from the local planning board. The application was roughly 100 pages long and cost more than $4,000 to compile.

"I have never worked so hard, so long, so consistently on anything in my life," she says. "They were 18-hour days—developing the plan, walking the site, taking measurements, digging holes, and meeting with groups of people about one thing or another."

Fund-raising was an enormous chore. Atwell knew that her teaching model would not hold water if she served only the typical private school clientele. To make sure her students represented the socioeconomic profile of rural Maine, she wanted to offer generous scholarships to offset the $3,350 tuition. So she sent a mass mailing to teachers she had come into contact with over the years, asking for donations. (She now receives about $10,000 a year in checks, ranging from $10 to $100.)

But she still needed more money to build the school. "It's been awful, the most humbling experience in my life," she says of her fund-raising effort. "I think I have this great professional reputation, and I go to foundations, and they have never heard of Nancie Atwell, they have never heard of *In the Middle*, and, after I explain my model for changing schools, they tell me they won't fund a local project."

Despite grants from the Bingham Trust, the Betterment Fund, and *The New York Times* Foundation, and a $50,000 no-strings-attached donation from veteran actor James Whitmore, she still had to collect her pension from Maine's teacher retirement fund to make a down payment on a mortgage. Some of her royalties from *In the Middle* go directly to the school. So far, she has received no pay from the center. Her husband keeps asking, half-jokingly, when she is going to draw a salary.

Despite her fiscal precariousness, Atwell is ready for a new challenge. She plans to open a secondary school by 1994. "If the model we have for the elementary school is powerful," she says, "the next level of work is going to be absolutely groundbreaking."

Others agree. Secondary education is her area of expertise, and there is a real paucity of models out there for middle and high school teachers. No matter what Nancie Atwell is doing, Donald Graves says, she provides a powerful example for others. "She expects so much of herself," he says, "that to hang around her you start to think, 'My god, am I carrying my weight?' She's not demanding that you do it, but you want to join her professionally."

The tough question is whether others can really follow in Atwell's footsteps. "You can't bypass the fact that she is one hell of a reader, writer, thinker, and learner," Graves says. "On the other hand, there are lots of teachers out there who are on the verge and who just need the chance to see a real pro at work." □

From Teacher Magazine, *May/June 1993*

61.

Daring To Be Different

Unhappy with her own performance as a teacher, Joan Riedl began a professional odyssey to find a better way.

By Elizabeth Schulz

Marilyn Bue remembers the shock she felt the first time sne visited Joan Riedl's classroom in North Elementary School in Princeton, Minn. "It wasn't like anything I had ever seen before," recalls Bue, who had a son in Riedl's 5th grade program at the time. "It looked like a beehive, with everyone talking and doing things and moving around. Joan would be talking to just a few students, and it confused me because I thought the whole class should stop and listen to her."

Bue's reaction is a common one. Parents don't know what to make of a learning environment that is radically different from the one they knew as students. But those who visit Riedl's classroom soon see for themselves, as Bue did, that children thrive in the setting she has created.

Riedl's classroom is set up like a resource room. The children are workers, responsible for synthesizing and using, rather than just reproducing, information. Riedl has relinquished some of her authority, giving her students choices and welcoming their comments about how the class is going.

The elementary school teacher has not always taught this way. A decade ago, a classroom visitor would have found Riedl at the blackboard talking to students seated in straight rows. But in the early 1980s, Riedl began to explore the uses of technology in the classroom. Her quest launched her on a journey. She read extensively, contacted and visited schools using innovative teaching approaches, observed her own students, and thought long and hard about what makes sense. All the while, she was fashioning her own approach to teaching.

Through this process, Riedl has learned that change comes at a price—but that there is a payoff, too. After overcoming some resistance in her school and community, Riedl recently persuaded the local school board to designate her program a "genuine learning alternative"—another name for a school within a school.

But she has set her sights even higher. Under a controversial new Minnesota law, a select number of licensed teachers from across the state will be allowed to design, start, and run eight "charter" public schools under contract with a local school board. Riedl wants to be one of them.

Smartly dressed in a crisp white blouse with brown twisted beads and a brown blazer, Riedl is describing the way she used to teach. For many years, Riedl says, she was a teacher cut straight from the traditional mold. She would stand in front of her classroom lecturing to children who had textbooks open in front of them. In those days, Riedl says, she made all the decisions in the classroom, and it was always quiet and orderly.

Then, in 1981, her elementary school acquired some computers. Riedl signed one out and wheeled it into her classroom. She put students on it for standard drill and practice and was surprised when they started coming in during lunch time to use it. "There has got to be more to this machine," she thought to herself. "But I don't know what it is." Seeing that technology had the power to motivate students, she wanted to find out more.

222

Riedl shopped around for a master's program in technology. After calling universities and telling them exactly what she wanted—a program that would teach her how to use some of the newest technologies as thinking and teaching tools—she settled on the College of St. Thomas in St. Paul. The program, designed for both elementary schoolteachers and businesspeople, taught those enrolled how to use technology in common sense ways as a natural learning tool.

The St. Thomas program introduced Riedl to the ideas of the software developer John Henry Martin, who created the IBM program *Writing to Read*. These ideas provided the groundwork for Riedl's re-created classroom. Setting up a classroom as a series of workstations, she reasoned, made good sense. If a teacher asks students to do real work at these stations and holds them accountable for what they accomplish there, the computer could be more than just something for them to play with after finishing their seat work. At a workshop on *Writing to Read*, Riedl heard that IBM was looking for someone to train teachers in schools that were implementing the program. After finishing her master's, Riedl took the job.

During her two-year master's program, Riedl had developed a vision for using technology in the classroom. But she found it difficult to translate that vision and transfer her enthusiasm to the teachers she was training for IBM. "The teachers were frustrated," she remembers. "They were thinking, 'Oh God, here are these machines; what am I going to do with them?'" So, after a year of teaching teachers, she decided she needed to return to the classroom and try out computers herself.

When Riedl got her own class in 1988, she was eager to make some changes. Technology got the ball rolling, but the transformation didn't end there. Riedl realized that to use computers in a common sense way, other aspects of her classroom would have to change, as well. And the master's program put her in the right mindset: It started her questioning her old approach. "I had to go away for a while before I could realize how cold my classroom was," she says. "I began to think of my classroom as an artist's palette. I take a bit of this color and bits of that and see if it blends; if it doesn't, I can wipe it out."

Over the next several years, Riedl used her new palette to paint a new classroom. This year, the changes have been more formally recognized by the district. Riedl's 4th and 5th grade class and a 3rd and 4th grade class that follows Riedl's approach have been made genuine learning alternatives within the school. What this means is that parents and students can choose to be part of the program. Still, the program is not independent of North Elementary. It must operate, for example, within the schedule imposed by the larger school.

Riedl once heard a quotation that she says describes the most important shift in her teaching: "Before I was a sage on the stage; now I'm a guide on the side." To get there, Riedl says she had to give up power. "I made it clear that the students' opinions matter," she says. "They know that this is their room."

It's true that students in Riedl's program have more control than most, but they also have more responsibility. Far from being passive recipients of knowledge, Riedl's students are workers, who must learn to manage themselves. Much of the day is spent with the class split up into groups working on projects or at technology "stations." Riedl works with one group at a time and fields questions from other students.

Students Voice Concerns

Today is a typical day. In one section of the classroom, a sandy-haired boy peers through a video camera with hand raised, five fingers spread. He signals a countdown: 5, 4, 3, 2, 1. The camera focuses momentarily on a blackboard where "Channel 11 News" is neatly printed. Another boy says, "Welcome to Channel 11 News" as he wheels the board away, revealing two other boys seated at a news desk. They introduce themselves and take turns giving summaries of the weather and local news.

At another station, four girls have clustered chairs around a videodisc player. One student, the group leader, holds the remote control. The leader asks, "Does everybody have a workbook and pencil?" They answer "Yes," and she starts a science video clip.

At the language arts station, a handful of students are writing in journals, summarizing books they've read. The students chose one of two books to read and decided as a group how many pages a day they would be responsible for reading. One group thought they could read 20 pages a day, so they could finish in a week. Most of them did; the rest finished over the weekend. "The peer pressure is greater than if I'm after them," Riedl explains.

The teacher herself runs a station called "How is it going?" Today, the group is discussing a chapter from a social studies book about colonial times. "I really believe in students learning how to talk and discuss and share insights on readings and responding to other people's ideas in a respectful way," she explains. They talk about the relationships between the Indians and the early settlers and hypothesize about how the introduction of tobacco may have led to slavery.

Riedl uses this station to gauge how the class is working for the students. Because she is very task-oriented, she explains, she has to set aside time to let the students voice concerns. Recently, a student told her that she felt overwhelmed, that there was just too much to do in class. Another student acknowledged that she, too, felt this way at the beginning of the year but that she had found a strategy to conquer it. She writes down everything the class is supposed to do during the week, looks at it, and then she decides what to do first, second, and third. "Kids love to hear other kids' solutions to handling the classroom," Riedl says.

Later in the day, the students disperse into math stations. Some go into an adjacent room, where today they watch "Square One," a math TV show, and answer questions on a work sheet. Another group works with tangrams, Chinese geometric puzzles.

But most of the students spend the time working through problems in the math book. Because it's an individualized math program, one student is working on remainders while another is on least common multiples. Students take pretests and then read a chapter and do problems. Riedl teaches skills that they can't seem to get on their own. Students move on to the next chapter after they conquer the end-of-the-chapter test.

Roland Benson, the principal of North Elementary, points out that with this interdisciplinary, project-oriented, individualized approach, Riedl must keep on top of the skill needs of her students. Her program assumes that children bring more to class than what they learned during the last school year. She must determine the areas the students can fly through and pinpoint where they need more extensive instruction. It isn't easy, he says, but Riedl seems to make it work. "If you are attuned to the sparkle of eyes, the smiles on faces, and the changes in the channels of energy," he says, "you see that children are getting involved in their learning because they want to be involved."

Parent Debbie Burroughs puts it this way: "She demands of the students and they end up demanding of themselves. I don't know how she does it."

Reshaping the Learning Environment

This school within a school has been a successful testing ground for other ideas Riedl intends to use in her charter school, if given the chance. In the past four years, she has given much thought to the design of classroom space, parental involvement, and student assessment.

In 1990, North Elementary, suffering from a space shortage, set aside money to transform an old locker room into a classroom. Riedl saw an opportunity to design a room that would suit her new teaching methods, and she seized it. She found an architectural firm that would donate its services, called a professor at the University of Minnesota who recommended books on designing spaces for children, and recruited a college senior studying interior design to help coordinate colors. Riedl organized a workshop that brought together these people and resources with students, school administrators, and parents.

Riedl fields questions from students as they work at interdisciplinary stations.

The group decided to keep the walls that separated the coaches' rooms and the showers from the locker room to cut down on noise when students work in groups. Carpeted floors at various levels, as well as movable carpeted structures that can be used as both tables or benches, were constructed. Today, the back of the main room looks like a library, with paperback books displayed on shelves and a circular rack and magazines on a flat rack. But there is also a homey touch: two white wicker chairs with quilted pillows. Riedl's desk is in one corner, with some shelves that give her a little private space without shutting her off from the classroom.

The presence of parents at the classroom-design workshop is in keeping with Riedl's novel approach to parental involvement. Before Riedl reshaped her classroom, she would only contact parents when a student was having problems. Now, much more is asked of parents, and they get much more in return. All the parents sign a contract agreeing to volunteer in the classroom half an hour each month. Riedl also asks them to attend information meetings, where they are introduced to some of the classroom workstations. This, she says, helps them understand how different the learning environment will be for their children.

Parents say the firsthand experience in the classroom helps them shake off their old notions of what a productive classroom should look like. Riedl recounts what one parent told the local school board when it was debating whether to designate her program as a bona fide "learning alternative." The parent said: "Listen, I came into Joan's room and I really didn't know what was going on. I was quite upset. But, my boy learned important organizational skills. He learned how to be responsible."

Riedl thinks parents learn from spending time in her classroom. But that is not why she wants them to come. The main reason, she says, is a bit more selfish. "To meet students' needs," she says, "I need help." Parents assist in running the stations, special projects, and field trips. And Riedl is convinced that having parents in the classroom sends a good message to the students. "Parents are the single most important people in these kids' lives," she says. "They can have a strong influence in how the students view school."

Every Monday, the students get a homework packet that must be completed by Friday. Parents are asked to check through the packet and sign it each week. That way, they know what their children are learning, they can see for themselves if their children are mastering the material, and they can encourage them to budget their time well. The homework packet can also act as a reality check for the teacher; Riedl asks the parents to write her a note if they find anything in the packet confusing or misleading.

In her dream school, Riedl would equip each classroom with a phone to make it easier for the teachers to contact parents during the day. She would also have someone take her class for a few days during the year so she could contact her parent volunteers to determine their skills and work out schedules.

Because communicating with parents is so important to Riedl, she is careful to assess her students in ways that the parents will understand. The teacher realizes that most are accustomed to academic progress being measured by tests. So, even though Riedl doesn't depend on basals to teach reading, she continues to use reading comprehension tests included in the books.

For the same reason, Riedl would continue to use standardized tests to assess students in her charter school, in addition to the more "authentic" evaluations she has developed over the past few years.

Traditional multiple-choice and standardized tests gave Riedl an adequate picture of her students' progress when her teaching was mostly lecture and textbook work. But since students in her redesigned classroom are expected to learn to communicate, organize their own learning, and demonstrate creativity, among other things, Riedl discovered that she needed measurements that more precisely chronicle their work and show their progress and performance. Now, students maintain portfolios of writing assignments and journals. The classroom video camera also archives the children's progress. A comparison between early tapes of the children's news summaries and a recent tape, for example, shows that their ability to synthesize and relay information effectively has greatly improved.

Gone, too, are the days when Riedl kept the standards for evaluation from the students. When making an assignment, Riedl always outlines how they will be evaluated on it. For an oral presentation of a project, for example, Riedl prints out a list of the points she will give them for such things as eye contact, self-presentation, use of visual aids, thoroughness of research, and content.

Riedl also asks students to evaluate themselves. "I want them to be able to say: I'm having problems with fractions or decimals. I need help on this," she says. She often asks them how they think they did on a project. The payoff comes when students gain the ability to evaluate their own work in order to improve it. Shortly after Christmas break, Riedl collected her students' journals. For the most part, she was pleased with their writing, but she told the class that she had asked a few students to rewrite sections. The surprise came when a student who had done satisfactory work approached her and said: "Mrs. Riedl, I was looking over this, and I was wondering if I should redo this part." Riedl let the student know that that is what real learning is all about.

For the past four years, Riedl has consciously set aside time to familiarize herself with the latest ideas in education. She has put many of her staff inservice days to use reading, attending workshops, and observing other classrooms. Last year, she even persuaded her school board to let her take every Friday off, unpaid, to continue these activities.

Riedl attributes much of her professional growth to her relationship with teachers in the Clara Barton Open School in Minneapolis and three schools in the Bellevue (Wash.) School District. "I haven't come up with all this on my own," she admits. "I take bits and pieces of what I know will work for me."

Riedl first read about the Bellevue schools in a software newsletter. Their work reinforced some of what she had been trying in her class, so she developed a telephone relationship with Marian Peiffer, a teacher at Ardmore Elementary School. Riedl would phone her and pick her brain about some details of the Bellevue program. "Do you use desks?" she once asked. Peiffer told her that they use tables. After talking about it awhile, both agreed that card tables, which could be folded up and put away, would be ideal.

In the fall of 1990, Riedl's district paid her airfare so she could visit Bellevue. She spent four days with the teachers there, watching how they had fine-tuned classroom management with technology. She noticed that they let the students work for long blocks of time, an option she had been wrestling with. "It was a great learning experience to follow other teachers, talk to them, tell them what I'm doing, and get their feedback," she says.

Riedl has also borrowed ideas from some of the more renowned minds in education. For example, she has customized some aspects of Mortimer Adler's Paideia Proposal in her classroom. "I'm not rigid Adler, but I like the framework," she says. "It's natural." Adler believes that teachers have to build students' knowledge base. So, every Thursday and Friday, Riedl offers something she calls "Choices," which gives students the opportunity to play games that expose them to geography, authors, artists, and architecture.

And Riedl has not been afraid to embrace some tried-and-true methods. "There are some traditional, old-fashioned ways of teaching that I believe in and put into the curriculum," she says. She thinks it is important, for example, to teach students how to take notes and write a business letter, narrative, and descriptive story. Riedl's principal notes that "she doesn't have fear of stepping out of the crowd or of stepping back into it if she sees that is the right way to go."

Riedl's proposal for a charter school is under consideration in both the Princeton and nearby St. Cloud school districts. If her dream school becomes reality, it would open in the fall of 1993 and would be shaped around her current teaching methods. At first, the school would serve 60 students, one class of 2nd and 3rd graders and another of 4th and 5th graders. The teachers would keep some of the same students for two years and would work as a team, sharing ideas and designing activities for use in both classrooms. Riedl's primary role would be to teach; she would share the administrative duties with the other teachers. Secretarial and janitorial duties would be shouldered by parents, teachers, and students alike, or contracted out. In the second year, Riedl would like to add a 6th and 7th grade classroom.

She believes that the creation of small, alternative public schools like the one she is proposing may be the only way to achieve real change in American education. "You've got to move with the people who can see the vision," she says. "Just like small-group instruction frees you up to do more with different children, change in schools may work better in small pockets."

Ideally, her charter school would be housed on or near a college campus that offers teacher education. Preservice teachers would be invited to apply for full-year apprenticeships that would give them more than a brief exposure to the ways technology and offering choices can motivate students. "People talk about experiential learning for children," Riedl explains. "I think it is real important that teachers experience different forms of teaching and learning."

The past four years have taught Riedl some lessons about the pace and pain of progress. "I have real enthusiasm for change—for getting quality, being cost efficient, and being a good consumer with tax dollars," she says. "But change is hard in any setting. I know that now."

Riedl didn't realize when she started rebuilding her classroom that she was sticking her neck out. She went in thinking she had discovered great new approaches to help kids learn and was surprised when other people didn't share her enthusiasm. She even met some resistance when she went to the board to have her program officially designated a school within a school; and now that she is seeking a charter the naysayers are raising their voices again. Says Bue, one of Riedl's converts: "Anytime you change something so dramatically and especially if tax money is going to support it, it has to be explained many, many times before it can sink in that it will work."

The process has taught Riedl how hard it is to try something different in a society that rewards conformity. "In upsetting the status quo, you take a risk," she says. "When you put forth your ideas, there is always the possibility that they might be ridiculed."

The battle is made tougher, she says, by the poor image many people have of teachers. "Elementary school teachers don't have a lot of status," she explains. "It's easy to believe sometimes that you have no right to speak your mind." Before major meetings, she gets psyched up by telling herself: "Listen, you are fine."

Nowadays, most parents, local educators, and school district officials agree that Riedl's risk-taking has earned her the respect of the community. "She has changed her school by what she has done in her classroom," says Benson, Riedl's principal. "She showed others that it is OK to do things differently as long as it better meets the needs of the kids."

Riedl says the leadership role has changed her. "Being out there, breaking new ground, and probing into new territory has made me stronger, more self-confident, more focused, more diplomatic, and more adaptable to working with the system in the decision-making process," she says. "My students are better for it, and I'm better for it." □

From Teacher Magazine, *March 1992*

62.

The Price Of Isolation

A major study finds that the most successful and flexible teachers belong to 'professional learning communities.'

By Ann Bradley

When Milbrey W. McLaughlin and Joan E. Talbert launched their five-year study of the factors that influence high schools and teachers, they began, like most researchers, with a set of assumptions about what would be important to ask.

But when they started interviewing teachers, the Stanford University researchers quickly learned that they were wrong. "What teachers taught me in the first year—much to my horror—was that we absolutely had to redo it," Ms. McLaughlin says.

Not surprisingly, the researchers had framed a set of questions that worked logically out from the classroom to touch on school, district, and state policies that might affect teachers' work. Teachers, they soon learned, "just don't see the world that way," Ms. McLaughlin says.

What the teachers wanted to talk about were the things that most directly influenced their work, like students and subject matter. So, the interviews were changed to let teachers tell their own stories, an approach the researchers call a "teacher's-eye view" of schooling.

In reframing their methods, the Stanford researchers moved to what observers call the "cutting edge" of social-science research. And their findings centered around the importance of relationships, organizations, and issues that are typically overlooked or taken for granted by traditional academic studies.

Most notably, the studies by the federally funded Center for Research on the Context of Secondary School Teaching, completed last year, revealed that teachers' participation in a "professional community"—whether through their academic department, school, or a network of like-minded colleagues—had a powerful effect on how successfully they were able to adapt their instructional strategies to meet their students' needs.

While other academicians have written about the importance of community for teachers, the center's studies were the first to look at communities as a specific context of teaching and to find a link between participation in a community and successful teaching, observers say.

Innovative Methodology

In using the term "context," the researchers refer to all of the variables that influence teaching: students, subject matter, academic departments, schools, parents, higher education, and the like. By examining how these contexts are "embedded" in one another, says Ann Lieberman, a professor of education at Teachers College, Columbia University, and member of the center's national advisory board, the center's work highlights the complexity of the environment that teachers and students work in.

"If we're serious about change and understanding how it takes place," she notes, "we have to understand context in a far deeper fashion." The studies, she adds, also provide a "serious look at how teachers see change."

"That's a perspective that has long been absent"

from education research, Ms. Lieberman continues, "and I don't think has ever been looked at in quite so thorough a fashion by people using an array of methods."

In fact, it was the innovative methodology used to conduct the research, Ms. Talbert says, that made some of the findings possible. To generate its primary database, the center conducted in-depth field research at 16 high schools in seven school districts in California and Michigan. Twelve of the schools were regular public schools, one was an alternative public school, and three were independent schools.

Almost 900 teachers in the high schools were interviewed each spring for three years. The center's researchers collected records from the sites and observed schools and classrooms. Various kinds of data also were collected for 48 students.

The studies generated voluminous data from the sites over the three years, including feedback from the teachers who were studied.

In an approach that the center's directors say is unique, the researchers then built "bridges" between the field data and two national longitudinal studies: the 1984 High School and Beyond surveys of teachers and the National Education Longitudinal Study of 1988.

The marriage of these two kinds of data is reflected in the center leaders' backgrounds: Ms. McLaughlin, the director, is a field researcher and education-policy analyst, while Ms. Talbert, the associate director, is a sociologist who does large-scale quantitative analysis. The people who conducted the center's various research projects also hailed from a wide range of disciplines, including anthropology, curriculum theory, political science, and teacher education.

"We all saw something different," Ms. McLaughlin says. "We had multiple lenses of different disciplines and perspectives."

'Crest of a Wave'

The "bridges" were constructed by replicating some of the same questions used on the national surveys in the field interviews, Ms. Talbert explains. That way, the researchers could gauge how representative the schools, departments, and individual teachers in their 16 schools were.

The NELS:88 survey asked about such factors as collegiality, workplace climate, and leadership. So, for example, if the field data showed big differences between academic departments in terms of collegiality, the results could be checked against the "yardstick" of the national surveys to insure that all attitudes would be represented in the study.

Because the 16 schools that were selected for the field study were chosen for specific purposes—and were not intended to be a representative sample of U.S. schools—using the national survey data also "lets us

have it both ways," Ms. McLaughlin says.

Gerald Sroufe, the director of government and professional liaison for the American Educational Research Association, calls the study's use of field data and national surveys "cutting edge." The research, he says, is "on the crest of the wave of combining qualitative and quantitative data to get a rich new perspective on things."

The center's findings will now have to be "tested through other measures to see how much you can generalize about it," he says.

The new methodology helped reveal the importance of "learning communities" for teachers. "It was really very much through the dialogue between the quantitative surveys and the interview data," Ms. Talbert says,

---

Rather than adhering to rigorous standards and failing many students, successful teachers found ways to actively engage their students in learning.

"that we began to see a lot of variation among teachers in the sample and their access to or participation in collegial groups that could support them."

In conducting their interviews, the researchers used what they called a "student-decline scale" that was derived from comments they heard from teachers. The scale included such assertions as "students don't try as hard as they used to" and "students are not able to master the material."

Within a school, academic departments with different degrees of collegiality turned out to contain teachers with very different scores on the student-decline scale, Ms. Talbert says. Teachers in departments with low levels of collegiality, they found, tended to have more negative views of students.

Similarly, teachers who had made the most successful changes in their practice and had more positive views about their students' capabilities turned out to have one thing in common: belonging to an active professional community that encouraged and enabled them to transform their teaching.

Rather than adhering unswervingly to rigorous standards and failing many students, or resorting to "dumbing down" their instruction, these successful teachers found ways to actively engage their students in learning. "These healthy, positive professional communities have said, 'Hey, let's stop trying to fit the kid to this, and fit what we're doing to the kid,' " Ms. McLaughlin explains.

By contrast, she says, "without support, many teachers fell back on their old practices or left the profession."

The importance of a sense of collegiality to a school's success was demonstrated vividly by comparing two schools in the same California district. Both served roughly the same student population and both lived under the same rules and regulations. The study found, however, that one school had high failure and dropout rates, while the other had among the highest test scores and sent 80 percent of its student to college.

The difference was reflected in the professional characteristics of the schools, Ms. Talbert says. In the school with the high failure rate, teachers complained frequently, came to work late and left early, and held meetings "at the mailboxes" if at all.

The successful school, she notes, held frequent schoolwide meetings to solve problems and develop innovative solutions, like an "adopt a student" program to provide more personal attention to students at risk of failure.

By adopting the perspectives of classroom teachers, the study also revealed some of the limitations of current education research, the center's directors say. Many studies look at entire schools, Ms. McLaughlin points out, which is too large a unit of analysis to pick up the differences among departments and classrooms that are central to the center's findings.

They also learned a number of things that contradict the way questions typically are framed in education research. Teachers are often asked about their sense of efficacy in their jobs, for example. But the center's work found that teachers' perspectives about themselves change depending upon what class period they are teaching: first period might be a breeze, but second period might be a constant struggle.

What those attitudes reveal, Ms. McLaughlin says, is that students are one of the most important contexts in teaching. As common-sensical as the notion sounds, she adds, "the policy world doesn't consider that at all."

But finding ways to help teachers deal with those contexts by creating professional communities may not be easy. "You can't command community," Ms. McLaughlin says, "and you can't concoct collegiality." □

From Education Week, *March 31, 1993*

63.

Relax, Reflect, And Renew

The North Carolina Center for the Advancement of Teaching nourishes the mind, body, and spirit.

By Karen Diegmueller

Deep inside a dark, dank cavern the size of a football field, a guide illuminates a few discreet lamps to accentuate dazzling rock formations. At just the right moment, when the two dozen explorers have grown still, the leader presses a button on the boom box he has been hauling around, and strains from the chorale of Bach's Cantata No. 78 pierce the air. Suddenly, the pitch-black home of bats, lizards, and 40-foot drop-offs is transformed into a majestic cathedral, proffering solace to its visitors.

For these North Carolina teachers, this journey into Tennessee's Tuckalee Cavern is one of many singular moments they will experience during their week-long stay at the North Carolina Center for the Advancement of Teaching. The only center of its kind in the nation, the NCCAT is beginning its second academic year in a new $7 million retreat in the Smoky Mountains of western North Carolina. At the NCCAT, the emphasis is on reward rather than reform. Teachers can participate in stimulating, intellectual discussions, fish in mountain streams, enjoy the camaraderie of fellow teachers from across the state, conduct scientific experiments, write chapters of a novel, or be transported back in time to the Victorian age.

And, at the end of their week, if the teachers return to their classrooms eager to try out what they've experienced, so much the better, says the center's staff. But that is not the NCCAT's mission. "At the NCCAT, we turn our attention to the renewal of teachers rather than to their reform," R. Bruce McPherson, former

director of the center, explained in a speech he delivered to the Minnesota Humanities Commission last year. "We do not seek to change people or their work environments, but rather to encourage them to rediscover and nourish their personal and professional strengths, the passion and the intellect that are their strongest allies in the daily business of teaching."

The NCCAT was the brainchild of Jean Powell, a North Carolina high school English teacher, who in November 1983 testified before the Governor's Commission on Education for Economic Growth about the need to instill pride, self-worth, and enthusiasm in teachers if the state wanted to retain and attract the best. "We have a governor's school for gifted students. Why not something similar for teachers?" she suggested. "We don't need any more educational methodology or the latest curriculum fads. We'd like to study the 'real stuff.'"

To Powell, that meant contemplating the Great Books, visiting art galleries, viewing plays, writing critical commentaries. "If that kind of learning experience doesn't turn on teachers, I don't know what will," she says. "That excitement will be communicated to students. Furthermore, being a student will give a teacher a renewed perspective of the student's role."

Her suggestion won the support of three of the state's most powerful forces: then Gov. James Hunt, the speaker of the House, and the president of the University of North Carolina. The trio shepherded the NCCAT through the state legislature, overcoming the opposition of the state National Education Association affiliate, which wanted the money to be used to increase teachers' salaries.

The center opened in the fall of 1986 and last year moved into its new quarters on 36 acres near the campus of Western Carolina University. The facility consists of three structures—two well-appointed residence halls, complete with fireplaces and full kitchens, and the main activities building. The latter houses seminar rooms, an amphitheater, a computer lab, a dining room, an exercise room, staff offices, and a combination lounge and library with a cathedral ceiling, skylights, a baby grand piano, and a spiral staircase. Teachers are also encouraged to use the university's library, swimming pool, tennis courts, and other amenities.

Teachers' stays at the NCCAT are built around seminars led by academicians or other experts hired by the center. A typical seminar involves between 20 and 25 teachers who meet for discussions and various other activities throughout the week. But not every second of every day at the center is scheduled. Time is set aside for teachers to relax, reflect, and recreate.

The NCCAT now orchestrates about 55 seminars during the 10-month school year, generally offering two simultaneously. A sampling of titles from last school year's winter-spring catalog includes: "The Culture of Ancient Greece," "Personal Investing," "At the Movies," "Appalachian Spring: Wildflowers in the Big Spectrum," "Cowboy Culture and the American Psyche," and "Americans in Paris." This last seminar transported teachers to the Paris of the 1920s; they read Hemingway, fished for trout, and became actors in a bistro—the dining room redecorated for a day.

Since the NCCAT began operating, some 3,000 teachers have gone through the center; it now accommodates about 1,200 a year. The state-funded center pays for both the teachers' travel expenses and a classroom substitute back home. Although North Carolina faces staggering budget problems, the center plans to continue operating its regular seminar schedule. Anticipating a cut of about 10 percent from their $3.4 million budget, the NCCAT officials say they will probably pare some of the center's ancillary programs.

A week at the NCCAT is meant as a reward for exemplary service to those who have taught in the state's public schools for at least three years. Teachers must submit a fairly rigorous and comprehensive application that includes essay questions and refer-

ences from their supervisor and a professional colleague. The program is popular; once a teacher is selected, it takes about a year before he or she actually arrives at the center. The wait is also a result of the NCCAT's attempts to pull together teachers from different regions of the state, grade levels, and areas of teaching expertise.

Despite the NCCAT's many attractions, it has had difficulty drawing men and minorities. Many male teachers in the state, McPherson says, double as

---

At the NCCAT, the emphasis is on reward rather than reform. Teachers can enjoy the camaraderie of fellow teachers from across the state.

---

athletic coaches, and while principals may be willing to release teachers from their classrooms, getting them to replace coaches with substitutes isn't easy in a state that takes its sports more seriously than most.

Attracting African-American teachers outside of the large metropolitan areas also poses a challenge. Many African Americans in North Carolina live on the state's coastal plain, a good 10-hour drive from the mountain hideaway. Some, McPherson says, are wary of traveling to an area where few African Americans live.

But most of the participants share the feelings of Lettie Polite, a middle school math and science teacher. Shortly before Polite's scheduled week at the NCCAT, she thought of canceling because she had so much to do. But her principal wouldn't hear of it, and Polite is now glad she didn't let anything get in her way. "It has given me so much insight," Polite says of her time at the NCCAT. "It just makes me feel like getting back in [the classroom]." □

From Teacher Magazine, *November/December 1991*

64.

For The Love Of Books

Across the country, teachers are getting to read and discuss books—both for classroom use and their own enjoyment.

By Debra Viadero

It is a little after 4 p.m., and eight teachers, a librarian, and a principal are gathered around a large oak table in the library of Armel Elementary School in Frederick County, Va. It looks like the sort of after-school gathering that might be discussing a troublesome student, parking issues, or some other matter of school policy.

The subject of discussion at this meeting, however, is books. "Good" books. Young-adult novels, adult fiction, professional-development books. Textbooks and readers are definitely not on this group's agenda. "Teachers can always find ways to use books in the classroom," says Anita Jenkins, the 4th grade teacher who leads this group. "But teachers almost never take the time to discuss books among themselves."

Teacher reading groups like this one, which meets monthly, are springing up in schools all over the nation this year. The groups are an outgrowth of a two-year-old program known as Teachers as Readers.

Initially begun by the Association of American Publishers' Reading Initiative and the Virginia State Reading Council, the program has an engagingly simple premise: Put books in the hands of teachers, encourage them to meet to discuss them, and, thus, rekindle in them a love of reading. The hope is that the teachers' enthusiasm for literature will eventually spill over into their classrooms and schools, as well. "If you can really hook children into reading in the early grades," says Mary Sue Dillingofski, who directs the AAP's Reading Initiative, "you hope that they become lifelong readers."

The Teachers as Readers program was launched in Virginia last year as an experiment involving 36 reading groups for elementary school teachers. The idea was loosely modeled on a project conducted in 1988 and 1989 by researchers at the Teachers College Writing Project at Columbia University. The researchers, Lucy Calkins and Shelley Harwayne, pulled together diverse groups of educators in New York City to read and discuss the works of Mary Gordon, Anne Tyler, and other contemporary authors. Five years later, Harwayne says, many of those groups are still meeting. "The intention was to give teachers an image of good 'book talk,' and, at some point later on, they begin to think about the implications for the classroom," Harwayne says. "How can we create this same experience for our students?"

The Teachers as Readers project, however, seeks a more direct link to the classroom. It specifies that the groups read at least four new children's books. The groups also can read one professional-development book. Dillingofski says the focus on children's books is important because so many are being published. The growth of the whole language movement, which calls for extensive use of literature in teaching reading, has helped make children's publishing a $1 billion-a-year industry. "Five thousand new children's books are published each year," she says. "Teachers just can't keep up, so they tend to rely on the same old chestnuts."

Beyond that restriction, however, there are few guidelines. The sponsors require only that the reading groups include a principal or a district administrator and that they meet at least six times. It is also suggested that groups include no more than 10 members. New groups receive $500 or more to buy books for members.

The simplicity and flexibility of the program have contributed to its rapid growth. Virtually all of the groups started in Virginia last year are still meeting this year with no funding from the program, although some have found funding elsewhere. In addition, dozens of other groups have sprung up in school districts throughout the state.

This school year, the project has expanded nationwide and enlisted the aid of such major national groups as the National Council of Teachers of English, the International Reading Association, and the American Library Association, which use their resources and large memberships to advertise the idea to teachers. At least 6,000 school districts have received information kits on the program.

Jenkins' group, which draws educators from both Armel and Virginia Avenue Elementary School in nearby Winchester, was one of the pilot groups formed last year. The group received $850 and read a variety of books, including *The Wretched Stone* by Chris Van Allsburg and Carolyn Reeder's *Shades of Gray*.

Each member of the group also read a different professional-development book and shared it with the others. This year, the group solicited a $200 grant from a local chapter of the Veterans of Foreign Wars to keep going.

At today's meeting, the subject of discussion is *Nothing but the Truth*, a young-adult novel by Avi. The story centers on a teenager who is suspended from school for humming along with "The Star-Spangled Banner" in class. The incident takes on major proportions as the media begin to report on it and the matter comes before the school board. The brouhaha has devastating consequences for both the rebellious student and his teacher. The narrative is told through the use of memos, transcripts of conversations, newspaper articles, letters, and journal entries.

The book's familiar terrain sparks a lively discussion for the reading group. Over coffee and cake, the educators talk about how the experiences recounted in the book compare with their own. They refer to points in the story where a coach, a counselor, or a principal should have acted differently, and they express sympathy for the teacher and the pupil. "What I liked about this book," one teacher volunteers, "is that you could really see both sides."

It does not matter so much, these teachers say, that some of the books they read are aimed at readers older than their students, who range in grade level from 1st through 4th. "Now I enjoy reading books I'll never use in my classroom," says Mary Lou Gulosh, a 3rd grade teacher at Armel. "In fact, I like some of the young-adult books more."

More important, these teachers say, are the other benefits the group derives from their meetings. "I don't think there's any doubt teachers need contact with one another to have some intellectual stimulation," says Kaleen Baker, a 4th grade teacher. "Now, you have the time set aside, you know you're going to do it, and, suddenly, you feel, 'Gosh, I'm a professional.'"

Melvin Pearson, Armel's principal and the only man in the group, says the talks have given him a new perspective on his job. "I don't work in a classroom every day," he says. "Being involved with a group of teachers and hearing them talk about things they enjoy has helped my perspective and has helped me stay a little more open-minded about things."

The involvement of principals or other administrators is key, Dillingofski says, because they typically set school budgets for children's books. In a survey of the 36 pilot groups, 74 percent of the principals said they planned to increase their budgets for children's trade books as a result of participating in the project.

What surveys cannot adequately measure, however, is whether the discussions are affecting the teaching going on in the classrooms of the teachers involved. The teachers in this group say their book talks are making a difference, whether it is simply using more picture books in class or modeling their enthusiasm for literature to their students.

Jenkins, who teaches at Virginia Avenue Elementary, says she has come to understand that learning literature is not a matter of coming away with one "right" interpretation. Pupils can develop their own perspectives. "My children," she says, "are now doing literature groups that I don't really feel I have to be a part of." □

From Teacher Magazine, *April 1993*

65.

Best-Kept Secret

A little known 'National Faculty' of college professors offers tailor-made staff-development programs to schools.

By Karen Diegmueller

Violet Anne Golden thinks she has discovered the secret to showing 7th graders how to do equivalent fractions. "They said, 'Miss Golden, that is not the way we learned it,'" she says. Undaunted, she explained to them, 'That is the joy of mathematics. You learn it a lot of ways."

On an even more fundamental level, the teacher at Arthur Richards Junior High School in St. Croix in the U.S. Virgin Islands explains what her deepening knowledge of mathematics has enabled her to do in the classroom: "It's to let the kids be creative, to reason in class."

Ms. Golden, to put it in terms that she most assuredly would appreciate, did not get from premise to conclusion on her own. She, along with other teachers in the Virgin Islands, had help from the National Faculty—a two-decades-old organization that links teachers and college faculty members to promote professional development. The group just might be one of the best-kept secrets in education. "We have worked very quietly," says Benjamin Ladner, the president of the Atlanta-based group. "We are not out to get people to pay attention to the National Faculty."

While the importance of preparing better teachers both before and after they get into the classroom has moved into the national forefront since the mid-1980's, the National Faculty has been working on-site with classroom teachers since the late 1960's. "We are radically committed to the centrality of teaching," says Mr. Ladner. "For so long, education reform focused on everything else, all of which is fine, but . . . what about

the teacher? Three days of in-service doesn't get it."

The National Faculty was the brainchild of Barnaby Keeney, the late president of Brown University, who, in the early to mid-1960's, conceived of a way to use university resources to benefit teachers. "The idea was very simple," says Mr. Ladner. "What if we establish a committee, simply take the best we have as college professionals, and approach schoolteachers as equals? By focusing on what we have in common as professionals, [we can] make our teaching better."

Funded primarily by the National Endowment for the Humanities and assisted by Phi Beta Kappa, the fledgling organization started on an experimental basis with a nucleus of 50 scholars. "What happened is, we touched a nerve that was quite remarkable," says Mr. Ladner. What makes it appealing, he says, is that the National Faculty offers teachers, who are largely isolated, the opportunity to talk about their work.

First, they form teacher teams, whose members decide what they need to shore up their teaching. If team members wanted to increase their knowledge of 19th-century history, for instance, the National Faculty would match them, say, with an expert from Stanford University. "We will find you the leading people in the field and bring them into your school," Mr. Ladner explains.

Since its modest beginnings, the organization has boosted its network of scholars to nearly 600 and has worked on projects in all 50 states as well as in the U.S. territories. It runs about 15 to 20 projects a year.

No two projects are alike, Mr. Ladner explains. They can range in scope from a single school to 60 sites within a district. No discipline is ruled out, but the focus clearly is on teaching content. "We think pedagogy arises out of content," says Mr. Ladner.

The length of time for each project varies from two to five years in order to ensure that it will leave a lasting mark. Typically, members of the National Faculty network hold week-long summer seminars; they are followed by two- to three-day monthly or bimonthly visits.

There are no curriculum guides, printed matter, or prescribed materials; each project is composed individually in collaboration with both the faculty and the local district. As Mr. Ladner explains, even though simultaneous history projects may be going on in Portland, Me., and Tucson, Ariz., they will be different because the people involved are different. "In a way, the concept is scandalous," he says. "We feel you have to reinvent the wheel each time we have a project."

The network, however, tries to learn through trial and error. One crucial lesson it has learned is the importance of local "ownership" of a project. "We try to be a catalyst, a resource, a friend," Mr. Ladner says.

Schools and districts are selected in a variety of ways. In some instances, funding organizations come forward with a specific project; in others, the National Faculty elects to take on a project in response to what it perceives as a targeted goal. Most often, a phone call from a school or district sets the process in motion.

Once a school or district is identified, the organization sends out a program officer to learn if the prospective client meets accepted criteria. First, it has to define its own needs. Then, officials must commit to systematic teacher involvement, a significant amount of time, participant release time, administrative support, and funding.

The Virgin Islands project began two years ago with the long-range goal of helping children of limited English proficiency improve their mathematical skills. To do so, teachers and administrators who were identified as potential math leaders were trained by National Faculty scholars. These leaders are expected, eventually, to train other teachers.

Two summers ago, 27 designated math leaders from St. Croix came together for an institute; this summer, 38 from St. Croix and St. Thomas received training. The way the program was designed for the territory, scholars visit the Islands every other month for two-day sessions. Funded by both the federal and territorial governments, the project cost about $52,000 the first year and $62,000 the second. "It is not a project that they picked up from California or New York. They tailor-made it for our specific needs," says Maria E. Sanes, the Islands' coordinator for bilingual and English-as-a-second-language education. The scholars involved have included a National Science Foundation official, an Ohio State University mathematician, and John Firkins, a mathematics professor at Gonzaga University in Spokane, Wash.

Mr. Firkins has gone to the Virgin Islands three times now, conducting two-day workshops as well as participating in a summer institute. With teachers observing him, he taught in the schools to children who spoke Crucian or Spanish, not English. He broke through the language barrier via the language of mathematics. He measured the 1st graders' smiles with pieces of string and then showed the children their smiles were the length of four lima beans.

"Part of the work I saw myself doing as a person from the National Faculty was to change the teachers' attitudes and the kids' attitudes," says Mr. Firkins. "I wanted the teachers to see the kids' reactions. Then I think they bought into what we were doing much more easily."

The district will not have hard data on the project until the end of this year, the third year of the project. Meanwhile, educators have to rely on their observations to judge the results. "The enthusiasm they have engendered in our teachers has been nothing short of miraculous," says Marion Gallo Moore, the district coordinator of mathematics for St. Croix. "Math is fun, and [the teachers] are infecting students with it."

Ms. Gallo Moore says she has observed more activity in the classroom, more interaction between teachers and students, and more use of the pedagogical techniques that the National Council of Teachers of Mathematics advocates.

Geared to limited-English-proficient students, the project nonetheless has aided other students, says Lionel Sewpershad, the assistant principal at Charles H. Emanuel Elementary School. "Where we have mixed classes, the same technique is being used with all these kids," he says.

No Universal Success

Not every National Faculty project has succeeded, Mr. Ladner acknowledges. Sometimes the fault has been the organization's, he says. Because of an error in judgment, the project may make a wrong match between scholar and site. Or a scheduling foul-up may sour the fragile beginnings of a new relationship.

At other times, he says, the fault lies with the school or district: Funding dries up, a new superintendent scotches the project, or the community gets in an uproar over a subject involving race or sex. Other projects have fallen to lengthy teacher strikes.

In the eyes of Violet Anne Golden, though, the project in the Virgin Islands is succeeding handsomely. Were it not for the scholars from the National Faculty, she says, she would not be where she is today. "Our teachers were inspired at those sessions," Ms. Golden says. "Language didn't mean anything for the first time in my life. The demonstrations were in our language—mathematics." □

From Education Week, *Dec. 4, 1991*

66.

Somebody To Lean On

We can't work alone as teachers; we need to divide the pain and multiply the pleasure.

Commentary By John Morris

If you happen to walk past my classroom at about 7:30 a.m. on a school day, chances are good that you will hear coming from my record player Bill Withers' song, "Lean On Me."

I often play this song when I arrive at school in the morning. It's message is simple and upbeat: Everybody needs a friend, from time to time—somebody to lean on. It has a great beat, so it helps me get moving as I start to prepare the room for the day. I do a bit of dancing as an antidote to the Oh-God-I'm-not-ready feeling.

Just as important as the dancing are the song's lyrics. I need to get that idea of mutual need up on the front burner of my brain every day. I need to admit that I can't work alone and that I won't get beyond all the inevitable failures if I only rely on myself. I need to look for partners with whom I can, as one of my colleagues says, "divide the pain and multiply the pleasure."

Several years ago, I began to feel that I was in a rut in terms of my teaching, and, as the saying goes, "The only difference between a rut and a grave is the depth of the hole." I realized that I had spent most of my career as a teacher in a self-contained classroom, which meant I had the freedom to create my own classroom environment and the opportunity to do spontaneous and crazy things if the moment seemed right. But the flip side of that kind of freedom and "self-containment" was a growing sense of isolation and loneliness. Feeling more and more buried in my classroom, I realized I had to reach out and form some kind of partnership. I needed someone to lean on. I was fortunate to have a colleague right across the hall who was feeling the

same way. After many informal conversations and brainstorming sessions, Judith and I decided to try doing a few things together, just to see how it might work. First, we scheduled storytime at the same time each day and gave the students a choice of listening to two different books. It worked. Suddenly, there was a new chemistry created in both classrooms. Each student had two teachers instead of one, and each teacher had a very different group of students to relate to for part of each day. It was a small step for us to take, but our dance had begun.

What began as a simple experiment blossomed into a much more ambitious attempt at team teaching. Judith and I tried all kinds of cross-grade groupings, multi-age activities, and interdisciplinary themes within the structure of our full-blown primary unit. As I reflect on the results of our four years of teaching together, the specific successes and failures are not the important things to recall. The crucial thing for me to remember is that both Judith and I needed someone to share the work of teaching with. It was like building a mobile: We started with one pair of balancing objects and then worked upward in order to construct something that became more and more complex. Without that first effort, that first careful and tentative balancing act, the thing never would have existed, and I would have sunk further and further into the sands of "self-containment."

This notion of interdependence is at odds with much of what our culture tries to teach us, especially those of us who are male. All too often in this country, we are trained to be self-reliant and independent, to go it alone and make things happen all by ourselves, to trust no one and compete with everyone. It is this tradition that leads us to celebrate the heroic adventurer who strikes out alone to conquer the wilderness or make a new scientific discovery or battle against all odds to win some victory. It is this philosophy that produces cultural heroes who are "tough" and who can "make it on their own" and who "don't need any help from anybody." So, we are encouraged to be like the athletes, entertainers, business executives, military leaders, and politicians who have achieved fame and fortune in our society by relying on their own talents and hard work in order to "make it."

In this environment, when the concept of "teamwork" does appear, it is usually for the purpose of teaming up in order to beat someone else's team. It is not surprising that the language of football, business, and the military interpenetrate each other. In these endeavors, we are taught that it is "teamwork" that gets the job done and enables us to compete successfully against our opponent, competitor, or enemy. But what about the notion that teamwork has value in and of itself? What about the idea that cooperation is not a weakness but is at the core of who we are as humans? What about the fact that to be "self-contained" and "independent" is also to be isolated, disconnected, and ultimately alienated from other people? If admitting that we need to lean on someone is perceived in our culture as a sign of weakness, is it any wonder that we have such high rates of chemical dependencies and addictive behaviors? Aren't they simply the end result of a philosophy that teaches us not to depend on anyone else? Our society produces a lot of rugged individuals, but it also produces a lot of lonely drinkers.

As I sit here in my study thinking about these things, I look at the poster hanging on the wall across from my desk. It is a poster a friend gave me after reading an essay I wrote comparing the work of teaching with the work of Sisyphus, the mythic Greek figure who endlessly pushes a rock up a hill. In one corner of the poster is a quotation from Albert Camus: "The struggle itself toward the heights is enough to fill one's heart." I agree with that idea, and I have felt in my teaching all of the strain and all of the exhaustion depicted in the beautiful line drawing of Sisyphus.

But I am now struck by the fact that the person pushing the huge boulder uphill is all alone. Sisyphus the self-reliant. Sisyphus the independent. But also, Sisyphus the lonely.

Next to this poster is a watercolor painting done by my wife. It is my favorite work of hers. Several years ago, I formally purchased it from her, just so it wouldn't be sold away from me. The painting is titled "Fred and Ginger," and it shows two lithe figures, against a background of muted blues and greens, dancing gracefully together. The effort of those two dancers is no less exhausting and will go on as endlessly as the effort of Sisyphus, but how much more wonderful it is to move and work and glide and turn and bend and push and balance together instead of all alone.

We all need somebody to lean on. □

John Morris teaches 1st, 2nd, and 3rd graders at Marlboro (Va.) Elementary School.

From Teacher Magazine, *October 1992*

67.

'Stars' And 'Quitters'

Professor Martin Haberman has developed a controversial technique for choosing successful urban teachers.

By Daniel Gursky

Martin Haberman has been telling anyone who would listen for more than 30 years that not all teaching is the same. Urban teaching is different, he says, and successful urban teachers exhibit a distinct mixture of skills and beliefs. For almost as long, Mr. Haberman has been arguing that schools of education cannot prepare enough effective teachers for America's city schools because faculty members themselves have virtually no urban teaching experience.

Considering his position as a professor of education at the University of Wisconsin at Milwaukee, Mr. Haberman's solution to the nation's chronic shortage of qualified urban teachers is rather unusual.

First of all, he would break what he calls education schools' "cartel" on the preparation of teachers, and open the profession up to all college graduates. But that alone is not enough, because there is no guarantee that arts-and-sciences graduates will make better teachers.

That is where Mr. Haberman's "urban-teacher selection interview" comes in. In three decades of using it to select candidates for various nontraditional teacher-preparation programs that emphasize practical, on-the-job training, Mr. Haberman claims that the interview has proved almost flawless at predicting would-be teachers' professional potential in the classroom.

By interviewing hundreds of "star" teachers around the county, Mr. Haberman has come up with what he considers to be the central attributes of good urban teaching. And to get a better idea of what not to look for in a teacher, he has talked to many self-described "quitters" who have left the profession.

The result is an interview process that looks more like a doctoral candidate's defense of a dissertation than a search for a teaching job. "Typical interview questions don't have any answers," Mr. Haberman complains. "For example, 'When did you decide to become a teacher?' That's like asking someone what their favorite color is. What are you going to do about the answer and what does the answer mean?"

And, he argues, if the interviewer loves children and wanted to be a teacher from the time she was a little girl, she will look for similar answers from teacher candidates. "What you have are very stereotypical questions that reflect the background and experience and prejudice of the questioner," he says.

In contrast, Mr. Haberman and his colleagues—the interview usually is conducted by two people—start by asking the candidate what she would do if one of her students was not doing his homework. The interview subject might suggest talking to the student, for example. But the questioners do not just accept that answer and move on. They repeat the scenario, saying that the teacher's suggestion worked for a short time, but the student has reverted to not doing his homework.

"So what do you do then?" they ask. It is a relentless process in which the teaching candidate has to keep coming up with additional suggestions. The point of the persistent questioning is to test just that—the person's persistence in handling a tough problem.

Other questions in the 30-minute interview are just as pointed and just as impossible to study for. Candidates are asked how they would deal with an authoritarian principal who wants them to discontinue an activity the children clearly love. They have to provide generalizations about teaching and apply them to themselves and other teachers. They are questioned about at-risk students, teacher burnout, and mistakes they might make in the classroom.

Perhaps the most unusual series of questions gets at a person's personal orientation toward teaching. "Is it possible to teach children you don't love?" the interviewer asks. And the converse, "Is it possible for children to learn from teachers they don't love?"

On each question or series of questions, Mr. Haberman has developed a continuum, with answers a star teacher would provide on one end and quitters' responses on the other. If the respondent provides the answer of a quitter on any question, he or she fails the interview. Successful candidates tend to provide answers that fall somewhere along the spectrum.

Mr. Haberman says he is trying to discover a prospective teacher's ideology and methods. "We get what a person thinks a teacher in a school serving poor kids is supposed to be doing and why, and also the behaviors they would engage in," he notes.

Martin Haberman uses his "urban-teacher selection interview" to select candidates for various nontraditional teacher-preparation programs that emphasize practical, on-the-job training.

In his vision of a good urban teacher, what emerges is a persistent, flexible, intelligent, resourceful, energetic person willing to admit his or her own fallibility. (And no, Mr. Haberman is not looking for people who think they have to love all children and be loved by them in return.)

After the interview, Mr. Haberman and the other interviewer classify the candidate as a "star," "high potential," "average potential," or "no potential."

"We don't miss 'no's' and we don't miss 'stars,'" he asserts. Some teachers that he predicted would be great turn out to be merely good, and vice versa, but all the teachers he picks turn out to be successful in the classroom, he adds.

Mr. Haberman is currently interviewing Milwaukee paraprofessionals for a program that will train them to become elementary- or middle-school teachers for the city's public schools.

All three paraprofessionals interviewed this day express some surprise after they leave the room. "I expected the interview to focus a little bit more on me," Robert Tilden says. "But I guess that's what they're

getting at by nailing you with difficult questions and seeing what you come up with." Mr. Tilden, who graduated from college almost 20 years ago with a degree in mechanical engineering, typifies the sort of older candidates with diverse experiences attracted to Mr. Haberman's training programs over the years. Since college, Mr. Tilden has worked as an industrial designer and hotel manager, and served two years as a missionary in Argentina.

Joel Koeper, another paraprofessional trying to get into the program, calls the process "a good technique" for selecting teachers. "Usually in an interview, you answer a question and they leave it alone, and you're pretty much finished," he says. "They were trying to dig a little bit deeper and see if there's anything there."

After going through Mr. Haberman's interview as part of another recent program, Carolyn Ealy is a big fan of the process. "The beautiful part about this interview is that it knows no race, color, creed, or age," says Ms. Ealy, a math and science teacher at Milwaukee's Thomas Edison Middle School.

In interviews for other jobs with the city's school system, she found she could fudge her answers, says Ms. Ealy, who now helps Mr. Haberman conduct some interviews. "This really gets to the heart" of what urban teachers do, she says.

Mr. Haberman estimates that about two-thirds of the paraprofessionals he selects for the current program will be minorities. This, he says, proves that plenty of qualified minority candidates want to become teachers. "We can find all the good minority teachers we want, provided we don't look in undergraduate schools of education," Mr. Haberman says. "In undergraduate schools of education, we're going to find less than 5 percent of the students are minorities, and they're going to be less bright than the minorities in the other schools and colleges."

Milwaukee does not use the term "alternative certification"—the paraprofessionals are applying for the Metropolitan Multicultural Teacher-Education Program—but the similarities are unmistakable. Mr. Haberman has trained administrators of other alternative-route programs—most notably in Texas—to use his interview, and he has recently been working with the Chicago Teachers' Union because teachers and principals there now have the authority to select teachers for their own schools.

Despite his claims of success, however, people are not exactly scrambling to get their hands on the interview form. Part of the problem, Mr. Haberman maintains, is that many urban systems do not want to screen out any potential teachers. "They want anybody who shows up," he says. "There are a lot of cities that would like to use this, but they can't because they need enough day-to-day subs."

And Mr. Haberman acknowledges that some people do not believe the interview works as well as he says it does. Part of that skepticism may be a product of his blunt criticism of the education establishment, which does not endear Mr. Haberman to some of his colleagues. Some teacher educators, in particular, have said the interview eliminates candidates who could develop into good teachers, even if they fail to show that during the interview. Other critics have said that good teaching is a personal, subjective matter that cannot be distilled into essential elements and tested in a half-hour interview.

"I can't describe 100 percent of what good teachers do," Mr. Haberman responds. "But I can describe 60 percent, and I'm happy with that."

The fact that he does not charge people to use his interview process also makes it suspect to some, he says. "It's very hard for people to believe it's a quality product if they get it for nothing," Mr. Haberman says. "I would like to make a lot of money, but I just don't know how." □

From Education Week, *April 1, 1992*

Please Give Us Your Opinion

Education Week and *Teacher Magazine* publish many more articles than we can fit into this reader, so we have to make choices. You can help us make sure we choose the most appropriate stories by rating those that appeared in this edition.

Please indicate your evaluation of each of the articles listed below, using the following scale:

1. This kind of article is most useful
2. This kind of article is somewhat useful
3. This kind of article is not terribly useful
4. This kind of article is not useful at all

We've also left space for you to indicate topics that you would like to see emphasized more in future editions.

____ America's Changing Students

____ Getting Ready For School

____ Teaching A Moving Target

____ Programs For Gifted Kids?

____ Kids Just Ain't The Same

____ The Baggage Of Abuse

____ Back Home In Indiana

____ The Mystery Of Learning

____ Thinking About Thinking

____ Madeline!

____ After Dick And Jane

____ A Course Of Action

____ Kids Learn When It Matters

____ The Unschooled Mind

____ Play Is Part Of Learning, Too

____ 'Full Inclusion, Not Exclusion'

____ The Mother Of All Networks

____ Computers Meet Classroom

____ Focusing On Outcomes

____ Voices Of Change

____ The True Road To Equity

____ Schools Are Not The Periphery

____ Verbal Confusion Over 'Tests'

____ The 'Common Core'

____ A Glimpse Into The Future

____ Reverse The Tide Of Mediocrity

____ Enemy Of Innovation

____ Basal 'Conspiracy'

____ Remapping Geography

____ The Meaning Of 'First By 2000'

____ Caught Between Two Worlds

____ Multicultural Perspectives I & II

____ Standing In The Winds Of Change

____ Boards Of Contention

____ Blurring The Line

____ Bureaucratic Gridlock?

____ Does 'Public' Mean 'Good'?

____ Schools Within Schools

____ Who's In Charge?

____ Taking Flight

____ Crossing The Tracks

____ Rear-Guard Reaction

____ A Perilous Odyssey

____ Under The Surface

____ Clock Watching

____ More Time, More Learning?

____ Where The Dollars Go

____ Savage Inequalities

____ Shortchanging Girls

____ Forging Policy For Harassment

____ The 'Radical Middle'

____ A Profession Evolving

____ By The Numbers

____ Forging A Profession

____ Standards For New Teachers

____ Assessing Teachers

____ The Spoils Of Success

____ Dynamic Duo

____ Consummate Professional

____ Daring To Be Different

____ The Price Of Isolation

____ Relax, Reflect, And Renew

____ For The Love Of Books

____ Best-Kept Secret

____ Somebody To Lean On

____ 'Stars' And 'Quitters'

_____

_____

_____

Tell Us About You

Name _____ Date _____

Are you an Instructor? _____ Student? _____ School Name _____

Department _____ School telephone number _____

Address _____

City _____ State _____ Zip _____

Do you own a personal computer? _____ Which one? _____

Do you own a VCR? _____ Do you own a CD-ROM drive? _____ If not, do you have access to one? _____

Would you purchase course-related materials on disk? _____ videotape? _____ CD-ROM? _____

Tell Us What You Think About This Book

For which course did you use this book? _____

Did you use another text along with this Reader? _____ Which one? _____

What are your general reactions to the Reader? _____

_____

_____

_____

May we contact you for editorial input? _____ May we quote you on related advertising? _____